Operational Financial Analysis: A Practical Handbook with Forms

Ronald R. Feiner

PRENTICE-HALL, INC. Englewood Cliffs, N.J.

*To my wife, Abby, whose constant encouragement
and assistance helped make this book a reality.*

Prentice-Hall International, Inc., *London*
Prentice-Hall of Australia, Pty. Ltd., *Sydney*
Prentice-Hall of Canada, Ltd., *Toronto*
Prentice-Hall of India Private Ltd., *New Delhi*
Prentice-Hall of Japan, Inc., *Tokyo*
Whitehall Books, Ltd., *Wellington, New Zealand*
Prentice-Hall of Southeast Asia Pte. Ltd., *Singapore*

© 1977 by

Prentice-Hall, Inc.
Englewood Cliffs, N.J.

Third Printing . . . . . December, 1979

*All rights reserved. No part of this book
may be reproduced in any form or by any
means, without permission in writing from
the publisher.*

Library of Congress Cataloging in Publication Data

Feiner, Ronald R
  Operational financial analysis.

  Includes index.
    1. Corporations--Finance--Handbooks, manuals, etc.
  2. Finance departments--Handbooks, manuals, etc.
  I. Title.
  HG4026.F44   658.1'5   77-943
  ISBN 0-13-637504-9

Printed in the United States of America

About the Author

Ronald R. Feiner is the Director, Planning and Control, for the Soft Drink Division of the Coca-Cola Bottling Company of Los Angeles. He has spent the past fifteen years developing an extensive background in the area of operationally oriented financial planning, analysis, and control systems. He has held positions both on the divisional and corporate levels which have provided exposure to many different industries and firms of varying sizes. His career has been specifically involved with business situations, where cost control, profit improvement, and accelerated cash flow were the prime objectives, and in some cases, were the key to the survival of the business and turnaround.

He has received a B.S. in industrial management and a M.B.A. from the University of Southern California. Mr. Feiner has written articles for *Managerial Planning* and is a frequent speaker before various professional societies and seminars.

What This Book Will Do for You

This handbook has been prepared for practitioners by a practitioner based on fifteen years of experience in diverse companies of varying size and organizational structures. The author has collected into one volume those everyday critical tools and applications which are required to systematically:

—Increase revenues which have profit potential.
—Streamline overall operations and cut costs.
—Monitor and improve the health of any business.
—Develop reliable plans, decisions, and actions.
—Create higher profits and business expansion.
—Detect and plug profit and cash flow leaks.
—Gain lasting profit improvements and growth through people involvement at all levels of the organization.
—Accelerate and increase cash flow on a continuing basis.

Today's financial managers and their staffs are assuming a greater role in their companies. They are being asked to do more than just keep the books, prepare financial statements, and be custodians of their company's assets. The controller and his staff are fully exercising what their job really implies—*control*. The treasurer has shrugged off his custodial mantle and has become active in managing the assets of his company.

Too often they are prevented from adequately performing their increased responsibilities because:

—they do not have the tools for expanding their functions and thus, they are bound to their more antiquated and classical roles.
—they are busy fighting fires and reacting to problems rather than evolving a systematic approach.

—their non-financial counterparts do not always understand financial results or what impact their actions are having upon the business.

—in smaller organizations, they are spread too thin, having to cover many financial and administrative functions.

—in many larger and successful companies, the financial, analytical, and control tools and systems have not kept up with the growth and/or technology of the business.

—finally, many financial managers have not been exposed to new skills and training.

A SYSTEMATIC APPROACH

Operational Financial Analysis fills the above void by providing a three-step systematic approach, which will provide readers with an:

1. Understanding and improved insight into their total business—the big picture.
2. Interpretation of the financial dynamics of their business.
3. Easy implementable approaches for solving specific profit eroding problems—"how to" tools.

This system works to generate bottom line results. Using these methods, diverse companies of varying size have slashed costs, improved profits, and quickly accelerated cash flow. While this handbook contains over 40 cases in point and approximately 130 support exhibits for driving home these concepts, there are numerous checkoff lists and point-by-point "how-to" examples incorporating the necessary forms and the steps to take in accomplishing such varied analytical and control applications as how to:

—develop a systematic approach to building profits (*Chapter 1*).

—use four tested questionnaires for collecting key data for gaining greater insight and understanding into your business (*Chapter 2*).

—incorporate the data and results from these key data questionnaires into an Action Intelligence Matrix (*Chapter 2*).

—initiate an effective communication tool for satellite locations—the President's letter (*Chapter 2*).

—install or improve the effectiveness of your planning mechanism (*Chapter 3*).

—establish solid business and planning objectives, which act as a basis for improving and expanding your business (*Chapter 3*).

—use a complete 28 point checkoff list for evaluating your firm's marketing plans (*Chapter 4*).

—use profit impact charting as a dramatic supplement to financial statements (*Chapter 5*).

—communicate financial and operating data to non-financial managers effectively (*Chapter 5*).

WHAT THIS BOOK WILL DO FOR YOU

—gain better insight into the relationship between pricing, cost, volume, and mix; and the effect they are having upon your gross profit margins (*Chapter 6*).

—insure that the production requirements outlined in your financial guideline reach the workbench (*Chapter 7*).

—make ABC inventory control part of your everyday material control and analysis vernacular (*Chapter 7*).

—better understand and use inventory turnover concepts (*Chapter 7*).

—quickly introduce or improve practical techniques for controlling material costs including complete instructions for how to take a complete and accurate physical inventory (*Chapter 8*).

—construct a step-by-step approach to implement an earned hours labor control and analysis program (*Chapter 9*).

—define cost centers and a cost collection hierarchy along functional and organization lines (*Chapter 10*).

—understand the cost/volume relationships between fixed, variable, and controllable costs (*Chapter 10*).

—pinpoint the breakeven point (*Chapter 10*).

—use contra-credits and unabsorbed costs as a powerful tool for measuring cost center effectiveness (*Chapter 10*).

—interchange three different methods of flexing your variable budget (*Chapter 11*).

—build your own handy to use Pocket Profit Projector (*Chapter 11*).

—convert an improved understanding of overhead allocation methods into the application of machine-hour rates (*Chapter 12*).

—ask 118 questions for detecting profit leaks (*Chapter 13*).

—improve profits through P.E.P., short for profit enrichment programs (*Chapter 13*).

—avoid writing an ineffective cost reduction memo (*Chapter 14*).

—involve people as the key for achieving lasting cost reductions (*Chapter 14*).

—spot and cure cash flow blockage (*Chapter 15*).

—do short and long range cash flow projections (*Chapter 15*).

—use 19 ways for accelerating cash flow (*Chapter 15*).

—realize that idle assets are not always idle (*Chapter 15*).

—identify, differentiate between, and economically justify big ticket items (*Chapter 16*).

—put discounted cash flow return on investment to work for you (*Chapter 16*).

—post audit and control big ticket item expenditures (*Chapter 16*).

—organize and staff an effective operationally oriented financial analysis staff (*Chapter 17*).

ZEROING IN ON YOUR PROBLEMS

Unfortunately, too many businesses are so caught up in their day to day activities that they fail to recognize or properly identify those problems which are impeding their firm's growth, reducing profits, and draining cash. In many instances, all that is required to spot those profit eroding problems is the asking of a few key or significant questions. These questions in turn help to refocus on other problems and thus the process is underway. Today's business executive does not need problems without identifiable solutions. In fact, he may need several alternatives. These alternatives in addition to solving specific problems may serve as idea generators for solving other problems.

With this concept in mind, the following list of 104 referenced major financial idea generators has been prepared. It has been prepared with the busy practitioner in mind, and is presented in a decision-table format. The left-hand section "Problem Area And/Or Issue" lists 23 general problem areas or issues which confront today's business and financial executives. The middle section "Alternative Solutions/Idea Generators" lists solutions, ideas, and approaches to the 23 general problem areas. The right-hand section of this decision table "Chapter Reference and Subsections" will show you how to immediately begin implementing the solutions to your problems.

Ronald R. Feiner

WHAT THIS BOOK WILL DO FOR YOU

List of 104 Referenced Major Financial Idea Generators

Problem Area and/or Issue	Alternative Solutions/Idea Generators	Chapter Reference and Subsections
1. What action should be taken to develop a stronger and more effective financial analysis staff, capable of increasing profits and cash flow?	1A. Develop an understanding of the changing role of the financial manager, his staff, and his management.	1. The changing role of the financial analyst and his management.
	1B. The staff should adopt a total systematic approach to operational financial analysis.	1. Three-step systematic approach to operational financial analysis.
	1C. The staff should cease being mere technicians and should apply a more diagnostic approach to analyzing their business.	2. M.D.ism—applying a diagnostic approach to your business.
	1D. Widen the analyst's perspective and increase his understanding of the business by defining, collecting, analyzing, and utilizing key data.	2. Four different and tested questionnaires for collecting key data.
		2. Converting your findings into an action matrix.
	1E. Conduct regular financial review meetings, which encourage a two-way communication between financial and non-financial managers and their staffs.	5. How review meetings using profit impact charts become the operational watchdogs.
	1F. Ingrain the "touching the hardware" concepts.	6. Come down from the ivory tower and touch the hardware.
	1G. Prepare a "charter," which properly defines and organizes this key management function.	17. Establishing goals and objectives.
	1H. Develop those specific skills which expand the current skills base.	17. Organizing and staffing. Various chapter subsections, such as flexible budgeting as a control tool in Chapter 11.

List of 104 Referenced Major Financial Idea Generators

Problem Area and/or Issue	Alternative Solutions/Idea Generators	Chapter Reference and Subsections
2. How can you determine if your current financial analysis approach is systematically and operationally oriented?	2A. Measure your current system against the 12 prerequisites of a total systematic approach to operational financial analysis.	1. Exhibit 1-1.
	2B. In the 4-phase evolutionary process, at what stage is your company achieving a total systematic approach?	1. Four-phase evolutionary process associated with achieving a total systematic approach.
3. How can we better involve the non-financial members of our management team in cost reduction and profit improvement.	3A. Develop an understanding at all levels of your organization of the changing role of the financial manager and his staff.	1. The changing role of the financial analyst and his management.
	3B. Conduct regular financial review meetings which encourage a two-way communication between financial and non-financial managers and their staffs.	5. A case guideline for implementing profit impact review meetings. Exhibit 5-28, 12-Point Checkoff List for Profit Impact Chart Review Meetings.
	3C. Convert financial and operating plans, results, and data into graphic form.	5. Charting as a dramatic supplement to financial statements. Exhibit 5-1, 8-Point Checkoff List for Considering Graphic Presentations.
		9. Interpreting results through graphic display.
	3D. Make your management aware of 118 profit leaks which they can plug.	13. What is P.E.P.?
	3E. Show first line supervision 23 ways they can stop eroding profits.	14. First level supervision—your first line of defense. Exhibit 14-1.

WHAT THIS BOOK WILL DO FOR YOU

List of 104 Referenced Major Financial Idea Generators

Problem Area and/or Issue	Alternative Solutions/Idea Generators	Chapter Reference and Subsections
	3F. Earn a 570% return on every dollar invested in a suggestion system.	14. Suggestion systems get everyone involved.
	3G. Combine personnel of different disciplines and approaches into special teams and task forces.	14. The values of special teams.
	3H. Consider sharing some of the profits with the employees.	14. Profit sharing plans, specifically, Exhibit 14-3, 9-Point Profit Sharing Consideration Checkoff List.
	3I. Consider forming a joint-venture or partnership between the company and its management at all levels.	14. R.O.I. management incentive plans, an 8 part step-by-step program.
4. How do you efficiently collect and interpret the key data required to build an effective operational financial analysis system; so as to better plan, control, and analyze the business?	4A. Effective data promotes new ideas along with better planning and control of your business.	2. Four different and tested questionnaires for collecting key data.
		2. Converting your findings into an action matrix.
5. Why should operational financial analysis be concerned about the planning mechanism?	5A. The planning mechanism and, in particular, the financial guide line (FGL) form the backbone for a dynamic and energetic program.	3. An effective financial guide line means greater profits, specifically note Exhibit 3-1, an 8-Point Checklist Defining the Need and/or Purpose of the F.G.L.

13

List of 104 Referenced Major Financial Idea Generators

Problem Area and/or Issue	Alternative Solutions/Idea Generators	Chapter Reference and Subsections
6. Does your company suffer from overplanning, underplanning or no planning?	6A. The key to achieving a balance between over- and underplanning is through the setting of business and planning objectives.	3. Establishing business and planning objectives—the critical step. 3. Case in point—the setting of business objectives can benefit the small as well as the large company. 17. Functional responsibilities and operating objectives.
7. How can you insure your company will have an effective financial guide line?	7A. There are basic financial planning fundamentals that must be incorporated.	3. Don't ignore the fundamentals, specifically Exhibit 3-2, which lists a 7-Step Process for Incorporating Financial Planning Fundamentals.
	7B. Be sure the financial guide line is: —Evaluated. —Presented to senior management. —Updated and tracked.	3. The financial guide line in action.
	7C. Recognize that if the F.G.L. is the backbone of an effective operational financial analysis system, then the marketing plan is the backbone of the F.G.L.	4. Introductory paragraphs.

WHAT THIS BOOK WILL DO FOR YOU 15

List of 104 Referenced Major Financial Idea Generators

Problem Area and/or Issue	Alternative Solutions/Idea Generators	Chapter Reference and Subsections
8. What constitutes an effective marketing plan, and how will you recognize one?	8A. If the plan meets certain prerequisites and you understand the criteria for each prerequisite, you will be able to recognize a well prepared and effective marketing plan.	4. What you should expect of your marketing plan.
	8B. The prerequisites are: —It must be written. —It must follow good planning. —It must be well organized. —It must be complete.	4. Exhibit 4-1, 28-Point Checkoff List for Preparing and Evaluating The Marketing Plan Content.
9. Why is the sales forecast a critical document?	9A. The sales forecast, besides being the key document in the preparation of the financial guide line, is also the ignition device for setting into motion several business controls.	4. Selecting the right sales forecasting method.
	9B. An incorrect assessment of your marketing situation can distort your plan and eventually, your business.	4. Two cases in point at the end of the chapter, show how two companies, rich in technical talent, failed to prepare or properly evaluate a sales forecast, and paid the consequence.
10. What sales forecasting methods are available?	10A. There are seven basic sales forecasting methods which are available for your selection.	4. The seven basic sales forecasting methods.

List of 104 Referenced Major Financial Idea Generators

Problem Area and/or Issue	Alternative Solutions/Idea Generators	Chapter Reference and Subsections
11. How can key financial information be presented and acted upon in a more effective manner?	11A. Consider supplementing financial reports with easy to comprehend graphic presentations.	5. Charting as a dynamic supplement to financial statements, especially Exhibit 5-1, 8-Point Checkoff List for Considering Graphic Presentations.
	11B. Consider adopting profit impact charts Series A (percentage of sales approach) or Series B (a functional approach), which act as operational watchdogs.	5. Profit impact chart component selection and Exhibits 5-2 and 5-3.
	11C. Consider conducting profit impact review meetings in order to implement a self-renewing, communicative planning, and control system.	5. A case guide line for implementing profit impact review meetings.
12. Do your financial analysis, cost accounting, sales, and manufacturing departments truly understand the interacting components, which improve or reduce gross profit margins?	12A. These departments should master or at least understand the two approaches to gross profit analysis.	6. What is gross profit margin? 6. Why analyze gross profit? 6. Two easy approaches to gross profit analysis.
	12B. Examine the effect of mix shift upon pricing, overhead absorption, etc.	11. The pocket profit projector. 12. The fourth point in the topic "Why does C. Lynn's management use and value the MHR?"
	12C. The financial analyst, besides analyzing costs, must be able to intrepret those interacting gross profit factors.	6. Come down from the ivory tower and touch the hardware.

WHAT THIS BOOK WILL DO FOR YOU 17

List of 104 Referenced Major Financial Idea Generators

Problem Area and/or Issue	Alternative Solutions/Idea Generators	Chapter Reference and Subsections
13. If the cost of materials is the largest item on your firm's income statement and your largest expenditure on your cash flow projection, then you better understand the composition of these dollars and control them.	13A. Convert the material usage projection used to prepare your financial guide line into a workable production and material control tool, i.e., bring the financial guide line to the workbench level.	7. Projecting material usage and inventory levels.
	13B. Utilize Pareto's Law and A.B.C. inventory control and analysis to improve the efficiency of your material cost and inventory usage.	7. A.B.C. inventory control and analysis.
	13C. Expand your view of inventory levels from a pure dollar value concept to the number of workdays required to turn the inventory.	7. Understanding Inventory Turnover.
	13D. If your firm expresses its inventory in terms of a turnover ratio, don't be lulled into complacency; speed them up!	7. Understanding Inventory Turnover.
	13E. Examine your scrap and rework levels as a possible source of profit erosion.	7. Benefiting from scrap reporting and analysis. Refer to Exhibit 7-3, 6-Point Checkoff List of Benefits from Scrap Reporting and Analysis.
	13F. Before you can begin to control inventory levels, turnover scrap, etc., you must be able to clearly identify the item you want to control.	8. Parts numbering—the first control step.
	13G. Stop duplicating and spreading the purchasing function over several departments and establish the responsibility of purchasing within one department.	8. Centralized purchasing—pays its way.

List of 104 Referenced Major Financial Idea Generators

Problem Area and/or Issue	Alternative Solutions/Idea Generators	Chapter Reference and Subsections
	13H. Don't ignore centralized purchasing as a cost cutter.	8. Centralized purchasing—pays its way, specifically, the subsection "Centralized purchasing as a cost cutter."
	13I. Introduce purchase commitment reporting. Know today, how many dollars will be spent tomorrow! Remember, it is easier to cut costs at the time the P.O. is written, than when the invoice has to be paid.	8. Purchase commitment reporting—today's view of tomorrow. Note the step-by-step introduction guide and forms.
	13J. The annual physical inventory count, if completed in an organized and systematic manner, can provide much needed information to be shared with other departments.	8. Physical inventory taking—is more than the motion of counting. Note, a complete set of inventory taking instructions are included.
14. Are you perplexed by the challenge of how to easily monitor the effectiveness and productivity of your labor force?	14A. Examine those areas not usually suitable for labor cost monitoring, and then consider earned hours.	9. The opening paragraph and the 5 applications which perfectly fit an earned hours application.
	14B. Understand how visibility can be gained in the area of labor efficiency without using complex industrial engineering-type standards.	9. Labor efficiency visibility without complex standards.
	14C. Implement the earned hours concept.	9. Implementing the earned hours system.
	14D. Communicate your results through graphic display.	9. Interpreting results through graphic display.
	14E. Investigate the impact of employee turnover upon labor efficiency and productivity.	13. Profit Leak Detection Questionnaire, section on employee turnover.

WHAT THIS BOOK WILL DO FOR YOU

List of 104 Referenced Major Financial Idea Generators

Problem Area and/or Issue	Alternative Solutions/Idea Generators	Chapter Reference and Subsections
	14F. Determine how standard operating procedures could increase your labor efficiency and productivity.	13. Profit Leak Detection Questionnaire section on standard operating procedures.
	14G. Be sure your employees are receiving first-rate supervision from a first level supervisor.	14. First level supervision—your first line of defense.
15. Does your firm truly understand its cost and expense structure?	15A. First step is to close the general ledger, and look at your operation; specifically. How does it perform its tasks and how is it organized?	10. Defining cost center along functional and organizational lines.
	15B. The next step is to assign a highly adaptable cost collection number scheme.	10. Cost collection hierarchy. Exhibit 10-4, the 12-Point Functional Review and Account Selection Checkoff Sheet.
	15C. Examine the account groupings within the hierarchy for cost relationships and controllability.	10. Understanding the relationship between fixed, variable, and controllable costs.
	15D. When examining labor costs, do not ignore payroll related costs.	10. Classifying labor and payroll related costs.
	15E. Identify what volume level is required to cover your "fixed nut" or what is required to just open the doors every morning.	10. Pinpointing the breakeven point.

List of 104 Referenced Major Financial Idea Generators

Problem Area and/or Issue	Alternative Solutions/Idea Generators	Chapter Reference and Subsections
16. Are you able to achieve and predict maximum cost effectiveness when the activity of your business varies?	16A. Investigate the use of flexible budgeting as a control tool.	11. Flexible budgeting as a control tool.
	16B. Evaluate how the effect of results measured against a static budget may be providing a poor performance picture.	11. Case in point—how budgeting cost control was made ineffective by using the static financial guide line.
	16C. If you are currently using a flexible or variable budget (or are considering one), carefully evaluate which accounts are to be flexed and by what factor.	11. Determining what accounts to flex.
		11. Avoiding the use of the wrong flexing factor.
	16D. Investigate the use of a flexible budget as a forecasting tool.	11. Flexible budgeting as a forecasting tool.
	16E. Why wait for final results? Provide your management with weekly projected income statements using flexible budgeting techniques.	11. Projection using flexible budgeting techniques. For a sample application, refer to Exhibit 11-6.
	16F. See how simple it is to develop a forecasting tool, which in seconds will give you the capability of making bottom line projections.	11. The pocket profit projector.
17. Do your financial and production people understand the overhead pool and the various methods for applying overhead?	17A. Study the composition of your overhead pool, and see if you are applying the overhead properly in order to obtain full absorption.	12. First step—understanding and applying overhead.
	17B. Evaluate the four methods of overhead application. Don't be afraid to mix them.	12. Four ways of applying the overhead pool.
	17C. When machines dominate the production and conversion process and a production facility is departmentized or arranged by machine center, then machine-hour rate can be the most desirable overhead application method.	12. Utilizing the machine-hour rate.

WHAT THIS BOOK WILL DO FOR YOU 21

List of 104 Referenced Major Financial Idea Generators

Problem Area and/or Issue	Alternative Solutions/Idea Generators	Chapter Reference and Subsections
	17D. Besides applying overhead, the MHR can provide management with valuable, decision-making information.	12. Why does C. Lynn's management use and value the MHR (concluding 7-point checkoff list in this chapter).
18. Do machines dominate your firm's production or conversion process?	18A. Explore organizing your cost collection hierarchy along functional lines based around machine centers.	10. Defining cost centers along functional and organizational lines.
	18B. Reevaluate your preventative maintenance program to see if it needs improvement.	13. Profit Leak Detection Questionnaire—Preventative Maintenance, Exhibit 13-8.
	18C. With the cost of energy becoming a dominant business expense, evaluate your utility conservation program.	13. Profit Leak Detection Questionnaire—Conservation, Exhibit 13-13.
	18D. Be sure that your first level supervision is not sanctioning the misuse of equipment.	14. First level supervision—your first line of defense, Exhibit 14-1, subsection on the misuse of machines.
	18E. Identify your true equipment requirements, so unnecessary equipment is not taking up valuable production or warehouse floor space.	15. Idle assets are not always idle.
	18F. Evaluate and beef-up, where necessary, your capital equipment, budgeting, evaluation, and post-audit programs.	16. Various chapter subsections and especially, Exhibit 16-2, Checkoff List for Developing a Framework for Evaluating Big-Ticket Items.
19. How can your organization make cost control and profit improvement a continuing way of life?	19A. Do not fall into the "you must cut costs by X%" trap and do not write an ineffective cost cutting memo.	13. Case in point—the cost reduction memo as an ineffective cost cutter.

List of 104 Referenced Major Financial Idea Generators

Problem Area and/or Issue	Alternative Solutions/Idea Generators	Chapter Reference and Subsections
	19B. Institute a profit enrichment program (P.E.P.) within an umbrella program capable of identifying profit erosion in varied organizations.	13. What is P.E.P.?
	19C. Do not confine your use of P.E.P. to industrial or commercial environments, because the concept is sufficiently open-ended in approach to spot and stop *cost drains* in hospitals, government agencies, and other institutions.	13. What is P.E.P.?
	19D. Begin by asking the 118 basic questions associated with the P.E.P. questionnaire plus the 23 points relating to first level supervision, and see how many weaknesses can be pinpointed.	13. P.E.P.'s 118 questions for profit leak detection. 14. Foreman and First Level Supervision Cost Erosion Prevention—23-Point Checkoff List, Exhibit 14-1.
	19E. Don't stop with the initial P.E.P. questioning, build a *successful* and on-going program—it's easy!	13. Questioning is not the end, but the beginning. 10-Point Checkoff List for Achieving a Successful Profit Enrichment Program, Exhibit 13-14.
	19F. Tap your most valuable resource for profit leak detection and the implementation of solutions—people!	14. Introductory material on people involvement, which opens this chapter.
20. What steps can be taken to effectively get people involved in cost reduction and control?	20A. First level supervision is your first line of defense against profit erosion, so provide them with the proper tools and teach them how to use these tools.	14. First level supervision—your first line of defense.
	20B. Establish a suggestion system, so that profit leak detection and profit improvement are not confined exclusively to the higher ranks of management.	14. Suggestion systems get everyone involved.

List of 104 Referenced Major Financial Idea Generators

Problem Area and/or Issue	Alternative Solutions/Idea Generators	Chapter Reference and Subsections
	20C. Organize special teams which have a prescribed approach and discipline, rather than general cost cutting teams, which are so prevalent and generally ineffective because they do not make lasting gains.	14. The value of special teams.
	20D. Begin by examining the function performed by incorporating value analysis techniques.	14. Value analysis teams.
	20E. Introduce work simplification, which has been described as an organized approach to common sense.	14. Work simplification teams.
	20F. Minimize production start-up problems by organizing a "production assembly team."	14. Production assembly teams.
	20G. Share the profits with the employees—introduce a profit sharing plan.	14. Profit sharing plans. Exhibit 14-3, 9-Point Profit Sharing Consideration Checkoff List.
	20H. Consider a group-oriented management incentive plan based on return on investment.	14. R.O.I. management incentive plans.
21. How can I generate greater profits for my firm by accelerating cash flow?	21A. Gain an understanding of how an accelerated cash flow will build profits.	15. How does accelerating cash flow build profits?
	21B. Put to use the simple four-step process for pinpointing cash flow blockage.	15. Pinpointing cash flow blockage.
	21C. Specifically, begin cash forecasting or shape-up your existing short and long term cash forecasting program.	15. Step 1—defining cash requirements (forecasting).
	21D. Don't stop with pinpointing cash flow blockage, take corrective action. Make current decisions—*now!*	15. 19 ways to accelerate cash flow. Case in point—how a large printer improved profits by analyzing and making cash flow timing decisions.

List of 104 Referenced Major Financial Idea Generators

Problem Area and/or Issue	Alternative Solutions/Idea Generators	Chapter Reference and Subsections
	21E. Examine your business for idle assets which are providing drag on your organization and thus impeding the profitability and growth of the business.	15. Idle assets are not always idle.
	21F. Periodically re-examine product lines and business endeavors to determine if vitally needed cash is not being wasted on marginal or unprofitable operations.	15. A final note on accelerating cash flow.
22. Is your firm properly addressing the analysis and evaluation of significant cash outlays on those big-ticket decisions?	22A. Determine which items and expenditures in your firm qualify for the title of big-ticket item.	16. Identify big-ticket items.
	22B. Develop a framework for evaluating big-ticket items.	16. A sample framework and method for evaluating big-ticket items.
	22C. Establish a proper capital budgeting procedure.	16. Capital budget items. A case in point—what can happen to a company which does not follow a capital evaluation framework.
	22D. Adopt a standard return on investment criterion and methods of evaluation, such as: —Time payback method —Discounted cash flow method *And stick to it!*	16. The method and establishing criteria for D.C.F.—R.O.I.
	22E. Remember, to post-audit and control the big-ticket item after you have acquired it.	16. A reminder to post-audit and control.

WHAT THIS BOOK WILL DO FOR YOU

List of 104 Referenced Major Financial Idea Generators

Problem Area and/or Issue	Alternative Solutions/Idea Generators	Chapter Reference and Subsections
23. How can you organize your financial analysis staff in order to develop a workable, systematic, operationally-oriented approach?	23A. Stop firefighting and place some order and direction into this activity.	17. When firefighting is the order of the day.
	23B. Set specific goals and objectives and hold those involved responsible.	17. The granting of an operational charter; Functional responsibilities and operating objectives.
	23C. Immediately, adopt improved planning and control techniques in order to achieve those specific goals in a timely manner.	17. Planning.
	23D. Remember, no matter how carefully you plan, the tasks to be done will require properly skilled people.	17. Organizing and staffing.
	23E. Determine the *modus operandi* which will maximize results.	17. Directing and controlling (Operational financial analysis in action).

CONTENTS

What This Book Will Do for You . 7

1 Systematic Approach to Profit Analysis—The Big Potential . 29

The Changing Role of the Financial Analyst and His Management . The Four-Phase Revolutionary Process Associated with Achieving a Total Systematic Approach . The Three-Step Systematic Approach to Operational Financial Analysis

2 Data Gathering and Implementation—Key Building Blocks in Operational Financial Analysis . 37

M.D.ism—Applying a Diagnostic Approach for Analyzing Your Business . Four Different and Tested Questionnaires for Collecting Key Data . Converting Your Findings Into an Action Matrix

3 Planning Mechanism—Blueprint for a Successful Operational Financial Analysis System . 58

An Effective Financial Guide Line Means Greater Profits . Establishing Business and Planning Objectives—The Critical Step . Don't Ignore the Fundamentals . The Financial Guide-Line in Action

4 Effective Marketing Planning—Objectives and Techniques in Operational Financial Analysis . 78

What You Should Expect of Your Marketing Plan . Selecting the Right Sales Forecasting Method

5 Profit Impact Charting for Improved Financial Reporting and Control . 85

A Case in Point—What One Company Learned About Planning and Control Techniques . Charting as a Dramatic Supplement to Financial Statements . Profit Impact Chart

CONTENTS

5 Profit Impact Charting for Improved Financial Reporting and Control (cont.)

Component Selection . A Recommended List of Charts for Getting Off to a Good Start . Profit Impact Charts Give Visibility to Deviation From Plan . What Happened After the Division and Corporate Managements Reviewed Red Ink Printing Company's Profit Impact Charts? . A Case Guide-Line for Implementing Profit Impact Review Meetings

6 Gross Profit Analysis—Eliminating the Confusion . 121

What is Gross Profit Margin? . Why Analyze Gross Profit? . Two Easy Approaches to Gross Profit Analysis . Come Down From the Ivory Tower and Touch the Hardware . How Well Do You Know Your Business?

7 Practical Techniques for Analyzing Material Costs . 131

Projecting Material Usage and Inventory Levels . A.B.C. Inventory Control and Analysis . Understanding Inventory Turnover . Benefiting From Scrap Reporting and Analysis

8 Practical Techniques for Controlling Material Costs . 141

Parts Numbering—The First Control Step . Centralized Purchasing—Pays Its Way . Purchase Commitment Reporting—Today's View of Tomorrow . Physical Inventory Taking—Is More Than the Motion of Counting

9 Earned Hours—An Easy Method for Controlling Labor Cost Through Operational Analysis . 168

Labor Efficiency Visibility Without Complex Standards . Understanding the Earned Hours Concept . Think Before You Implement . Implementing the Earned Hours System . Interpreting Results Through Graphic Display . How the Earned Hours Reporting Package Can Be Applied to Your Organization

10 Expense Categorization—A Prelude to Improved Profits Through Streamlined Operational Analysis . 186

Defining Cost Centers Along Functional and Organizational Lines . Cost Collection Hierarchy . Understanding the Relationship Between Fixed, Variable, and Controllable Costs . Pinpointing the Breakeven Point . Using Contra-Credits and Unabsorbed Costs to Measure Cost Center Effectiveness

11 How to Use and Benefit From Flexible Budgeting—Prime Analytical Tool . 200

Flexible Budgeting as a Control Tool . Avoiding the Use of the Wrong Flexing Factor . Flexible Budgeting as a Forecasting Tool . Projection Using Flexible Budgeting Techniques

12 Machine-Hour Rates—Proven Profit Generator . 216

First Step—Understanding and Applying Overhead . Utilizing the Machine-Hour Rate

13 Plugging Those Oft-Time Overlooked Profit Leaks with Profit Enrichment Programs . 220

Questioning is Not the End But the Beginning

14 People Involvement—Key to Lasting Cost Reductions . 230

First Level Supervision—Your First Line of Defense . Suggestion Systems Get Everyone Involved

15 Generating Profits Through Accelerated Cash Flow . 243

How Does Accelerating Cash Flow Build Profits? . Pinpointing Cash Flow Blockage . 19 Ways to Accelerate Cash Flow . Idle Assets Are Not Always Idle

16 Operational Financial Analysis and the Economic Justification of Big-Ticket Items . 254

Identifying Big-Ticket Items . A Simple Framework and Method for Evaluating Big-Ticket Items . A Reminder to Post-Audit and Control

17 Systematic Profits Via Operational Financial Analysis—An Organizational Case Study . 270

Establishing Goals and Objectives . Planning . Organizing and Staffing . Directing and Controlling [Operational Financial Analysis in Action]

Index . 282

1

SYSTEMATIC APPROACH TO PROFIT ANALYSIS—THE BIG POTENTIAL

The theme of this handbook is how to systematically build profits through the application of operationally-oriented financial analysis and control tools. This chapter positions you, the reader, as if you were beginning a footrace, by placing you in the starting blocks. This positioning is accomplished by defining:

1. Your objectives in reading this book, which we hope are to build a better understanding of how to:
    —Increase revenues, which have profit potential.
    —Improve overall operations.
    —Maintain and improve the general health of the business, and cure certain specific ills.
    —Develop reliable targets, plans, decisions, and actions.
    —Create higher profits and increase cash flow.
2. The changing role of the modern financial analyst/manager and his management.
3. The prerequisites for a total systematic approach to financial analysis.
4. The evolutionary process associated with achieving a total systematic approach.
5. The three-step systematic approach to operational financial analysis.

THE CHANGING ROLE OF THE FINANCIAL ANALYST AND HIS MANAGEMENT

Until the 1940's and early 1950's, the controller and the management accountant were cast in the role of the historian, reporting financial results in an impartial manner without concern for how these results impacted or could be interpreted by the other segments of the business. Similarly, the treasurer's role was rigid and custodial in nature. It was confined to the areas of investment, credit, and collections.

Recently, the controller and his staff have begun to fully exercise what the job really implies—*control*. The treasurer has shrugged off his custodial mantle and has become active in managing the assets of his company. As the roles of the controller and treasurer continue to expand, so have the roles of their fellow executives. In the past they knew very little about accounting, financial analysis, budgets, business planning, asset management, and control. All members of the management team are now acquainted and involved in the use of these skills. Regardless of an executive's specialty, whether it lies in marketing, manufacturing, or engineering, he is a contributor and to a greater extent dependent on these approaches and techniques. He also needs the information provided by these various techniques in order to analyze, understand, and evaluate the performance of his functional responsibilities, as well as how well the total company is performing. Performance is more than just profitability and can only be determined by continually asking:

1. What has been our past track record and what factors can be attributed to this record?
2. What is our current position—strengths and weaknesses?
3. What factors are leading to our current success or lack of it?
4. Where are we going from here and how are we going to get there?

To effectively answer this abbreviated list of thought-provoking questions and a myriad of others, a total systematic approach toward financial analysis is required.

EXHIBIT 1-1
The Twelve Prerequisites Of a Total Systematic Approach to Operational Financial Analysis

1. *Active* in that the financial analyst does not sit back and watch the passing parade, but is an active participant. The analyst is not an idle numbers cruncher or historical commentator, but should provide complete information and conclusions which spawn decisions for management at all levels. The system and approaches he uses are interlocking, interdisciplinary, and reactive to changing conditions and needs.

2. *Balanced* in that there must be a correlation between the effort expended to achieve a result. Peter Drucker states it best in his familiar quote—"Nothing is as bad, as to do the useless thing with great efficiency."

3. *Communicative* in that the system fosters feedback which must be a two-way communication of current results-oriented financial and operating data suitable for use by all those who have a need to know. Suitable means it is timely and is presented

in a manner which is easily interpretable by both financial and non-financial executives.

4. *Forward Looking* in that it realizes historical analysis is not the end product, but the beginning. A total system strives to do away with the conception of the financial analyst and/or the business planner as an individual with his eyes on the past, who backs into the future. A total system should attempt to recognize the ultimate effect of today's actions upon tomorrow's events and results.

5. *Interdisciplinary* in that the control and analytical tools of areas, such as the ABC material control concept or the methods simplification approaches of the industrial engineer, etc., are all adoptable in developing a total system. By not understanding, adopting, and/or interlocking these so-called foreign or non-financial approaches, the financial analyst will operate in a "turtle-world," which will do both himself and his firm a disservice.

6. *Operational* in that it reflects what is happening in the organization. The approach must be to get behind the numbers and determine what factors are truly shaping current and future results. The analyst must not be desk-bound, but must be familiar with current production processes, distribution patterns, R&D developments, etc.— i.e., the analyst must be willing to get out and touch the hardware.

7. *People Oriented* in that people make things happen through a system and not vice-versa.

8. *Preventative* in that those firms which lack a systematic approach with accompanying support tools usually have a firefighting atmosphere. The effort spent in developing such an approach will pay a very high return on the time invested for many years to come, while the time invested to resolve the firefight is shortlived, and it may have no return at all.

9. *Questioning* in that it should cause issues and problems to pop to the surface and not remain hidden in the detail. The analyst must place into daily practice, what some have quoted as the definition of effective management, "the art of asking significant questions."

10. *Reiterative* in that the approach and system have the ability to repeat or regenerate themselves.

11. *Systematic* in that it is a set of tools and approaches. Although they can be operated and used independently, when combined and interlocked they form a more powerful whole.

12. *Supplementary* in that it should supplement and support existing financial reporting methods and statements. The analyst should recognize when a single column added to an existing report suffices instead of generating another analytical report.

THE FOUR-PHASE EVOLUTIONARY PROCESS ASSOCIATED WITH ACHIEVING A TOTAL SYSTEMATIC APPROACH

In order to better evaluate your financial analysis system and to communicate its strengths and weaknesses or general status to other members of your management team, it is helpful to understand how a total and complete system for financial analysis evolves. The evolutionary process can be described in four phases:

1. The Observation Phase
2. The Understanding Phase
3. The Modification or Correction Phase
4. The Objective Phase

These phases are best understood when paralleled to the growth of an emerging business and are explained in the following case in point.

A case in point—how Marquee Plastic Letter Company evolved a total systematic approach

THE OBSERVATION PHASE

Marquee Plastic Letter Co., as their name implies, began as a manufacturer of plastic letters for theater marquees. The business, although incorporated, was a sole proprietorship in concept and organization. The firm's financial statements were prepared by a small accounting firm. When the results were reviewed by the founder and his outside accountant, he was content as long as there was enough cash in the bank and the business was making some sort of minimal profit. Thus, he was purely in the observation phase and his financial statements were maintained strictly for recording results, filing tax returns, and supporting very small working capital loans. As Exhibit 1-2 shows, he was in a two-step cycle or network consisting of actions and results.

EXHIBIT 1-2
Financial Analysis System Evolution
Observation Phase

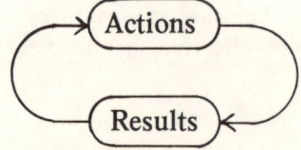

In this two-step sequence, there was no action taken to overtly modify or change the results. I.e., the business was run by the seat of the founder's pants; and to a great extent the business ran itself.

THE UNDERSTANDING PHASE

The founder decided to expand and improve his business. He began by expanding his product offerings into lines which could use his existing equipment. He then found it was necessary to pay more attention to his financial results and hired a controller to evaluate his financial results. As Exhibit 1-3 shows, another sequence was added to the system.

Even though he understood a great deal more about his business and why it performed in a certain manner, he remained historically oriented and made no overt attempt at reshaping future results. One might describe him by saying that with his eyes on the past, he was backing into the future.

SYSTEMATIC APPROACH TO PROFIT ANALYSIS

EXHIBIT 1-3
Financial Analysis System Evolution
Evaluation Phase

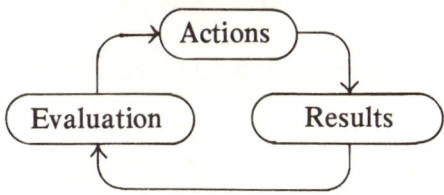

MODIFICATION PHASE

As the business expanded, he found he was not able to have his finger on every operation, and his attention was being drawn to larger and less detailed responsibilities. These responsibilities included working with key customers, suppliers, and with his bank for expansion capital. When his sons entered the business, the day-to-day operations were turned over to them. Thus, the business had become complex, and there was now a need and a desire on the part of the founder and his sons to do more than just understand, but to know what had happened and why. As Exhibit 1-4 shows, another loop was added to the chain—the attempt to modify results.

EXHIBIT 1-4
Financial Analysis System Evolution
Modification Phase

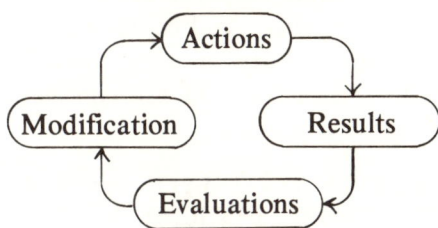

OBJECTIVE PHASE

When they first attempted to preshape results, they found it was necessary to define their objectives and goals and prepare written plans on how they were going to obtain these objectives. They referred to their objective and planning activities as "goals." In order to successfully secure their goals, the controller, who was now V.P. of Finance, added the vital ingredient of communication, which was previously non-existent. The founder now saw the need to communicate his goals to other areas and individuals within the firm. Certain systems and approaches had to be changed or added in order to meet these goals. They agreed that the evaluation of financial results would have to be more operationally-oriented for them to achieve their objectives. Exhibit 1-5 shows still another link added to the network. Also, the evaluation step was widened to include the measuring of objectives and plans.

With the addition of the "goals link" and the "evaluation link" being expanded to measure these results, a "feedback loop" has been created. Once this feedback loop was

EXHIBIT 1-5
Financial Analysis System Evaluation
Objective Phase

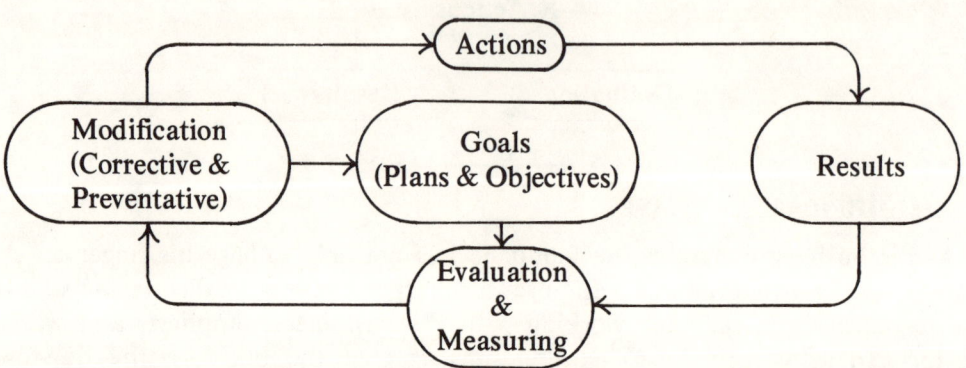

operative and strengthened, the system became reiterative, self-perpetuating and even self-improving.

It must be kept in mind businesses do not have to evolve to have an operationally-oriented, totally systematic approach to financial analysis. Unfortunately, too many businesses—large and successful have evolved to their current size and success but have failed to evolve their financial analysis systems and approaches. A natural response would be that these firms have achieved some form of success and prominence. The retort would be, "How much more successful could they have become?" Far too many firms are still statement-oriented and are ignoring operational conditions and factors. They are not preventative in orientation and are conducting single shot exercises in response to numerous firefighting requests.

THE THREE-STEP SYSTEMATIC APPROACH TO OPERATIONAL FINANCIAL ANALYSIS

The method

The transition to a more operational and systematic approach to financial analysis and the rewards of improved profits and cash flow requires three steps:

STEP 1.—UNDERSTANDING THE TOTAL BUSINESS

Before examining any of the detailed components of an organization, a complete overview and understanding of how the total business functions is required. This is often referred to as the *conceptual* or *big picture analysis*. No matter what it is called, it means you must first understand the whole before you can examine and interpret its parts, because the sum of its parts when combined together tend to present a different picture than if they were examined separately.

STEP 2.—UNDERSTANDING THE FINANCIAL DYNAMICS

Once you have gained the ability to successfully monitor, analyze, and control the

SYSTEMATIC APPROACH TO PROFIT ANALYSIS

business in its entirety, you are then in a better position to analyze the financial dynamics of the business. The financial dynamics is an expression of those components, resources, and by-products, which are consumed and produced by any functioning organization. A manufacturer sells a product and produces a gross profit. This gross profit is a result of pricing, the consumption of resources in the form of labor, material, and overhead dollars, and the adjusting of inventory levels, etc.

STEP 3.—"HOW TO" TOOLS

The key to steps one and two is the word *understanding*. Understanding can only be gained by having and applying a matched set of tools which will produce this effect. The term "matched" is used because each tool can be used independently, yet when combined, interlock to form a strong systematic approach for gaining an in-depth understanding of your business.

Profits don't happen, they are engineered

The remainder of this book shows you how to weave a series of tools and techniques into a systematic network for improving the financial condition of your business. The first five chapters are conceptual in nature. They introduce you to a series of "how to" tools for understanding, monitoring, analyzing, and identifying problems along with controlling the overall business.

The remaining chapters are concerned with the application of specialized tools for handling specialized areas. These areas form the financial dynamics of a business and consist of:

- Gross Profit
- Labor Costs
- Material and Inventory Control
- Indirect Cost and Expenses
- Cost Reduction and Profit Improvement
- Cash Flow
- Capital Expenditures
- Business and Product Line Expansion

The three-step process forms an overall approach which causes the analyst to continue to review his business and its components. As he learns, he develops an expanded view, as shown in Exhibit 1-6. This focusing is required because profits don't happen, they are engineered. The operational analyst is the engineer who skillfully maneuvers his understanding and analytical tools toward improving the overall financial condition of his company.

36　　SYSTEMATIC APPROACH TO PROFIT ANALYSIS

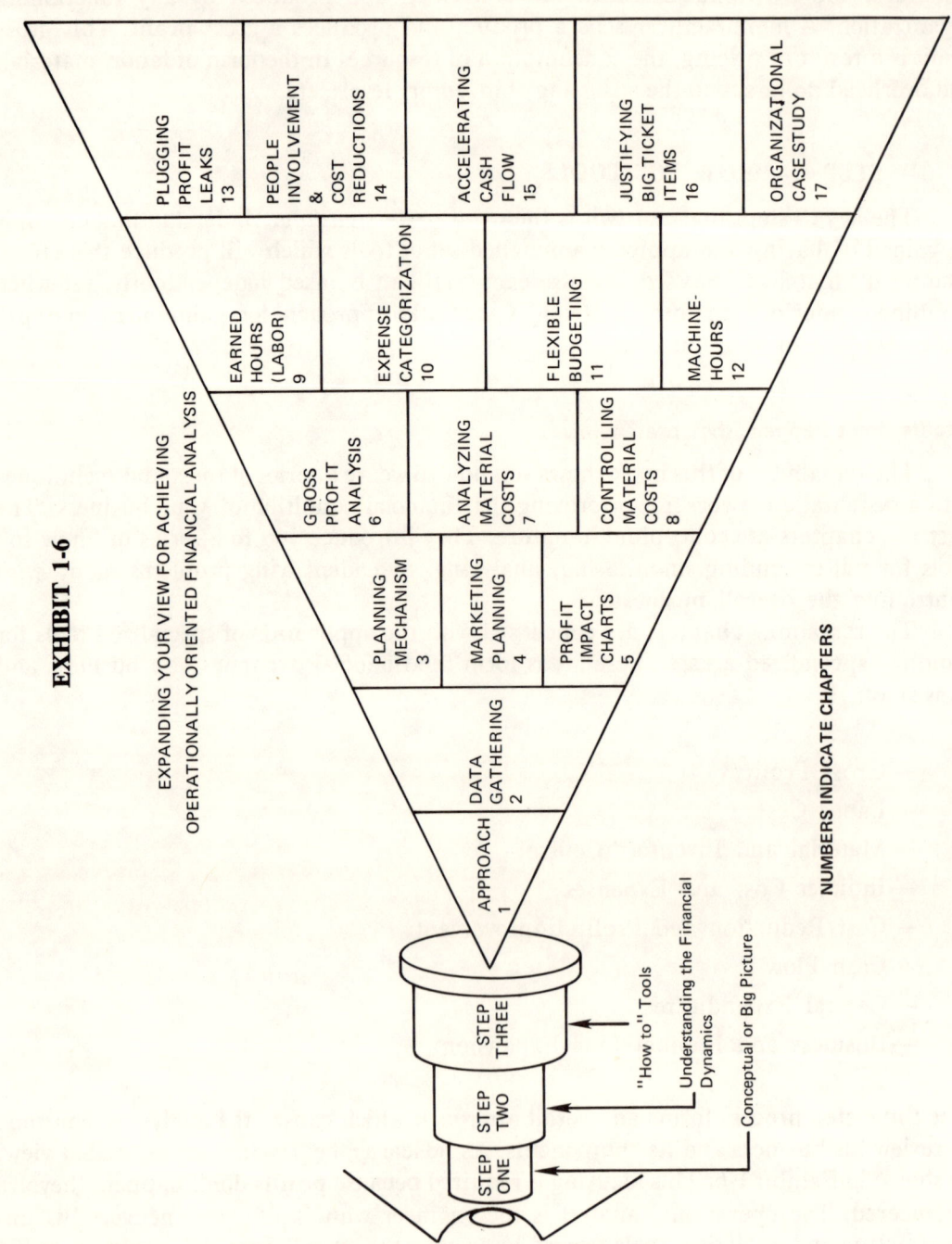

EXHIBIT 1-6

2

DATA GATHERING AND IMPLEMENTATION—KEY BUILDING BLOCKS IN OPERATIONAL FINANCIAL ANALYSIS

This chapter takes you, the reader, out of the starting blocks and moves you further toward your objective of systematically building profits through the application of operationally-oriented financial analysis and control tools. The first step in achieving this objective is to adopt a diagnostic approach referred to as M.D.ism. In order to successfully master this diagnostic approach and intelligently maximize the applications presented in the remainder of the book, the reader needs operational data and information. Agreed, every company has data, but we are seeking data which generates understanding, relationships, and ideas.

This information is provided by utilization of tested questionnaires that can be easily transferred and adapted to your firm's needs. Once the data has been collected, it must be assembled into an action matrix. Thus, the data does not remain in a static state because the action matrix will highlight and assist in identifying:

1. Organizational relationships and reporting structures.
2. General strengths and weaknesses.
3. Product data (types, mix, relationships, gross profit).
4. Inefficiencies (production, distribution, office, etc.).
5. Systems deficiencies, bottlenecks, breakdowns.

6. Profit eroders.
7. Cash drains.
8. Fixed and variable cost relationships.
9. Corrective actions.

This questionnaire/matrix technique is very useful for individuals:

1. Who are new to a firm and wish an easy and organized approach for developing more than just a surface understanding.
2. Who have had a new firm or division added to their responsibility as a result of a reorganization or business acquisition.
3. Who are assigned as auditors, troubleshooters, or consultants.
4. Who are members of senior management and require an easy tool or reference point for making, evaluating, and following up on decisions, changes, and improvements.
5. Who are moving up in their organization and want to know how their business operates and functions.

M.D.ism—APPLYING A DIAGNOSTIC APPROACH FOR ANALYZING YOUR BUSINESS

The diagnostic approach or M.D.ism

We are all acquainted with the diagnostic approach our personal physician takes during an office visit in ferreting out the cause of our physical complaint or illness. The diagnostic approach consists of a four-step process:

Step One — The patient describes his own troubles.
Step Two — The doctor conducts a physical examination of the patient.
Step Three— Additional investigations and special tests are conducted as required.
Step Four — The facts gathered above are combined to form a statement concerning the patient's health.

The data received are analyzed and evaluated and a prognosis and cure can be prescribed.

Applying M.D.ism to your business

The same diagnostic approach can be applied to analyzing the overall health of your business and the solving of those problems which are weakening the health and condition of the business. Whereas the doctor maintains a medical history of each of his patients, the company's financial statements and accompanying commentary, which highlight the major changes from prior periods or plans, serve as part of the history or condition of the firm. The other part of the history has to be maintained and updated in the form of key data. The gathering of key data can serve both as a means of providing

DATA GATHERING AND IMPLEMENTATION

the supplemental or base information and is a vital aspect of the diagnostic process. The individual who is gathering the data must also develop an understanding of how these facts relate to the function of the business. It is not uncommon to find decisions and actions based on a set of facts and conditions which in reality have slowly changed and are no longer truly valid or appropriate. Think back five years and see how your business has changed from yesterday, and then try to visualize how your business will be conducted five years from now. Changes in technology, products, customer requirements, internal systems, etc., will guarantee you will be conducting your business in a different manner tomorrow from how it is conducted today.

FOUR DIFFERENT AND TESTED QUESTIONNAIRES FOR COLLECTING KEY DATA

If data gathering and implementation is a key building block toward establishing a systematic approach to operationally-oriented financial analysis, then the data which is to be collected must be *key* data. Key in that it provides insight and understanding. The data and information which is collected at this stage of the process will be instrumental in structuring your financial guideline and even in pinpointing those areas which will require future corrective action. Thus, the data which is collected must be meaningful and key to your organization.

Four different questionnaires or checkoff lists are provided. To some extent, they are similar and yet they are different. They have one common fact; they all have stood the test of the business firing line. You may choose to select certain items from each of the different formats and prepare your own individualized list tailored to your particular business.

Profit enrichment program questionnaire (exhibit 2-1)

P.E.P. is short for Profit Enrichment Program and is the subject of Chapter 13. The 118 questions for identifying profit leaks listed in Chapter 13 originally began as the six page questionnaire (included as Exhibit 2-1). This questionnaire was originally developed by a highly diversified company as an umbrella program that would attempt to find a common denominator or approach in cost improvement for similar but unrelated businesses. P.E.P. was their first attempt at a systematic approach. The program at first was designed to provide an answer to the division manager's or controller's question—"But how can we improve our division's profits and performance, and how can you evaluate our true performance when you don't understand our business?" In the same breath they usually added—"And anyway, our business is unique."

Thus, the P.E.P. questionnaire was conceived out of necessity to provide an answer to the "our business is unique" syndrome. The task was easy: simple identify those types of expenditures and functions which are common to all organizations. The questionnaire was organized around each division's undisputable common denominator, which was the set of financial statements each division was required to submit each month. Thus the basic organization of the P.E.P. questionnaire corresponds to a typical income statement.

EXHIBIT 2-1

Profit Enrichment Program Questionnaire

SALES AREA

List 10 Highest Offerings to Public DESCRIPTION	PER UNIT PROFIT %	Realized Profit (Check off ✓)		
		LOW YIELD	AVERAGE YIELD	HIGH YIELD
1.	1.	1.	1.	1.
2.	2.	2.	2.	2.
3.	3.	3.	3.	3.
4.	4.	4.	4.	4.
5.	5.	5.	5.	5.
6.	6.	6.	6.	6.
7.	7.	7.	7.	7.
8.	8.	8.	8.	8.
9.	9.	9.	9.	9.
10.	10.	10.	10.	10.

1. What steps are you taking to reduce costs on the low yield items listed above?

2. What additional sales volume can be generated with present capacity by new products introduction?

COST OF SALES AREA

1. What is the cost of sales breakdown on an average unit in each product line offering?

PRODUCT LINE	MATERIAL %	LABOR %	OVERHEAD %	TOTAL %
1.	$	$	$	$
2.				
3.				
4.				
5.				

COST OF SALES (Continued)

2. How can you reduce your cost of sales by 10%?

MATERIAL	LABOR	OVERHEAD EXPENSES
1.	1. *Direct:*	1. *Fixed Expenses*
2.		
3.		
4.	2. *Indirect:*	2. *Controllable* (*Variable*)
5.		
6.	3. *Supervision*	
7.		

DATA GATHERING AND IMPLEMENTATION

MATERIAL AREA

3. How have you reduced costs in the material area in the past six months?
3A. How effective have you been in increasing the inventory turnover rate in the past six months?
4. How do you control purchasing to make certain buys are in economical quantities without increasing unnecessary levels of inventory on hand?
5. Are F.O.B. points on purchases negotiated to avoid unnecessary shipping costs?
6. What items in your processing cycle do you send outside due to limitations of your equipment (i.e., machine-heat treat chrome, etc.)?
7. Have you checked into the capabilities of other divisions to furnish this service and to what extent do you utilize Company facilities?

LABOR AREA: FACTORY

8. What is the relationship between direct labor and indirect/support labor?
9. What steps have you taken to improve this relationship and reduce costs in the past six months?
10. What steps have you taken in the past six months to reduce overtime?
11. Is labor cost and material cost clearly defined to permit accurate evaluation to cost of sales?
12. What effort has been expended during the past six months in the product redesign area or value analysis area to substantially reduce the cost of production?

OVERHEAD

13. What has been accomplished in the past six months to delegate responsibility to the foreman level to insure cost awareness at a level where greatest savings can be effected?
14. Has all equipment considered surplus been made available on the Corporate Surplus List for possible transfer to another entity or a decision to dispose of or sell?
15. Are records kept on the relative maintenance costs on all major critical pieces of equipment?
16. What efforts do you exercise to cut utility costs to the bare minimum?
17. How do you handle rental equipment, and who has the authority to obligate your division?
18. What controls are established to insure supplies are judiciously purchased only when needed?
19. What controls are now enforced to avoid pilferage and deterioration of supplies in the factory and office area?
20. How have you accomplished elimination of shipping and delivery expense by changing F.O.B. point to F.O.B. shipping point?
21. What material handling and automotive equipment should be deemed surplus?

SELLING—MARKETING EXPENSES

22. How much additional sales volume per head and per representative in the sales area has been generated in the past six months?
23. Has an analysis been made to determine whether there is a cost saving to be gained by changing marketing and distributions, i.e., sales vs. distributors or manufacturers' representatives or salary vs. commission, etc.?
24. What method do you use to evaluate the effect of your advertising programs?

25. How do you determine which items to feature in your advertising approach?
26. What guidelines and limitations have you set for expense accounts?
27. Do you discourage collect telephone calls?

GENERAL AND ADMINISTRATIVE EXPENSE
28. What have you accomplished to reduce controllable costs in this area in the last six months?
29. What systems or procedures have you instituted to standardize techniques, eliminate confusion and reduce costs?
30. Has a review of surplus office furniture and equipment been conducted and have you declared the items as surplus to the corporation?
31. What controls do you have over petty cash expenditures?
32. How effective have you been in reducing receivables turn days in the past six months?
33. How effective have you been in reducing the cost of collection expense or bad debts in the past six months?
34. Is the postage account controlled and monitored?
35. Is the cost feedback adequate for you to manage your business? If not, what is missing that needs attention?
36. Have you been able to resolve problems by cross pollenization of ideas with other General Managers in your corporation? If so, what type of challenges were successfully mastered?
37. Would an official communication organ be of help to broadcast cost improvement ideas adopted at one location for possible adaptation by your location?

OTHER INCOME AND EXPENSE
38. How successful have you been in the past six months in obtaining more favorable discount terms from your suppliers?
39. What controls have you established to make certain all monies earned on discounts are a portion of your profit enrichment program?

Divisional cost systems survey (exhibit 2-2)

As the Diversified Company conducted its P.E.P. survey, they discovered a majority of its smaller divisions were lacking in effective cost collection and analysis systems. Thus the divisions did not have a firm grasp of their pricing policy in relationship to their market place. As a result of these questionnaires, many of the divisions surveyed requested and were provided with assistance in upgrading their cost collection and analysis process. Eventually one of the key team members, who had conducted these surveys and installed new cost control systems, left the Diversified Company and joined another multi-division company as a troubleshooter. He combined the two questionnaires and used them as a starting point for unscrambling some other involved and uprofitable problems.

Cost of sales questionnaire (exhibit 2-3)

Expanding upon the old bromide that nothing happens until a sale is made, there is no chance of a reasonable profit unless there is a reasonable gross profit. The cost of

DATA GATHERING AND IMPLEMENTATION

sales questionnaire examines the components associated with the cost of sales for a manufacturing firm—labor, materials, overhead, manufacturing variances, change in inventory, etc. The last categories are covered under "Other."

EXHIBIT 2-2
Example Corporation
Divisional Cost Systems Survey

I. *General*
    Division Name_____
    Planned Sales_____ Planned NBT_____ %_____

Major Product Lines	*% of Planned Sales*	*Gross Profit%*	*Headcount*
_____	_____	_____	_____
_____	_____	_____	_____
_____	_____	_____	_____
_____	_____	_____	_____
_____	_____	_____	_____
_____	_____	_____	_____
_____	_____	_____	_____
TOTAL _____	_____	_____	_____

Listing of Customers by Major Product Lines is Attached_____.
Organization Chart is Attached_____.
Chart of Accounts is Attached_____, including narrative. Description_____.
List of Cost Centers is Attached_____.
Cost Centers are divided into direct and indirect areas_____.
Indirect Cost Centers are segregated into Overhead and G & A centers_____.
Employees are segregated by Cost Centers_____.
Expenses are segregated by Cost Centers_____.
Do departmental budgets exist for direct_____ and indirect areas_____?
Is the budget feedback adequate?_____
_____
_____.

If not explain. _____
_____
_____
_____
_____
_____.

II. *Manufacturing Area*
    Does Supervision understand the Chart of Accounts and Budget Feedback?_____
    _____
    _____.

Comments on the ability of the following departments to aid the cost system:
Production_____.
Production Control_____
_____
_____.

Material Control_____
_____
_____.

Purchasing Control_____
_____
_____.

Quality Control_____
_____
_____.

Engineering_____
_____
_____.

How is work scheduled?_____
_____
_____.

How is manufacturing notified of a new job?_____
_____
_____.

How is accounting notified a job is completed?_____
_____
_____.

III. *Cost System*
Is there a cost accumulation system in effect for production_____,
engineering_____, construction in progress_____.
If yes, Job Cost__, Process Cost__, Standard Cost__, Other____.
If no, how is cost of sales computed?_____
_____
_____.

and inventories valued?_____
_____
_____.

Can present personnel handle the cost system?_____
_____
_____.

General Comments on cost system _____
_____
_____.

IV. *Estimating and Pricing*
Is a statement of work prepared before each quote?_____
_____.

What is the basis for the labor estimate?_____
_____
_____.

DATA GATHERING AND IMPLEMENTATION 45

What is the basis for the material estimate?_____
_____
_____.

How are overhead and G&A applied?_____
_____
_____.

Who applies the profit?_____
_____
_____.

Who approves the quote?_____
_____
_____.

Who compares the sales order to the original quote?_____
_____
_____.

Does the quote become the production and engineering budget?_____
_____
_____.

Comments & Recommendations: _____
_____
_____.

EXHIBIT 2-3
35-Point Cost of Sales Questionnaire

Material Costs

1. What percent of sales are direct materials?
2. How is the standard cost for materials established?
3. How often are these costs reviewed and by what procedure?
4. Are "free stock" items included as a direct or indirect cost?
5. How effectively and accurately are purchase parts invoiced and material (stores) requisitions processed?
6. Is a part numbering system maintained?
7. Does cost accounting's purchase price agree with purchasing's current records and if not, what corrective action is required?

Direct Labor Costs

8. What percent of sales is direct labor?
9. What percent of total salary and wages is direct labor?
10. Which departments (cost centers) are being measured by performance reports, and are line managers making effective use of these reports?
11. Are standard labor hours based on historical actuals or industrial engineering standards?
12. How current are these standards?
13. How accurate are the standard dollar labor rates, and do they reflect shift differentials?
14. How is cost accounting notified of changes in the labor rate or in the standard hours?

Overhead Costs

15. What percent of sales is overhead?
16. What percent of overhead is classified as indirect labor and is it all truly indirect?
17. What percent of the overhead represents variables, semi-variables, and fixed costs?
18. How is overhead applied, and is there more than one rate?
19. Is any of the overhead pool applied to materials and is the rate sufficient to fully absorb actual expenses?
20. Do overhead expenses exist by department?

Variances

21. How are variances reported—by job, standard production runs, or on an exception basis?
22. Are material variances segregated from labor variances?
23. Are labor variances segregated by rate and efficiency factors?
24. Are material variances segregated by price and usage?
25. Are variance results oriented so that causes can be quickly identified and corrected?
26. How effective are variance reports? Who receives, reviews, and analyzes these reports?
27. Is sufficient data provided so all jobs can be adequately reviewed?
28. Who determines which jobs or production runs will be reviewed?
29. Is cost estimating plugged into your variance reporting?
30. Can any of these variances be honestly billed to the customer to reflect changes, etc.?

Inventory Related

31. Are book to physical adjustments booked as discovered?
32. Are inventory cycles conducted, and how often?
33. How are production losses and shrinkages controlled, reported, and booked?

Other

34. Are gross profit margin analyses performed on a regular basis?
35. Are product line profit and loss statements prepared and shared with those who can make a definite contribution toward improving future results?

President's operating report (exhibit 2-4)

This final document is really a supplement to the other three questionnaires. It is submitted by the chief operating officer of the business unit. He may hold the title of President, Division Manager, General Manager, etc. Although the format has financial overtones, it is not a substitute for the financial commentary which accompanies the statement package. This report is an operational analysis highlighting what has happened during the period in question set against the financial results for the same time period. Whereas it is not geared toward gathering the basic key data about the operation, it does serve to provide a background or frame of reference as to what is occurring at the location in question. This type of report is useful for monitoring the accomplishments of key business objectives and general business performance. Another consideration could be to introduce the P.O.R. first, then gear your questionnaire format to coincide with the format of the letter, thus providing the reader of the president's letter with a better understanding of what is being presented. The example included as Exhibit 2-4 was first introduced to provide a newly appointed group vice-president in a newly assembled operating group with a communication tool between him and his division operating heads.

EXHIBIT 2-4
Example & Format
President's Operating Report

COMPANY: DATE:

GENERAL

	ACTUAL	%	PLAN	%	VARIANCE
Orders (Sales Booked)					
Net Sales					
Prime Cost (Labor & Material)					
Overhead					
Selling & G.&A.					
Operating Profit					
Net Non-Operating Items					
N.B.T.					
Receivables					
Inventory					
Head Count					

SALES

Billings varied from plan because two large jobs for General Motors and IBM were not finished on time because of customer-caused delays amounting to $35,000 in volume which will be picked up next month bringing us back to anticipated sales and profit levels.

Incoming sales for the month are at anticipated sales levels but we are a little worried with the change in management at our fourth largest customer which may bring some buying practice changes. We will watch them closely.

LABOR & MATERIAL

July was a disappointment from the standpoint of sales, but satisfaction may be gained from production performance. With labor and materials at 58.89% of sales (3% below Budget) and with total overhead within $240 of Budget, the breakeven point was at $139,448 producing N.B.T. $8,778 before taxes, despite the low revenue. From the logical premise that any additional sales would generate no additional burden, it can be deduced that budgeted sales of $200,000 would have resulted in a profit of more than 12% before taxes. Spoilage for the month was 1.18% of sales; or viewed in a more alarming perspective, spoilage consisted of almost 2% of other labor materials.

OVERHEAD—Was on target except for:

Current Factory Expenses—suffered from extraordinary repairs of equipment: No. 3 press was repaired at a cost of $1,088. Also departmental and general factory supplies rose $645 above budget.

Shipping and delivery expense—has continued to show improvement and the savings this month have offset the higher current factory expense to the extent that the net factory overhead is within budget.

SELLING EXPENSE is well within limits except for speculative art, which has been mounting. If this trend continues we will lay off some people in that department.

GENERAL & ADMINISTRATIVE EXPENSES reflect excesses in executive salaries for vacation pay to Mr. X (which we forgot to budget for), telephone of $300 and $375 in taxes and licenses. The latter account was charged with a deficiency assessment of $556 for city business license fees for past years based upon audit of deliveries made within the city during those years so should be in line in the future.

Only $754 of *Other income* was received in commission from Joe Doe Co., while an average of $2,875 per month has been realized from this source in the past and should be in the future.

LABOR RELATIONS

No problems. Union contracts on covered departments do not reopen until late next year and there has been no organizational activity in the open departments. Availability of labor pool still all right.

CAPITAL NEEDS

No capital requests needed at this time. However, we may need a new folding machine about December or January at a cost of approximately $15,000 after trade-in.

ACTIVITY ITEMS

Color Separation Dept.—We still have some problems with the installation of the new equipment in this department as well as a few minor crewing problems. We turned out some separations but they are not of required quality and of course they are costing us too much because of our inexperience. We are making progress however and by the end of next month should hit the breakeven point as anticipated.

Wage Plans—Have reviewed the first draft with our Personnel Director and the cost of implementation would be more than we could afford so we are in the process of refining the wage section as well as certain job classifications and will have our final draft for submission to you within two weeks.

BASIC BUSINESS PLAN

We are still looking for the right man to pursue the financial printing field business and are having a lot of trouble finding the right man within the budget. We may have to raise our horizons on what we are going to have to pay this man in the beginning until he becomes self-liquidating.

RECEIVABLES

Collections continue to be tough but we are meeting our 45-day goal primarily because our major customers have been paying very well and we have given some extra effort on some of the stragglers.

"STOP LOSS" OR "INVESTMENT" AREAS

The two salesmen we have in training are progressing nicely, but we are still investing about $700.00 per month in this program. If everything goes right they should hit the breakeven in another three months.

Our concession at the pilot Sears Roebuck Store is costing more than we anticipated by about $300.00 a month (total costs $2,300 per month) but we are not sure yet that it would be wise to close it.

CONVERTING YOUR FINDINGS INTO AN ACTION MATRIX

The previous section has shown you how to collect key data in an organized manner. The next step is often omitted by even the most sophisticated analysts and business consultants, and yet it is a most essential step—converting your findings into an action matrix. What happens in too many cases is the key data is assembled and either:

1. Remains in a reference notebook with limited access or use.

2. Develops into an analytical summary, which is better than the previous point.

3. Develops into a recommendation which is geared for action such as:

    —Gross profit needs to be improved in order to cover fixed costs.
    —Fixed costs must be reduced in order to improve profits.

DATA GATHERING AND IMPLEMENTATION

—Industrial technology should be transferred to the development of a high margin commercial product offering.
—Other.

but fails to define an action plan with measurable milestones of how the recommendations should be accomplished, completion dates, and who in the organization is to be held responsible.

As an operationally-oriented financial analyst, your aim is to analyze and convert your key data from simply data to usable "intelligence." This is not unlike the U.S. Government's Central Intelligence Agency which has a section whose purpose is to collect random bits of information, analyze them, and form data into a usable and workable intelligence. Like the C.I.A., you can use your newly developed intelligence level to ask significant questions and make worthwhile decisions and recommendations.

The Action Intelligence Matrix (Exhibit 2-5) is designed to fit the findings and conclusions derived from gathering your key data into nine function areas which are associated with almost any form of business endeavor:

1. General Management—Setting of policy, providing overall direction, staffing, etc.
2. Developing Marketing—Defining new markets or expanding established ones.
3. Selling—Providing customers within these defined markets with goods and services.
4. Pricing and Gross Profit—Insuring that the products which are sold are profitable.
5. Product Research and Development—Innovation—the need to continually develop new products and concepts in order to keep the competition at bay.
6. Production Management—The coordination of methods, tooling, facilities, labor, or vendors.
7. Financial Management, Internal—Controllership—the planning and control of profits.
8. Financial Management, External—Treasury—the raising and managing of funds.
9. Employee Relations—The full gamut of personnel, labor relations, etc.

Just to fit or file your findings and conclusions into the appropriate functional area would not direct or aim this intelligence in any particular direction or toward improving your decision-making ability.

A four-step conversion process transforms your intelligence into a set of actions. Using a combined marketing function as the functional area, let's proceed through the steps:

Step One—Define one or more *key objectives*. E.g.: institute marketing and selling improvements.

Step Two—Define or describe the *specific end result* or target. E.g.: achieve a more organized approach for rifling in on high profit accounts. Bring selling costs within the budgeted 3% of sales as specified in the financial guide line.

Step Three—Establish an *action plan* which spells out the tasks required to achieve steps one and two. E.g.:
- Pursue more strategic management level selling.
- Develop a more detailed and systematic approach to selling via annual sales plan and target accounts.
- Incorporate cost reductions and staff reorganization.

Step Four—Specify timing and due dates. E.g.:

1. May 31st —Cost Reductions
2. June 15th—Reorganizations
3. July 31st —Strategic Selling
4. July 31st —Annual Sales Plan

The following case in point illustrates three approaches for gathering key data and implementing the intelligence gained from the gathering. Although the approaches refer to three different organizational levels, they can be interchanged or mixed depending on your goals. In reviewing this case study, you will note the theme is the same—gather the key data so that a complete diagnosis can be made of the general health of the business, more intelligent and significant questions can be asked, decisions made, and an action plan developed and implemented.

A three-part case in point—how the gathering and implementing of key data acted as the first steps in affecting the turnaround of a badly battered business.

BACKGROUND

The Diversified Company mentioned earlier in this chapter began as a highflying mini-conglomerate. After completing an acquisition binge which saw them acquire over seventy small- to medium-size companies. Diversified's management decided it was necessary to stop functioning as a loosely knit holding company and to consolidate its efforts into four primary business areas. These areas were not based upon any business growth prescription or according to a set of written business objectives, but were chosen by sorting out what they owned and forcing a fit into four so-called synergistic but unrelated groupings. Each of these groups were equal in sales dollar volume (the only true common denominator).

The group directors were charged with the charter of tying together these loosely knit companies into viable business units which could eventually be spun off as separate independent companies. Diversified's management realized that to implement their charters, a large injection of capital equipment was required. The division presidents, many of whom had sold their businesses to Diversified on the promise of expansion capital, rallied to the cause, and Diversified began a capital spending binge which is discussed in more depth in Chapter 16.

In addition, Diversified embarked upon several of its own internally generated business development activities. While many of the ideas had merit and in time would prove worthwhile, Diversified failed to realize that innovative ideas and fledgling technologies take time to mature. Thus, they became impatient; and instead of being

EXHIBIT 2-5
Format for Preparing Your
Action Intelligence Matrix

Functional Area	General Objective	Specific End Result	Action Plan	Timing
GENERAL MANAGEMENT				
MARKETING MANAGEMENT (DEVELOPING MARKETS)				
MARKETING MANAGEMENT (SELLING THOSE MARKETS)				
PRICING & GROSS PROFIT				
PRODUCT RESEARCH & DEVELOPMENT				
PRODUCTION MANAGEMENT				
FINANCIAL MANAGEMENT, INTERNAL				
FINANCIAL MANAGEMENT, EXTERNAL				
EMPLOYEE RELATIONS				

content with a few eggs in one basket, they kept adding more developmental type projects until they became too numerous and complex to manage and finance.

Part of the financial problem could have been eliminated earlier in Diversified's history if the President, who was then one of the largest stockholders, had been willing to allow a secondary stock offering. It would have provided some liquidity to the business, but still would have not solved their problem which was the inability to manage the uncontrollable growth. The growth came to a sudden halt when the fledgling plants and technologies did not come on-stream fast enough, the general economic boom quieted, and money became tight. This forced the ouster of the President, and his successor began a rebuilding program.

I. GATHERING AND IMPLEMENTING KEY DATA AT THE CORPORATE LEVEL TO ASSIST IN EFFECTING A TURNAROUND

In actuality, the building program had begun earlier with the attempt by the group directors and certain corporate staff officials to weld their companies into the viable business units mentioned above. The first and most critical step was to inventory and analyze the strengths and weaknesses and institute corrective actions where possible. This activity consisted of four phases:

Phase One—57 Preliminary Divisional Surveys were conducted using the Profit Enrichment Program Questionnaires (Exhibit 2-1). In addition to completing the document, support papers were included which provided insight into the Division's products, equipment, skills, key personnel, salary structure, internal financial reports, etc. This data was not gathered to form a thick report, but to provide as complete a picture as possible of each Division's potential.

Phase Two—48 Cost Methods Evaluations were conducted using the Divisional Cost Systems Survey (Exhibit 2-2). This survey and analysis showed only fifteen of the systems analyzed to be adequate. Of the thirty-three remaining, only twenty-two were eventually repaired.

Phase Three—33 Pricing/Cost Estimating Evaluations were conducted as an outgrowth of the work completed in Phase Two. Of the thirty-three evaluations, eleven were analyzed, three systems were installed, and nine special studies were conducted. At least one-third of the special studies resulted in the re-negotiation and/or early institution of corrective actions which averted severe financial exposure on several large contracts.

Phase Four—6 Cost and Cash Flow Stop Gaps were instituted into smaller units for planning, controlling, and analyzing material purchases and labor. The tool for controlling material purchases was the purchase commitment system discussed in Chapter 8 and controlling labor by the earned hours approach discussed in Chapter 9.

The results of this four-phase approach were to define problems areas and take corrective steps when and where possible. In many cases, the Division's management was simply too close to the problems or firefights to see or take the time to implement solutions. The activity which took place in steps two through four was part of the on-scene first aid which was given to the patient until major surgery could be performed.

II. GATHERING AND IMPLEMENTING KEY DATA AT THE GROUP LEVEL TO ASSIST IN EFFECTING A TURNAROUND

As the individual groups began to evaluate each of the units and determine which of the units were salvageable and which should be discontinued, the gathering of key data became more refined and was eventually fashioned into a business profile for each unit of the company. A typical profile exclusive of financial data is described as Exhibit 2-7. In reviewing this profile, note the similarity to the narrative portion of the President's Report previously discussed (Exhibit 2-4). These business profiles can be used as the first step toward instituting this type of reporting format. With the writing of these business profiles, the group director could begin to understand the relationship between short and long range planning and its organizational structure in determining what was required to achieve its goals.

Typical Company was part of a group which anticipated sales in excess of $75 million and consisted of 14 companies, 17 plants, operated in 7 states, had one million square feet of facilities, and employed close to 2,000 people in manufacturing four product lines.

The group objectives were to:

—Operate profitably.

—Double each division's sales and profits in five years.

—Set profit targets of at least 10 percent on sales before taxes.

—Set R.O.I. targets of at least 25 percent before taxes.

—Grow internally and externally within the four existing product lines.

—Develop a capable organization to implement the above goals.

What they found was that the individual businesses within the group had to continually plan to reduce the gap between dying product lines and the introduction of new products and new markets. To accomplish this and insure profitable growth, they needed to build an organizational structure which was capable of simultaneously:

1. Watching over existing business to insure continued growth and profitability.
2. Looking into new products and markets, developing these opportunities coincident with the phasing out of the older and unprofitable products and enterprises.
3. Monitoring the group's position as it relates to the industry, the economy, and competition.
4. Reinforcing communications between the group management and the division presidents.
5. Avoiding financial surprises which could impair the profitability and potential of the group.

Thus the group was able to:

1. Gather data and refine it.
2. Produce business profiles for each unit in the group, which described the unit, its problems, its potential, and its business plan.
3. Define a set of operating objectives which were compatible with the parent company's goals as well as the potential and current circumstance of the individual units which form the group.
4. Define the type of organizational structure which would be required in order to

implement the goals and unleash the potential of the surviving units in the group.

III. GATHERING AND IMPLEMENTING KEY DATA AT THE DIVISION LEVEL TO ASSIST IN EFFECTING A TURNAROUND

Once the group structure began to function and the incurable companies were either sold or closed, the job of curing the walking wounded began. In Chapter 5, you will meet another of Diversified's companies—Red Ink Printing Co. Their profit impact charts read like a bad set of hospital X-Rays and definitely classified them as a bad case of the walking wounded. Although labor control was a key problem, it was necessary to collect additional information in order to diagnose all of the problems affecting Red Ink, so a complete healing job could be performed. The results were finalized into an Action Intelligence Matrix, very similar to the one shown in Exhibit 2-5. As the entire matrix is too extensive to be included, certain facets have been selected as "how to" illustrations.

Illustration #1: The following objectives were included under each of the following functional areas:

General Management
—Institute a true organizational change.
—Insure full-time administrative management.
—Develop a simple, balanced operating formula.

Sales
—Institute selling and marketing improvements.

Pricing/Gross Profit
—Formalize job recap overview.

Production Management
—Conduct a precise evaluation of the manufacturing operation.
—Maximize production and quality.

Financial Management
—Cash management.

Illustration #2: If you will refer back to the four-step conversion process for transforming your intelligence into a set of actions, you will recognize the Red Ink action plan for instituting selling and marketing improvements.

Illustration #3: Exhibit 2-6 duplicates the action plan associated with the general management's general objective—develop a simple, balanced operating formula.

SUMMARY

Diversified, with the help of a lot of people and long hours, was able to refinance and reorganize itself into a profitable operating company.

EXHIBIT 2-6
One Column Illustration of
Red Ink Printing Company's
Action Intelligence Matrix

AREA	General Management
OBJECTIVE	Develop a simple balanced operating formula.
SPECIFIC END RESULT	1. Provide frame of reference for improving decision making. 2. Motivate and control all levels of management on a self-renewing basis. 3. Cause department managers to initiate on their own cost improvements and short cuts. 4. Influence pricing and job costing.

ACTION PLAN	1. Install as a way-of-life, the following P&L financial guidelines:
	    Labor & Material 66% of sales
	    Overhead 18% " "
	    G&A 4% " "
	    Selling 3% " "
	    Profit 9% N.B.T.
	2. Adjust cost center P&Ls and profit sharing to basic P&L formula.
	3. Relate pricing and job cost review to P&L formula.

TIMING	May 15th— Orientate division management to concept. June 1st— Tie formula to multiple cost center concept. August 1st— Tie formula to departmental profit sharing.

EXHIBIT 2-7
Business Profile—Example

The Typical Metal Company
(Subsidiary—A California Corporation)

Staff

A. Shore—President
M. Thomas—Exec. Vice-President
B. Sangray—Vice-President & Controller

Locations

Plant	Warehouse
123 Manufacturing Road	456 Storage Place
Profit, California	Profit, California

Products & Services

Hot rolled and fabricated steel angles and flats.

Markets Served

Metal working—manufacturing and processing industries.

Capabilities

Engineering design, rolling, fabrication, steel processing and stamping.
Presses up to 250 tons, roll forms.

Marketing

Typical Metal Company has recently completed a detailed analysis of the steel fabrication industry and/or their product mix as affected by changing trends in this industry. They feel their overall sales growth will continue because of the demand for finished steel parts and a loosening up of money in 19X1. Historically, their business has fluctuated along with the automotive industry.

Manufacturing

Typical Metal Company is presently operating a partial second shift on all lines which they plan to round out by March and continue throughout the year. The hiring of two additional foremen to run a full second shift will be required. The added cost of the foremen is recoverable through increased operating efficiency, elimination of overtime, and reduced scrap of 8%.

Purchasing

A steel strike is anticipated in the third quarter, and thus stock piling has begun. Material prices are anticipated to be slightly less than the past year as a result of a recently negotiated foreign steel contract. The negotiations resulted in a $5/ton decrease in price for a major portion of Typical's steel requirements.

Engineering

All engineering on equipment is being performed by manufacturing, thus no plant engineering is anticipated. Customer engineering is supplied as required.

Industrial Relations

The current labor contract ends 3/9/X1 and no strike is anticipated, but a modest rate increase is expected which will be recoverable through pricing and improved plant efficiency.

Organization

No major changes to their current organization chart is anticipated. Typical has provided for succession planning and has instituted appropriate training programs to insure its realization.

Facilities Summary

    Land Area (acres)
    Building Area (thousands of square feet)

DATA GATHERING AND IMPLEMENTATION

    Capital Investment (net)
    Property Taxes—annual $
    Building Rental—annual $
    Equipment Leased—annual $
    Insurance—annual $

Performance Indexes Data

    Number of employees by key labor classification
    Square feet of facilities
    Accounts Receivable
    Inventory
    Accounts Payable
    Total Assets
    Equity
    Backlog
    Current year's sales, profit before taxes
    Plan sales, profit before taxes
    Prior year's sales, profit before taxes

Statistics

    Sales per asset
    Sales per employee
    Sales per square foot
    Number of days in receivables
    Inventory turnover
    Return on assets

3

PLANNING MECHANISM— BLUEPRINT FOR A SUCCESSFUL OPERATIONAL FINANCIAL ANALYSIS SYSTEM

The how to systematically build profits through the application of operationally-oriented financial analysis theme is continued in this chapter by addressing one of the most important links in this process—the planning mechanism. The planning mechanism and in particular the annual Financial Guide Line (F.G.L.) form the backbone for a dynamic and energetic program. The planning mechanism described in this chapter is more than just long-range planning or budgeting; it serves as a blueprint for expressing:

—How the business will be operated.
—What is important to the successful operation of the business.
—What are the objectives to be accomplished.
—How will these objectives be achieved.

This "how to" chapter provides those individuals who have never installed a planning mechanism with the essentials for installing a successful system. For those individuals who have a planning system currently in force, ideas and pointers are provided for making it a more productive and effective system.

AN EFFECTIVE FINANCIAL GUIDE LINE MEANS GREATER PROFITS

The importance of a written financial guide line

The F.G.L. is the written financial expression of the business blueprint previously discussed. As financial analysts and executives, you may be required to explain or even

PLANNING MECHANISM

sell the need for a written F.G.L. to various levels of your organization. The following checklist has been prepared as an aid in answering the question—What purpose is served or need fulfilled by preparing a written F.G.L.?

EXHIBIT 3-1
8-Point Checklist Defining the Need and/or Purpose of the F.G.L.

1. The need to plan is incumbent upon all levels of management because we are not able to foretell what the future holds for each of us.
2. The need for a written F.G.L. is vital in converting ideas and dreams into actionable plans.
3. The need for an action plan which delegates responsibility to every member of the management team, so they know and understand their commitment as to:
   — What has to be accomplished.
   — When it has to be accomplished.
   — What is required in time, services, and materials in order to achieve this accomplishment.
   — Who is responsible.
4. The need to have a roadmap for monitoring the different activities which are underway and their progress.
5. The need to know what corrective productive action must be taken when we start going away from the F.G.L.
6. The need to direct all available resources which are found in a manufacturing environment—the five M's of manufacturing—men, materials, machinery, methods, and money.
7. The need to identify problems before they occur and set into motion the appropriate corrective action. In this type of situation, your F.G.L. may be modified into alternative plans such as "go or no go" plans or recovery plans.
8. The need to coordinate the efforts of various profit centers and/or cost center within these profit centers and to assure these functions are all heading in the same direction. An example would be insuring that a total company (profit center) is producing the right product mix.E.g., a large quantity of Product A is produced when all we can sell is Product B, and to what extent will the engineering work being performed on Product C impact tomorrow's sales and the sales on A and B.

The goal, after a point in time, of the F.G.L. is to have your management asking:

—What does this decision or course of action ultimately cost our company?

—What does it save the company?

—How am I appreciating the profits of the corporation, my division, or my department?

Overplanning vs. underplanning

The development of the F.G.L. has to be a happy medium between overplanning and underplanning. The financial planning package that you send out to each reporting unit must be designed to achieve this happy medium. Management at all levels must know that this is your goal.

There can be overplanning when elaborate reports and graphs are requested and prepared beyond any need that exists for improving the decision-making powers of the individual managers. Another example of overplanning is a manager being overcautious about making necessary and important decisions.

On the other hand, underplanning is the failure to take into account significant events that are predictable and that should be within the purview of the well-informed manager. Underplanning may also take place when the manager makes only a crude guess with regard to matters that should be more thoroughly studied.

The F.G.L. should be a picture of what each profit center can achieve, not what the center feels the corporate or head office wants to see. Also, a plan submitted by a reporting unit's management to show itself as heroes at the end of the year, because they beat their F.G.L. by a 50% margin, is a F.G.L. that does a disservice to both the reporting unit and to the headquarter's staff, who will be reviewing the plan during the year. As the preparer of the F.G.L., you must stress to your management that many different levels will be reviewing his plan during the year with many different objectives in mind. Many decisions will be based upon what is stated in the F.G.L. When comparing the actuals to the planned activity, the reader in a far distant headquarter's office may decide that a certain reporting unit has enough available resources to complete the task, and thus a badly needed piece of equipment or working capital may have been denied a reporting unit, all because there was a lack of thoroughness in preparing the business plan and its written financial expression—the F.G.L.

A "reporting unit" depending upon your function and level in your organization can vary. If you reside on the corporate staff, a reporting unit could be the various profit centers which make up your corporation. A profit center for this definition is an independently self-supporting subsidiary or division of a multi-division firm. At the profit center level, a reporting unit could be an entire plant, cost centers, or departments within the plant or profit center.

ESTABLISHING BUSINESS AND PLANNING OBJECTIVES— THE CRITICAL STEP

The key to achieving a balance between over and underplanning is the setting of business and planning objectives. Planning objectives are those factors, techniques, and considerations which reflect how your firm will be able most effectively and efficiently to plan and control the business. The partial list of points which follows is a mixture of both procedural and conceptual considerations. Remember, the following list of planning objectives is not complete; it is only the beginning:

— What time periods will be covered and how much detail will be presented? E.g.: How "big picture" should your long range plan be or how much detail should your annual F.G.L. contain in regards to account level, summary account level, statement level, by month, by quarter, etc?

— What objectives, benefits, and purposes are expected from each level of planning? E.g.: Is the F.G.L. level satisfactory for controlling your organization or do you need detail departmental budgets to effect the level of control which is desired?

— What resources are available such as time, manpower, computerization, etc?

PLANNING MECHANISM

- —What area of the business will be first to benefit from the installation of an improved planning and control system and by what method?
- —How will the planning be updated and maintained?
- —What is management's top priorities in the planning and controlling of the business?
- —How can you insure that the planning process will generate new ideas, while properly addressing basic everyday "how do we better run the business" problems?
- —What steps must be taken to insure there is a true interrelationship between the results achieved from the long range planning process and the actions which are reflected in the F.G.L. and its supporting set of departmental budgets?
- —Remember, the planning and reporting methods must coincide.

Business objectives are the results of management's defining and developing a total and complete business strategy. In reviewing the growth and success of the American industrial giants such as General Motors, Sears, et al., they all have a common hallmark—successful strategies. This point is best proven by General R.E. Wood, former board chairman of Sears, Roebuck & Company, who stated it best of all in his familar quote: "Business is like war in one respect, if its grand strategy is correct, any number of tactical errors can be made; and yet the enterprise proves successful."

Thus, a workable blueprint, which stresses a true balance between over and underplanning can be achieved by properly:

1. Identifying your planning objectives, framework, and procedures.
2. Establishing definite business strategies.
3. Developing business objectives which are based on these strategies.
4. Converting these objectives into actionable operating plans.
5. Expressing these plans financially in the form of a financial guide line.
6. Extrapolating the F.G.L. into departmental budgets to insure action at the lowest possible levels.

A case in point—how two diverse and profitable companies incorporate functional objectives and operating responsibilities into a workable and effective blueprint

In the last chapter of this handbook, you will be introduced to how the Abron Company has organized to implement a systematic operationally-oriented approach to financial analysis. Abron, which offers a regionally well-known consumer goods product, and an industrial manufacturer and supplier, who has built an equally profitable business, have a mutual approach. They both have introduced into their organization the setting and defining of business and planning objectives as a critical step in the control process. While Abron is relatively new at the process, the industrial products company, which has been at it for several years, has doubled its sales in each of two consecutive five-year periods. They attribute their sales and organizational growth to having a planning and control system which is keyed to the defining of clear-cut functional responsibilities and setting of operating objectives or goals.

In a nutshell, the difference between a functional responsibility and an operating objective is the difference between a routine assignment and a new and innovative approach requiring a definite action, which will impact the general profitability and liquidity of the firm. The industrial products company, which Abron patterned its approach after, feels there are between 125 and 150 functions required to operate a business. E.g.: If a business sells on terms, it will require the administration of a credit function. The specific operating objective for a given period could be that the accounts receivable level should never be more than 15% of average monthly sales. The percentage could vary depending upon business conditions. (Refer to Chapter 17 for a further explanation and example of one set of functional responsibilities and operating objectives in action.)

The overall goals and objectives initiated at the corporate level are narrowed and translated downward throughout the organization. Eventually, parts of these goals will become the individual manager's annual incentive goals. Thus, the goals do not remain stagnated at the top of the organization, but are placed into action at the proper time and level.

Abron adopted this approach as a solution to meeting two needs:

1. A need to generally improve the caliber and relativeness of planning to keep pace with both the rapid product and organizational expansion Abron was experiencing.
2. A need to improve the caliber, effectiveness, and profit relativeness of the setting of goals by department and section managers.

The key to implementing solutions to the above mentioned problems was the separation of a manager's functional responsibilities and his operating objectives. E.g.: The manager of plant engineering and maintenance replaced "Painting the warehouse ceiling" as an operating objective with "Prepare a program which reduces machine down time by 20%. (Painting the ceiling is covered under his functional responsibilities as a routine task.)

How Abron updates and tracks the accomplishment of its annual operating goals is covered in the last case in point in this chapter.

A case in point—the setting of business objectives can benefit the small as well as the large company

Abby, Inc. is a small but profitable metal fabricator and processor. The founder/president discovered that as his business grew, his problems also were growing at a much faster rate. He was continually in a cash bind and found that the hours required to tend the store were increasing to a point that he was even working Sundays. These actions prompted him to step back and analyze his business and how it compared to others in his industry. His analysis showed his business to compare very closely to others in his industry group including those bigger in size. His analysis was not confined to financial and operating problems and conditions. His list of key problems and conditions showed that plants of his size suffered from:

—continued firefighting
—long hours required by key people

—constant scrambling for orders

—always being short of working capital

To correct this situation, he invoked the following three-step formula:

1. Set both company and personal goals.
2. Determine and take the necessary steps required to achieve these goals.
3. Relate each decision to the goal.

The last point became his overall operating philosophy. If a decision did not bring him closer to reaching a desired goal then the answer to the decision in question was NO! With this operating philosophy in hand, he established the following objectives and parameters for conducting his business:

1. Each job, regardless of size, must be profitable. Marginal jobs, which would at least help to absorb fixed costs were discouraged, because they could "turn sour."
2. Their products would be service and quality, not fabrication and processing.
3. Customers would be solicited on the basis of their requirements for quality, special handling, and service.
4. Pricing would be fair to their customers, while profitable to Abby, Inc.

Abby, Inc.'s president had as his overall objective the establishment of a firm which was in essence a business free from competition. To support this concept, this firm discouraged any customer who did not meet their desired customer profile. The practice of submitting bids was all but discontinued in the pursuit of developing this type of business. Prices were only quoted as an accommodation to customers.

Over the years, the sales force was all but eliminated as customers became aware of the proven service and intuitively chose Abby over the other vendors. The key to operating in this manner was the firm's continued commitment to excellent service and fair pricing. Because they were actively involved in the success and profitability of the business, the employees fostered and adhered to this overall business philosophy and its operating objectives. This was attained through their participation in the company's profit sharing program. (For comments on how profit sharing programs can be the key to lasting profits, refer to Chapter 14.)

This case has been included to drive home the point that setting business objectives or goals is not confined to the large companies with extensive staffs. If you truly wish to engineer profits and remove some of the risk from your business by adopting a systematic approach, then the first step is the setting of a realistic set of business objectives.

DON'T IGNORE THE FUNDAMENTALS

The one unpardonable sin for those who are charged with coordinating the preparation of the F.G.L. is committed when they appear to be disorganized and show signs of not having planned their activity. This will occur when basic fundamentals and details, which may appear mundane, are overlooked or totally ignored. These fundamentals are presented in Exhibit 3-2 which lists a 7-step process which should be easily implementable into your organization.

EXHIBIT 3-2
7-Step Checkoff List of Financial Planning Fundamentals

Step 1— Issue a complete planning calendar and timetable. This step is essential since it serves as a preplanning activity, which will identify potential problems, bottlenecks, key dates, staffing, and most important serves as a checkoff list for insuring that all areas, steps, and functions have been included and evaluated. *Example:* One large company has determined that the preparation of its annual business plan, capital budget, financial guide line, and operating departmental budgets require 77 major steps and accompanying milestone dates. The process begins the first workday after the July 4th recess and culminates with the final presentation to the chairman of the board on the Tuesday prior to Thanksgiving. As this firm makes greater use of its computer timesharing capability, the process time is predicted to be shorter.

Step 2— Design and issue simple, easily understood formats and forms. The forms should be simple instead of a volume of 10 or 15 sheets as is so often the case. This should be the case for both your long range planning financial projections (Exhibits 3-3 through 3-6) and your annual financial guide line. The F.G.L. can be kept to two legal size, double-width pages. One page having to do with P & L items, and the second having to do with balance sheet items.

    First let's discuss the P&L—Exhibit 3-7. The top part of this page should show a development of orders; starting when the orders will be brought into the house and their effect on backlog. This is the basis for a detailed sales figure. From there you derive your net sales and your necessary expenses. If you wish to have statistical information such as sales and profit based on headcount, square footage, etc., this data should be contained at the bottom of this page.

    The next page is the balance sheet—Exhibit 3-8. You should show the following: The development of cash flow, your receipts and disbursements, which then becomes the first line of the balance sheet showing the amount of cash, and how the cash was arrived at. Another section is the derivation of inventory levels. This should be in the same format, showing additions and reductions of inventory. If space permits, and you are interested, you may do the same thing for accounts receivable and payable.

    In addition to your P & L and balance sheet, the most important page to any financial plan is the assumptions or criteria page. This should be filled out in great depth. Its value will come in analyzing the variances from your plan, in evaluating alternative plans, and as a general basis for your thinking for future plans. Another document which is essential is your list of capital expenditures for plant and equipment, buildings, leaseholds, land. This list should include every item of a capital nature and should tie in with your balance sheet and show the date of acquisition of each asset. Justification sheets should back up each capital item. This document should show payback period, discounted cash flows, and return on the gross assets. (This is covered in greater detail in Chapter 16.)

    You may wish to have other supporting schedules. These may include the development of products, the phasing out of old products, more detailed information on receivables and inventory, backlog and sales projections. These schedules should be kept to a minimum and be selective.

EXHIBIT 3-3

LONG-RANGE FINANCIAL PLAN
INCOME STATEMENT

(DOLLAR AMOUNTS IN THOUSANDS)

	EST. Current	PLANNED 19X1	19X2	19X3	19X4	19X5
SALES	$	$	$	$	$	$
GROSS PROFIT						
(% of Sales)	%	%	%	%	%	%
EXPENSES:						
Marketing						
General and Administrative						
Other						
INCOME BEFORE TAX						
Income Tax						
NET INCOME	$	$	$	$	$	$

% GROWTH

SALES	%	%	%	%	%	%
Compound Sales Growth						%
NET INCOME	%	%	%	%	%	%
Compound Income Growth						%

EXHIBIT 3-4

LONG-RANGE FINANCIAL PLAN
KEY DATA AND RATIOS

(DOLLAR AMOUNTS IN THOUSANDS)

	EST. Current	PLANNED 19X1	19X2	19X3	19X4	19X5
ADJUSTED GROSS ASSETS	$	$	$	$	$	$
GROSS ASSET TURNOVER						
% RETURN ON SALES	%	%	%	%	%	%
ROAGA	%	%	%	%	%	%
EMPLOYEES						
UNITS SOLD PER EMPLOYEE						
PERSONNEL COST PER EMPLOYEE	$	$	$	$	$	$
UTILIZATION OF PRODUCTION CAPACITY:						
Maximum Capacity	%	%	%	%	%	%
Peak Season Capacity	%	%	%	%	%	%
CASH RETURNED TO CORPORATE AS A % OF INCOME	%	%	%	%	%	%
E.P.S. CONTRIBUTION						
COMPOUND GROWTH — E.P.S.						%

PLANNING MECHANISM

EXHIBIT 3-5

LONG-RANGE FINANCIAL PLAN
FUNDS FLOW STATEMENT

(DOLLAR AMOUNTS IN THOUSANDS)

	EST. Current	PLANNED 19X1	19X2	19X3	19X4	19X5
FUNDS PROVIDED BY:						
Net Income	$	$	$	$	$	$
Depreciation						
Disposals of Property						
Deferred Taxes						
Other						
Total Funds Provided						
FUNDS APPLIED TO:						
Capital Expenditures						
Returns to (from) Corporate						
Debt Service						
Other						
Total Funds Applied						
INCREASE (DECREASE) IN WORKING CAPITAL						

CHANGES IN WORKING CAPITAL:						
Cash and Securities	$	$	$	$	$	$
Receivables and Inventories						
Current Liabilities						
Other						
Total Changes						

EXHIBIT 3-6

LONG-RANGE FINANCIAL PLAN
CAPITAL EXPENDITURE PROJECTION

(DOLLAR AMOUNTS IN THOUSANDS)

	EST. Current	PLANNED 19X1	19X2	19X3	19X4	19X5
Land & Buildings	$	$	$	$	$	$
Lab & Test Equip.						
Machinery and Equipment						
Improvements						
Office Equipment						
Fleet						
Special Projects:						
1.						
2.						
3.						
4.						
5.						
Total Special Projects						
Contingency						
Total Capital Expenditures						
% of Net Income	%	%	%	%	%	%

PLANNING MECHANISM 69

EXHIBIT 3-7

FINANCIAL PLAN (Page 1)

STATEMENT OF INCOME AND SUPPLEMENTARY DATA
(IN THOUSANDS OF DOLLARS)

#	DESCRIPTION	COMP. CODE	NOV.	DEC.	JA... UG.	SEPT.	OCT.	FOURTH QUARTER	12 MONTH TOTAL
1	BACKLOG								
2	NEW BOOKINGS								
3	SALES PROJECTION (Detail)								
4									
5									
6									
7									
8									
9									
10									
11									
12	TOTAL SALES PROJECTION								
	INCOME STATEMENT								
13	GROSS SALES	1301							
14	SALES DISC., RETURNS & ALLOWANCES	1302							
15	NET SALES								
16	COST OF SALES								
17	DIRECT LABOR	1303							
18	DIRECT MATERIAL	1304							
19	OVERHEAD	1305							
20	CHANGE IN INVENTORY	1306							
21	TOTAL COST OF SALES								
22	EXPENSES								
23	SELLING EXPENSE	1307							
24	GENERAL & ADMINISTRATIVE EXPENSE								
25	CORPORATE CHARGE								
26	Subtotal G & A & Corp. Chg.	1308							
27	TOTAL SELLING & G & A EXPENSE								
28	OPERATING INCOME								
29	NON-OPERATING INCOME								
30	INTEREST	1309							
31	RENTS	1310							
32	DIVIDENDS	1311							
33	OTHER	1312							
34	TOTAL NON-OPERATING INCOME								
35	NON-OPERATING EXPENSE								
36	INTEREST	1313							
37	OTHER	1314							
38	TOTAL NON-OPERATING EXPENSE								
39	INCOME BEFORE INCOME TAXES								
40	STATE & LOCAL INCOME TAXES								
41	FEDERAL INCOME TAXES								
42	TOTAL INCOME TAXES	1315							
43	NET INCOME								

EXHIBIT 3-7 (cont.)

INTERCOMPANY ITEMS									
44 NET SALES									
45 INTEREST INCOME									
46 INTEREST EXPENSE									
47 RENTAL INCOME									
48 RENTAL EXPENSE									
49 DIVIDEND INCOME									
50 CORPORATE CHARGE									
51									
52 DEPRECIATION INCLUDED ABOVE									
SUPPLEMENTARY DATA									
53 **NUMBER OF EMPLOYEES**									
54 DIRECT									
55 OTHER									
56 **TOTAL NUMBER OF EMPLOYEES**									
57 **SPACE** – UTILIZED (IN SQUARE FEET)									
58 – VACANT (IN SQUARE FEET)									
59 **TOTAL SPACE** (in square feet)									
60									
61 **ANNUAL BUILDING RENTAL**									
62 **ANNUAL EQUIPMENT RENTAL**									

PLANNING MECHANISM   71

EXHIBIT 3-8

FINANCIAL PLAN (Page 2)

FISCAL YEAR _____

BALANCE SHEET AND RELATED STATISTICS
(IN THOUSANDS OF DOLLARS)

	DESCRIPTION	COMP. CODE	OCT. CURRENT YEAR	NOV.	AUG.	SEPT.	OCT.
	CASH PLAN						
1	BEGINNING CASH BALANCE						
2	CASH RECEIPTS						
3	ACCTS RECEIVABLE COLLECTIONS						
4	INTERCOMPANY COLLECTIONS						
5	SALE OF FIXED ASSETS						
6	OTHER						
7	INTERCOMPANY ADVANCES						
8	**TOTAL CASH RECEIPTS**						
9	CASH DISBURSEMENTS						
10	GROSS PAYROLL						
11	ACCOUNTS PAYABLE PAYMENTS						
12	INTERCOMPANY PAYMENTS						
13	PURCHASE OF FIXED ASSETS						
14	TAXES						
15	OTHER						
16	INTERCOMPANY ADVANCES						
17	**TOTAL CASH DISBURSEMENTS**						
18	**NET CASH BALANCE**						
	INVENTORIES						
19	RAW MATERIALS						
20	PURCHASED PARTS						
21	WORK-IN-PROCESS						
22	FINISHED GOODS						
23	OTHER						
24	**TOTAL INVENTORIES**						
	BALANCE SHEET						
25	CASH	0201					
26	MARKETABLE SECURITIES	0202					
27	ACCOUNTS & NOTES RECEIVABLE	0203					
28	INVENTORIES	0211					
29	PREPAID EXPENSES	0218					
30	**TOTAL CURRENT ASSETS**						
31	RECEIVABLES DUE AFTER ONE YEAR	0219					
32	CSV OF LIFE INSURANCE – NET OF LOANS	0220					
33	INVESTMENTS	0221					
34	DEFERRED CHARGES	0222					
35	PATENTS, TRADEMARKS, ETC.	0223					
36	INTANGIBLES VIA ACQUISITION – NET	0224					
37	PROPERTY, PLANT, & EQUIPMENT						
38	LAND	0225					
39	BUILDINGS	0226					
40	MACHINERY & EQUIPMENT	0227					

EXHIBIT 3-8 (cont.)

41	LESS ACCUMUL. DEPRECIATION	0228
42	**Net Property, Plant & Equipment**	
43	OTHER ASSETS	0229
44	**TOTAL ASSETS**	
45	BANK LOANS	0301
46	ACCOUNTS & NOTES PAYABLE	0302
47	ACCRUED—PAYROLL & RELATED EXP.	0303
48	INCOME TAXES	0304
49	OTHER EXPENSES	0305
50	CURRENT PORTION—LONG TERM DEBT	0306
51	**TOTAL CURRENT LIABILITIES**	
52	ADVANCES (TO) OR FROM AFFILIATES	0307
53	ADVANCES (TO) OR FROM CORPORATE	0308
54	DEFERRED—INCOME TAXES	0309
55	OTHER	0310
56	MORTGAGES PAYABLE	0311
57	OTHER LONG TERM DEBT	0312
58	**TOTAL LIABILITIES**	
59	DIVISION EQUITY	0317
60	RETAINED EARNINGS—THRU LAST YR.	0320
61	CURRENT YEAR EARNINGS	
62	**TOTAL EQUITY**	
63	**TOTAL LIABILITIES & EQUITY**	

PLANNING MECHANISM

Step 3— Prepare and issue a detailed instruction or planning manual.

Now that you have decided on a form that you are going to use, you must now go through and analyze each form for completeness. As you do this, a planning manual should be written. This planning manual should conceive of every possible question that a remote division might ask on how to do its planning.

It should be a line-by-line description showing what has to be placed on each line. An example of the completeness that is required is shown below for the balance sheet included as Exhibit 3-8.

Line 26 MARKETABLE SECURITIES

Investments in the form of stocks, bonds, and other securities owned by the entity and which are readily marketable or mature within one year.

Line 27 ACCOUNTS AND NOTES RECEIVABLE

Claims (excluding intercompany) arising in the ordinary course of business which are reasonably expected to be realized in cash during the normal operating cycle of the business, usually within one year. Uncollected progress billings, and installments and deferred payment items are also fully included, regardless of the terms of collection. Miscellaneous receivables, such as amounts due from employees and notes receivable are classified on this line. Any allowance for doubtful accounts is offset to this account.

Line 28 INVENTORIES

This line serves to describe lines 19 through 23 and requires no entry.[1]

Line 19 RAW MATERIALS

Cost of tangible commodity purchased for use which requires additional processing, fabricating or finishing.

Line 20 PURCHASED PARTS

Cost of fabricated or manufactured parts which are purchased from outsiders, and which are ready for assembly without substantial further manufacturing.

Line 21 WORK IN PROCESS

Cost of tangible property in the process of production, or raw material and purchased parts directly charged to production on which processing may not have started.

Your planning manual should not be looseleaf, so the pages cannot get lost. It compels the planning section to correct and compile a newly updated book each year or each planning cycle.

Step 4— Develop the necessary computer software programs.

If the corporation is quite large or if there are multidivisions, some computing capability is required. The computing capability should be used to generate all the statistical information. The profit center should not take the time to do these calculations. Time should be directed toward doing a good job of planning.

---

[1] No entry is required because the computer program will automatically retrieve the total of lines 19 thru 23.

Also, you will need to have a computer program that consolidates all of your various plans by groups and sub-groups, and gives you a final total. Your computer program can perform elementary checks such as, taking the net profit line and converting it to the balance sheet. If the balance sheet does not balance, it gives you an error message.

A final point on your computer program is that your forms should be coded to the computer program, so that the documents can be key-punched directly as received from the profit center and thus eliminating the extra coding step.

In harnessing the computer, do not forget to include computer timesharing capabilities. Because of computer timesharing's highly interactive mode, the operational-oriented financial analyst is able to:

— Handle lengthy calculations, such as manpower staffing requirements and associated labor costs.

— Manipulate data files, interrelationships, conditions that would otherwise be time consuming if performed manually or even in a computer batch mode, because of the slow turnaround.

— Play the "what if" game. E.g.: If my costs drop X% and I incur a mix shift of Y, what will happen to my gross profit Z?

— Perform projections based on historical data and actuals.

— Analyze the company's future in light of its past.

For a demonstration of how two firms in two totally different industries effectively apply timesharing in preparing their financial guide lines and support budgets, refer to the case in point following this checkoff list.

Step 5— Allow enough time for the printing and distributing of forms to the reporting units.

Most people do not allow enough time for preparation of the form by the printer. This includes checking the roughs and finals, and then allowing ample time for the forms to be printed. Once the forms have returned from the printer and the packages have been prepared, a cover letter should be written from the President, stressing to division management the importance of planning to the corporation.

Step 6— Allow enough time for the reporting units to complete their requirements.

Remember in many instances the individual at the reporting unit will have to complete his financial projections in addition to his regular duties, so allow enough time. In addition, preplanning should be done to allow for proper follow-up and control. No matter how much we try to avoid it, there will always be one or two reporting units which will be delinquent in submitting their plans. You may wish to have a detailed follow-up procedure ready, including a series of letters reminding those who are preparing the F.G.L. and budgets of the deadlines which have to be met and the importance of the project.

Step 7— Allow enough time for performing routine clerical evaluations and adjustments.

When the plans return, they should be clerically checked to assure that computer time will not be wasted because of an out-of-balance condition. (This assumes your program uses a trial balance format.)

If ample time is not allowed for making final adjustments, mistakes and

PLANNING MECHANISM

omissions can and will occur. Because it is the last phase, it is the phase that will stick in everyone's mind and could be the basis on which they judge your entire planning function. Leave enough time because it is the capstone to your entire activity.

One more consideration, do not make any adjustments, no matter how small, without discussing them with the preparers, because you plan to hold them accountable for the F.G.L. and budgets being achieved. The evaluation phase is discussed in the next section of this chapter following the case in point.

A case in point—how two diverse and profitable companies incorporated computer timesharing and saved both time and money, while producing an improved F.G.L.

Do you have enough time to adequately prepare and analyze your company's F.G.L. and support departmental budgets? In most cases, the response would indicate that there is not sufficient time. Those charged with preparing the F.G.L. at Abron Company and at the industrial products company (both of which are subjects in the opening case in point) were faced with solving this type of problem.

Their solution was to add computer timesharing terminals and selective programs to their arsenal of financial analysis capabilities. Initially, the terminal was used to process mathematical routines which used to consume many hours of the analyst's and clerical staff's efforts. Once this number crunching activity was bedded down, the analysts were able to approach more sophisticated comparative and analytical routines. Eventually, the analysts at Abron were able to set up a "war room" to prepare very simple financial models, which they used in making summary level financial projections and playing "what if" games.

Specifically, Abron felt they initially saved a little over $8,000 in "hard dollar savings" and an additional $16,000 in "soft dollar savings." These soft dollar savings represented the additional temporary financial analyst costs which would have had to be incurred, if they were to curtail the overtime effort which is currently being incurred but not paid, because the analysts are classified as salaried exempt.

Beyond the dollars, the true savings were the flexibility and added "think time" which the terminal provided. The analysts, who were charged with preparing the budget, could analyze results and concepts and not continually be bogged down in the crunching of numbers.

Specifically, the industrial products company was able to reduce its joint headquarters plant's budget review sessions from an average of two plus days to just over one-half of a day. This was accomplished by first identifying each account as either a variable account, which was related to production, or a fixed account, which did not vary. They also determined that those accounts which were classified as semi-variable were in reality either variable or fixed. Then they proceeded to prepare timesharing computer programs, which analyzed three years of dollar activity by month for each variable account and converted the data into a cost per production unit rate for each variable account. This rate was based on one foot of product produced. E.g.: If they were budgeting for the plant and equipment maintenance account for the month of May and May's production estimate showed the Los Angeles plant producing 1,500,000 equivalent feet of product, the terminal would extend the equivalent feet to be produced by the agreed upon rate of 3¢ per equivalent foot equaling $45,000.

With the actual three-year history for each account plus an understanding of the inflation factor which had to be applied to each account for the next year, they were able to cut down the debate time between headquarters and plant personnel.

Thus each of these dynamic firms was able to automate its budgeting activity and to curtail its number crunching effort. Consequently, they increased their analytical and review time with the assistance of timesharing.

THE FINANCIAL GUIDE-LINE IN ACTION

Once the F.G.L. has been received from the various reporting units or you have assembled the individual budgets into the F.G.L., it needs only to be evaluated and presented to your senior management team.

Evaluating the F.G.L.

While the F.G.L.'s were being prepared, corporate headquarters management should have defined what is to be expected from each one of its reporting units in each crucial area; sales, new bookings, net before tax, cash generation, etc. The corporation should know what it expects from each one of its divisions, but these goals should not be a dictation of what the reporting unit is to submit. It is only a means of comparing the plan to what the corporation expects from each one of its divisions. This area has to be treated very, very carefully, so that the reporting units do not feel that corporate headquarters has dictated to them, because no management team should be held responsible for a business plan and accompanying F.G.L. which they have not developed. On the other hand, as evaluators, it is your job to determine the extent to which the plan is attainable.

Another point to be stressed in this section is that the evaluation procedure should not be based solely on historical data and trends, but on the facts which are going to shape the functioning of the profit in the next fiscal period. The plan should be neither a pie-in-the-sky forecast which could never be reached, nor a plan that can be achieved in a breeze. The objective is a plan which reflects the best thinking and efforts of the preparers.

While the reporting units were preparing their F.G.L., you should prepare a summary document called an Evaluation Sheet. This document should be condensed by quarter, showing the plan, the actual year to date, the previous year's plan, prior year's results, and any other relevant data. This should highlight sales, net before tax, receivables, cash or any other pertinent information that you think is important. Also, it should have a goal section in order to interpret how well the unit will be able to meet the corporate or headquarter's goal, which was discussed above.

Remember, as an operationally-oriented financial analyst, don't just process the numbers, but try to understand the facets of the business, the industry it operates in, its cost structure, its ability to raise prices, etc.—don't just crunch numbers!

Presenting the F.G.L. to senior management

Do not neglect to make a formal presentation to management of the business plan for the forthcoming year and its accompanying financial guide lines once it has been consolidated and finalized. Management should be presented with an indexed booklet containing the complete plans and the important subsections to that plan. Once the booklet has been prepared and distributed and management has had a chance to digest

PLANNING MECHANISM

the report and form questions, a briefing meeting should be held. The purpose of this meeting is to breathe some life into the figures and explain the whys and wherefores that will contribute to the next financial period's results.

Updating and tracking the F.G.L.

As next year's financial results develop, you will need to track the progress of these results against the F.G.L.; Chapter 5 is devoted to one method of tracking the F.G.L.—profit impact charts. Another approach may be to hold quarterly reviews, at which time a current projection of how the current year is shaping up may be in order. Remember, if you do consider having these quarterly updates, reporting unit managers are still to be required to explain in detail any deviation from their original F.G.L. submission. If this adherence to the original F.G.L. is not upheld, sloppy and weak planning will occur in both the defining of business strategies, setting of objectives, and forming of the business plan.

A case in point—how Abron tracks and updates its F.G.L. using a simple two-step process

The first case in point introduced you to the Abron Co., and how they began the formation of their F.G.L. by basing it upon a set of annual operating objectives. Abron Company is also the subject of Chapter 17.

Abron's Director of Financial Analysis and Budgets feels very strongly that the business planning process, which results in the F.G.L., is a continuous process. Unfortunately, too many businesses view the preparation of the F.G.L. as an interruptive process, which is undertaken once a year. To insure the F.G.L. does serve as a business blueprint, the Director and Abron's management have instituted the following updating and tracking procedure:

1. The financial statements and budget vs. actual variances are each supported by supplementary commentary which provides an in-depth understanding of the numbers.
2. A quarterly progress report is prepared and presented to senior management. The quarterly review analyzes the progress made to date against the F.G.L. plus a current outlook for the remainder of the fiscal year.

Part of this quarterly review process is a progress report pertaining to the status of the current year's operating objectives. Each functional manager is asked to submit a briefly written paragraph explaining the accomplishments to date, as pertains to each of the various operating objectives. Functional managers are also asked to identify and track future topics which will eventually become tomorrow's operating objectives.

Applying this simple two-step process, Abron is able to easily track the progress of actual results in relation to the financial guide line and to update its operating objectives. In addition to these two major steps, Abron has instituted a modified series of profit impact charts for tracking one of its operating units which is located outside of the continental United States. Abron's financial analysis staff has discovered that by using these charts in conjunction with the financial statements, they are better able to adequately monitor and control this unit's performance against its F.G.L.

4

EFFECTIVE MARKETING PLANNING—OBJECTIVES AND TECHNIQUES IN OPERATIONAL FINANCIAL ANALYSIS

As the financial guide line is normally prepared by accounting-oriented individuals, there is a tendency for the preparers to overlook and underevaluate the thought process used to develop the marketing plan. Even sophisticated analysts fail to realize that:

1. The marketing plan is the key to their financial guide line and business plan.
2. As an operationally-oriented financial analyst, he should and want to become involved in the operational decision-making process which will effect tomorrow's business and profits.
3. What is outlined in today's marketing plan will impact tomorrow's evaluations and analytical assignments.
4. With his involvement in the development of various data bases and their manipulations, the analyst could well become the co-preparer of the marketing plan.

This chapter provides a series of checkoff lists suitable for the financial and marketing analyst. The financial analyst can use these lists as a guide to becoming a more constructive evaluator of his company's marketing plans. The marketing analyst can use them as a guide to preparing his marketing plan or as a tool for finding and correcting any deficiencies in the current planning system.

EFFECTIVE MARKETING PLANNING

WHAT YOU SHOULD EXPECT OF YOUR MARKETING PLAN

It must be written!

The first objective of any business is to create the ability to generate customers and have these customers purchase your goods and services. It is an aphorism that "Nothing happens until someone sells something to someone else." Thus, we have marketing; and marketing to be effective must have a written marketing plan, because a written plan:

1. Forces an *organized approach* to analyzing markets, market share, products, pricing, customers, and setting of objectives.
2. Improves *communication and decision-making,* because all levels of the organization are equally informed. Also, key factors and variables are thus presented in a format, which will provide challenging exchanges of ideas and comments.
3. Results in an early *warning device* to alert management to deviations from the plan, which brings about corrective action.
4. Provides a *management performance* tool for evaluating people, products, and programs.

It must follow good planning precepts!

Before conducting an in-depth examination of the marketing plan, it should be reviewed from an overall basis by asking the following questions:

1. Are assumptions clearly defined?
2. Have internal limitations and external factors been considered in setting goals and objectives?
3. Have alternative courses of action been considered and are they included?
4. Have tasks and programs been defined, scheduled, and has responsibility for achievement been clearly established?
5. How is the plan to be measured?
6. How does the plan compare to long-term objectives and needs?
7. Does the plan have top-management support?

It must be complete and well organized!

The marketing plan to be effective must be well organized. If it is well organized, you increase your chances of having a complete and accurate plan. The elements of a good annual plan are listed below and can serve as the basis of a table of organization for your company's plan:

1. *Preface*—Includes an introduction and summary of the plan to be presented.
2. *Prior Year Review*—Contains a complete review and synopsis of the prior year's planning, its successes and failures.
3. *Current Market Situation*—Evaluating your market situation begins by analyzing the total available market. This analysis continues by determining

how much or what percentage of this total market you intend to command.

4. *Opportunities*—Defines all opportunities, restrictions, and problems which enter into the formation of your plan.
5. *Goals and Objectives*—Goals and objectives must be specific and include both descriptive and quantitative goals.
6. *Strategy*—Includes the overall strategies, individual tactical plans, and programs which will be necessary in order to achieve the goals and objectives set in the previous sections.
7. *Implementation Plan*—The detailed timetable for completing the individual tasks which are required to implement your strategy.
8. *Financial Data*—In this section, unit sales, forecasts by product line, territory, etc., should be converted to sales dollar forecasts. In addition, support budgets for adverting, sales incentives, promotions, and sales training must also be completed in order to understand the cost associated with gaining these sales.

It must be complete!

Today's marketing plan besides being the basis for preparing the financial guide line will also be the first link in setting into motion a causal chain of events (similar to the domino effect) which could lead to new products and markets, reorganization and retraining, etc.

EXHIBIT 4-1

28-Point Checkoff List for Preparing and Evaluating Marketing Plan Content

Basic Business
1. What is the nature of our business?
2. What factors are causing us to be successful or retarding success?
3. Do we have a basic marketing philosophy?
4. What are the interrelationships of our markets, businesses, ventures, and products?

Markets
5. What broad markets ought we or should we be penetrating, i.e., industrial, consumer, institutional, foreign, etc.?
6. Which segments of these markets should we be aiming for?
7. What is our potential in each of these segments?
8. How does our current and future product mix fit into these market segments?
9. What opportunities and problems are associated with these markets, and how will they effect our future?
10. Who and what are the characteristics of the prominent customers in these markets? A customer profile should be developed which includes markets, numbers, size, location, buying patterns, etc.
11. Have we correctly defined the buying needs of these customers, and how can we satisfy these needs?

EFFECTIVE MARKETING PLANNING

Products

12. What basic products should we offer?
13. How do our products measure up in the market place?
14. Which products should be modified, eliminated, or repackaged?
15. Are our products priced properly, and do they provide the proper gross profit margin?
16. What new products and technologies need to be developed and at what cost?
17. Within each product group who is the competition?
18. What are their strengths and limitations?
19. What is our basic approach to meeting the competition?

Selling and Distribution

20. How good is our sales and distribution network, and what advantage does it offer us over our competition?
21. Are we using the proper and most efficient selling and distribution methods?
22. Are our sales and distribution organizations properly staffed, trained, and compensated?

Advertising and Sales Promotion

23. What method is employed to measure advertising and sales promotion effectiveness?
24. What strategy dictates the use of media, direct mail, displays, promotions, publicity, etc.?
25. What is our company and product image, and is it satisfactory?

Marketing

26. Are the marketing organization and programs organized and staffed properly to execute their plans?
27. Is the total company organized to execute the marketing plan? (Can production meet delivery quotas, are distribution channels adequate for foreign market penetration, etc.?)
28. How good are our market research, planning, and measurement tools?

SELECTING THE RIGHT SALES FORECASTING METHOD

The sales forecast, besides being the key document in the preparation of the financial guide-line, is also the ignition device for setting into motion the controls which regulate the:

—setting of sales quotas

—setting of budgets

—flow of production

—levels of inventories

—spending of purchasing dollars

—the borrowing of short and long term capital

For these reasons, a sales forecast must be produced which is timely and reasonably accurate. As an operational financial analyst, you need to be familiar with the basic marketing forecasting tools which are available in order to accomplish this goal.

The seven basic sales forecasting methods

1. *Polling Key Executives*—Although it is based on the opinion of several key executives, the poll can be completed quickly and easily without the use of statistics. It also expedites the approval process, because those who ultimately are held responsible for planning and running the organization are the ones who are providing the input. E.g.: A consumer products company is headed by a very knowledgeable marketing man, who, because of his industry expertise, provides his marketing and planning staff with his knowledge and insight as to what extent he feels the market will grow or contract. Based on this key assumption, they begin to build their sales forecast for the forthcoming year.

2. *Polling the Salesforce*—This technique taps the information which exists in the territory being served. Once the sales forecast has been prepared, sales personnel will usually have greater confidence in it, because they have provided the input used in its preparation. Since salesmen are usually poor estimators in regard to demand, they will tend to be self-serving, especially when sales quotas will be based on the forecast. Careful review of the data is required at successive levels.

3. *Polling Customers*—This procedure is especially advantageous where products are few, easily identified, or located where the seller maintains customer inventory levels. The seller can then determine the total demand for the product and extrapolate his share or portion of the demand.

4. *Delphi Technique*—While this technique is used primarily for long range forecasting, it should not be overlooked for shorter range planning. The Delphi technique eliminates experts, appointed heads, strong personalities, who because of their status or personality would otherwise dominate or intimidate the results of a poll. A panel is assembled and polled, the group's answers are compiled, and a composite summary is prepared. This approach masks the identity of the responders and allows for the presentation of all viewpoints and conclusions.

5. *Extrapolation Techniques*—These mathematical techniques put to use time-series decomposition for preparing forecasts based on trend, cyclical and seasonal analysis, and exponential smoothing for the fitting of growth curves. Exponential smoothing is a form of moving averages which applies a weighted sum of all past numbers in a time series, while placing the heaviest weight on the most current or recent information. Thus, these methods can be used to analyze past movements and interactions of the basic influences which largely determine the pattern of your firm's sales, such as long-term growth trends, cyclical movements, seasonal variations, and irregular movements.

6. *Correlation Technique*—This technique measures the relationship between two or more factors. As a sales forecasting tool, it utilizes past relationships between the variable to be forecasted and other variables, i.e., what factors are influencing current sales, such as disposable income. This method forces the preparer to qualify the assumptions underlying his estimates, thus making it

EFFECTIVE MARKETING PLANNING

easier for management to check the results. There is an inherent danger in placing too much reliance on the correlation relationships while totally ignoring the need for an independent appraisal of future events.

7. *Econometric Technique*—This method is based on developing a set of relationships between your business or industry and a set of economic variables. Once the theory of relationships has been developed, a set of equations which form a model for interpeting and converting the economic variables is prepared. In the not too distant future, with the aid of computer timesharing, marketing forecasters and business planners will have the ability to link their internal (company) forecasting models. So, when designing your forecasting system, this future capability should be kept in mind.

Cases in point—how an incorrect assessment of the marketing situation can distort your sales forecast and eventually cause you to lose control of your business

The next two cases in point demonstrate how two companies, which were rich in technical talent, failed to prepare or properly evaluate a sales forecast and paid the consequences.

CASE IN POINT #1—BUDGET STEREO SET COMPANY

Budget Stereo Co. was an independent corporation which was a captive supplier for a large retail furniture store chain selling quality products to primarily low income families. As middle income families recognized the quality plus low prices offered by the chain, their Hi-Fi Stereo business began to grow, and Budget Stereo also grew. Budget Stereo, realizing their product was superior to their competitors, decided to expand. Their sales forecast was based on the belief that with their superior quality, budget minded consumers would rush to purchase their product. Based on this sales forecast, they acquired a silent partner to finance this expansion and began to increase their inventory levels in anticipation of increased sales.

At first the expansion occurred and then declined. They also began to incur delivery problems, which drew their attention away from their eroding sales order backlog. Realizing their inability to deliver was a result of production problems, they decided to bring in an outside consultant. He recommended improvements in their production control system. He also directed them to get out into the field and determine what was their true market potential, what percentage of that market was available to them, and who were their customers. They refused to do this because it would divert their attention from solving their production problems, which they felt were their true problems. Meanwhile, the silent partner, who ceased to be silent, placed his own management in the firm.

The new management promptly conducted the survey, prepared a detailed marketing forecast, and realized that the product they offered could not compete successfully in the middle income market. The new management used existing inventories as holiday promotional specials to expand and secure their customer base in the budget market.

The original owners walked away with a token settlement, wishing they had listened to the consultant, but happy their business did not fall under the auctioneer's hammer.

CASE IN POINT #2—CORROSIVE TIMER COMPANY

Corrosive Timer Co. had developed a small, electro-chemical timing device which combined electrical current and chemical corrosion. This device was very useful in measuring the elapsed time between equipment maintenance or major overhaul efforts. This technology was primarily sold to the military. Corrosive Timer decided to expand their minuscule commercial business by selling a commercial version of their timer as a between car service (oil-change—lubrication) measuring device.

The timing device was test marketed and a very optimistic sales forecast was prepared. On the other hand, the controller thought the test was limited and not truly representative of the market, but he felt it was not his job to challenge this overly optimistic forecast. A financial guide line was prepared in great detail and submitted to their venture capital source for further financing. The venture capital firm, lulled by the previous growth of the military business, quickly provided the funds; and in exchange, the founders relinquished further control.

Sales did not materialize as expected. The founders, who were now minority stockholders in their own firm, began to re-examine how the forecast had been put together. They realized they had entered a market they truly knew very little about. They had developed a sales forecast based on weak information (improper market test area).

The venture capital company, realizing the potential loss to themselves, sold their interest to a large, high technology firm who treated the business as just another product line. The founders, like the Stereo Co. founders, were content to walk away with a little cash and a lot of broken enterpreneurial dreams.

5

PROFIT IMPACT CHARTING FOR IMPROVED FINANCIAL REPORTING AND CONTROL

Chapter Five provides an important link in how to systematically build profits through operational financial analysis. It shows you how to expand that column of information on the income statement labeled "Variance from Financial Guide Line" into an easy and effective means of:

1. Better communicating actual results and deviations from plans and goals to non-financially oriented managers at various levels within the organization.
2. Immediately pinpointing problems and opportunity areas, especially in their earliest stages of development.
3. Defining action points and tracking them to their successful completion.

To achieve this objective, two series of profit impact charts suitable for immediate installation within your organization are described and explained by the use of case examples. Chart series A reflects a top-down approach to analyzing the course of your business; while Chart series B is more detail oriented and views the conduct of the business from a bottom-up approach.

As the chapter unfolds, you will see the uniqueness of the approach is not confined to the charts alone, but to the manner in which they are incorporated into how you analyze and evaluate results and incorporate your findings into the decision-making processes of the business. The chapter opens with a much overlooked concept—that no firm or division of a larger company should consider itself too small to have and effectively use business planning and control systems.

A CASE IN POINT—
WHAT ONE COMPANY LEARNED ABOUT PLANNING
AND CONTROL TECHNIQUES

Unfortunately, many smaller firms or units of larger corporate organizations do not feel there is a need for even the simplest planning and control systems in their organizations. The best way to dramatize the irrationality of this thought process is to describe a discussion I held with the president of a small firm that manufactures heating and air-conditioning components. He informed me that while attending a small business seminar at one of the local universities, the participants were asked if their firms would like to take part in a case study. This study was to determine if budgeting, cost control, and profit planning techniques which are used advantageously by larger firms could be adapted for use by smaller companies. His firm chose to participate in the case study. In discussing the results of the case study, two facts were apparent:

1. Size is not a limitation

The techniques his firm learned as a result of the case study participation are applicable to smaller business units.

This fact was demonstrated when an economic slump forced many of his competitors out of business. However, by using the techniques learned in the case study, he was able to adjust his business to current economic conditions.

2. Many managers of smaller units are reticent

There is a basic reticence displayed by most small business units toward the techniques used by their larger counterparts. This point was demonstrated by the fact that of all the participants at the seminar only the heating and air conditioning manager volunteered his firm to be used in the case study. Most of his fellow participants felt these techniques could not be used successfully by their firms because there was no workable vehicle available to them for implementation.

Arguments for and against

The main argument offered by the manager of the smaller business unit is his organization is small enough to be planned and controlled by himself and/or a few key people in the organization. In a form of rebuttal, the manager of the smaller business needs an effective and efficient vehicle for planning and control in order to allow for orderly growth. As the business grows it becomes more complex both technically and organizationally, and the manager finds it difficult to keep his finger on every area of the firm. He is then forced to hire others to carry out some of these tasks. Eventually, the small business manager becomes so deeply involved in the other areas such as financing, sales, marketing, new product development, and a higher level of administration and leadership, he becomes removed from the day-to-day activities.

Although we have spent some time building a case for the adoption of a good planning and control vehicle in the smaller business units, we should not lose sight of its

PROFIT IMPACT CHARTING

value in the larger corporate environment, because it is in these environments, due to the size, complexity, and fragmentation into individual departments, that profit impact charting backed up by a well thought-out financial guide-line is imperative.

CHARTING AS A DRAMATIC SUPPLEMENT TO FINANCIAL STATEMENTS

Another weak argument offered by some managers is the financial statements are all they need to control their operations. In truth, it takes more than financial statements to control operations. The successful manager must develop a means of binding together every member of the management staff and move them toward a common goal: achievement of the financial guide-line. Most financial people overlook an essential element when they are designing a planning and control system, namely the system needs to motivate the user into some form of constructive action. The proper use of effective charting permits a system to be self-renewing. It gives a manager parameters to make confident decisions. As an example in point, the manager who only relies on his financial statement can develop the false belief he is doing the best possible job, and thus the only decision he makes is to maintain the current course of action. I.e., no change in business strategy, organization, or approach is required at this time.

Profit impact charts as the vehicle

Consider the concept of profit impact charting as a graphic approach to financial planning and control. The operational manger, whether he is in engineering, production, or marketing, is not an accountant. Therefore, he needs clearly synthesized financial information to manage his segment of the operations. Many companies use charts as puff and not as analytical tools for communication and decision making. The profit impact charting concepts provide the user with a complete series of charts that guide inter-relationships, depict trends, and detect deviations from plan.

EXHIBIT 5-1
8-Point Checkoff List for Considering Graphic Presentations

1. Vividly isolates trends and pinpoints deviations.
2. Shows the relationship between financial and non-financial data.
3. An effective means of isolating and presenting selected portions of the financial condition of the business without revealing the entire financial condition.
4. Operational conditions need not be masked by bookkeeping entries.
5. A communication tool for holding regular review meetings.
6. The charts can be the major framework for writing monthly operational activity reports or supplementary monthly financial statement commentary.
7. Placing financial data into a common form that is easily understood by both financial and non-financial personnel.
8. An easy educational tool for teaching non-financial managers the impact of their operating actions upon the financial condition of the company: i.e., building a financial statement awareness.

PROFIT IMPACT CHART COMPONENT SELECTION

The question may enter your mind—Where do I begin to determine what data I should include in my profit impact charting package? In fact, you have started this process in the previous chapters.

A RECOMMENDED LIST OF CHARTS FOR GETTING OFF TO A GOOD START

EXHIBIT 5-2
Chart Series A—Percentage of Sales Approach

Chart Number	Description
A-1.	Sales Dollars YTD/N.B.T. Dollars YTD
A-2.	Sales Monthly/N.B.T. Monthly
A-3.	Net Before Taxes as a % of Sales
A-4.	Direct Labor
A-5.	Material
A-6.	Overhead
A-7.	Selling Expense
A-8.	G & A Expense
A-9.	Head Count by Department
A-10.	Cash Flow—Monthly
A-11.	Receivables
A-12.	Inventories

Chart Series B—A Functional Approach

Chart Number	Description
B-1.	Orders in Units
B-2.	Orders Mix in Units
B-3.	Shipable Orders
B-4.	Shipment in Units
B-5.	Shipment Mix in Units
B-6.	Sales in Dollars
B-7.	Contribution to Sales & Profit by Product Line
B-8.	Profit Before Taxes
B-9.	Head Count & Staffing Analysis
B-10.	Administration—Indirect Expenses
B-11.	Engineering & Research Expenses
B-12.	Manufacturing—Indirect Expenses
B-13.	Marketing Expenses
B-14.	Maximum and Minimum Inventory Levels
B-15.	Maximum and Minimum Backlog Levels
B-16.	Pro-forma Balance Sheet
B-17.	Cash Flow
B-18.	Facility Requirements

To achieve your financial guide line you had to go through the necessary steps of gathering key data. With this data already in hand, you need only select the format.

PROFIT IMPACT CHARTING

Exhibit 5-2 shows two lists of charts which can be used independently or mixed, as suits the needs of your organization.

The charts present two different ways of looking at a business: from the top-down or bottom-up. To select the series of charts most suited to your organization, you must be fully acquainted with your needs and the conclusions you wish evaluated and acted upon.

Chart series A is better suited for high level reviews: at the group level in the multi-company firm. This series could be the basis for your monthly activity report to the home office. It can also be used as a supplement to monthly financial statements, a means of breathing life into the otherwise dry statements. Chart series A provides a top-down or a more conceptual approach to managing the business than Chart series B. Examples of Chart series A formats and their relationship to the percentage goals concept are shown in Exhibits 5-6 to 5-16.

Chart series B is more functional in approach and thus more suited for conducting internal operational review meetings and writing financial commentary at the division or plant level. At this level the financial man is more concerned with product mix, product line, gross profit contribution, R & D costs, etc. Chart series B provides a more in-depth look at the components that make up the business: a bottom-up approach. Examples of chart series B formats and their applications in holding operational review meetings are shown as Exhibits 5-18 to 5-26.

PROFIT IMPACT CHARTS GIVE VISIBILITY TO DEVIATION FROM PLAN

One question that is very often asked by operational managers in functional areas is "How are we doing against plan?" or "Am I making my goals?" The best way of tackling these questions is to provide these managers with graphic presentations of how they are doing in meeting their goals. This can be depicted on the profit impact charts by measuring the distance between the broken line (Plan) against the solid line (Actual). See Exhibit 5-3.

Breathing life into the charts

In order to activate these charts, a few easy refinements need to be added:

The first is to list the key data that went into developing the chart.

The second is to include trends that point to possible problems or suggest opportunities. A missed opportunity can do more harm to a firm's growth than all the problems incurred during the year. This trend is usually shown as an extension of a solid actual line crossed by a dotted line. See Exhibit 5-3.

The third is to add mind joggers. Mind joggers are key words that serve as reminders and/or explanations of why deviations of plan occur. They are important to the results-oriented managers, who are caught up in the *now,* and often forget the details or causes that brought them about.

A few examples of mind joggers are:

—Breakeven point pierced

—Wildcat strike

—First delivery—government contract

EXHIBIT 5-3

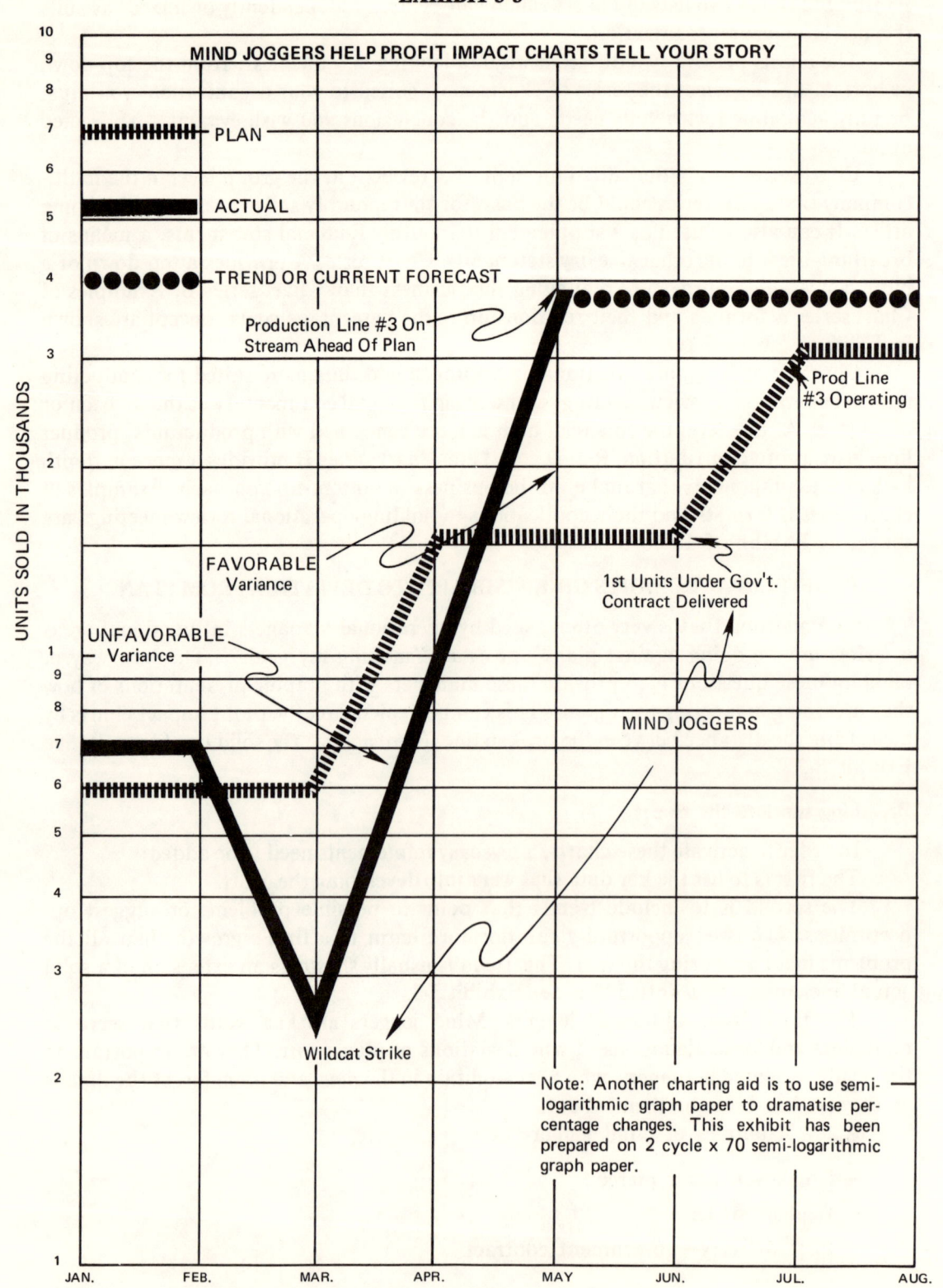

PROFIT IMPACT CHARTING

—Profit impact charting introduced

Exhibit 5-3 illustrates how these aids can be included.

Sharpening your use of profit impact charts

It was previously stated that the value of these charts lies in their interrelationships. The concept of how to best use the interlocking nature of these charts is best accomplished by reviewing the live data contained in the next case in point of the Red Ink Printing Co. Imagine you are analyzing the charts for the first time and attempting to define an appropriate action program.

A case in point—how Red Ink Printing Company used the interlocking nature of profit impact charting to uncover and solve its problems

Red Ink Printing Company's main market is a highly competitive regional area where high quality and extra service are required. This firm requires an intensive capital investment and is midway through a three-year new plant start-up program. Red Ink has determined that its ultimate goal is to continue to build profitable volume and strive for an 11% before tax return on sales. The future financial guide line income statement goal is shown as Exhibit 5-4.

EXHIBIT 5-4
Red Ink Printing Co.
Future P & L Percentage Goal

Sales		100%
Labor	18%	
Material	48%	
Overhead	18%	
Total C/S		84%
Gross Profit		16%
Selling Expense		4%
G&A Expense		3%
Net Before Taxes		9%

While striving toward its ultimate goal, the firm has developed via its financial guide line, a current year's goal of doing better than breaking even. By examining what the firm did for the last reported month, March, we can compare it to the future (long range) and current goals; see Exhibit 5-5.

EXHIBIT 5-5
March Actual vs. Goals

	March Actual	Current Goal	Future Goal
Labor	22.5%	17.6%	18.0%
Material	51.4	50.9	48.0
Overhead	19.9	19.6	18.0
Total C/S	93.8	88.1	84.0

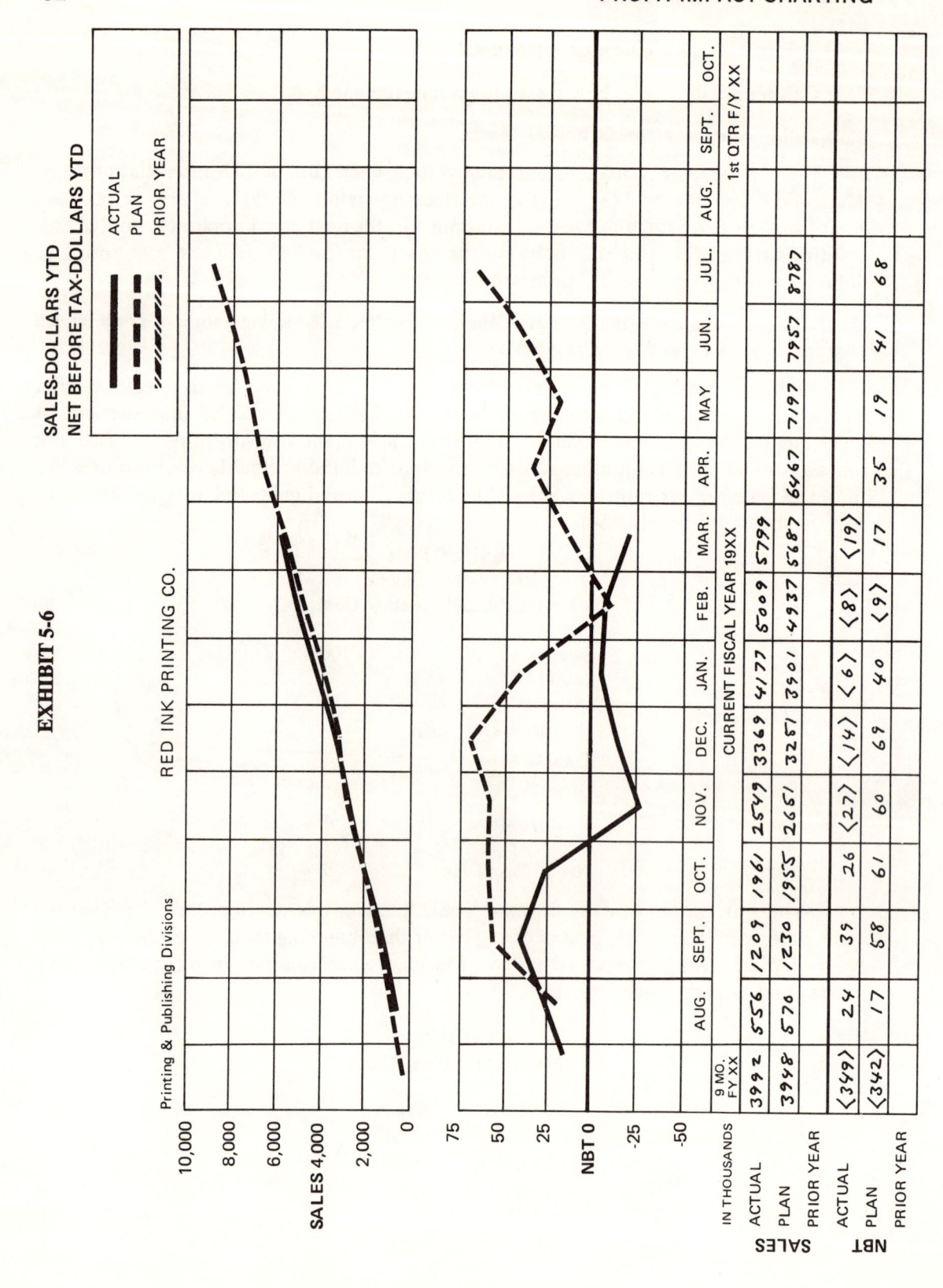

EXHIBIT 5-6

RED INK PRINTING CO.
Printing & Publishing Divisions

SALES-DOLLARS YTD
NET BEFORE TAX-DOLLARS YTD

- ACTUAL (solid)
- PLAN (dashed)
- PRIOR YEAR (hatched)

IN THOUSANDS	9 MO. FY XX	AUG.	SEPT.	OCT.	NOV.	DEC.	JAN.	FEB.	MAR.	APR.	MAY	JUN.	JUL.	AUG.	SEPT.	OCT.
SALES ACTUAL	3992	556	1209	1961	2549	3369	4177	5009	5799							
SALES PLAN	3948	570	1230	1955	2661	3261	3901	4937	5687	6467	7197	7957	8787			
SALES PRIOR YEAR																
NBT ACTUAL	⟨349⟩	24	35	26	⟨27⟩	⟨14⟩	⟨6⟩	⟨8⟩	⟨19⟩							
NBT PLAN	⟨342⟩	17	58	61	60	69	40	⟨9⟩	17	35	19	41	68			
NBT PRIOR YEAR																

CURRENT FISCAL YEAR 19XX — 1st QTR F/Y XX

PROFIT IMPACT CHARTING

Gross Profit	6.2	11.9	16.0
Selling Expense	4.3	5.2	4.0
G & A Expense	4.3	4.0	3.0
Net Before Taxes	(2.4)%	2.7%	9.0%

Putting the charts to work

By studying Exhibit 5-5, it is quite evident that direct labor is out of control. This factor coupled with near misses in the other profit and loss areas are keeping Red Ink Printing Co. from achieving its current percentage goals. As a supplement to Chart series A, there are self-explanatory comments regarding their interaction.

EXHIBIT 5-6

Comments

Year to date sales since November continue to be ahead of plan. The realization of planned profits at first glance appears to be unattainable. The Y.T.D. profit dollars (lower section of the chart) are almost the exact opposite of the financial guide-line goal. A planned profit of $17,000 is in reality an actual loss of $19,000. Although monthly sales (next exhibit—monthly sales) seem to be running ahead of plan, their ability to generate turnaround profits seems doubtful. If you do not investigate further, using both charts concurrently, the typical year-end results would be as follows:

	Plan	*Forecast*[1]	*Difference*
Sales $	8787	8899	112
Profit $	68	(41)	(109)

Preliminary Conclusions

The planned sales level is obviously not buoyant enough to float profits above the breakeven level. The causes may be that there are in-house job losers or the plant can not produce efficiently.

Questions to Management

1. Are all the "buy-in jobs," which had a known breakeven or low profit contribution potential, out of the orders backlog? If not, how soon will they be out?
2. Are current job estimates being priced with enough profit?

[1] The commentary for the next exhibit shows how the estimate was derived.

EXHIBIT 5-7

Comments

Monthly sales are running ahead of plan, but they fail to produce profits. Profits since December are in a continual decline. If the profit line is to be trended out (not shown), the monthly losses by July would be substantial. In order to determine if this trend conclusion is correct, the year-end results could be forecast using the data relationships shown on the charts as follows:

PROFIT IMPACT CHARTING

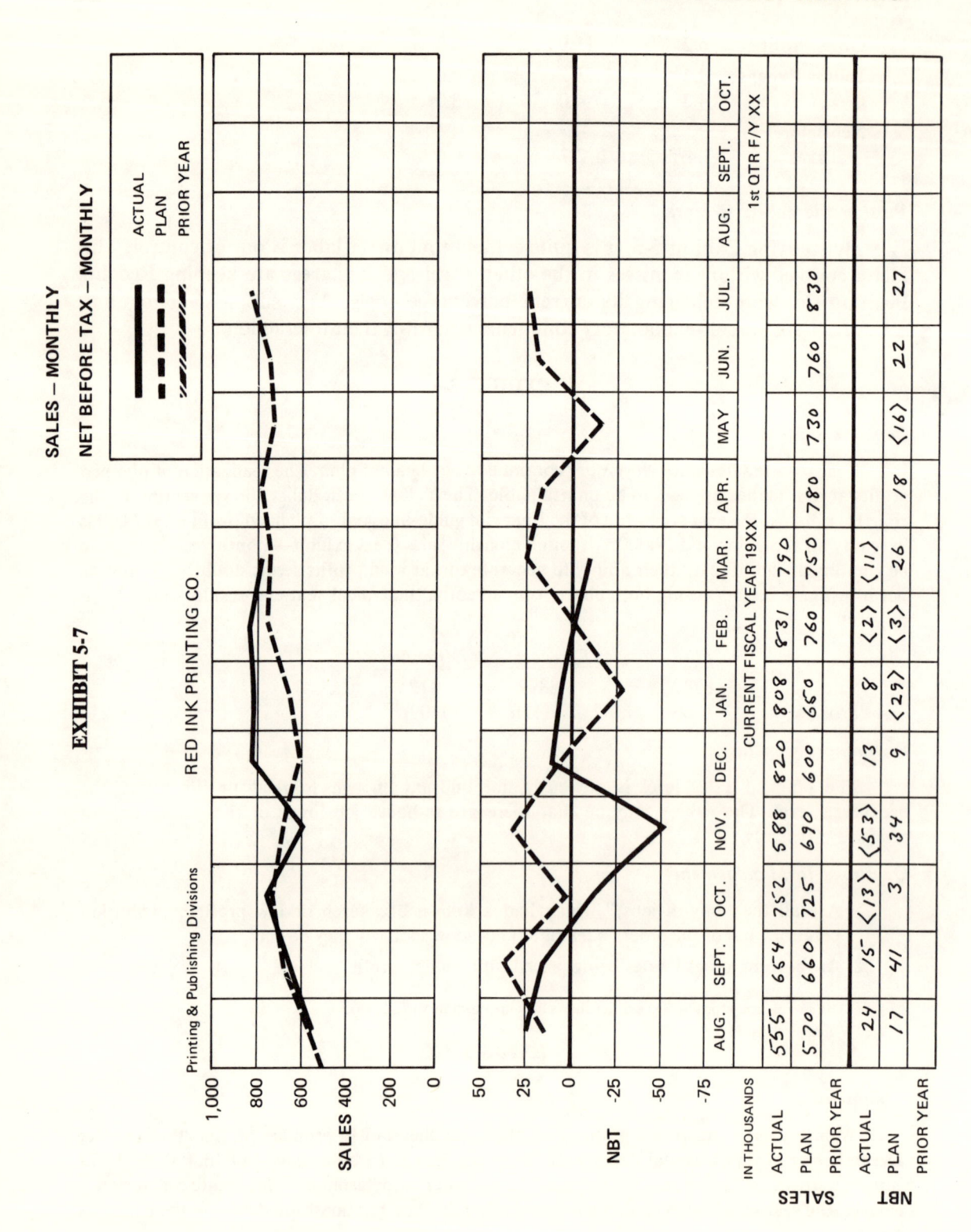

EXHIBIT 5-7

SALES – MONTHLY

NET BEFORE TAX – MONTHLY

Legend: ACTUAL (solid), PLAN (dashed), PRIOR YEAR (dash-dot)

RED INK PRINTING CO.

Printing & Publishing Divisions

IN THOUSANDS		AUG.	SEPT.	OCT.	NOV.	DEC.	JAN.	FEB.	MAR.	APR.	MAY	JUN.	JUL.	AUG.	SEPT.	OCT.
SALES	ACTUAL	555	664	752	588	820	808	831	790							
	PLAN	570	660	725	690	600	650	760	750	780	730	760	830			
	PRIOR YEAR															
NBT	ACTUAL	24	15	⟨13⟩	⟨53⟩	13	8	⟨2⟩	⟨11⟩							
	PLAN	17	41	3	34	9	⟨29⟩	⟨3⟩	26	18	⟨16⟩	22	27			
	PRIOR YEAR															

CURRENT FISCAL YEAR 19XX   1st QTR F/Y XX

PROFIT IMPACT CHARTING

HOW YEAR-END PROFITS ARE FORECAST USING DATA FROM THE CHARTS

Sales Actual YTD through March	$5799
Plus Plan for Remaining Four Months	3100
Total	$8899

HOW YEAR-END SALES ARE FORECAST USING DATA FROM THE CHARTS

NBT Actual YTD through March	(19)
April (Based on March)	(10)
May (April + May with a little Cushion)	(20)
June (Based on Feb./Mar. Actual)	(5)
July (Similar to Dec. Actual)	13
Forecast Loss	(41)

Critical Observation

When sales for Red Ink fall below the $800,000 point, the Profit Red Alert Stage begins. If sales continue to drop, the breakeven point is reached at $700,000. When operating within the profit red alert area, there is little room for production cliches or bad-debt write-off, etc.

EXHIBIT 5-8

Comments

Exhibit 5-8 is particularly valuable when used in conjunction with the monthly sales data shown on Exhibit 5-7 in order to evaluate and confirm breakeven levels. This exhibit also serves as a reference point or jumping-off place for analyzing the remaining charts. The next five charts allow you to individually analyze the profit and loss components that contribute to the return on sales percentage.

EXHIBIT 5-9

Comments

Exhibit 5-9 is the major key to the problems affecting Red Ink Printing Co. In March, the direct labor was almost 5% above the plan, and when compared to prior periods, it is trending contrary to plan. Exhibits 5-14 and 5-15 are the keys to understanding this chart.

Question to Management

Is the increased labor the result of added heads or overtime?

EXHIBIT 5-10

Comments

At first glance, material costs seem to be holding closely to plan. This chart has to be watched very carefully because its figures represent the biggest portion of the expendable dollars. On monthly sales of just under $800,000, a 1% variance in this area could account for the difference between Red Ink showing a profit or a loss.

EXHIBIT 5-8

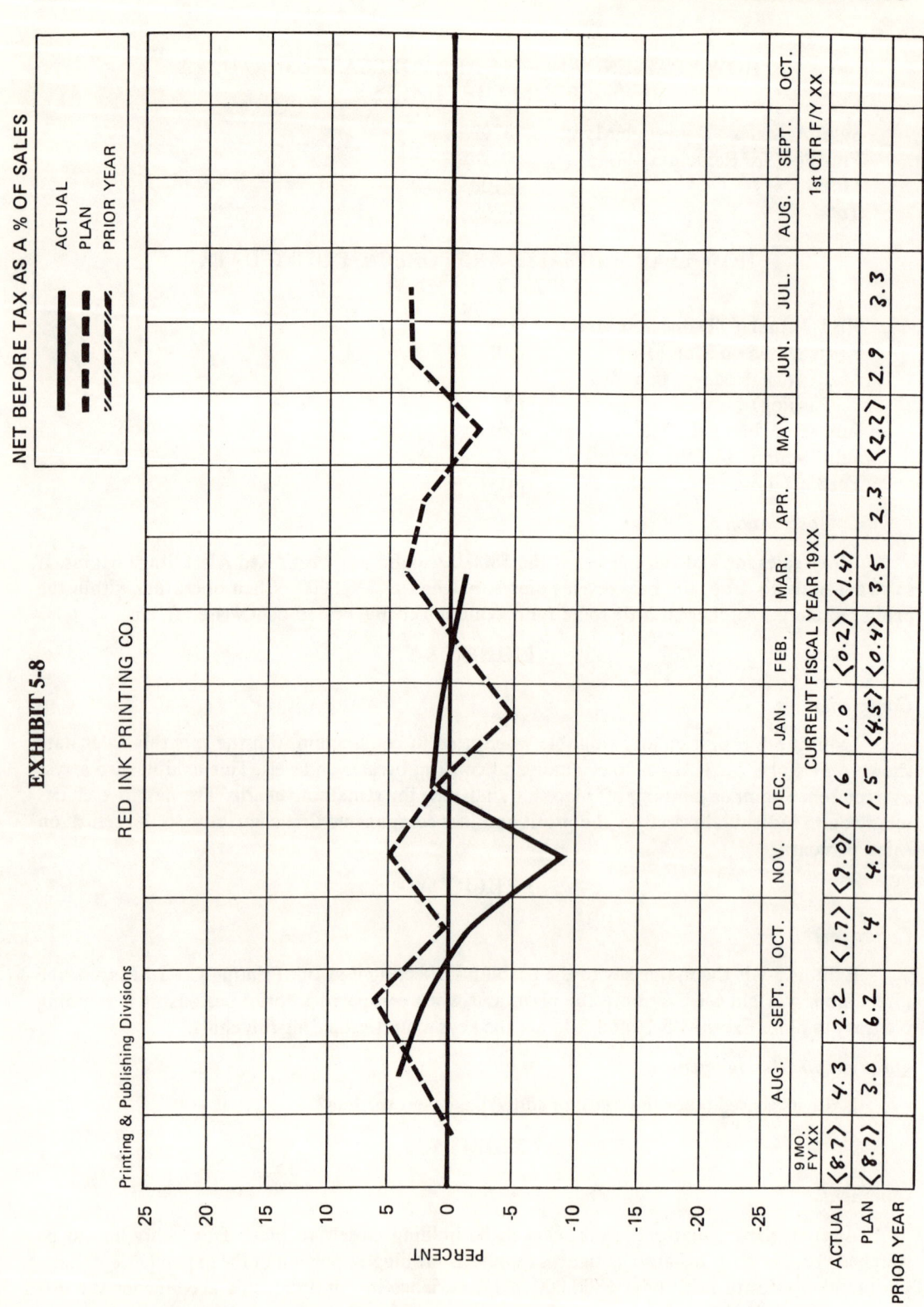

RED INK PRINTING CO.

Printing & Publishing Divisions

NET BEFORE TAX AS A % OF SALES

— ACTUAL
--- PLAN
///// PRIOR YEAR

	9 MO. F/Y XX	AUG.	SEPT.	OCT.	NOV.	DEC.	JAN.	FEB.	MAR.	APR.	MAY	JUN.	JUL.	AUG.	SEPT.	OCT.
ACTUAL	⟨8.7⟩	4.3	2.2	⟨1.7⟩	⟨9.0⟩	1.6	1.0	⟨0.2⟩	⟨1.4⟩							
PLAN	⟨8.7⟩	3.0	6.2	.4	4.5	1.5	⟨4.5⟩	⟨0.4⟩	3.5	2.3	⟨2.2⟩	2.9	3.3			
PRIOR YEAR																

CURRENT FISCAL YEAR 19XX | 1st QTR F/Y XX

PROFIT IMPACT CHARTING

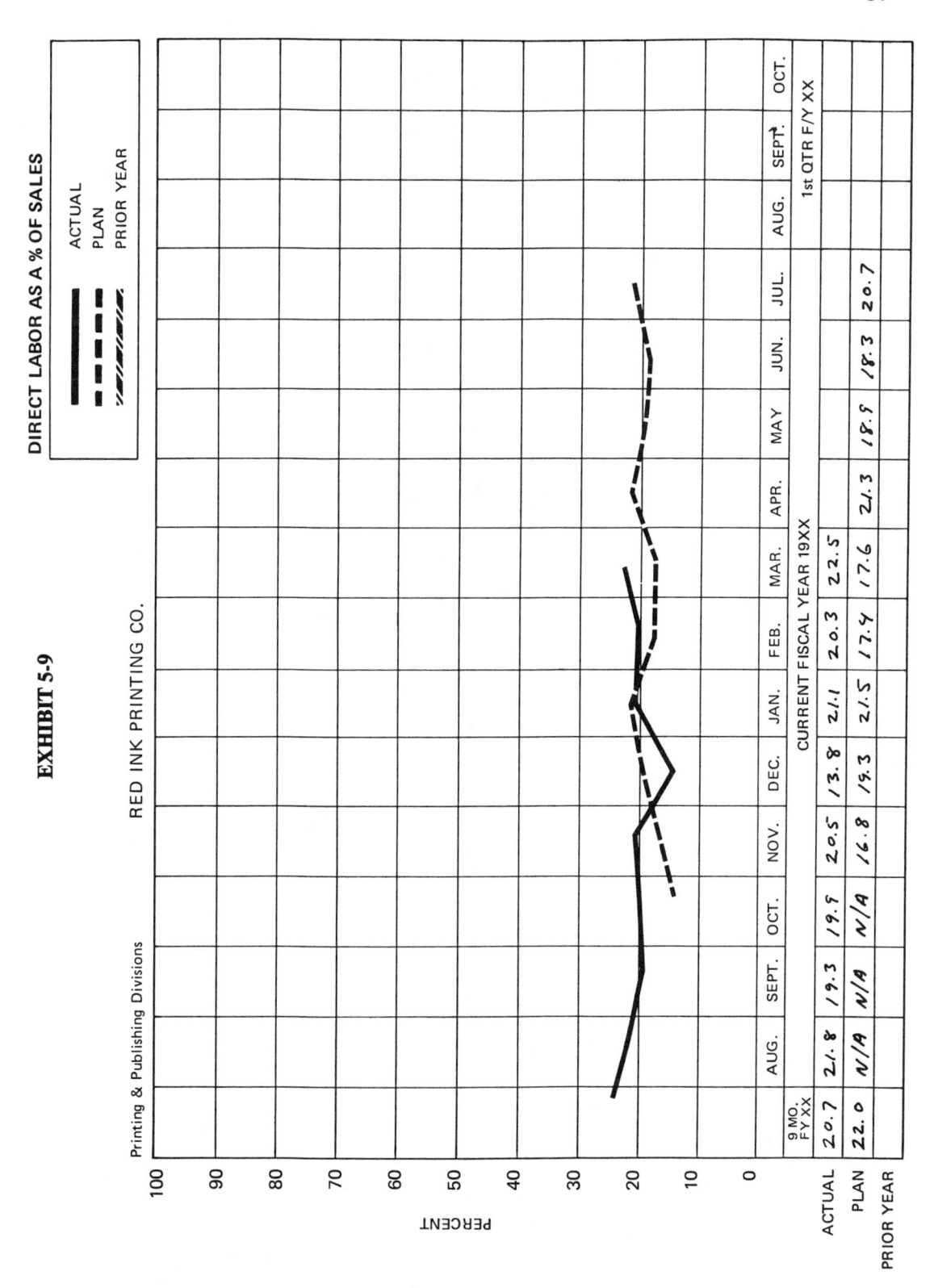

EXHIBIT 5-9

RED INK PRINTING CO.

DIRECT LABOR AS A % OF SALES

- ACTUAL
- PLAN
- PRIOR YEAR

Printing & Publishing Divisions

	9 MO. FY XX	AUG.	SEPT.	OCT.	NOV.	DEC.	JAN.	FEB.	MAR.	APR.	MAY	JUN.	JUL.	AUG.	SEPT.	OCT.
ACTUAL	20.7	21.8	19.3	19.5	20.5	13.8	21.1	20.3	22.5							
PLAN	22.0	N/A	N/A	N/A	16.8	19.3	21.5	17.4	17.6	21.3	18.5	18.3	20.7			
PRIOR YEAR																
					CURRENT FISCAL YEAR 19XX									1st QTR F/Y XX		

EXHIBIT 5-10

MATERIAL AS A % OF SALES

———— ACTUAL
- - - - PLAN
░░░░ PRIOR YEAR

RED INK PRINTING CO.

Printing & Publishing Divisions

	9 MO. FY XX	AUG.	SEPT.	OCT.	NOV.	DEC.	JAN.	FEB.	MAR.	APR.	MAY	JUN.	JUL.	AUG.	SEPT.	OCT.
ACTUAL	50.2	50.4	49.4	53.8	63.6	54.6	50.4	49.9	61.4							
PLAN	49.9	N/A	N/A	N/A	50.0	50.0	50.0	52.1	60.9	51.0	51.0	51.2	51.0			
PRIOR YEAR																

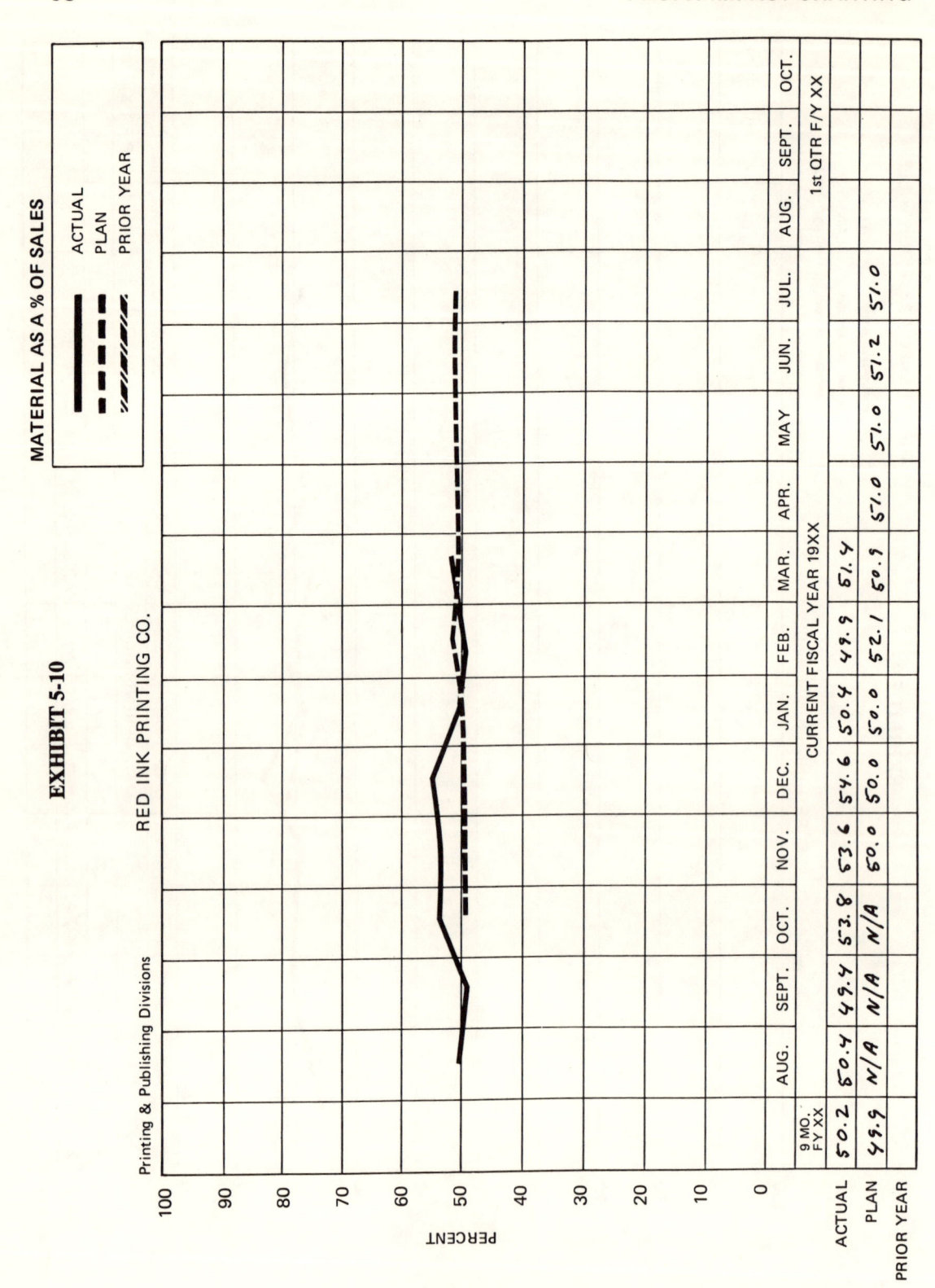

CURRENT FISCAL YEAR 19XX | 1st QTR F/Y XX

PROFIT IMPACT CHARTING

EXHIBIT 5-11

Comments

The main observation to be made regarding this chart is the effect upon overhead absorption when sales fall below the breakeven point. You will see that in November, due to the inability to develop enough sales, the overhead as a percent of sales rose by almost ten percentage points.

EXHIBITS 5-12 and 5-13

Comments

These both show that expenses are running slightly over plan. With the other problems facing Red Ink Printing Co., it is easy to ignore these minor variances and assume that they are acceptable. To the contrary, when a plant is operating as close to the loss line as this one is every unfavorable variance is important. In fact, until the direct labor problems are resolved, every area of the company has to operate on or below its target point.

EXHIBIT 5-14

Comments

The P & L is being eroded in the area of direct labor because of a head count problem. This is not to rule out the fact that overtime and excessive re-work might also be problem makers.

Before we can draw any basic conclusions, we need to determine what are the staffing requirements at different volumes.

EXHIBIT 5-15

Comments

The first step upon reviewing this chart is to determine what is the ideal staffing of this plant at current volume. At that point you can better evaluate the large addition to the staff which has taken place since August.

The first department to be investigated is bindery, because it is the largest direct labor department. This department requires an extensive amount of hand labor for stacking, sorting and repair work.

Questions to Management

1. Why has head count's growth exceeded sales growth?
   (May—$555,000 vs. March—$790,000)
2. Is the bindery having to perform excessive re-work due to poor quality control in the other departments?
3. Is the bindery organized properly and is the foreman in control?

PROFIT IMPACT CHARTING

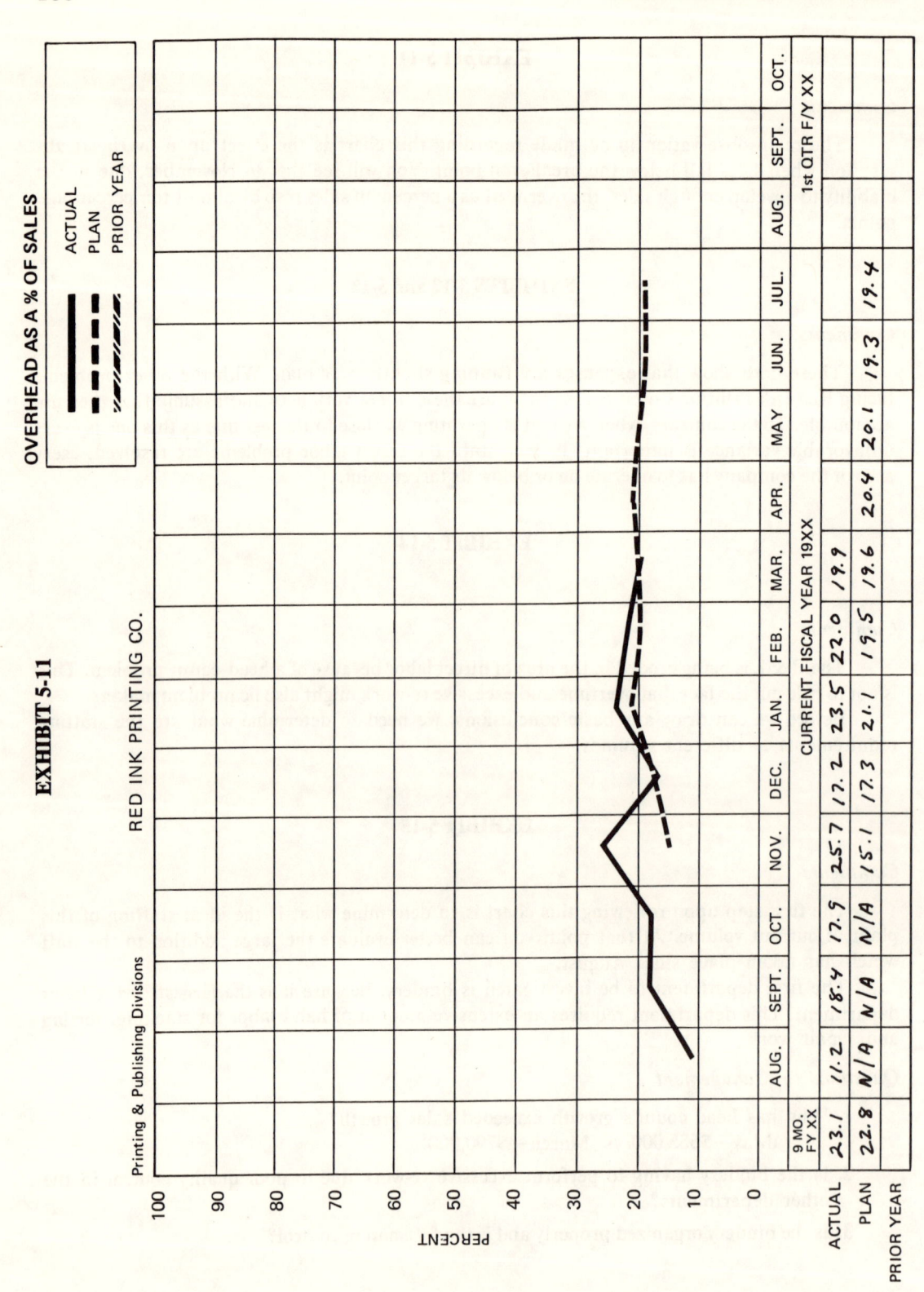

EXHIBIT 5-11

RED INK PRINTING CO.

Printing & Publishing Divisions

OVERHEAD AS A % OF SALES
— ACTUAL
--- PLAN
/// PRIOR YEAR

	9 MO. FY XX	AUG.	SEPT.	OCT.	NOV.	DEC.	JAN.	FEB.	MAR.	APR.	MAY	JUN.	JUL.	AUG.
ACTUAL	23.1	11.2	18.4	17.9	25.7	17.2	23.5	22.0	19.9					
PLAN	22.8	N/A	N/A	N/A	15.1	17.3	21.1	19.5	19.6	20.4	20.1	19.3	19.4	
PRIOR YEAR														

CURRENT FISCAL YEAR 19XX | 1st QTR F/Y XX

PERCENT: 0, 10, 20, 30, 40, 50, 60, 70, 80, 90, 100

PROFIT IMPACT CHARTING

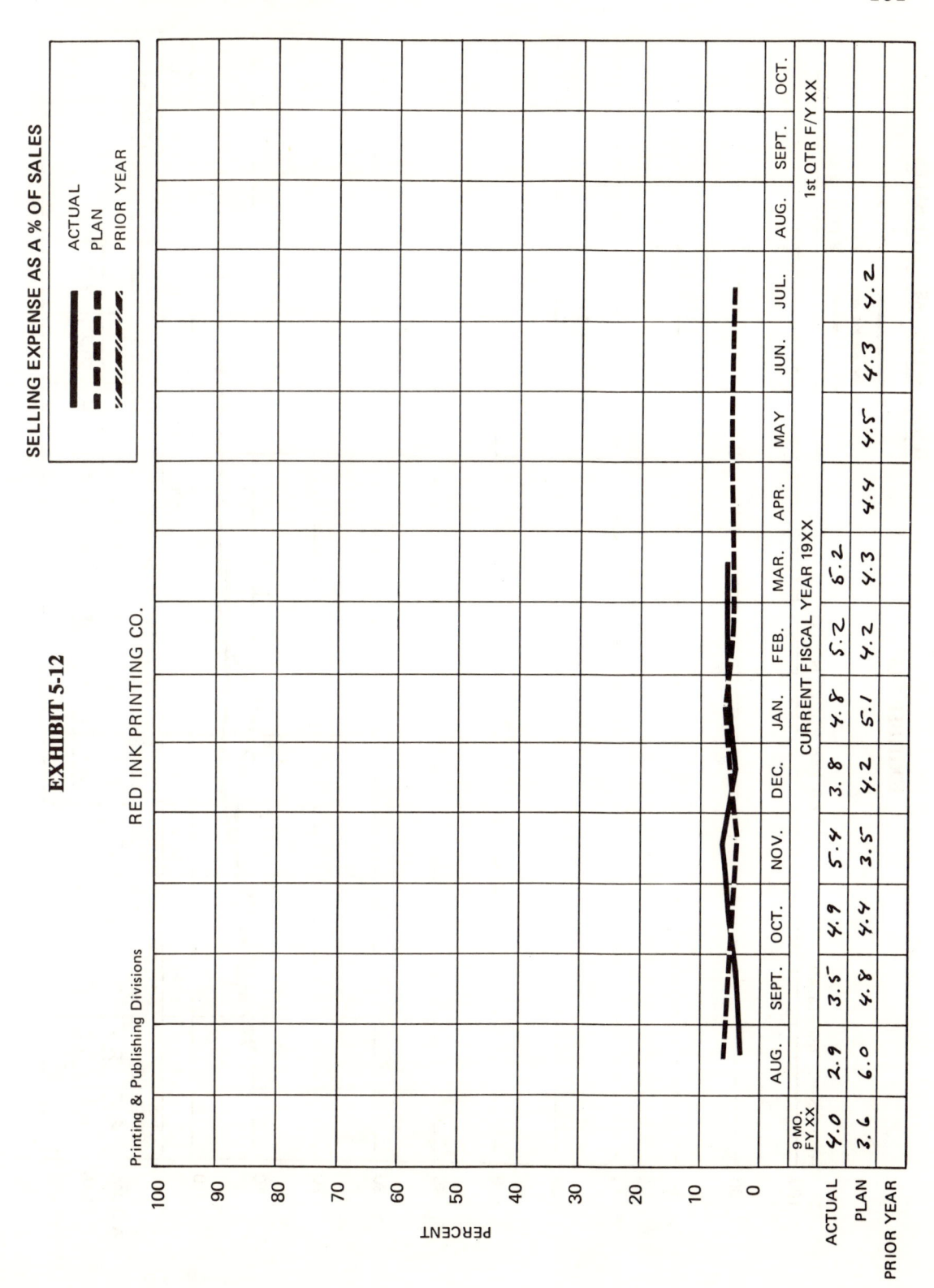

EXHIBIT 5-12

SELLING EXPENSE AS A % OF SALES

RED INK PRINTING CO.
Printing & Publishing Divisions

Legend: ACTUAL (solid), PLAN (dashed), PRIOR YEAR (hatched)

	9 MO. FY XX	AUG.	SEPT.	OCT.	NOV.	DEC.	JAN.	FEB.	MAR.	APR.	MAY	JUN.	JUL.	AUG.	SEPT.	OCT.
ACTUAL	4.0	2.9	3.5	4.9	5.4	3.8	4.8	5.2	6.2							
PLAN	3.6	6.0	4.8	4.4	3.5	4.2	5.1	4.2	4.3	4.4	4.5	4.3	4.2			
PRIOR YEAR																

CURRENT FISCAL YEAR 19XX | 1st QTR F/Y XX

PERCENT (0–100)

PROFIT IMPACT CHARTING

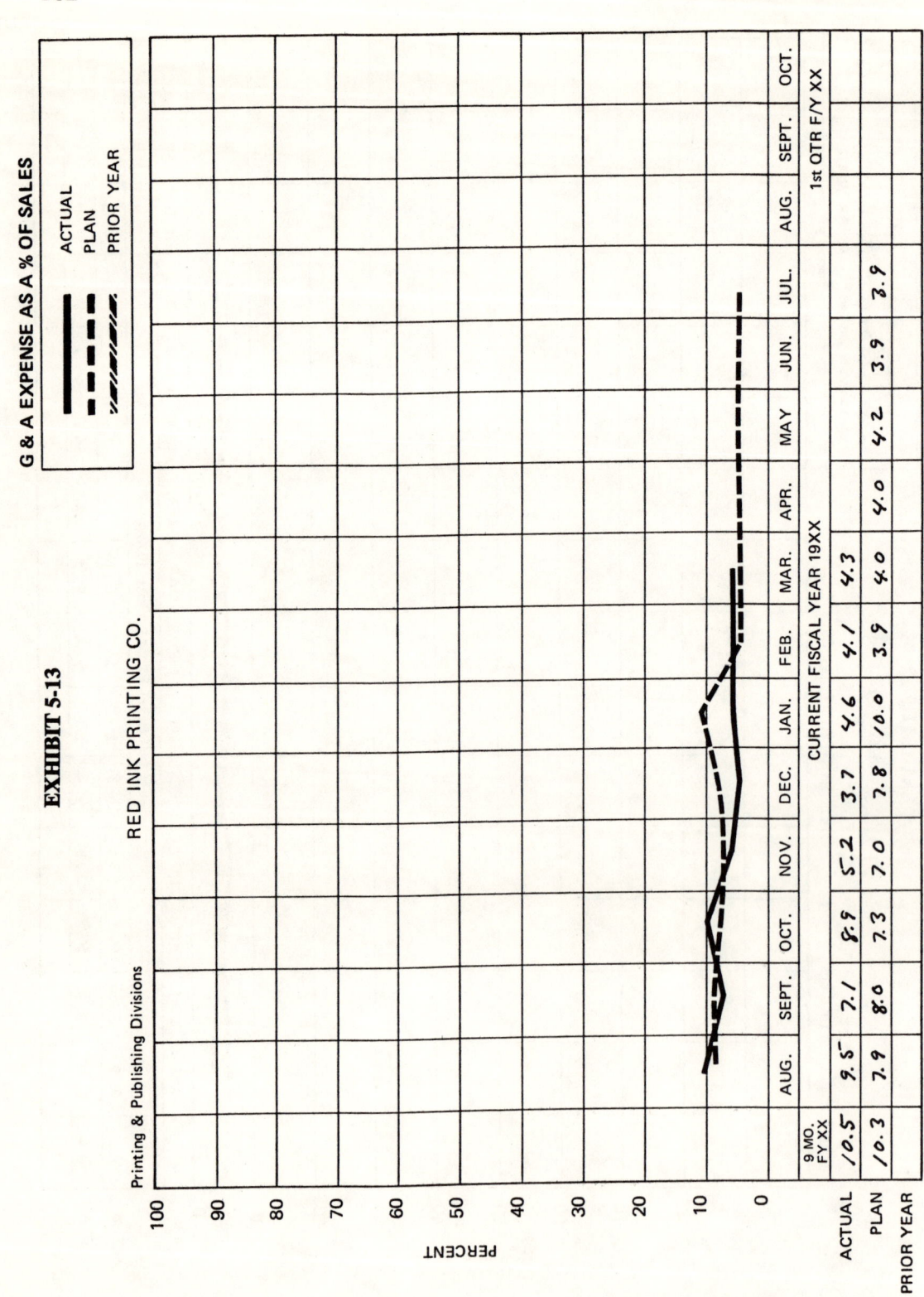

EXHIBIT 5-13

RED INK PRINTING CO.

Printing & Publishing Divisions

G & A EXPENSE AS A % OF SALES
- ACTUAL (solid)
- PLAN (dashed)
- PRIOR YEAR (hatched)

	9 MO. FY XX	AUG.	SEPT.	OCT.	NOV.	DEC.	JAN.	FEB.	MAR.	APR.	MAY	JUN.	JUL.	AUG.	SEPT.	OCT.
ACTUAL	10.5	9.5	7.1	8.9	5.2	3.7	4.6	4.1	4.3							
PLAN	10.3	7.9	8.0	7.3	7.0	7.8	10.0	3.9	4.0	4.0	4.2	3.9	3.9			
PRIOR YEAR																

CURRENT FISCAL YEAR 19XX — 1st QTR F/Y XX

PERCENT (0–100)

PROFIT IMPACT CHARTING

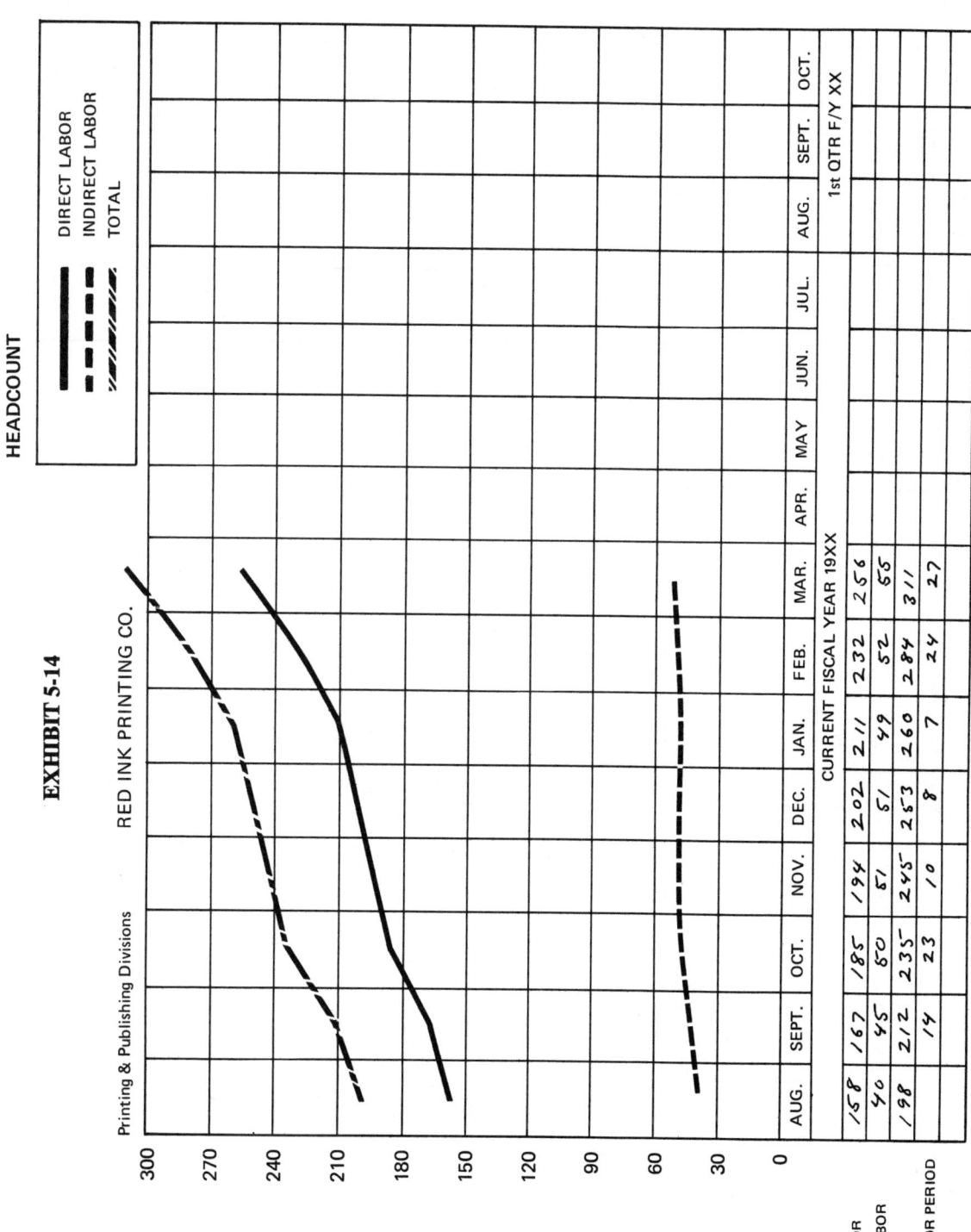

EXHIBIT 5-14

RED INK PRINTING CO.
Printing & Publishing Divisions

HEADCOUNT

Legend:
- DIRECT LABOR (solid line)
- INDIRECT LABOR (dashed line)
- TOTAL (hatched line)

	AUG.	SEPT.	OCT.	NOV.	DEC.	JAN.	FEB.	MAR.	APR.	MAY	JUN.	JUL.	AUG.	SEPT.	OCT.
DIRECT LABOR	158	167	185	194	202	211	232	256							
INDIRECT LABOR	40	45	50	51	51	49	52	55							
TOTAL	198	212	235	245	253	260	284	311							
CHANGE PRIOR PERIOD		14	23	10	8	7	24	27							
PRIOR YEAR															

CURRENT FISCAL YEAR 19XX — 1st QTR F/Y XX

EXHIBIT 5-15

HEADCOUNT BY DEPARTMENT

RED INK PRINTING CO.

Printing & Publishing Divisions

	AUG.	SEPT.	OCT.	NOV.	DEC.	JAN.	FEB.	MAR.	APR.	MAY	JUN.	JUL.	AUG.	SEPT.	OCT.
G & A	20	20	20	22	24	24	24	24							
Sales	20	25	30	29	27	25	28	31							
Total Indirect	40	45	50	51	51	49	52	55							
Indirect Plant	15	17	18	19	20	23	28	28							
Comp.	15	16	16	24	24	25	29	29							
Litho Prep.	20	23	24	21	22	25	27	27							
Press	44	47	49	47	47	47	49	49							
Bindery	64	64	78	83	89	91	99	123							
Total Direct	158	167	185	194	202	211	232	256							
GRAND TOTAL	198	212	235	245	253	260	284	311							

PROFIT IMPACT CHARTING 105

EXHIBIT 5-16

Comments

The cash flow figure depicted on this chart is computed on a receipts and expenditures basis. Based on the wide deviations that are occurring, a further investigation is mandatory in order to level the peaks and valleys in the cash flow.

Required Management Action

Immediate attention should be given to the aging of the accounts receivable, inventory levels, and the payment rate for accounts payable.

WHAT HAPPENED AFTER THE DIVISION AND CORPORATE MANAGEMENTS REVIEWED RED INK PRINTING COMPANY'S PROFIT IMPACT CHARTS?

Red Ink Printing Co. is part of a diversified printing group which has sales in excess of $75 million. In reviewing Red Ink's charts it was determined that the greatest profit contribution could be achieved by further identifying the factors increasing labor costs. Three separate analyses were conducted:

1. A comparison of sales history to direct labor staffing using the line of best-fit method to analyze and determine relationships.
2. Bindery crewing study was based on the rated capacities and speeds of the bindery equipment. This analysis was undertaken in order to determine the true impact that this department was having upon the total work force.
3. An analysis of overtime required per direct labor employee to meet delivery schedules was completed.

The first analysis was designed to pinpoint excessive crewing and to show that Red Ink was manning for peak production levels. Once hired, these employees were seldom cut back to adjust to production peaks and valleys; i.e., head count exceeded normal needs by thirty-eight (38) direct workers. The conversion of this head count reduction to dollar savings is computed as follows:

Reduction in personnel	38
Total hours worked—YTD	58,240
Average hourly rate	$ 3.62
Direct Labor Savings	$210,829
Payroll related costs at 17% (see note)	+ 35,840
Total Savings	$246,669

The second study showed that of the 38 excess direct labor personnel, 30 were in the bindery. The third analysis showed that each employee on a weekly basis earned an average of $50.53 per week in ovetime; i.e., for the first eight months of the year, Red Ink spent $355,620 in direct labor overtime. If the overtime could be cut in half after the 38 people were terminated, the following savings would be derived:

EXHIBIT 5-16

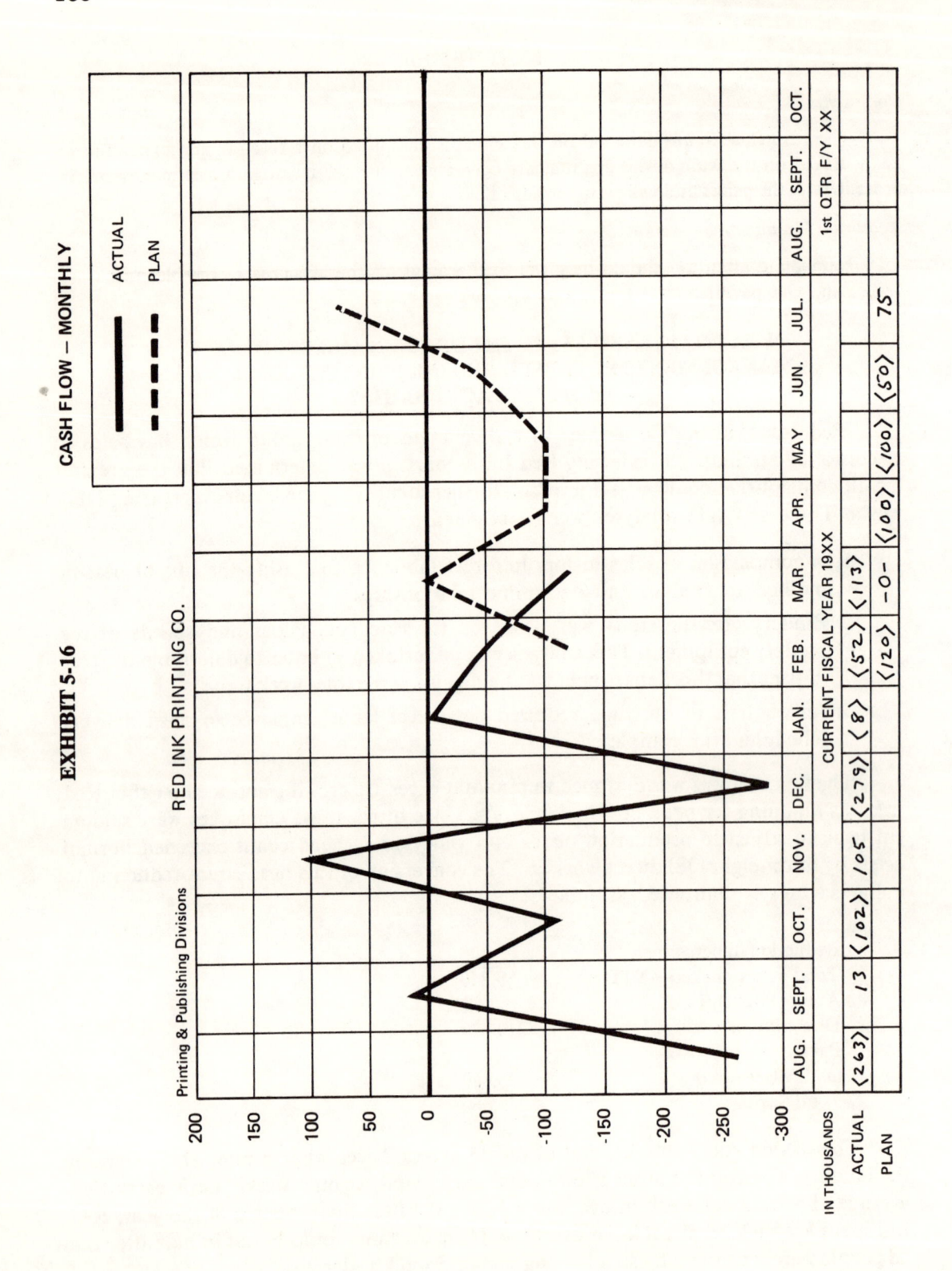

RED INK PRINTING CO.

Printing & Publishing Divisions

CASH FLOW — MONTHLY

ACTUAL ———
PLAN - - - - -

IN THOUSANDS	AUG.	SEPT.	OCT.	NOV.	DEC.	JAN.	FEB.	MAR.	APR.	MAY	JUN.	JUL.	AUG.	SEPT.	OCT.
ACTUAL	⟨263⟩	13	⟨102⟩	105	⟨279⟩	⟨8⟩	⟨52⟩	⟨113⟩							
PLAN							⟨120⟩	-0-	⟨100⟩	⟨100⟩	⟨50⟩	75			

CURRENT FISCAL YEAR 19XX | 1st QTR F/Y XX

PROFIT IMPACT CHARTING

Revised head count	218
Current annualized O.T. cost per employee (52 X $50.53)	$2628
Potential savings	$572,804
Less 50% for special jobs and emergencies	($286,402)
Total Savings	$286,402

At first glance, it would seem absurd for any company to allow hiring and overtime to run rampant as it had at Red Ink, but they were caught up in the day-to-day activities, which were compounded by unusual start-up problems. Thus, people were added and overtime allowed in the guise of growing pains. If they had *initially* implemented a series of profit impact charts, they would have been able to view the business in its entirety and could very well have avoided draining the business of $523,071, or an additional pre-tax return on group sales of approximately 8%.

Note: In addition to direct labor being affected by the high and continually increasing head count, overhead costs were also feeling the impact, especially payroll related costs which ran at 17% due to the plant being unionized.

How review meetings using profit impact charts become the operational watchdogs—holding the right meetings

Does your company have too many meetings? Are these meetings generally worthwhile? If you have answered "Yes" and "No" respectively to these questions, you may wish to consider holding a few effective profit impact chart review meetings instead of many less useful ones. At such meetings, you would be able to assign Critical Action Tasks (CATs) to various functional managers. At subsequent meetings you could follow-up and review the CATs. As the organization adjusts its course toward resolving the CATs, the meetings develop direction and become more purposeful. You will find that managers are lifted out of the daily routine by these meetings. They have time to get some perspective on the business and become alert to potential dangers and, of course, new opportunities. They will not waste their energies responding to individual indicators such as an increase in semi-finished parts in inventory or some other blurb on the management's radar screen. They will start to view the business as an integrated system. This concept is best described as operating under the banner of no surprises. See Exhibit 5-17.

A CASE GUIDE-LINE FOR IMPLEMENTING PROFIT IMPACT REVIEW MEETINGS

An effective way of illustrating the use and implementation of the profit impact charting system as an operational watchdog is by reviewing how Unison Computer approached this task.

A case in point—how Unison Computer Division implemented profit impact charting as its operational watchdog

In accordance with management's blueprint for acquisitions, highly technically-oriented computer science firms have been acquired over the past three-year period.

EXHIBIT 5-17

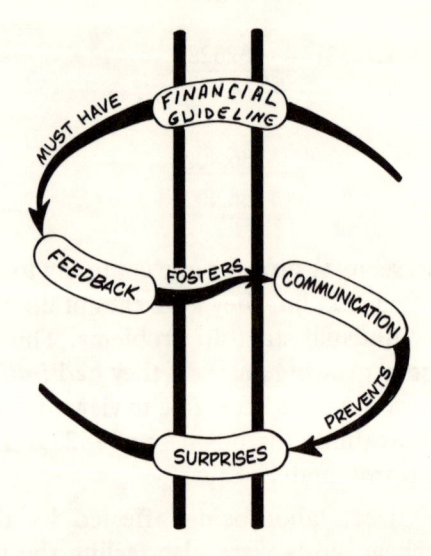

[Diagram: A dollar sign ($) with labeled bubbles — "FINANCIAL GUIDELINE" at top, "MUST HAVE" arrow leading to "FEEDBACK", which "FOSTERS" "COMMUNICATION", which "PREVENTS" "SURPRISES".]

Management felt it was more practical to use existing technology and markets than to start from scratch. Until last summer, these plants were operated on a highly independent basis and managed from corporate headquarters by a group co-ordinator. In order to align the like businesses, corporate headquarters decided to combine these entities. Combining the companies under one banner accomplishes the following:

1. Addresses the market place as a single force.
2. Enjoys the benefit received from the economies of scale.
3. Achieves maximum results from the resources available.

A group of men were assembled, and with the aid of a management planning and control system a dynamic team resulted. The group controller became the new division controller, and the senior planning officer became the new division general manager, etc.

The steps taken to implement a self-renewing, communicative planning and control system are described as follows:

STEP 1. FINANCIAL GUIDE-LINE PREPARATION

The formation of the financial guide line was no problem because the new entity, Unison Computer, was required by corporate policy to submit a plan. The forecast operating statement (income statement) is shown as Exhibit 5-18.

STEP 2. CHART SELECTION

The current planning meeting's agenda revolves around the preparation and review of the mid-month P & Ls and balance sheets. Through the process of elimination, the general manager decided to use several charts. His selection varied from meeting to meeting. Chart series B was the format introduced, because it matched their functional approach towards business. Refer to Exhibits 5-18 to 5-26.

PROFIT IMPACT CHARTING

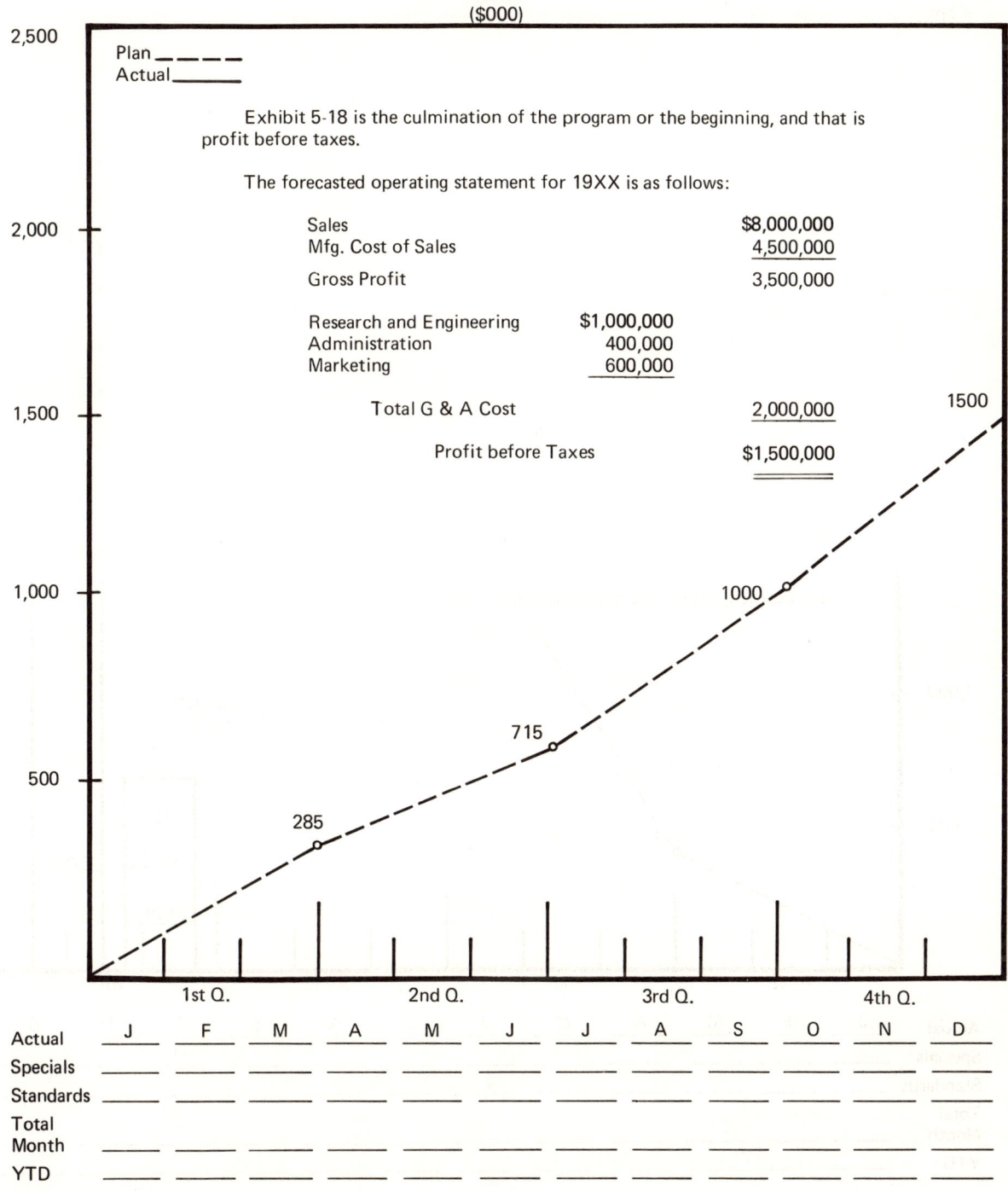

EXHIBIT 5-18

UNISON COMPUTER
PROFIT BEFORE TAXES
19XX
($000)

Exhibit 5-18 is the culmination of the program or the beginning, and that is profit before taxes.

The forecasted operating statement for 19XX is as follows:

Sales		$8,000,000
Mfg. Cost of Sales		4,500,000
Gross Profit		3,500,000
Research and Engineering	$1,000,000	
Administration	400,000	
Marketing	600,000	
Total G & A Cost		2,000,000
Profit before Taxes		$1,500,000

Plan _ _ _ _ _
Actual _____

Plotted points: 285, 715, 1000, 1500

	J	F	M	A	M	J	J	A	S	O	N	D
Actual												
Specials												
Standards												
Total Month												
YTD												

PROFIT IMPACT CHARTING

EXHIBIT 5-19
UNISON COMPUTER
19XX
ORDERS
(Units)

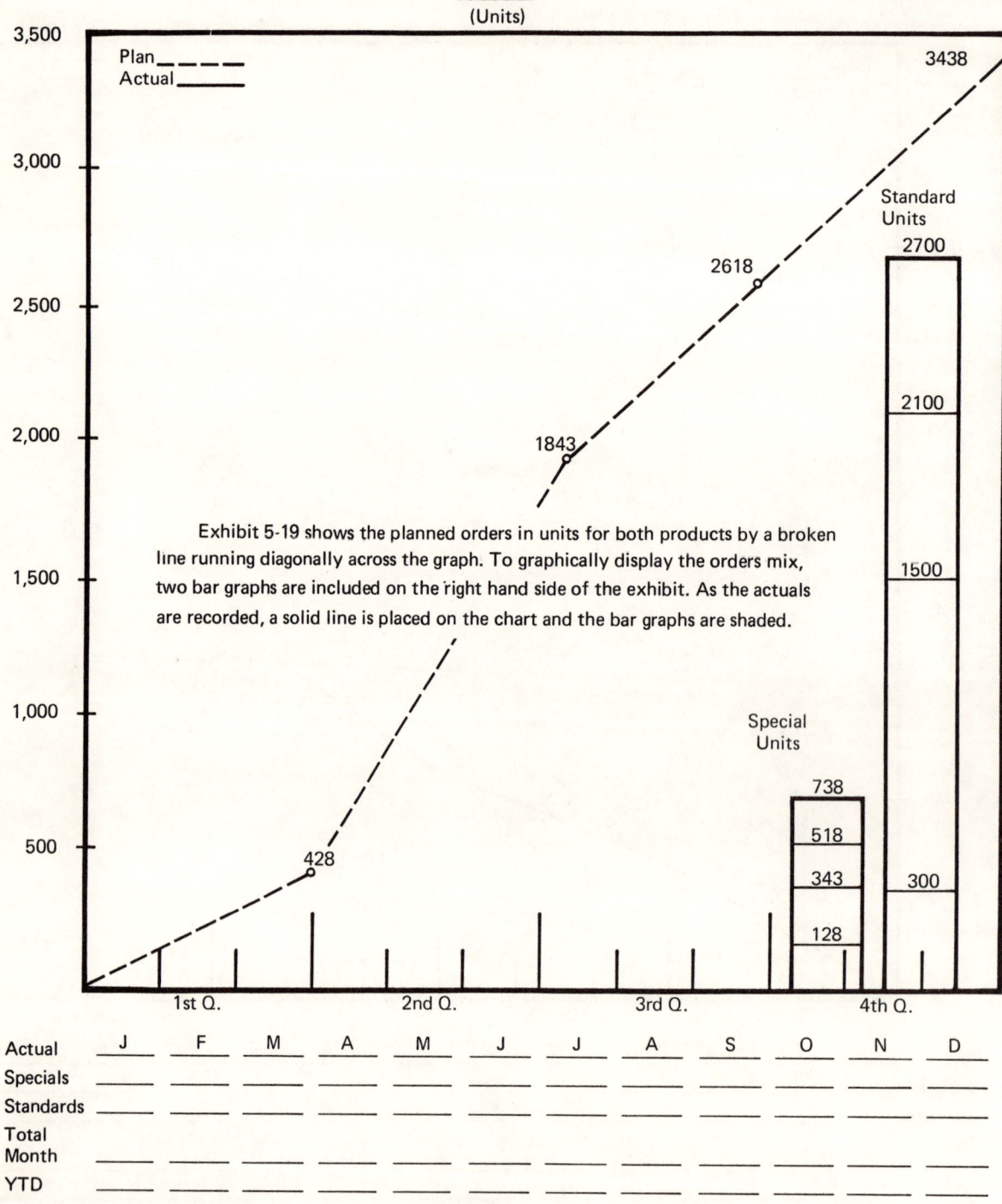

Plan _____
Actual _____

Exhibit 5-19 shows the planned orders in units for both products by a broken line running diagonally across the graph. To graphically display the orders mix, two bar graphs are included on the right hand side of the exhibit. As the actuals are recorded, a solid line is placed on the chart and the bar graphs are shaded.

Standard Units: 2700, 2100, 1500, 300

Special Units: 738, 518, 343, 128

Plan line points: 428, 1843, 2618, 3438

Quarters: 1st Q., 2nd Q., 3rd Q., 4th Q.

	J	F	M	A	M	J	J	A	S	O	N	D
Actual												
Specials												
Standards												
Total Month												
YTD												

PROFIT IMPACT CHARTING

EXHIBIT 5-20

UNISON COMPUTER
19XX
ORDERS MIX
(Units)

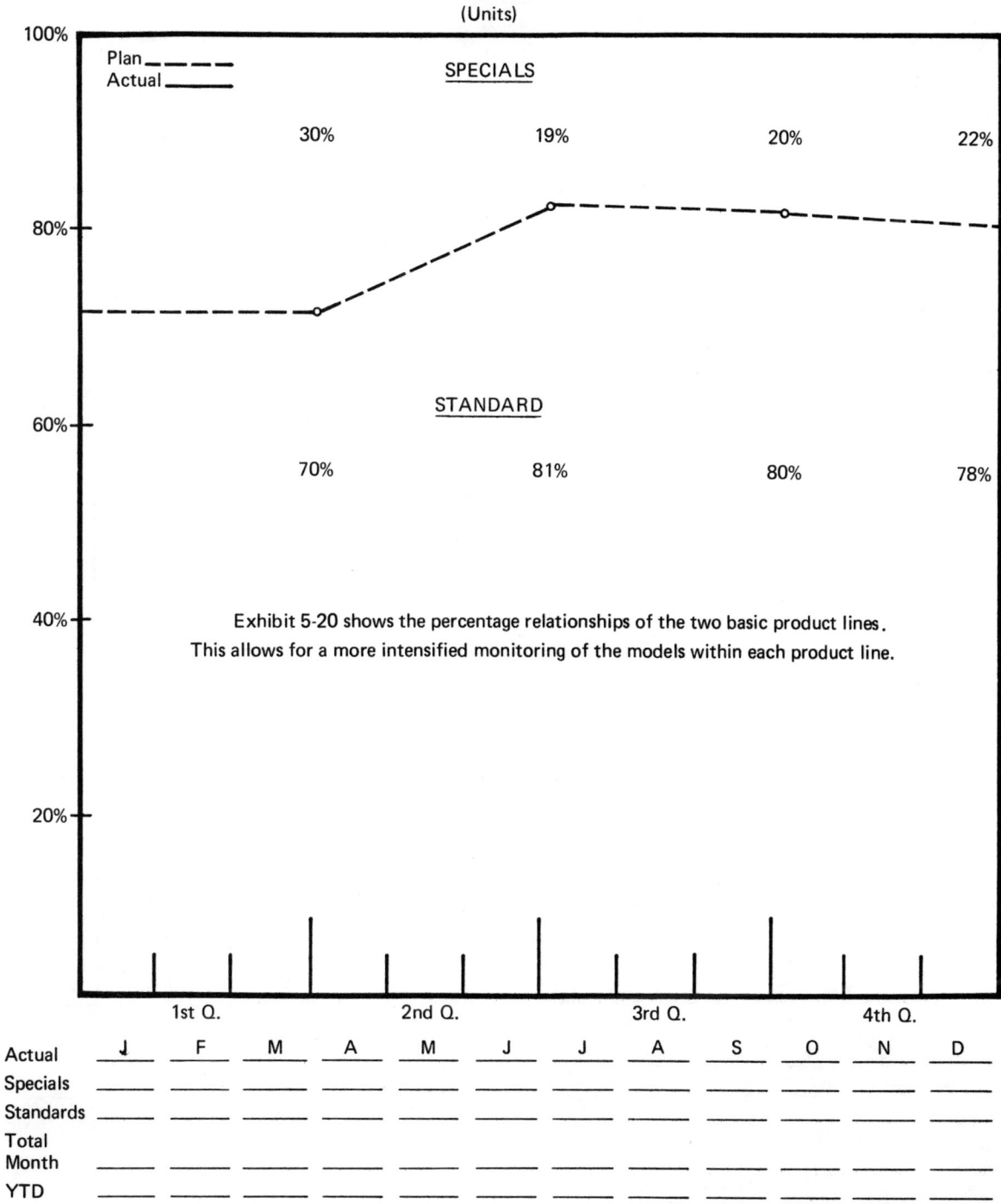

Plan -----
Actual _____

SPECIALS

| | 30% | 19% | 20% | 22% |

STANDARD

| | 70% | 81% | 80% | 78% |

Exhibit 5-20 shows the percentage relationships of the two basic product lines. This allows for a more intensified monitoring of the models within each product line.

1st Q.   2nd Q.   3rd Q.   4th Q.

Actual   J   F   M   A   M   J   J   A   S   O   N   D
Specials
Standards
Total Month
YTD

EXHIBIT 5-21

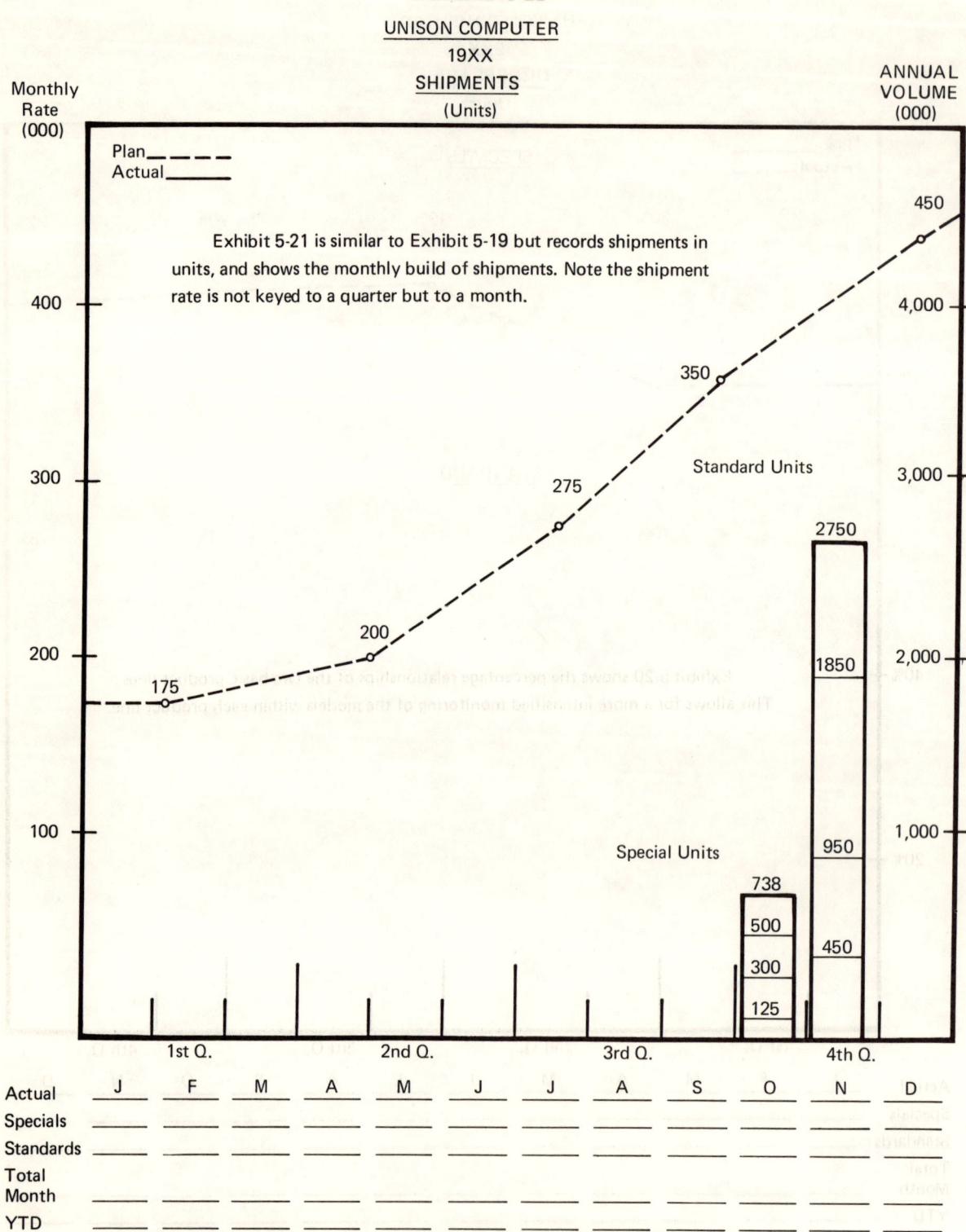

UNISON COMPUTER
19XX
SHIPMENTS
(Units)

Exhibit 5-21 is similar to Exhibit 5-19 but records shipments in units, and shows the monthly build of shipments. Note the shipment rate is not keyed to a quarter but to a month.

Plan — — — —
Actual ———

Monthly Rate (000) / Annual Volume (000)

Plan points: 175, 200, 275, 350, 450

Standard Units stacked (4th Q): 2750 / 1850 / 950 / 450
Special Units stacked (3rd Q): 738 / 500 / 300 / 125

	J	F	M	A	M	J	J	A	S	O	N	D
Actual												
Specials												
Standards												
Total Month												
YTD												

1st Q.   2nd Q.   3rd Q.   4th Q.

PROFIT IMPACT CHARTING 113

EXHIBIT 5-22

UNISON COMPUTER
19XX
SHIPMENTS — MIX
(Units)

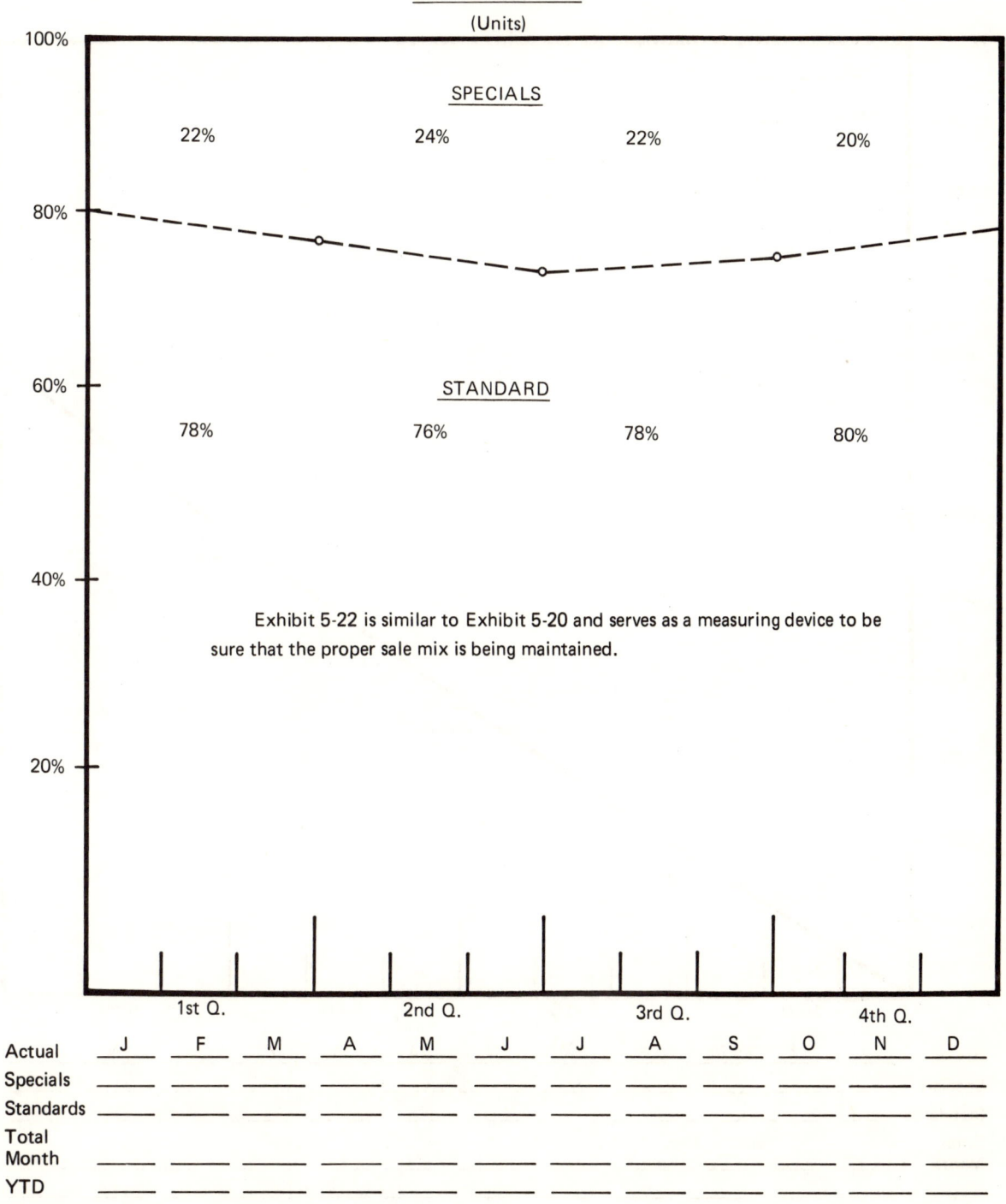

	1st Q.	2nd Q.	3rd Q.	4th Q.
SPECIALS	22%	24%	22%	20%
STANDARD	78%	76%	78%	80%

Exhibit 5-22 is similar to Exhibit 5-20 and serves as a measuring device to be sure that the proper sale mix is being maintained.

	J	F	M	A	M	J	J	A	S	O	N	D
Actual												
Specials												
Standards												
Total Month												
YTD												

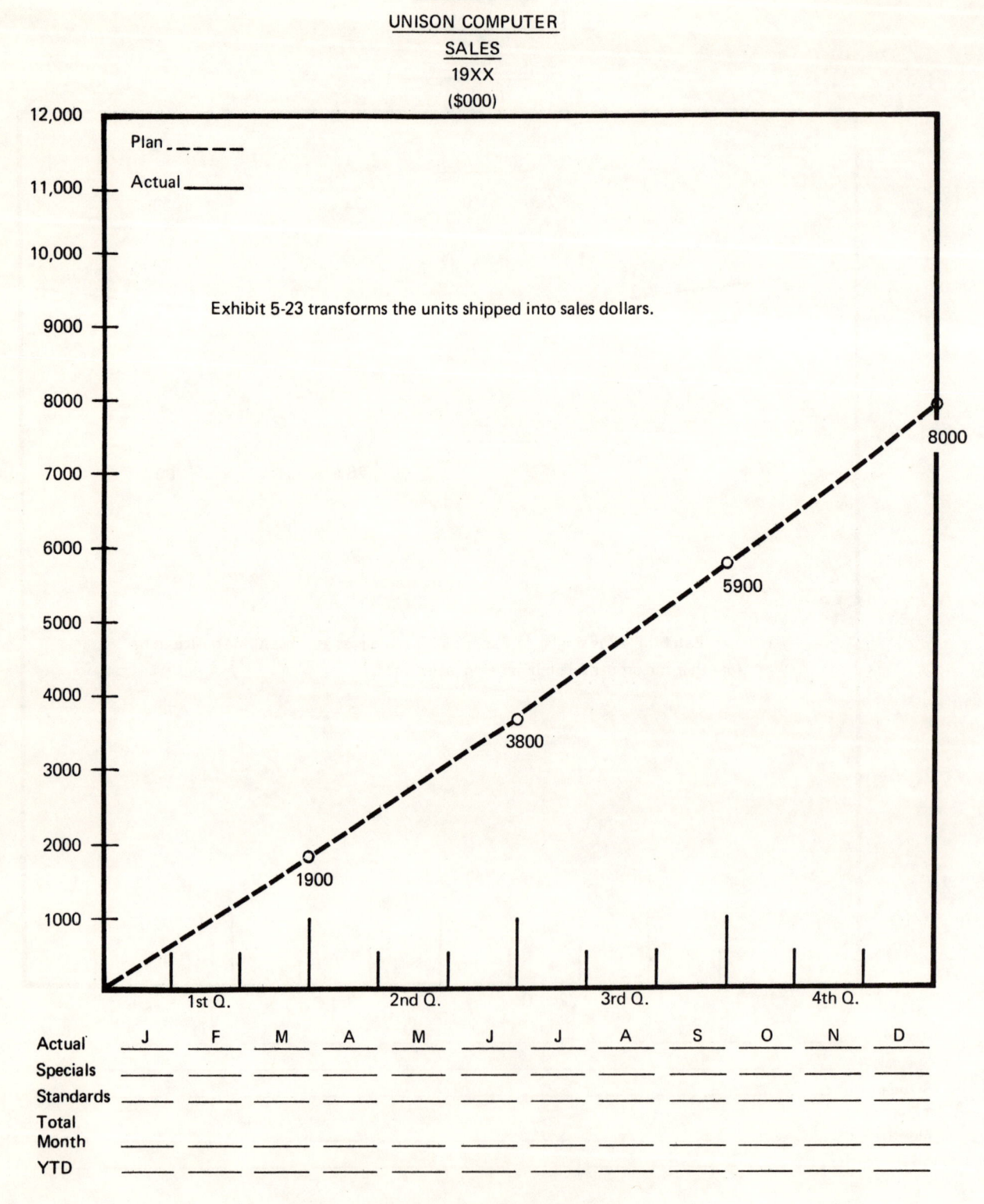

EXHIBIT 5-23

UNISON COMPUTER

SALES

19XX

($000)

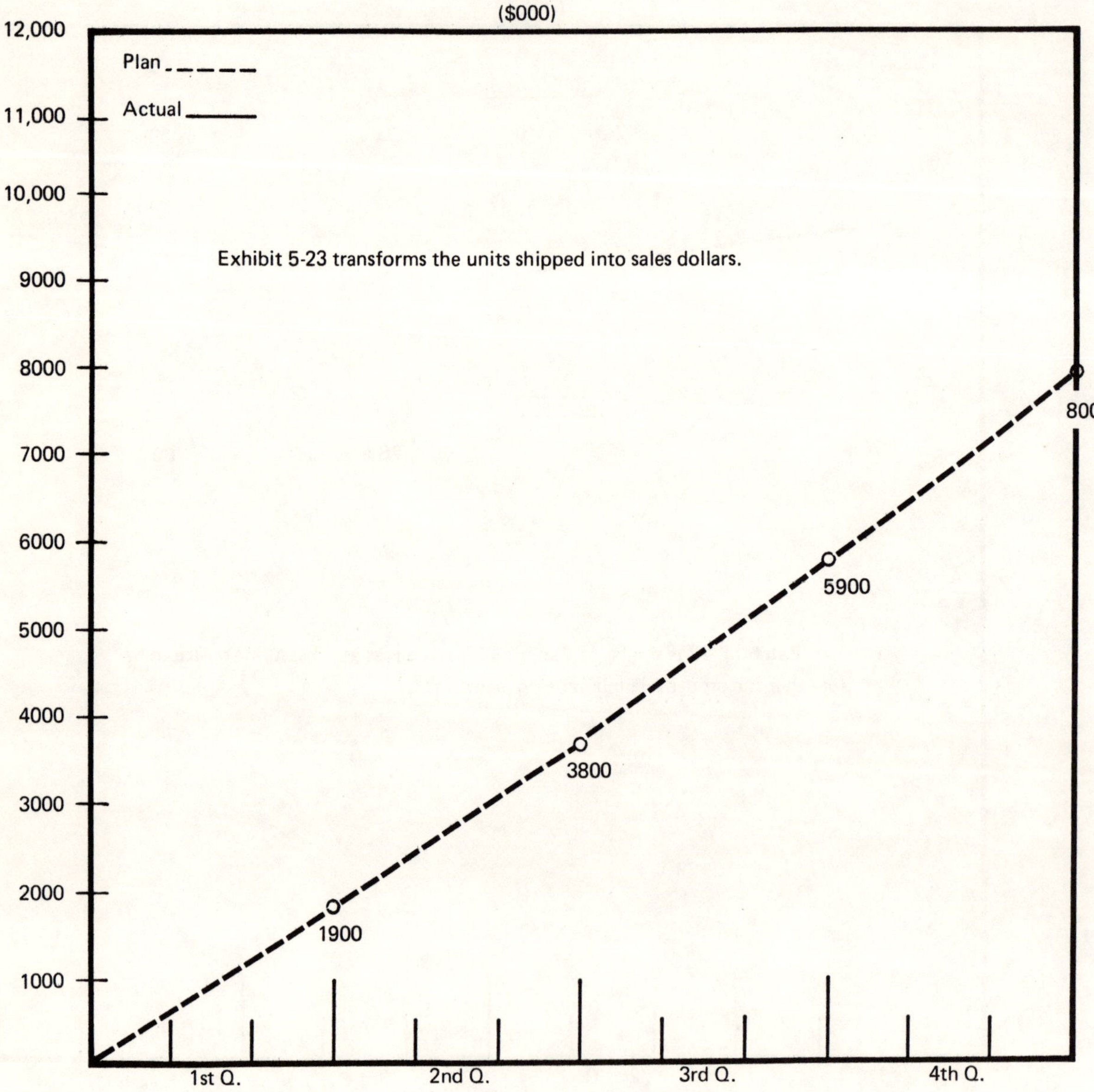
12,000
11,000
10,000
9000
8000
7000
6000
5000
4000
3000
2000
1000
Plan
Actual
Exhibit 5-23 transforms the units shipped into sales dollars.
8000
5900
3800
1900
1st Q.
2nd Q.
3rd Q.
4th Q.

Actual	J	F	M	A	M	J	J	A	S	O	N	D
Specials												
Standards												
Total Month												
YTD												

PROFIT IMPACT CHARTING

EXHIBIT 5-24

UNISON COMPUTER
CONTRIBUTION TO SALES AND PROFIT BEFORE TAXES
19XX
DOLLARS

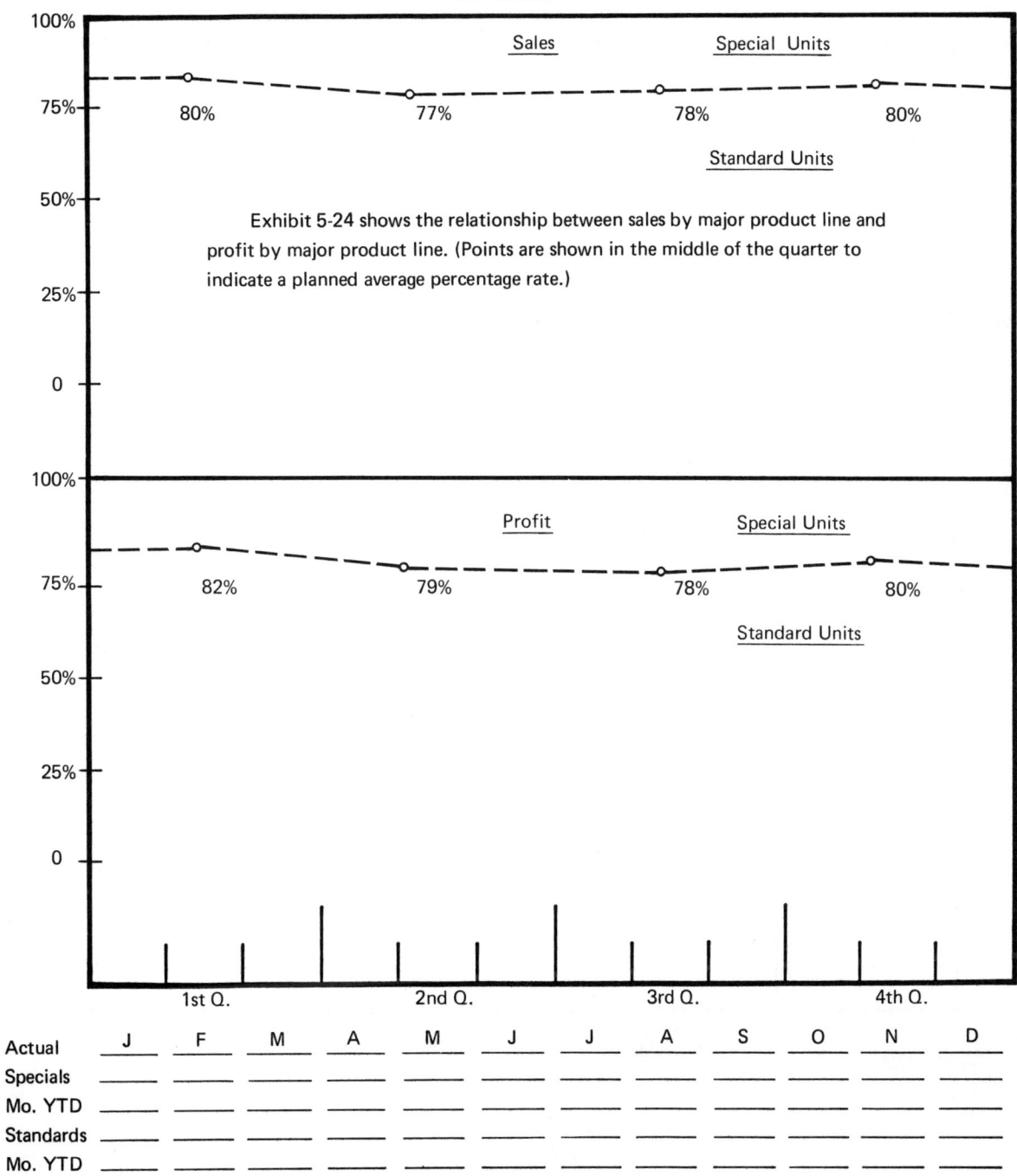

Sales — Special Units: 80%, 77%, 78%, 80%

Standard Units

Exhibit 5-24 shows the relationship between sales by major product line and profit by major product line. (Points are shown in the middle of the quarter to indicate a planned average percentage rate.)

Profit — Special Units: 82%, 79%, 78%, 80%

Standard Units

1st Q. 2nd Q. 3rd Q. 4th Q.

Actual: J F M A M J J A S O N D
Specials
Mo. YTD
Standards
Mo. YTD

EXHIBIT 5-25

UNISON COMPUTER
EXPENSES BY AREA
MARKETING ($000)

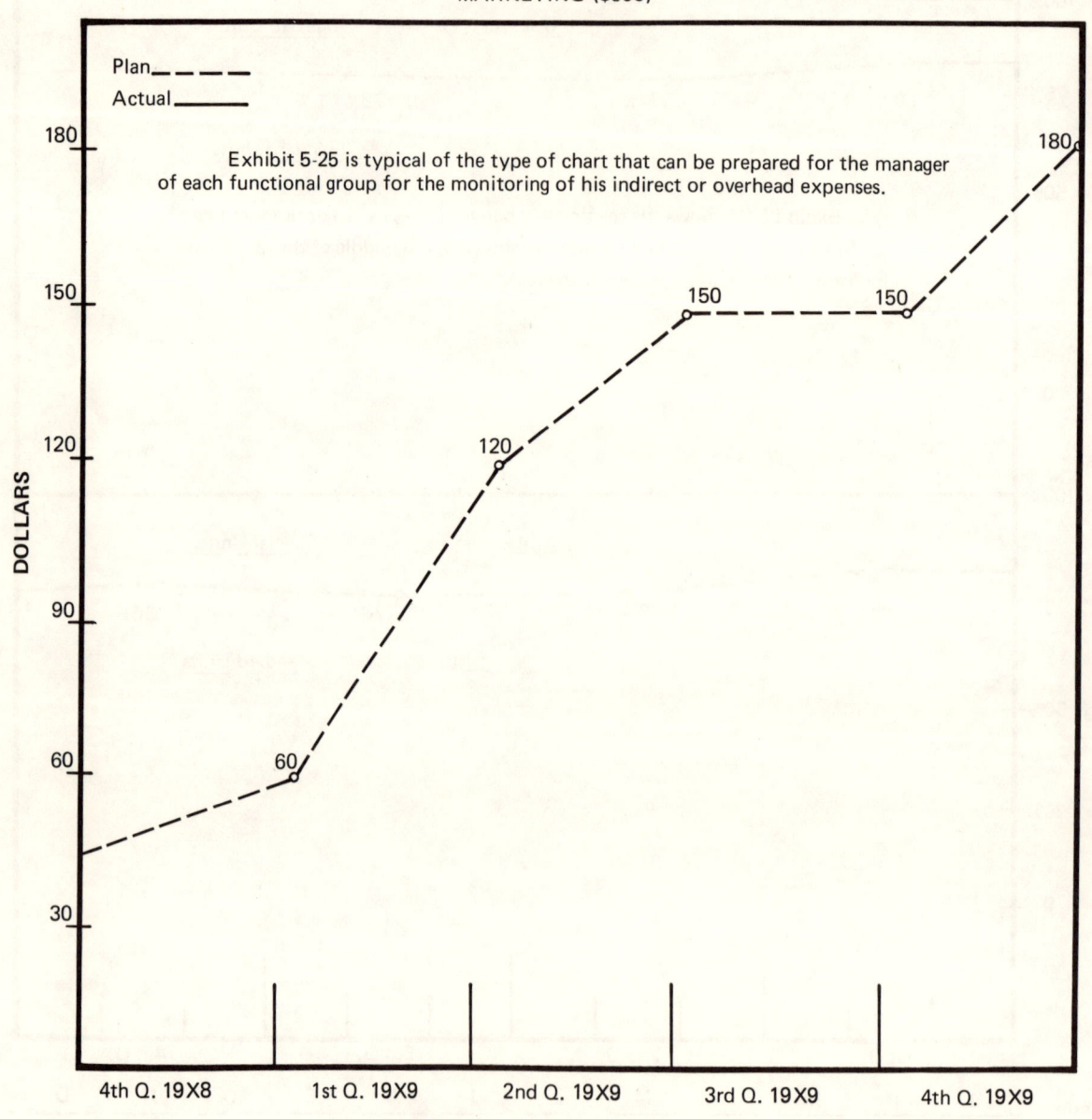

Plan _ _ _ _ _
Actual _____

Exhibit 5-25 is typical of the type of chart that can be prepared for the manager of each functional group for the monitoring of his indirect or overhead expenses.

PROFIT IMPACT CHARTING

EXHIBIT 5-26
Unison Computer
Head Count and Staffing Analysis
19XX

Head Count	*Plan*	*Actual*	*Variance*
Administrative	32		
Technical Staff	52		
Technicians	18		
Design & Drafting	4		
Assemblers	75		
Other	10		
TOTAL	191		

Staffing			
Administration	10		
Operations	125		
Engineering	20		
Research	20		
Marketing	16		
TOTAL	191		

Exhibit 5-26 is included to show that proper planning and utilization of human resources should also be mentioned. Proper head count and staffing are vital to a small industrial plant.

At this point we should discuss the problem of presenting data succinctly. At Unison, after several false starts, the non-real time information was estimated and adjusted as the data became available. This combined the real-time approach with the integrity of recorded data.

STEP 3. MEETING STRUCTURE

Exhibit 5-27 describes the two basic types of review meetings, which differ in structure and attendance.

At Unison, the general manager was in charge of the managers' meeting and decided to meet on Saturdays until the combined operation was running satisfactorily. After the general manager's meeting, cost center meetings were conducted using the same charting approach. The controller was responsible for all of the chart presentations and attended each of the cost center meetings in order to provide continuity and lend authority to the meetings.

The lower box labeled *Next Monday Review Meeting* has been included only to stress the necessity of follow-up on action points set up in prior meetings. If the follow-up phase is not an integrated part of the meeting format, much of the purpose and impact of the meeting is lost. To insure that your meetings get off to a good start, use the checkoff list shown as Exhibit 5-28.

EXHIBIT 5-27

ATTENDANCE AT REVIEW MEETINGS

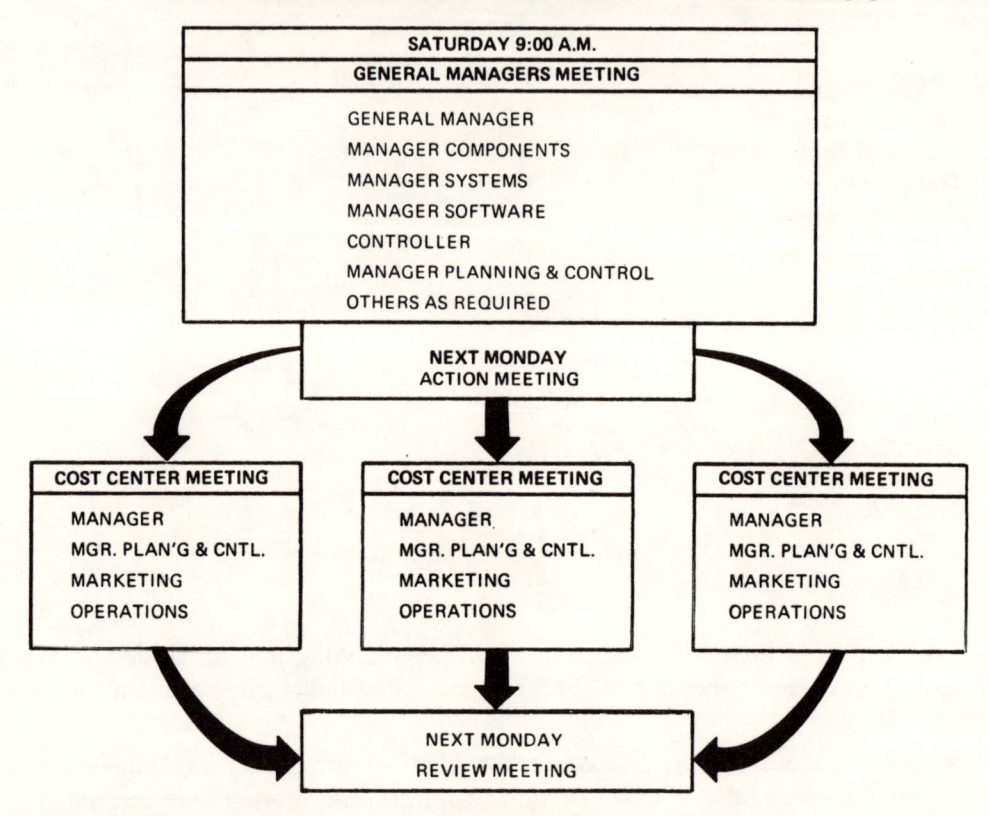

```
SATURDAY 9:00 A.M.
GENERAL MANAGERS MEETING

GENERAL MANAGER
MANAGER COMPONENTS
MANAGER SYSTEMS
MANAGER SOFTWARE
CONTROLLER
MANAGER PLANNING & CONTROL
OTHERS AS REQUIRED
```

NEXT MONDAY ACTION MEETING

COST CENTER MEETING	COST CENTER MEETING	COST CENTER MEETING
MANAGER	MANAGER	MANAGER
MGR. PLAN'G & CNTL.	MGR. PLAN'G & CNTL.	MGR. PLAN'G & CNTL.
MARKETING	MARKETING	MARKETING
OPERATIONS	OPERATIONS	OPERATIONS

NEXT MONDAY REVIEW MEETING

STEP 4. MEASURE YOUR ACHIEVEMENTS

Once a quarter take a step back and measure your achievements. Unison did this and found out that they have a vehicle that provides them with a watch-dog approach. They were able to achieve the following:

— Conversion of a group of independent entrepreneurs into a solid team.
— Reduction in non-productive staff.
— Reduction in conflicting activities.
— Reduction in non-essential expenses and teams of certain services.
— Acceleration of "bird in hand" sales efforts.

EXHIBIT 5-28
Checkoff List for Profit Impact Chart Review Meetings

1. Set up a regular schedule and maintain it. Intially the meetings should be held weekly, then bi-weekly.
2. Review minutes of the previous meeting.

3. Discuss actions taken on previous assignments.
4. Vary the agenda of each of the meetings by discussing different charts or special projects. Insist on continuity and incorporation of the current data.
5. Develop a style that fits your organization, but keep give-and-take on target, i.e., stick to the meeting objectives.
6. Build a team, don't grade each member.
7. Invite only people involved in the matters to be discussed.
8. Provide participants with an agenda of things to be discussed, and copies of necessary reference materials prior to the meeting.
9. Set a timetable to begin and end the meeting on time.
10. Reach definite conclusions.
11. Assign responsibility for follow-up action.
12. Remember time is money, so use your meeting time effectively. A meeting that wastes 15 minutes of 10 executives' time earning $15,000 or 10.4 cents per minute, wastes 2-1/2 man hours and costs $15.60.

The next two cases in point, which conclude the chapter, demonstrate how two diverse companies have benefited from using the approaches discussed in this chapter.

A case in point—how profit impact charts helped save $150,000 by the reduction of material costs

A manufacturer had built a successful plastics business around the vacuum forming process when he decided to expand his business. His plan for expanding the business was to introduce the polyfoam process. At the start, he recognized two problems. First, he had to do the pioneering in this relatively new field. Secondly, while the vacuum form scrap could be ground up and recycled, the polyfoam could not be reused. Simultaneously with the introduction of the new line, the present vacuum form business seemed to grow by leaps and bounds. Financially, though, he began to experience a deterioration of his normal 31% gross profit. The real problem that he faced was that he could not identify from his financial statements the causes for the decline in his gross profit other than the fact that his material cost had sharply increased.

In order to gain a quick grasp of the situation, the series A profit impact chart package was prepared along product lines. By splitting the vacuum forming and the new polyfoam lines for analysis, he immediately saw that the gross profit for the vacuum forming line (including new orders) increased by 35% while the polyfoam line was running a negative 60%. Thus, by the use of the impact charts, the plastics producer knew where to begin to attack his problem.

The manufacturer of the equipment was called in for consultation. The rewards were two-fold. The equipment manufacturer discovered that he needed to improve his product in order to make it more salable. Our plastics producer found out that:

1. He was now confident he could accept the extra vacuum forming business without the fear of eroding his profits.

2. He increased the polyfoam production from 175 mediocre units per hour to 600 good units.

3. He realized an improved gross profit percentage which meant a savings in material costs of $150,000.

A case in point—how an electronics firm used profit impact charting as a communication tool and rallying factor for effecting a $2 million turnaround

A southern California computer peripheral equipment manufacturer had been supplying the majors with 60% of their needs. Then suddenly two of its largest customers decided to drop their computer lines. After the smoke cleared they found out that their backlog was depleted by $10 million, pre-tax loss for the year was $2 million, and a large inventory that had been accumulated in anticipation of future growth was now questionable. As they approached their new fiscal year, the board of directors had authorized a total reshaping of the company. In addition to improving the financial health of the business, the thrust was toward new product introduction, building a larger backlog, reducing inventory levels, etc.

The board requested the business plan be updated in detail and be provided to them on a monthly basis. It was decided to build all communications and monitoring of goals and objectives around series B profit impact charts. Although a form of profit impact charts had been used as a supplement to their financial reports, they had never been used as a communication tool nor a rallying point for directing and challenging the management team. By using the charts to co-ordinate the various business strategies that were needed to effect a turnaround, the company saw the following dollar savings:

	Prior Year	Current Year	Change Gain/ (Reduction)
Pre-tax Profits	$ (2092)	$ 83	$ 2175
New Orders	$13,326	$15,543	$ 2217
Inventory Levels	$ 7,465	$ 6,332	$(1133)

(thousand of dollars)

The lasting benefits were:

—An increased level of responsiveness and planning that filtered downward into the organization.

—The ability to pinpoint problems and take corrective actions early in the game.

—The knowledge that new products can be developed and introduced in a shorter period of time.

6

GROSS PROFIT ANALYSIS—ELIMINATING THE CONFUSION

This chapter serves as a transition or bridge between the first five chapters and those remaining. The first five chapters introduced you to a series of "how to" tools and approaches for understanding, monitoring, analyzing, and controlling the overall business. While the previous chapters may be termed conceptual, the remaining chapters are specific, as they deal with specialized areas such as labor and material costs, expenses, cash flow, etc. Chapter Six, Gross Profit Analysis, is a conceptual chapter because it deals with more than one area—revenue and costs. It is definitely a supplemental tool for gaining a better insight into your income statement. It is also a specific chapter because it relates to a single unique financial analysis area—gross profit.

WHAT IS GROSS PROFIT MARGIN?

Gross profit is simply the difference between sales less cost of sales on the income statement. In a manufacturing environment, the cost will include direct labor, direct material, and factory overhead. Whereas in a distribution firm, there will be no labor or overhead expenditures, only the products purchased for resale. Similarly in a service business cost of sales could be limited to labor only.

To analyze gross profit margins is simply to understand those interacting factors which contribute to gross profit. The three main factors which contribute to gross profit changes are:

Pricing— the price of the product or service sold.

122 GROSS PROFIT ANALYSIS

Cost — the cost of the units sold. In a manufacturing environment, this would represent labor, material, and plant overhead.

Volume—the number of units sold and the composition or mix of these units. If you are offering various services, you may wish to use hours rather than units.

WHY ANALYZE GROSS PROFIT?

The analysis and understanding of gross profit margin is a vital key because it can unlock otherwise hidden problem areas such as insufficient volume or pricing, cost increases, or mix shift. In many instances, you can do an excellent job of controlling expenses, but are not able to develop sufficient gross profit margin to cover the expenses and a reasonable profit. Some companies continue on in spite of themselves, attacking expenses, staying ahead of creditors, but failing to address fundamental problems such as the generation of adequate gross profit margin.

A Case In Point—Anonymous Chemical Company—Cutting Costs While Ignoring Gross Profit Margins

Anonymous Chemical Co. is a small, publicly-held company. In its recent financial statements to its stockholders, the following three statements have been paraphrased from the accompanying commentary:

Paragraph 1

During the recent year, we have completed a consolidation of operations. The $212,307 operating loss reported for the year includes the cost of these changes. Included in this cost reduction activity was the closing of our Southeastern warehousing and operations. It will now function only as a sales office.

Paragraph 2

Your Company currently shows an overall sales increase of $123,108. This is a result of the growth in our remaining two metropolitan areas. Sales were lower in the Southeast reflecting its reduced activity. Your Company benefited from the overall reduction in total operating costs.

Paragraph 3

We are now in the process of valuing the current mid-year inventory, and the data indicates an inventory adjustment which will reduce or eliminate any profit in the current fiscal year. We are beginning to see the light in that the severe operating losses of prior years have been substantially stopped and sales have held up during this recession. Your management is hopeful that in a better general business climate, there will be further improvement.

Hoping will not be enough! As Exhibit 6-1 shows, selling and administrative expenses have decreased 12% between 19X6 and 19X5, but there has been no improvement in their gross profit margin which remains at 31%. With interest expense increasing every year, the auditor's statement rings like a fire-bell in the night:

The Company's continuance in business is dependent upon the success of future operations and/or the ability of the Company to obtain additional working capital required.

EXHIBIT 6-1
Anonymous Chemical Co.
Three-Year Comparative Income Statement

	19X7 $	19X7 %	19X6 $	19X6 %	19X5 $	19X5 %
Net Sales	$1,786,284	100.0	$1,652,980	100.00	$2,179,254	100.0
Cost of Sales	1,232,657	69.0	1,139,982	69.0	1,701,340	78.1
Gross Profit	553,627	31.0	512,998	31.0	477,914	21.9
Selling & Administrative Expenses	733,873	41.1	876,595	53.0	883,406	40.5
Loss From Operations	(180,246)	(10.1)	(363,597)	(22.0)	(405,492)	(18.6)
Other Income (expense)						
Interest Expense	(51,541)	(2.9)	(36,787)	(2.2)	(13,707)	(.6)
Other Expense	19,480	1.1	13,596	.8	(21,169)	(1.0)
Total Other Income (expense)	(32,061)	(1.8)	(23,191)	(1.4)	(34,876)	(1.6)
Loss from Continuing Operations Before Federal and State Taxes	$(212,307)	(11.9)	$(386,788)	(23.4)	$(440,368)	(20.2)

TWO EASY APPROACHES TO GROSS PROFIT ANALYSIS

Calculating the effect of mix shift

Earlier in this chapter, volume was described as the number of units sold and the composition or mix of these units. E.g.: If your firm planned to sell 1,000 cases of canned peas and 500 cases of canned corn, but in actuality you sold 500 cases of peas and 1,000 cases of corn, you would still have sold the same anticipated volume of 1,500 cases. You would have experienced a mix shift away from peas to corn. If the selling price and costs were the same for both peas and corn, you would not be concerned, because the dollar impact would be zero. It is switches among products which force you to investigate what effect mix shift may have on your gross profit.

If your firm has a long and varied product line and you *do not* have access to computerization to extend each product sold by its representative selling price and cost, you should consider using approach number 1.

Approach Number 1 incorporates an average selling price and cost concept. Thus the effect of mix shift is spread within the price, cost, and volume figures. This averaging disguises the effect of mix and it is not discernable.

Approach Number 2 matches the true price and cost by line item. This forces the mix shift into volume where it can be isolated from the true volume or quantity sold. Approach number 2 should be used when you have a narrow product line, which can be extended manually or when you have access to computerization. The computerization is required to match selling prices and cost data bases to units sold and maintained, and to update this data on an on-going basis.

APPROACH NUMBER 1—IGNORING MIX

Step 1—Decide on the two periods you wish to compare and calculate the variances between them. In making the decision of what to compare, there are basically four options or alternatives available. In each of these options you are making comparisons between a current period and a base period.

Current Period		*Base Period*
Actual	vs.	Budget
Current Actual	vs.	Prior Actual
Current Budget	vs.	Prior Actual
Current Budget	vs.	Original Budget

For this illustration, actual vs. budget has been selected, and the variances have been calculated and displayed in the next example:

(UNFAVORABLE)

	Actual	*Budget*	*Difference*
Units	22,800	21,800	+1,000
Sales	$102,600	$100,400	+$2,200
Cost	70,110	60,240	(9,870)
Gross Profit $	$ 32,490	$ 40,160	$(7,670)
Gross Profit %	31.7%	40.0%	-8.3%

Step 2: Calculate the *actual* average selling price and costs per unit.

Selling price $\quad \dfrac{\$102,600}{22,800 \text{ units}} = \$4.5000$

Cost $\quad \dfrac{\$ 70,110}{22,800 \text{ units}} = \$3.0750$

Step 3: Calculate the *budgeted* average selling price and cost per unit and gross profit.

Budgeted per Unit Averages

Selling Price $\quad \dfrac{\$100,400}{21,800 \text{ units}} = \$4.6055$

Cost $\quad \dfrac{\$60,240}{21,800 \text{ units}} = \underline{\$2.7633}$

Gross Profit $\quad \underline{\$1.8422}$

Step 4: Calculate the three gross margin factors—price, cost, and volume.

Price: Actual units multiplied by the unit price difference.

GROSS PROFIT ANALYSIS

$ 4.5000   Actual/Unit Price
  4.6055   Budgeted/Unit Price
($ .1055)   Difference/Unit[1]
X 22,800   Actual Units
($ 2,405.4) Unfavorable Pricing

[1]Unfavorable because actual unit price is lower than anticipated.

Cost: Actual units multiplied by the unit cost difference.

$ 3.0750   Actual/Unit Cost
  2.7633   Budgeted/Unit Cost
($ .3117)   Difference/Unit[2]
X 22,800   Actual Units
($ 7,106.8) Unfavorable Cost

[2]Unfavorable because actual cost was higher than anticipated.

Volume: Volume difference multiplied by the budgeted unit gross profit.

22,800   Actual Units Sold
21,800   Budgeted Units Sold
 1,000   Difference[3]
X1.8422   Unit Gross Profit
$1,842.2 Favorable Volume

[3]Positive, because more units were sold than planned.

Step 5: Summarize the three gross margin factors from Step 4, and check total to gross profit difference in Step 1. -$(7670.0)

Price	$(2405.4)
Cost	$(7106.8)
Volume	$1,842.2
	$(7670.0)

APPROACH NUMBER 2—SEGREGATING MIX

Step 1: Same as step 1, approach 1.

Step 2: Approach number 2 requires the preparation of two worksheet formats to facilitate calculating the gross margin factors. Worksheet A prepares the basic data to be entered on the gross profit analysis summary, Worksheet B. Thus step 2 is to prepare the two worksheets.

Step 3: Calculate the actual selling price by items. The actual units sold are multiplied by each line item's unit actual selling price (Cols. 1 X 2 = 3 on Worksheet A). Enter the answer $102,600 on Worksheet B (Exhibits 6-2 and 6-3).

Step 4: Calculate the actual cost by item. The actual units sold are multiplied by each line item's actual unit cost (Cols. 1 X 4 = 5 on Worksheet A). Enter the answer $70,110 on Worksheet B.

Step 5: Calculate the budgeted selling price. The actual units sold are multiplied by each line item's unit budgeted selling price (Cols. 1 X 6 = 7 on Worksheet A). Enter the answer $100,320 on Worksheet B.

126   GROSS PROFIT ANALYSIS

Step 6:   Calculate the budgeted cost. The actual units sold are multiplied by each line item's budget cost (Cols. 1 X 8 = 9 on Worksheet A). Enter the answer $60,192 on worksheet B.

Step 7:   Calculate the average budgeted gross profit for the actual units sold.

This does not require using Worksheet A and is accomplished in two easy parts.

A. Compute average budgeted gross profit.

$$\frac{\text{Budgeted Gross Profit } \$40,160}{\text{Budgeted Units Sold } 21,800} = \$1.8422 \text{ average budgeted gross profit}$$

B. Multiply the actual units sold by the average budgeted gross profit; and enter your answer $42,002 on Worksheet B.

```
     22,800 actual units sold
X  $1.8422 average budgeted gross profit
    $42,002
```

Step 8:   Calculate the budgeted gross profit. The budgeted units which were anticipated to be sold are multiplied by each item's budgeted gross profit (Cols. 10 X 11 = 12 on Worksheet A). Enter the answer $40,160 on Worksheet B.

Step 9:   Summarize Worksheet B to determine the gross profit margin factors. This worksheet shows you the factors to be:

Price increase of	$ 2280
Cost increases of	(9918)
True volume increase of	1842
Unfavorable mix shift of	(1874)
Total change in gross profit	$(7670)

As a result of mix shifts, you get a different view of what occurs between budgeted and actual results. As an operational financial analyst, you need to keep your management abreast at least once a quarter of what effect mix shift is having upon your business. Marketing can use this data to analyze past sales and promotional activity and further use this data to generate new sales and marketing activities. Engineering and manufacturing can put this information to work in cutting costs, and all segments of the business including finance can use this insight to sharpen their business planning and budgeting.

Remember, approach number 2 works best when your product line is lengthy and you have access to computerization for doing your heavy number crunching. If you do not have access to an in-house computerization, consider Time Sharing. If no computerization is available for handling extensive product lines employ Pareto's Law (see Chapter 8)—identify those items which constitute 80% of the volume and assign them an average unit cost and selling price, because they only represent about 20% of the value. The remaining 20% volume should be priced and costed exactly because they represent about 80% of the dollar value.

GROSS PROFIT ANALYSIS

EXHIBIT 6-2
Gross Profit Analysis Worksheet—A

Products Sold	1 Actual Units Sold	2 Actual Selling Price	3 1X3	4 Actual Cost	5 1X5
Small	4,560	3.10	14,136	2.00	9,120
Medium	6,840	4.10	28,044	2.75	18,810
Big	6,840	5.10	34,884	3.50	23,940
Large	4,560	5.60	25,536	4.00	18,220
TOTALS	22,800		$102,600		$70,110

6 Budgeted Selling Price	7 1X7	8 Budgeted Cost	9 1X9	10 Budgeted Units Sold	11 Budgeted Gross Profit	12 10X11
3.00	13,680	1.80	8,208	3,000	1.20	3,600
4.00	27,360	2.40	16,416	6,000	1.60	9,600
5.00	34,200	3.00	20,520	6,000	2.00	12,000
5.50	25,080	3.30	15,048	6,800	2.20	14,960
	$100,320		$60,192	21,800		$40,160

EXHIBIT 6-3
Gross Profit Analysis Worksheet—B

Step	Description	Price	Cost	Volume	Mix	Proof
2-3	Actual Qty. @ Actual Prices	+102,600	XXX	XXX	XXX	+102,600
2-4	Actual Qty @ Actual Cost	XXX	−70,110	XXX	XXX	70,110
2-5	Actual Qty @ Budgeted Prices	100,320	XXX	XXX	+100,320	-0-
2-6	Actual Qty @ Budgeted Cost	XXX	+60,192	XXX	60,192	-0-
2-7	Actual Qty @ Average Budgeted Gross Profit [4]	XXX	XXX	+42,002	−42,002	-0-
2-8	Budgeted Qty @ Budgeted Gross Profit	XXX	XXX	40,160	XXX	40,160
2-9	Summarize	2,280	(9,918)	1,842	(1,874)	(7,670)

A case in point—how a large soft drink bottler harnessed the computer for analyzing gross profit margin and how they use this information

At one time, this bottler had only two packages—regular and king-size, both in returnable bottles. Via acquisitions and change in consumer preference from returnable to one-way packaging, their two-product-line data base grew to a very lengthy pricing and packaging configuration. With the large number of items in their product list, they were no longer able to manually isolate the effect mix shift was having upon their gross

---

[4] This step establishes the common factor used to separate the volume variance into true volume and mix.

Note: All plus and minus signs are functional and not conditional.

profit margins. The financial and marketing staffs also wanted to know the effect promotional activity was having upon mix shift and how big a factor mix really was in contributing or eroding gross profit margins. Because of the lengthy product offering and varying regional pricing and costs, mix shift was considered by some to be extensive.

In the preparation of their financial guide line (annual budget and business plan) this firm makes extensive use of product pricing and costing computer data bases. These data bases are also used for various daily computations along with the monthly closing. Thus, it was very easy for this firm to simply extend its actual cases sold by the budgeted selling price and cost to prepare the basic data required to analyze mix shift between actual and budget. To analyze mix shift between current and prior periods, they extend on a line item basis the actual cases sold to prior year's selling prices and costs.

Not all solutions to complex problems have to be complex. This one was easy. The soft drink bottler examined the data they had available and put it to use in solving a problem which could not be solved manually in a timely manner. After this system was operational, this firm found that mix shift did not possess the impact expected. With mix shift isolated, the firm was now better able to interpret the true effect of each of the three elements—pricing, cost, and volume—and how they played in adding to or detracting from gross profit margins.

Currently this data is presented to senior management on a quarterly basis and used to validate and analyze annual and quarterly financial projections. As this firm is very bottom line oriented, it uses the results of these analyses to determine pricing moves in this highly competitive business. The V.P.-Controller uses this data to help direct the actions and interpret the results of the packaging committee, a group of key individuals who are responsible for finding and evaluating cost reductions.

COME DOWN FROM THE IVORY TOWER AND TOUCH THE HARDWARE

As an operational financial analyst your job is not finished when you have completed the gross profit analysis. The true test of your analytical skills is your ability to interpret the interacting factors which caused the relationship between price, cost, volume, and mix to occur. This ability can only be developed by touching the hardware, i.e., coming out from behind your desk, leaving the ivory tower and finding out what happens:

—in the marketplace to effect sales and pricing.
—in production to effect costs and delivery.
—in distribution to effect efficient and inexpensive delivery.
—in engineering for tomorrow's products.
—in marketing for tomorrow's sales.

A mini-case in point—how a budding financial analyst learned to touch the hardware

An electronics firm was awarded a twenty million dollar development and production subcontract to develop a specialized memory system for a large computer company. To handle this contract, a program manager was hired, and a program team assembled. As part of this team, a young financial analyst was assigned to the program manager. A task-oriented, financial reporting package was installed to control and analyze the progress of the program. The young analyst, who thought he was doing a superb job, was surprised by the results of his performance review. The program

GROSS PROFIT ANALYSIS

manager informed him, although his reports were complete and accurate, they were also dry and stuffy and were not providing him with a clear in-depth understanding of the financial condition of the program. Taken aback, the young man wanted to know how he could develop his reports into worthwhile management tools. The program manager informed him he was like Harold Hill, the instrument salesman in the musical *The Music Man*, who could never reach his true potential as a salesman because he didn't know the territory. The program manager directed the analyst to get out from behind his desk and learn first hand what was happening in engineering, production, and Q.C. The term he used to describe this process was "touching the hardware."

This program manager was a results-oriented individual; and to insure his young analyst would follow his advice, he assigned him to a specific time and tour path. Fairly soon, the analyst was able to incorporate his new found operational awareness into his financial and analytical reports. Not only had the analyst become more interested in his work, but his financial reports were making a greater contribution to the program.

Touching the hardware requires consistency of effort and the willingness to pursue questions to a logical conclusion.

HOW WELL DO YOU KNOW YOUR BUSINESS?

The following checkoff list is designed to get you started in a repetitive, self-generating program. This type of program forces you to keep up with changing conditions and trends. We all know about the proverbial path that is paved with good intentions.

EXHIBIT 6-4
12-Point Checkoff List for Gaining Greater Operational Awareness
(AKA—Touching the Hardware)

1. Marketing

Do you have a key individual in marketing who keeps you abreast of what constitutes your firm's current market, future market, and their approaches for reaching the market through new products, pricing, promotional activity, advertising, etc?

2. Sales

Do you visit outlying sales branches and meet with branch managers to gain an understanding of their particular problems and needs?

3. Engineering

How often do you have lunch with the chief engineer or key engineering personnel in order to keep up with the changing technical side of your industry?

4. Pre-production Activity

When you last visited the prototype shop, how were they coming along in readying next year's product entries in relation to finalizing tooling, production documentation, etc?

5. Production and Material Control

Have you taken a few minutes to have someone briefly explain the major sub-assemblies, major parts, cost, and availability of same in conjunction with an exploded master bill of material and a production assembly hierarchy (goes into chart)?

6. Production—Procedures

Can you identify and have you kept up-to-date with the key operations in your production job or process flow?

7. Production—Floor

When was the last time you toured your operations with an intent of being brought up-to-date on bottlenecks, changes, problems, and future equipment needs?

8. Quality Assurance

Are you up-to-date on the latest major quality assurance programs which are in effect to insure product reliability and customer acceptance?

9. General Accounting

Does the accounting manager keep you and other members of the financial analysis staff abreast of changes in the accounting process and systems?

10. Cost Accounting

Have you taken the time recently to review the standard cost file for labor and material cost changes?

11. Systems & Procedures

Are you on distribution for receipt of all major system and procedure changes which could affect your knowledge of how your firm operates?

12. Financial Administrator

If you are a group controller or manager do you hold quarterly review meetings or staff meetings? Are these meetings held at the same location or are they rotated so all members of your group can view and become acquainted with the other operations and problems in the group and thus foster an exchange of ideas?

7

PRACTICAL TECHNIQUES FOR ANALYZING MATERIAL COSTS

If the cost of materials is the largest item on your firm's income statement and your largest expenditure on your cash flow projection, then you need to understand the composition of these dollars. The most practical method for understanding this dollar area is through several easy analytical applications such as:

— Projecting Material Usage

— Understanding Inventory Turnover

— Using A.B.C. Inventory Analysis

— Benefiting from Scrap Reporting and Analysis

PROJECTING MATERIAL USAGE AND INVENTORY LEVELS

The value of plan your work, work your plan

Here is an area where implementing the concept of "plan your work, work your plan" can pay off. Most companies have some form of production planning and control, whether it be conducted by a formal department or by a departmental foreman. In many cases this planning is tied loosely to the sales projection and in rare cases to the financial guide line. Thus many commonplace production inefficiencies occur such as:

— intermittent, inefficient, and short production runs.

— double handling because materials were not available when needed.

- proper tooling methods are not developed, because production runs are not long enough.
- true benefits of the learning curve are not realized.
- quantity discounts are missed.
- economical quantity orders are not defined.
- production lines or machines are idle or slowed down awaiting a critical part[1] that winds up being installed on overtime to meet schedule.

Thus, in order to obtain your goals, it is critical to tie your production planning to your financial guide line.

A case in point—how the systematic projection of material cost and usage greatly improved gross profit margin by 7.3%

Meredith Electronics, a medium-size electronics manufacturer, was finding it difficult to make timely and profitable shipments.

On forecast shipments of 695 units, they were projecting:

	Total	Avg./Unit
Sales	$20,818,000	$29,954
Cost of Sales	15,655,000	22,525
Gross Profit	$ 5,163,000	$ 7,429
Gross Profit %	24.8%	

The gross profit percentage return on sales was not sufficient to provide an adequate bottom line profit. A thorough investigation revealed the fact that the production schedule did not agree with the sales forecast used in the preparation of the financial guide-line, which indicated a much higher gross profit percentage. Further analysis of the job cost records showed that the finished cost of the units was exceeding its original material and labor estimates. After a meeting with the production manager, it was estimated that the excess production costs occurred because units were being worked on intermittently. This was occurring because in many instances, vital parts and subassemblies were not on hand when the order came in from marketing. The production manager alluded to the fact that the problem was due to marketing's erratic shipment projections and insufficient delivery lead times.

The solution was to force marketing to define a more realistic and firm sales projection, which turned out to be 120 units lower than previously forecast. Once the new financial guide line with its improved sales projection was approved by senior management, it was then converted into a production shipment schedule. This generated a definite plan for purchasing parts and sub-assemblies, which became the basis of a sub-assembly master production schedule. This is the identical process described in Exhibit 7-1.

With the new forecast, improved production scheduling and shipment capabilities, the gross profit percentage improved by 7.3 percentage points. This was based on the following figures:

---

[1] Remember the major airframe company, who could not ship its new short range jet until the galley sub-assemblies arrived and were installed.

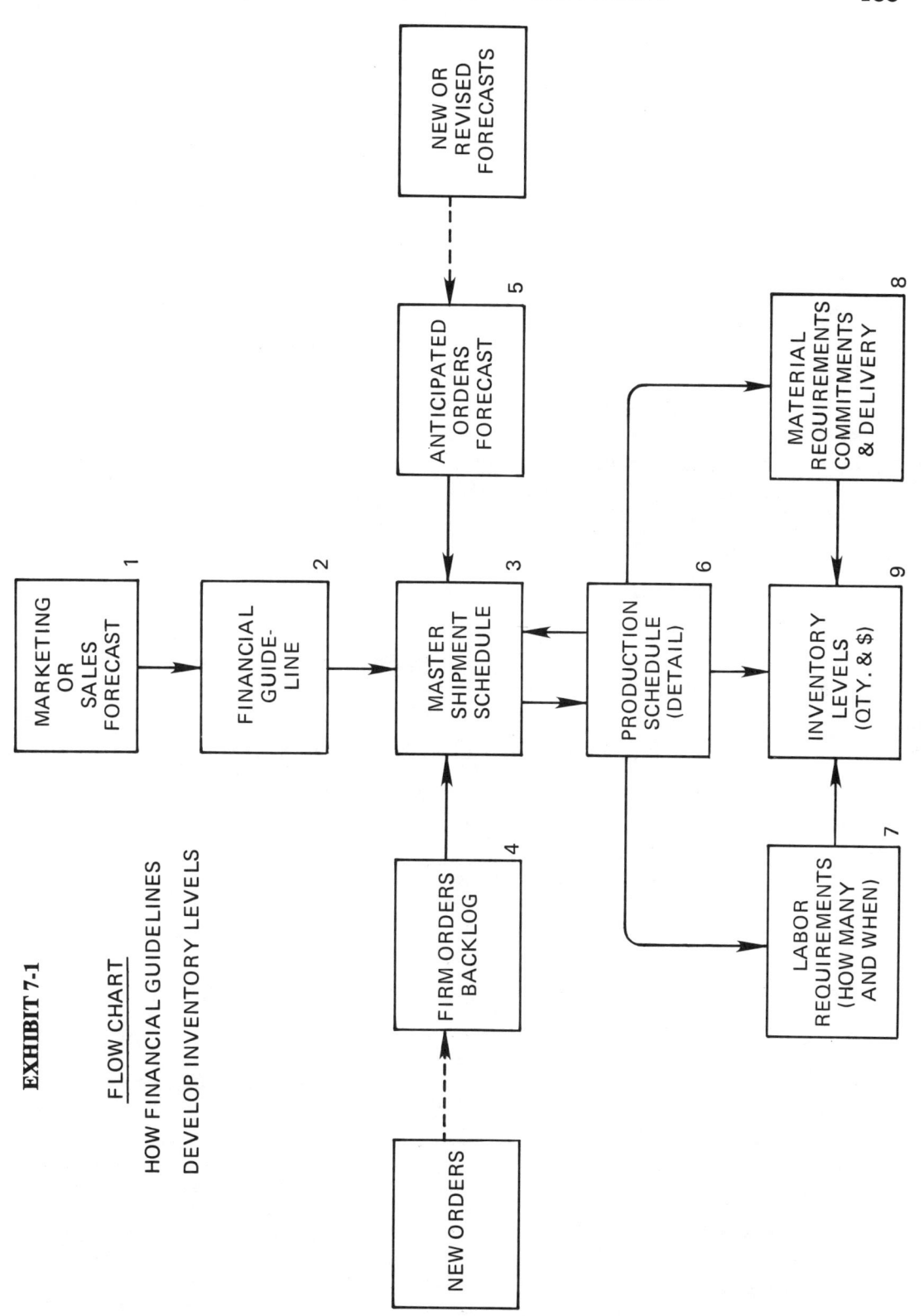

PRACTICAL TECHNIQUES FOR ANALYZING MATERIAL COSTS 133

EXHIBIT 7-1

FLOW CHART
HOW FINANCIAL GUIDELINES
DEVELOP INVENTORY LEVELS

1. MARKETING OR SALES FORECAST
2. FINANCIAL GUIDELINE
3. MASTER SHIPMENT SCHEDULE
4. FIRM ORDERS BACKLOG
5. ANTICIPATED ORDERS FORECAST
6. PRODUCTION SCHEDULE (DETAIL)
7. LABOR REQUIREMENTS (HOW MANY AND WHEN)
8. MATERIAL REQUIREMENTS COMMITMENTS & DELIVERY
9. INVENTORY LEVELS (QTY. & $)

NEW OR REVISED FORECASTS

NEW ORDERS

	Total	Avg./Unit[2]
Sales	$18,782,000	$32,664
Cost of Sales	12,751,000	22,176
Gross Profit	$ 6,031,000	$10,488
Gross Profit %	32.1	

Another cost savings benefit derived from a more realistic and systematic approach to material projection and production scheduling was the cutting back on indirect support personnel who were no longer needed to fight fires.

Bringing the financial guide line to the work bench

In many companies, the final production portion of the financial guide line never reaches the desks of those individuals who must implement the plan, such as the production managers, warehouse superintendents, transportation managers, quality directors, etc. Hopefully, when these managers submitted their inputs to the F.G.L., they should have developed detailed production assembly and shipment schedules and departmental budgets based upon the *finalized* marketing forecast in the F.G.L.

The flow chart in Exhibit 7-1 shows the sequence of events that take place in converting the F.G.L. into a workable production control tool:

—1st Step— converting the sales forecast into a master shipment schedule (3)[3].

—2nd Step— continually updating (4 & 5).

—3rd Step— resulting in a detailed production schedule (6). This would show the availability of labor and material required to complete the forecast.

—4th Step— updating the inventory (9). For ease of control, planning, and analysis, inventories should be segregated by:

    raw materials
    components
    sub-assemblies
    work-in-process
    finished goods

A.B.C. INVENTORY CONTROL AND ANALYSIS

The concept of A. B. C. inventory control has its base in Pareto's Law. Pareto was an Italian mathematician who stated that the major items in any particular group normally make up a relatively small portion of the total items in the group, i.e., a majority of the items in the group, even in the aggregate, will have little or no impact upon the total and thus will be of little importance or significance.

What Pareto's Law says is that 80% of the items in a group usually account for only 20% of the total value. Conversely, 20% of the items in the same group will constitute 80% of the value.

Even in reviewing your daily work load, you will see that only about 20% of the

---

[2] Reflects improved mix shift and pricing.

[3] Numbers in parentheses represent numbers on the flow chart.

PRACTICAL TECHNIQUES FOR ANALYZING MATERIAL COSTS

items you tackle during the day are not delegatable and the payoff is greater than other items. These we could class as Group A items. The other 80% break down into two lesser categories of importance. Group B items fall somewhere below Group A in importance while Group C tasks should be delegated to someone else or totally ignored.

Most managements fail to recognize the need for applying varying degrees of control to various segments of their inventories. Many companies apply the same effort to controlling a valuable electric motor as they do a barrel of inexpensive flat steel washers.

The items that constitute the high dollar usage should receive management's attention while the low dollar usage items should require very limited attention.

Usage is computed by multiplying the quantity used during the year by the unit cost. To demonstrate the relationship, these different items have a similar annual unit or quantity usage.

Class	Description	Quantity	Unit Cost	Annual Usage
A	Motor	4,250	$6.250	26,563
B	Clamp	3,509	$ .450	1,579
C	Pin	4,520	$ .050	226

Industrial practice is to divide the inventory into three groups, varying degrees of control applied to each group.

Items	Usage	Control	Reviews
A	High Dollar	Extensive	Currently
B	Medium Dollar	Moderate	Monthly
C	Low Dollar	Limited	Quarterly

Exhibit 7-2 shows the percentage of parts in one company's inventory and how these parts based on usage break down into the three groupings.

UNDERSTANDING INVENTORY TURNOVER

Inventory turnover is a simple ratio to compute that can have a major impact upon judging how well you are operating your business. This ratio reveals how many times during the period you sold, shipped, or replaced products. The calculations are as follows:

Turnover Ratio

Finished goods

$$\frac{\text{Cost of Goods Sold}}{\text{Average Finished Goods Inv.}} \quad \frac{\$385,000}{\$ 65,000} = \text{Turnover of 5.92 times}$$

Raw Materials

$$\frac{\text{Raw Materials Consumed}}{\text{Average Raw Material Inv.}} \quad \frac{\$135,000}{\$ 17,000} = \text{Turnover of 7.94 times}$$

Many managers find it easier to relate to the turnover ratio if it is expressed in workdays. This is accomplished by dividing the ratio into the number of workdays in a year.

EXHIBIT 7-2

INVENTORY CONTROL
ABC ANALYSIS METHOD

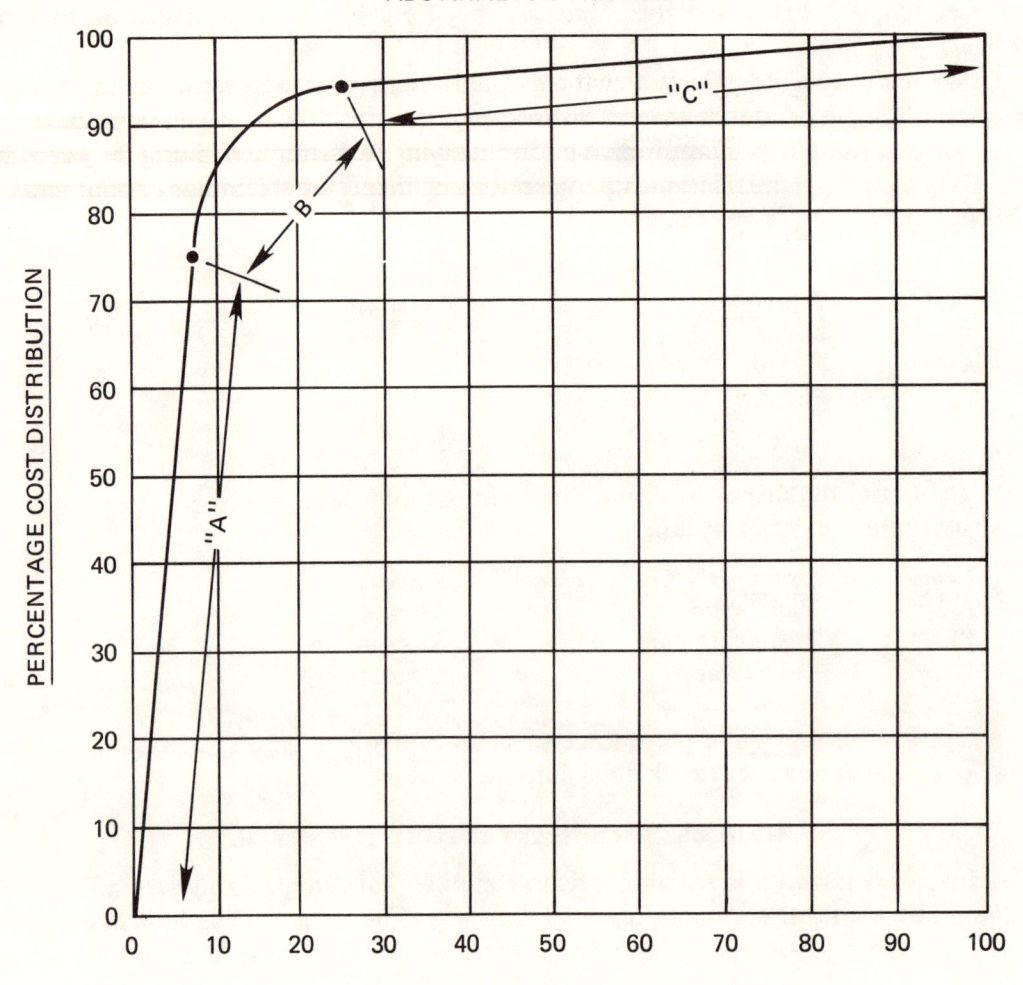

PERCENTAGE COST DISTRIBUTION (y-axis, 0–100)

PERCENTAGE DISTRIBUTION OF PARTS IN INVENTORY (x-axis, 0–100)

CLASS	% PARTS	% COST
A	8	75
B	25	20
C	67	5

PRACTICAL TECHNIQUES FOR ANALYZING MATERIAL COSTS

Turnover Ratio Expressed In Workdays
42.7 days of unsold finished goods
31.9 days in raw materials

We used average inventories for our example, but what about highly seasonal businesses or businesses where severe fluctuations occur? To answer this question, it is necessary to compare your company to similar companies in your industry group. This data can be obtained from your bank or trade association.

This next example shows the diversity that can exist between industry groups. At first glance, how does your company compare?

Industry Group[4]	Turnover	Days
Bottlers—Soft Drink	9.7	37
Children's Clothing	4.9	73
Drugs and Medicines	3.5	103
Industrial Chemicals	6.4	56
Ball & Roller Bearings	4.6	79
Fabricated Structural Steel	6.0	60
Valves and Fittings	3.0	119
Commercial Printing—Litho	12.1	30

The turnover ratio will vary in regard to the size of the firm and the financial capability of your management. The range that exists for the soft drink bottlers is illustrated in a study of 184 bottlers:

Upper Quartile	14.1	26 days
Medium Quartile	9.7	37 days
Lower Quartile	6.6	55 days

Don't be lulled into complacency because your statistics are better than your industry group. Your goal is to speed up your turnover ratio and thus improve profits and cash flow. This can be accomplished by being mindful of the following:

—understanding your industry group.
—knowing the causes and factors that contribute to your ratio.
—establishing a reasonable goal and the steps required to achieve that goal.
—working your plan.

BENEFITING FROM SCRAP REPORTING AND ANALYSIS

The benefits

At first glance, it appears that scrap reporting and analysis belongs in the quality control section of a production handbook. Unfortunately, scrap and excessive re-work are profit eroders. Initially, it is the job of the financial analyst to get behind the causes

---

[4]Represents manufacturing companies, not wholesale or retail firms.

of these profit eroders. He should establish programs that set up a scrap allowance and monitor the progress against the goals. The benefits to be achieved by instituting this monitoring and analytical function are listed in the next exhibit.

EXHIBIT 7-3
Six-Point Checkoff List of Benefits from Scrap Reporting and Analysis

1. Keep scrap losses at minimum, maximizing profitability.
2. Compare production efficiencies and yields to the amount of scrap generated and re-work required.
3. Appraise management of trouble spots in the production cycle for remedial action.
4. Recover costs from vendor.
5. Better utilization of materials.
6. Consistent approach to reporting techniques.

The scrap ticket

In order to initiate the consistent approach mentioned in point 6 of the previous checkoff list, the scrap tickets described in Exhibits 7-4 and 7-5 are used. These scrap

EXHIBIT 7-4

PRINT I.R. DO NOT WRITE

INSPECTORS REPORT
MATERIAL REJECTION

№ 39905

PART NAME	PART NUMBER		QTY. INSP.	QTY. REJ.	TRAVELER NO.	OPERATION NO.
REJECTING INSPECTOR	STAMP NO.	LOT FAB. SERIAL NO.	PROJECT	MJO		DATE
VENDOR	PURCHASE ORDER NO.		MODEL	REJ. IN DEPT.		DEPT. RESPON.

REASON FOR REJECTION-EXPLAIN IN DETAIL

DISPOSITION

USE AS IS	REPAIR	REWORK	SCRAP	RTN. TO VENDOR	CHARGE BBC	CHARGE VENDOR
☐	☐	☐	☐	☐	☐	☐

GIVE DETAILS-LIST ITEMS SCRAPPED

CORRECTIVE ACTION TAKEN | DATE | SIGNATURE

QUALITY CONTROL	DATE	STAMP NO.	CUSTOMER	DATE	ENGINEER	DATE	P.M.R. ☐ MRB ☐

☐ HYTECH
☐ SANTA MONICA

DISTRIBUTION
BLUE-Q.C. WHITE-PURCH. YELLOW-ACCT. PINK-RCVG. HARD-MATERIAL

PRACTICAL TECHNIQUES FOR ANALYZING MATERIAL COSTS 139

tickets can be used anywhere within the production cycle. For analysis purposes, these tickets can be summarized on a worksheet or key punched, sorted, displayed by part number, cause of reject, or final disposition. Remember, don't stop with the analysis; put your data to work seeking a cure to the causes of the reject.

EXHIBIT 7-5

MATERIAL REJECTION TAG	Nº 11901

REQUEST FOR MATERIAL REPLACEMENT

PART NO.	DESCRIPTION	ACCOUNT	QTY.
ASSEMBLY NO.	ASSY DESCRIPTION		ASSY ORDER NO.

REASON FOR REJECTION

	RECORD CHECK	REJECTED BY	DATE

REPLACEMENT

FROM ACCT.	TO ACCT. 644-4468	QTY. REQ'D	QTY. B.O.	ISSUE OR B.O. BY	REC'D BY
QTY. ISSUED	UNIT COST	UNIT	AMOUNT	POSTED - M.C.	POSTED - ACCTG.

SALVAGE REVIEW

QUANTITY	DISPOSITION	TO MATERIAL REVIEW BOARD FOR DISPOSITION	RESPONSIBILITY
	USE AS IS — RETURN TO STK.		☐ ENGINEERING
	REWORK — SEE BELOW	DATE	☐ MANUFACTURING
	SCRAP	BY	☐ VENDOR

REWORK INSTRUCTIONS (USE REWORK ACCOUNT BELOW)

REWORK ACCOUNT	DISPATCHER	SALVAGE REVIEW BY	DATE

REWORK ACTION

REWORK COMPLETED BY: DATE:	REWORK ACCEPTED BY: DATE:	
QTY. RETURNED TO STOCK: (CREDIT 2512-207 ON S.R.)	QTY. REJECTED FROM REWORK:	MFG. ADM.

REQUISITION COPY

A case in point—how a firm saved $173,000 by using a material rejection tag system

Shortly after Meredith Electronics adopted a more systematic approach to projecting material usage they were beset with another material-related problem. One of their products was an electro-mechanical control unit. This unit contained five magnesium castings costing $600 each. They were obtained from a single source, which was very dependent on Meredith's business for its survival. The current production schedule called for the assembly of 240 completed units. Unfortunately the shipment schedule was slipping, because 30% of the castings were being rejected. These defective castings contained hollow interior pockets that could only be discovered during the machining cycle.

The following data demonstrates the degree of Meredith's financial exposure if the failure rate were to continue.

Total castings required (240 X 5)	1,200
Rejected castings @ 30% failure rate	360
Value of raw castings @ $600.	$216,000

In addition to the cost of the scrapped raw castings, Meredith had to scrap any machining costs that occurred prior to encountering the faulty pockets. This high dollar exposure brought about the design and installation of a material rejection tag and system. The system portion is very important, because without its implementation, all you would have is a lot of bad parts with pretty tags, where before you simply had bad parts. The system portion is very simple in that the data contained on the tags would be summarized, analyzed, and acted upon by a special material review board. Prior to the implementation of this system, rejected parts or problems were inconsistently noted on the production work order or an entire sub-assembly was pulled out of the regular production cycle and assigned a re-work production work order.

Under the new system, a material rejection tag was filled out stating the nature and location of the imperfection and at what point in the machining process the failure was detected. The data from these tags was summarized and studied by both the casting company and Meredith's material review board. Together, they made basic changes to the design of the castings, method of casting, and the final machining process. These changes forced the rejection level to drop to 2% or a projected scrap level of $43,200 as compared to the original $216,000 projection. Besides these dollar savings, Meredith was guaranteed a continuing supply of reliable castings, and the vendor continued to have a viable business relationship with his customer.

8

PRACTICAL TECHNIQUES FOR CONTROLLING MATERIAL COSTS

The previous chapter provided you with four beneficial analytical tools for sharpening your insight and understanding of material cost and inventory levels. Now that you have the ability to get behind the numbers, you are ready to get ahead of the numbers by adapting four easily implementable approaches:

— Parts Numbering—The First Control Step
— Centralized Purchasing—Pays Its Way
— Purchase Commitment—Today's View of Tomorrow
— Physical Inventory—Is More Than the Motion of Counting

Most companies do not adopt a preventative profile and chose to ignore all or part of the above mentioned systems until they are faced with a deterioration in their income statement or cash flow. They fail to realize the continuing payoff of lower material cost and expenditure levels by implementing these beneficial concepts.

PARTS NUMBERING—THE FIRST CONTROL STEP

Know what you are controlling

Before you can begin to control inventory levels, turnover, scrap, etc., you must be able to clearly identify the item you want to control. This is accomplished by instituting a uniform part numbering system that tells a story. The part numbering system should be both general and specific in description.

142 PRACTICAL TECHNIQUES FOR CONTROLLING MATERIAL COSTS

A General Description—Is it raw material, semi-finished part, sub-assembly finished part, or assembly purchased part, etc?

A Specific Description—If the part is electrical, what type part and the specifications?

Exhibit 8-1 demonstrates how the part numbering system used by a large fleet department tells a complete and detailed story about the items in their inventory. Prior to the installation of this system, this department was either losing, out of, or never seemed to have the right part in stock. Time was being lost by ordering the part or by making a special trip to pick it up.

EXHIBIT 8-1
Example of a Part Numbering System That Tells a Story

A part numbering system that tells a story for an automative fleet maintenance shop would be as follows:

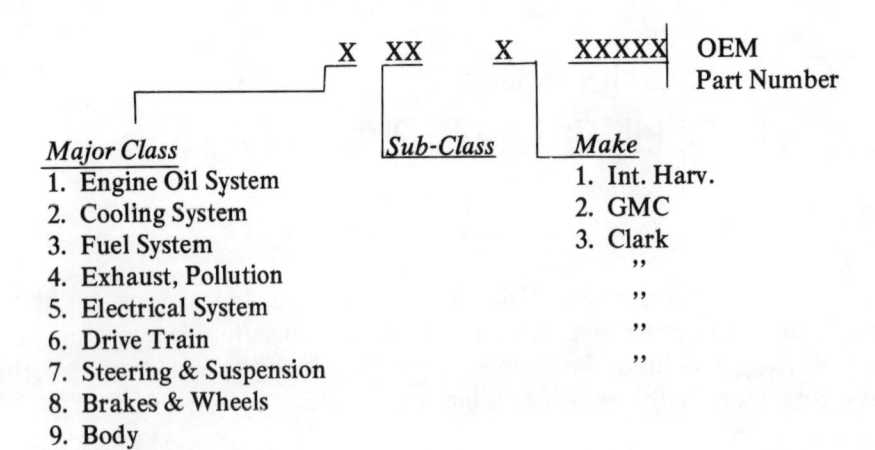

```
        X XX    X    XXXXX  OEM
                           Part Number
```

Major Class   *Sub-Class*   *Make*
1. Engine Oil System   1. Int. Harv.
2. Cooling System   2. GMC
3. Fuel System   3. Clark
4. Exhaust, Pollution   "
5. Electrical System   "
6. Drive Train   "
7. Steering & Suspension   "
8. Brakes & Wheels
9. Body

To illustrate the benefits of an intelligent pre-fix code, 13 International Harvester part numbers were pulled at random:

258 387	C1	Tail Pipe
291 869	C91	Center Bearing
111 775	3	Generator
389 279	C91	Gasket Set
358 921	C1	Muffler
268 574	C92	Rotor
360 514	C1	Distributor
389 280	C91	Kit-Carb.
877 978	R92	Clamp
360 700	C1	Condenser
379 475	C91	Carburetor
361 764	C1	Points
877 313	R92	Dist. Cap

Sorting them as you would on a manual or EDP system, high order, left to right, the 13 part numbers would look like this:

PRACTICAL TECHNIQUES FOR CONTROLLING MATERIAL COSTS

111 775	3	Generator
258 387	C1	Tail Pipe
268 574	C92	Rotor
291 869	C91	Center Bearing
358 921	C1	Muffler
360 514	C1	Distributor
360 700	C1	Condenser
361 764	C1	Points
379 475	C91	Carburetor
389 279	C91	Gasket Set-Carb.
389 280	C91	Kit-Carb. Repair
877 313	R92	Dist. Cap
877 978	R92	Clamp

The limitations of this sorting are quite apparent in that you have a tail pipe sorted in between a generator and a rotor, a center bearing and a muffler laced between a rotor and a distributor.

A pre-fix code will give you some logical groupings:

Fuel System	311 1	379 475	C91	Carburetor
	318 1	389 279	C91	Gasket Set-Carb.
	319 1	389 280	C91	Kit-Carb. Repair
Exhaust System	411 1	358 921	C1	Muffler
	413 1	258 387	C1	Tail Pipe
	414 1	877 978	R92	Clamp
Electrical	521 1	111 775	3	Generator
	531 1	360 514	C1	Distributor
	534 1	877 313	R92	Dist. Cap
	535 1	268 574	C92	Rotor
	536 1	360 700	C1	Condenser
	537 1	361 764	C1	Points
Drive Train	643 1	291 869	C91	Center Bearing

Int. Harv. OEM Part Number

Now that you have a logical sequence and have converted your inventory card and/or eventually an EDP master file, you can add other helpful complementary data as:

1. *Location*—(Shelf, branch, service trucks, machine shop, fork-lift shop, etc.)
2. *On Hand Quantity*
3. *Purchase Quantity*
4. *Usage Quantity*
5. *Vendor ID*—(Sources of Supply)
6. *Cross Reference*—to equivalent, non-DEM part number (NAPA, United, etc.)
7. *Standard Cost*

The concepts that are shown in the above examples are easily transferrable to most organizations. In a manufacturing company, the sub-class digits can be used to designate whether a part is:

1. Purchased
2. Machined or fabricated
3. Sub-Assembly—Partial
4. Sub-Assembly—Complete
5. Final Assembly—Partial
6. Final Assembly—Complete

Also the original equipment manufacturer's number (OEM) can be deleted and replaced with a common part number if the parts are similar. An example of how one company saved money and confusion by switching to a pre-fixed inventory number follows:

A case in point—by the assignment of common part numbers, out of stock conditions were alleviated and quantity discounts were granted

In the previous chapter you were introduced to Meredith Electronics which had encountered material-related business problems. Well, here is still another material-related problem that plagued Meredith.

They seemed to be continually out of stock on many of what their material control department had designated as their 50 most critical parts. In order to inaugurate some control of these items, they instituted a "hot sheet" to keep track of them. They found the hot sheet difficult to use because of the dissimilarity between the vendor part numbers. In order to simplify the use of the hot sheet, these fifty items were organized into a specialized uniform part numbering system. Now the hot sheet with its new uniform part numbering system became a vital material and production control document for isolating shortages and future needs. The hot sheet also began pinpointing which parts were truly interchangeable and substitutable, since the vendor part numbers were grouped by the Meredith number. The substitution factor caused the items on the hot sheet to be reduced from 50 to 35.

Unfortunately, the engineering drawings and production and assembly documents remained unchanged and continued identifying parts by vendor number or name. This conflict caused the company to adopt a uniform part numbering system that would tell the same story to everyone and force a reduction in the number of duplicate parts. Part specifications were written and a four-digit number was assigned with a letter prefix such as M1865. M1865 would now replace Company A's 1051938 or Company B's Electro charge-68, etc.

The new system in addition to the above:

— reduced line items per bill of materials.
— facilitated a faster and easier bill of material explosion which was used for determining total parts required.
— reduced the number of items being tracked on the hot sheet.
— simplified inventory and material control procedures.

With fewer items to handle and track coupled with better planning, they were able to eliminate their out-of-stock condition.

Since Meredith was now buying fewer items but in larger quantities, purchasing was now able to negotiate improving pricing (remember the total number of parts per assembly didn't increase, only the bill of material line items decreased). For example, Meredith needed 50,000 units of what we now refer to as M1865. Prior to the new system, they would have concluded three separate purchase orders for a total of $46,250 and had to track each of them.

Qty	Part #		Cost	Total
25,000	#1051938's	@	.9000 ea for	$22,500
10,000	#52639's	@	1.1000 ea for	11,000
15,000	#E.C.-68	@	.8500 ea for	12,750
50,000	Avg.	@	.9250 ea for	46,250

With Meredith's combined buying power, they were able to select the lowest unit price and achieved a 5% price reduction, which saved them $5,875 (85c per unit less 5% = .8075 per unit X 50,000 = $40,375. $46,250 less $40,375 = $5,875). Now they just had to keep track of one P.O.

CENTRALIZED PURCHASING—PAYS ITS WAY

What it is

Centralized purchasing establishes the purchasing function and responsibility under one department and location rather than having it duplicated within a multi-plant operation or by a user department within a single plant location. In many large companies, user departments may still continue to order their specialized requirements, but under the control of a blanket purchase order issued by the purchasing department.

How to effectively use blanket purchase orders

A blanket purchase order establishes the purchasing of a wide variety of items from a single vendor source over a specific period of time. A blanket purchase order differs from a master purchase order in that a master purchase order is used only by Purchasing to order and control the future delivery of specific materials. This is done through a series of releases to the master purchase order as the items are required.

The concept of the blanket purchase order is to provide a source of supply for a user department with a minimum amount of paperwork and delay. This delegation of authority to the user department to issue releases to the blanket purchase order does not relieve the purchasing department of its authority or responsibility in the selection of vendors and establishment of prices and terms. In fact, purchasing will work very closely with the user in the selection of the vendor to be covered under the blanket purchase order.

Blanket purchase orders are issued for a stipulated time period and include specific terms and conditions. An example of the wording contained in a typical blanket P.O. would be:

> TO COVER THE PURCHASE OF SERVICES OR PARTS AS REQUIRED BY THE FLEET DEPT. OF THE C. LYNN DISTRIBUTION CO.
> Period: Jan. 1, 19X7 thru Dec. 31, 19X7—Term 2%—10th Delivery—Via Supplier Truck Invoices will be submitted in triplicate with appropriate purchase order number indicated. Packing slips must also show purchase order number.
>
> This agreement may be cancelled by either party upon written notice.

Releases against the blanket P.O. should cover any additional information that is not previously covered by the blanket P.O.

Centralized purchasing as a cost cutter

Since the purchasing function touches all phases of the company, by centralizing this function its cost savings potential is extensive. The savings are derived as follows:

ENJOYING THE BENEFITS OF SPECIALIZATION

Line managers can now devote full-time to operating their respective areas, rather than spending time on purchasing and its related problems. Purchasing specialists can be developed!

RESPONSIBILITY IS PINPOINTED

Functional responsibility for purchasing is fixed under the direction of a single individual and not spread throughout the organization. Senior management can better evaluate their firm's overall purchasing policies, priorities, and procedures.

CLERICAL EFFORT IS CUT

Paperwork duplication is reduced because fewer orders are processed for the same number of times and the entire cycle handles less paper (purchasing, receiving, material control, accounting, etc).

BETTER INVENTORY CONTROL

Better inventory control is achieved because one department or plant's excess may be another's needs. Min/max levels are better maintained and obsolescence is reduced.

EARLY INSIGHT INTO NEEDS AND PROBLEMS

Under a centralized purchasing concept all of a company's material and supply needs can be realized and evaluated, thus doing a more realistic job of projecting how a company will or will not be effected by price changes or shortages. Changes can be identified early in the game and the necessary corrective action, if any, can be implemented.

IMPROVED PRICE NEGOTIATIONS

If a company's needs are consolidated, identified, and projected, you will be able to approach your supplier and ask for and get quantity discounts. They will be more receptive to offering you their best possible price because they can gear their production or buying levels to your future commitments.

Case in point—how combining and standardizing four plants' requirements for wiping cloths saved $41,539 in the first year

Yes, wiping cloths. A large air-frame manufacturer decided to adopt a centralized purchase function and began to identify items that were used in more than one plant location in substantial quantities. In their first year of operation, with only a staff of two, they were able to identify approximately 30 of these items and placed company-wide agreements and saved 1.4 million dollars or 13.0%.

One of these agreements was for specialized wiping cloth material. Upon investigation, it was discovered that the size, texture, and quality varied from plant to plant. If any savings were to be achieved, a uniform size, texture, and quality must be agreed upon. As Exhibit 8-2 shows, it took two years to achieve complete standardization and the lower cost per case savings that come from purchasing:

— a standard cloth.
— a smaller, but no less useful and effective cloth.
— a combined buying power of four plants.

EXHIBIT 8-2
Cost Savings from Centralized Purchasing
Standardization & Combined Purchasing Power

Industrial Wiping Cloths

Plant	Prior to corp. agreement Size	Price/ Case	1st year agreement Size	Price/ Case	Savings/ Case	2nd year agreement Size	Price/ Case	Savings/ Case
A	9x10	$57.30	9x10	$52.65	$ 4.65	8x9	$42.49	$14.81
B	9x10	55.35	9x10	52.65	2.70	8x9	42.49	12.86
C	18x12	59.40	9x10	52.65	6.75	8x9	42.49	16.91
D	36"RLS	90.00	9x10	52.65	37.35	8x9	42.49	47.51

Savings Impact First Five Years

1st year	$ 41,500
2nd year	79,800
3rd year	17,200
4th year	17,000
5th year	132,000
Total	$287,500

Exhibit 8-3 shows that this same company by instituting centralized purchasing concepts saved 18.3 million dollars over their first five years of operation with a very limited staff and relatively few agreements in force.

EXHIBIT 8-3
Cost Savings from Centralized Purchasing
First Five Years Accomplishments—Large Air Frame Co.
(Dollars In Millions)

	Agreements in Force			Savings		
Years	Manpower	Qty	Value	Annual	Cumulative	
1st	2	30	$10.1	$1.4	13.0%	$ 1.4
2nd	2	57	23.6	2.1	15.5%	3.5
3rd	5	97	28.0	3.9	10.8%	7.4
4th	6	147	41.5	4.9	12.2%	12.3
5th	6	187	41.9	6.0	13.7%	18.3

PURCHASE COMMITMENT REPORTING—TODAY'S VIEW OF TOMORROW

What it is

Purchase commitment reporting is an operationally-oriented financial tool that allows you to get ahead of the numbers and see what is coming down the road both from an expense and a cash expenditure point of view. Even though this is a technique for monitoring and controlling cash expenditures, it is included here to put some teeth in your projecting and monitoring of material usage. Specifically, this system tells you at a glance what is your current unpaid purchase order dollar commitment by major procurement classification. In addition you are able to measure your purchases in relation to current sales activity, so that there is no excuse for over-committing. In many instances, this report is used in conjunction with the earned hours report to monitor major prime cost inputs so that evaluation and control can be effectively applied on a real time basis assuring greater profit ability and improved cash flow.

This reporting system measures the business exposure in regard to outstanding purchases of a controllable nature. Utility bills, rent, taxes, etc.—items of a fixed nature are not involved in these computations. The installation is simple and uses two forms:

— Purchase Commitment Daily Log (Exhibit 8-4)
— Purchase Commitment Balances Report (Exhibit 8-5)

The Purchase Commitment Daily Log is designed to record daily purchases by the purchasing agent or his equivalent. Its purpose is to assist in the completion of the Purchase Commitment Balances Report.

The Purchase Commitment Balances Report includes the following sections:

A. Opening Commitment Balances (Ending balance previous period)

This balance is the total dollars in the accounts payable open items and the open purchase orders.

B. Current Period Purchase Order Commitment

This column results from the totals of the monthly purchase commitment daily log.

C. Current Period Invoices Paid

The total placed in this area is recorded from actual accounts payable paid during the month, covering controllable items.

D. Current Period Balance

a + b - c = d

E. Summary Information

Self explanatory.

F. Remarks

Reserved for the division general manager to explain major increases or decreases before report is forwarded to corporate level.

EXHIBIT 8-4

RON MANUFACTURING CO.

PURCHASE COMMITMENT DAILY LOG

MONTH OF MAY 19X7

DAY	ENDING BALANCE	GIDGET	IDIDGET	PRODUCTION OUTSIDE	SUPPLIES FACTORY	SUPPLIES OFFICE	OTHER	OTHER MISC
		50,000	20,000	25,000	5,000	500	2,000	500
1ST WEEK								
1		3,000	12,735	475				
2		5,000		325				
3				4,325				
4		5000		490	250			
5		—	5,248	650				
6								
2ND WEEK								
1		8,150	3,465	2,912	400			
2		4,000	—	925				
3		2,050		600		300		
4				870				
5			8,148	1,650				
6								
3RD WEEK								
1		7,000	1,642	292	100			
2		5,000		3,721				
3		4,000		246				
4		3,000	461	587			250	
5		8,800		650				
6								
4TH WEEK								
1		6,000	478	950	250			
2		10,000	2,045	1,700				
3		2,500	528	350				
4		800	—	250				
5		200		282				
6								
5TH WEEK								
1								
2								
3								
4								
5								
6								
TOTAL		70,000	35,000	22,000	1,000	300	250	—
ADD END BALANCE & TOTAL		120,000	55,000	47,000	6,000	800	2,250	500
SUBTRACT ACCOUNTS PAYABLE		65,000	40,000	15,000	4,000	400	750	500
BALANCE CURRENT MONTH		55,000	15,000	32,000	2,000	400	1,500	-0-

EXHIBIT 8-5
PURCHASE COMMITMENT BALANCES REPORT

RON MANUFACTURING CO.
MONTH ENDING MAY, 19X8

	PRIOR PERIOD BALANCE	%	CURRENT PERIOD PURCH. ORDER COMMIT.	CURRENT PERIOD INVOICES PAID	CURRENT PERIOD BALANCE	%
SALES	$302,000	100.00			$350,000	100.00
PRODUCTIVE MATERIAL:						
GIDGET PRODUCTION	$ 50,000	16.56	$ 70,000	$ 65,000	$ 55,000	15.71
WIDGET PRODUCTION	20,000	6.62	35,000	40,000	15,000	4.29
OUTSIDE PROCESSING	25,000	8.28	42,000	15,000	52,000	14.86
TOTAL PRODUCTION	95,000	31.46	147,000	120,000	122,000	34.86
SUPPLIES:						
FACTORY	5,000	1.66	1,000	4,000	2,000	.57
OFFICE	500	.16	300	400	400	.11
OTHER	2,000	.66	250	750	1,500	.43
TOTAL	7,500	2.48	1,550	5,150	3,900	1.11
OTHER PURCHASES	500	.17	—0—	500	—0—	
GRAND TOTAL	$103,000	34.11	$ 148,550	$125,650	$125,900	35.97

DOLLAR COMMITMENT (INCREASE) DECREASE — ACTUAL THIS PERIOD $(22,900)

% (INCREASE) DECREASE 22.23

PLANNED COMMITMENT FIGURE IN PROFIT PLAN $ 105,000

% 30.00

ACTUAL BALANCE (OVER) UNDER PLAN $(20,900)

% 19.90

REMARKS

PRACTICAL TECHNIQUES FOR CONTROLLING MATERIAL COSTS

Step by step installation

STEP 1

The installation is simple. An inventory of outstanding unfilled orders plus open accounts payable items are taken at month's end. When calculated, the figures form the basis for the beginning open commitment figure.

STEP 2

On a second sheet, each day the purchasing representative enters the commitment total by classification of each buy request.

STEP 3

At month's end, the commitments are added to the beginning balances arriving at a sub-total.

STEP 4

The actual accounts payable on controllable items paid for the period is subtracted, leaving the new open commitment balance to be reported.

STEP 5

Dollar commitment increase or decrease plus variance from profit plan information is calculated.

STEP 6

The monitoring of this report allows management to take corrective profit enrichment action before expenses become a *permanent* liability and reduction to revenue.

As in the case of the earned hours application, blank forms of the above-mentioned two reports are provided (Exhibits 8-6 and 8-7) to assist you in getting off to an easy start in controlling your commitment levels.

PHYSICAL INVENTORY TAKING—IS MORE THAN THE MOTION OF COUNTING

Taking periodic physical inventories, whether it's counting production parts or supplies, is one of the oldest financial tasks. In most companies it is not approached in a very systematic manner. Taking physical inventories has been included in this handbook because there is a definite need for a canned approach that is usable and readily installable in most companies. The value of applying an organized and systematic approach is more than meeting your annual audit requirements. The data received from this task can inform you as to:

— the degree of obsolescence in your inventory.
— identification of slow and fast moving items.
— classification of the inventory by ABC class.
— the starting point for investigating the causes of lost or excess items.
— basis for the development of a sales program for moving slow items.
— other.

EXHIBIT 8-6
PURCHASE COMMITMENT DAILY LOG

MONTH OF _____

DAY	WEEK	ENDING BALANCE	PRODUCTION	SUPPLIES FACTORY	SUPPLIES OFFICE	OTHER	OTHER MISC
	1ST WEEK						
1							
2							
3							
4							
5							
6							
	2ND WEEK						
1							
2							
3							
4							
5							
6							
	3RD WEEK						
1							
2							
3							
4							
5							
6							
	4TH WEEK						
1							
2							
3							
4							
5							
6							
	5TH WEEK						
1							
2							
3							
4							
5							
6							
	TOTAL						
	ADD END BALANCE & TOTAL						
	SUBTRACT ACCOUNTS PAYABLE						
	BALANCE CURRENT MONTH						

EXHIBIT 8-7
PURCHASE COMMITMENT BALANCES REPORT

MONTH ENDING

	PRIOR PERIOD BALANCE	%	CURRENT PERIOD PURCH. ORDER COMMIT.	CURRENT PERIOD INVOICES PAID	CURRENT PERIOD BALANCE	%
SALES						
PRODUCTIVE MATERIAL:						
TOTAL PRODUCTION						
SUPPLIES:						
FACTORY						
OFFICE						
OTHER						
TOTAL						
OTHER PURCHASES						
GRAND TOTAL						

DOLLAR COMMITMENT (INCREASE) DECREASE — ACTUAL THIS PERIOD

% (INCREASE) DECREASE

PLANNED COMMITMENT FIGURE IN PROFIT PLAN

%

ACTUAL BALANCE (OVER) UNDER PLAN

%

REMARKS

A case in point—how an acquiring firm bought a business and received a bonus of 50,000 partially completed units

A multi-divisional company decided to divest itself of its after-sale automotive business and had negotiated a sale to a leader in the industry. One of the elements that determined the sale price was, of course, the value of the inventory on hand at the time of sale. At the onset of the sale negotiations, the division had taken a physical inventory which coincided somewhat with the book number. The terms of the sale agreement stipulated that a final inventory be taken to insure the buyer that the minimum inventory figure used to establish the sale price was valid. The inventory instructions included as Exhibit 8-8 were used. When the inventory was completed, tallied, and organized by class, two things were apparent:

1. The minimum inventory dollar level stipulated in the sale agreement was there and the sale was finalized.
2. In fact, there was more work in process on hand then was shown on the books. The buyer received a windfall of approximately 50,000 units. This allowed the buyer to shut down portions of his sub-assembly operations for four months and complete final assemblies out of inventory.

Planning for inventory day

Taking of physical inventory need not be the dreaded occasion it is made out to be. A good inventory can be error free, easy to take and analyze, and have multiple uses by others than accounting personnel. This objective can be achieved if the emphasis is on pre-planning and the proper assignment of responsibilities and tasks. This is the function of the inventory team captain. This individual can be from general accounting, cost accounting, material control, etc, just as long as he is acquainted with the production process and the items to be counted. To get you off to a good start, first find an individual who is hard working and fits the above criteria, and then hand him Exhibit 8-8—Production Physical Inventory Procedure Instructions.

EXHIBIT 8-8
Production Physical Inventory Procedure Instructions

I. *Scope*
   This instruction presents a guideline to be used in the preparation and execution of physical inventory requirements established by your corporation.
   Corporation policy dictates that a complete physical inventory must be taken at least once a year, or may be taken more often if circumstances warrant. The inventory will cover raw materials, stores, work in process, finished goods, and supply items.

II. *Functions Affected*
   Corporate, group, division and plant management levels.

III. *Operations Affected*
   A. Your corporation
   B. Group—divisions within your corporation
   C. Wholly-owned subsidiaries

IV. *Forms Requirement*
    A. Inventory tickets — Exhibit (G)
    B. Pre-inventory tickets — Exhibit (F)
    C. Inventory Ticket Control Log — Exhibit (C)
    D. Inventory Control Audit Sheet — Exhibit (D)
    E. Inventory Release Form — Exhibit (E)

V. *General Guidelines*

The general manager is delegated the responsibility to see that the inventory is taken according to the principles set forth in this instruction and also the principles set forth by good accounting practices. He may in turn delegate responsibilities within his organization to see that the following requirements will be accomplished:

  A. *Inventory Times*

    The date of the inventory, the starting time, the lunch time and the quitting time will be established and all personnel should work to the same schedule.

  B. *Inventory Personnel*

    A list of personnel assigned to conduct the inventory including the following areas of responsibilities:
      1. auditor
      2. area supervision
      3. control desk log clerk
      4. counters
      5. recorders

  C. *Floor Plan—Exhibit A*

    To be furnished to the corporate controllers' office and the plant auditor one week prior to inventory date to substantiate the area to be counted. It should be noted here that all off-site locations should be included which have company material on their premises, either for processing or storage.

  D. *Ticket Requirements*

    An estimate of the number of tickets needed for each location or section of the floor plan must be submitted to the auditor at least four days prior to the inventory date. This time requirement allows the proper planning prior to the date of inventory to make certain that tickets and controls have been firmly established.

  E. *Parts List Descriptions*

    To be made available to all inventory personnel involved three days prior to the inventory date. This allows all personnel to review and ask questions if necessary before the date of the inventory.

  F. *Inventory Aids*

    Provisions must be made to have the necessary aids on hand (i.e., scales, tape, rope, pencils, etc.).

  G. *Pre-Inventory Instructions*

    To conduct the necessary instruction meetings to make certain all employees have a clear conception of their job responsibility. The amount of pre-planning definitely affects the quality of the inventory.

VI. *Specific Guidelines*
    A. *Housekeeping*

All like materials should be stored in the same area wherever practical. All bins in storage facilities should be cleared of rubbish. All scrap shall be accumulated and disposed of before the date of the inventory. If disposition has not been made, all scrap must be placed in a neutral area for ready identification and identified.

    B. *Statistical Information*

The following list should be made available for the corporate controller's office or the public auditor's:

1. Prior to inventory cutoff time:
   a. Last number purchase order assigned.
   b. Last number sales invoice issued.
   c. Last number receiving report assigned.
2. After inventory clearance time:
   a. First number purchase order assigned.
   b. First number sales invoice issued.
   c. First number receiving report assigned.
3. List of the open purchase orders to vendors not received as of close of business day prior to the inventory.
4. List of open sales orders not filled as of close of business day before inventory.
5. List of finished goods recorded as sales prior to cutoff time, still physically in plant and not shipped. (These items will have "do not inventory" tags affixed on them physically by inventory personnel.)
6. List of the finished goods actually shipped but not billed as of the cutoff date.

    C. *Cutoff*
      1. *Receiving:*

Receiving of all purchase parts will be cut off at close of business the day before the inventory date. All paperwork received on the day before the inventory date will be stamped "before inventory." All incoming inventory on the date of the inventory will be kept separate in a specified area on the receiving dock with "after inventory" tags placed in a conspicuous spot physically on the material for easy identification. All paperwork received on the date of the inventory will be stamped "after inventory." (The auditor assigned will review the paperwork and attest that this was done).

No movement of this material in the receiving area will take place until the total plant has been released by the auditor in charge of the inventory.

      2. *Shipping:*

Shipment of all goods will be cut off at the close of the working day prior to the date of the inventory. Beginning at the opening of business prior to the date of inventory, all paperwork relating to shipments will be stamped "before inventory" to insure a proper cutoff point for inventory evaluation. The shipping log will be reconciled at the end of the day to make certain all documents tie in and proper cutoff has been established. After the auditor has released the plant for inventory, all shipping documents for at least one day after the inventory will be stamped with an "after inventory" stamp.

    D. *Assembled Customer Finished Goods Orders Shipments on Inventory Date*

The assembly of these customer orders will be made up prior to the closing cutoff time on the day before the inventory date. All paperwork involved must be stamped "before inventory." These shipments will be placed in a distinct separate area and will be considered part of the inventory to be taken. Serialized, Xeroxed, or offset copies of the delivery slips may serve as inventory tickets and will be audited before the shipment is released. The auditors will sign these copies and remit them to the inventory control desk for inclusion in this inventory.

E. *Material Movement*

No material movement will be allowed within the total plant, off-sight locations, or departments after closing time the day prior to the inventory. Two exceptions to this general policy may be:
1. Assembled customer finished goods orders will be shipped from the specific location after clearance by audit to satisfy customer needs.
2. Weight counted items. It may be necessary to transport a skid to the scale to be counted. After the count, the skid will be returned immediately to the same area using the inventory tickets designated for that area.

F. *Slow-Moving Inventory Areas*

Some areas have little or no movement for a length of time. These areas may be counted during the week prior to the inventory cutoff time if agreed upon by the auditor in charge and the plant manager. No material will move either in or out of the area if this agreement has been made. Pre-inventory tags may be used to facilitate count (see Exhibit F).

G. *Scrap*

All scrap material must be segregated and disposed of prior to the close of business on the day before the inventory. Any scrap which inadvertently is left on hand and has not been written off should have the scrap ticket attached and a definite appraisal value assigned. This material must be placed in one area and inventory tickets will be written on the items giving full information as to the value attached.

H. *Counts*

All material will be counted. Hand counting where practical, and by weight counting where volume and size negate hand counting. If a part is to be weight counted, it must be transferred from its present container to a clean skid or box to make certain rubbish, rags, steel straps, etc., are not included in the count. Any container containing rubbish will automatically be rejected by the auditor as an invalid item. Predetermined weight conversions (i.e., carton box, price, etc.) factors can be arrived at prior to the inventory date making it possible to record only weight at the time of inventory. (This area is optional.) Unbroken vendors' cartons, steel packets, drums, etc., may be counted using vendor information. All open containers, cartons, drums will require detail count, either by hand count or weight count.

I. *Customer Consigned Material on Site*
Government Consigned Material on Site

This material should be segregated into workable, controllable locations. *"Do not inventory"* tags should be placed in a predominant spot to make certain inventory tickets are not written. (Memo inventory action may be advisable, however, to reconcile customer and plant records.) The choice of action is the responsibility of plant controller (auditor).

J. *Returnable Containers: Skids—Pallets*

They should be segregated into a definable area. Separation of filled drums from empty containers is advisable. Material content of tapped drums should be inventoried to the closest estimate (i.e., 1/2 barrel). Separate tickets must be issued to separate material and containers.

VII. *Definitions—Responsibilities*
   A. *Plant or Division Manager*
      1. Responsible for successful accomplishment of inventory.
      2. Responsible to see that adequate staffing is available for an orderly inventory process.
      3. Responsible to see that pre-inventory meetings are held with his inventory staff to communicate management requirements for successful execution.
      4. Responsible to see that material movement is frozen on the date of the inventory until the auditor releases the plant.
      5. Furnishes necessary data called out to the corporate controller's office and the auditor:
         a. Floor plan (see Exhibit A).
         b. Personnel listing (see Exhibit B).
         c. Quantity of tickets required for a section.
         d. Parts number and parts description (if possible).
         e. Statistical data—(see VI, Section B).
      6. Responsible to see proper cutoff points are established and adhered to by all personnel.
   B. *Inventory Auditor*
      1. Responsible to see orderly, accurate inventory is taken.
      2. Responsible for issuance of inventory tickets, maintaining log of tickets, and through audit, assuring all tickets are accounted for (see Exhibit C).
      3. Responsible for exception audit of all locations to attest to the accuracy of count. All tickets must be initialed that have been audited.
      4. Responsible to write up any discrepancies found on the auditors log (see Exhibit D).
      5. Initiates the area clearance ticket when satisfied that the inventory is proper in the particular section (see Exhibit E).
   C. *Inventory Team*
   Consists of two people; 1 counter, and 1 recorder assigned by plant management from the plant working force. The personnel selected for these teams must be:
      1. Knowledgeable of the area to be inventoried.
      2. Able to identify items by part number and by part description whenever possible.
      3. Responsible for supplying correct count, part number, and part descriptions on all materials in their assigned areas.
      4. The counter is responsible for identifying the items and counting same.
      5. The recorder will repeat the part number, part description, and count to the counter as he records the counters' findings on the inventory tickets. The recorder must legibly transcribe this information so the inventory ticket can readily be read for pricing purposes.
      6. The recorder and the counter will affix their team number in the "by" square area to attest to the accuracy of their count.
   D. *Inventory Tickets* (*see Exhibit G*)
   A two-part form serially numbered for control purposes packed in lots of 50 serialized units:
      1. Part 1 is taped to the carton, container, or part being counted for audit reference. At this time, the accounting section, part 2, remains intact.
      2. Part 2—perforated portion of ticket with all the pertinent data on it.
   The following numbers explain the use of the ticket:
      1. Part number—Insert the part number wherever possible from the parts list

EXHIBIT A
Floor Plan — Ron Mfg. Co.

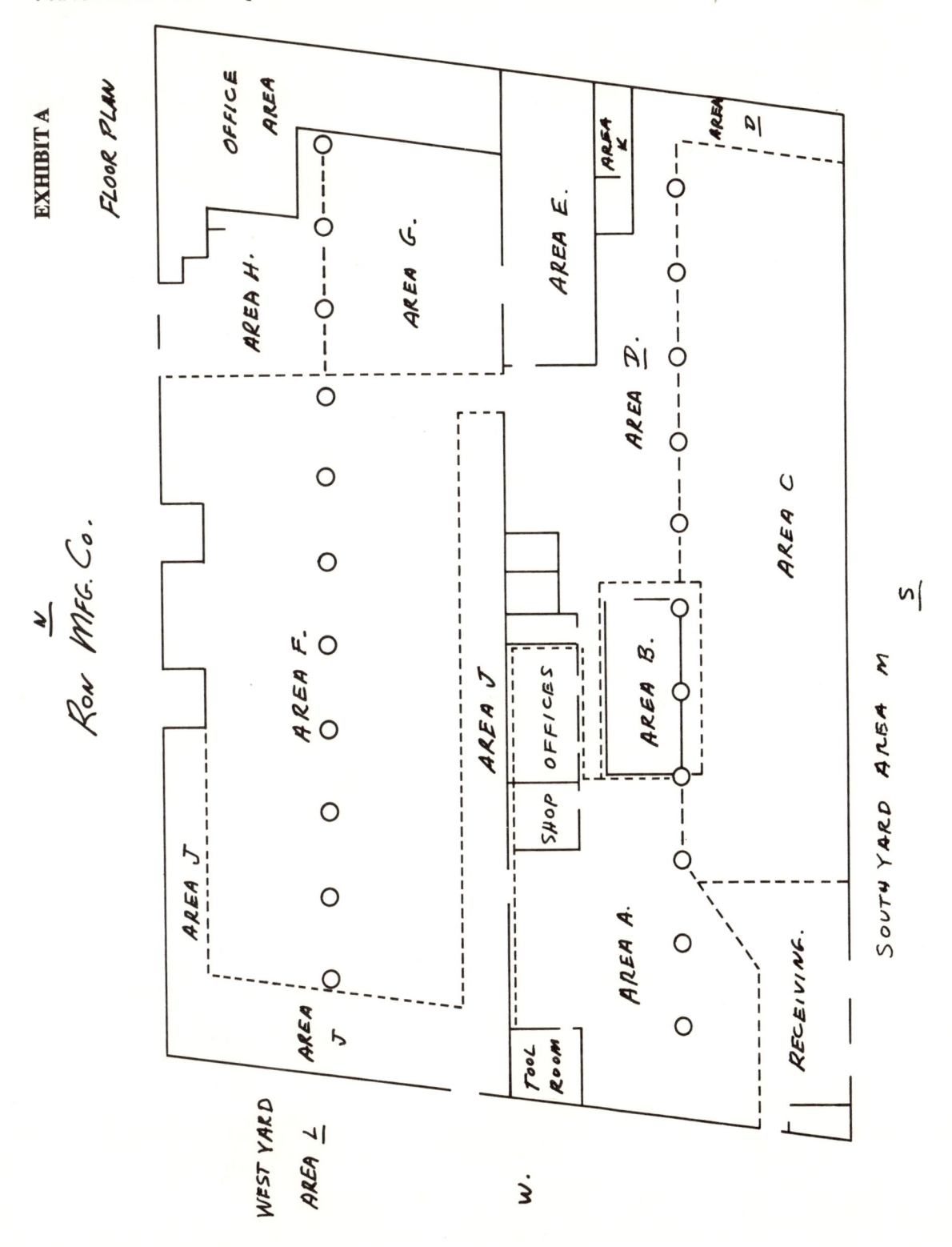

EXHIBIT B

Ron Manufacturing Co.
197_ Annual Physical Inventory Personnel Roster

Counters-Recorders Teams:

	Team		Assigned Area
	#1	R. Solarzano	
		O. Lopez	
	#2	C. Ellis	
		N. Nunez	
	#3	V. Parra	
		A. Mendoza	
	#4	S. Polizzi	
		Z. Cordova	
	#5	F. Jaster	
		A. Teller	
	#6	D. Smith	
		B. Jones	

Lot Control
Sharon Carter — Area Supervisor

Price & Extension
G. Rowland
A. Abrams
W. Smith — S. Pook

Auditors
G. Hadley
P. Howard

Alternates:
E. Abena
F. Alambata
S. Jacks
S. Ursan
F. Soto
R. Pish
K. Mays

EXHIBIT C

Division: Roh MFG. Co. — Inventory Ticket Control Log.

Ticket Numbers From — To	Area	Supervisor	Area Assigned	Date	Time Issued	Date	Time Rec'd	Count Audited	Remarks

162

EXHIBIT D

AREA	TICKET #	PART N°.	DESCRIPTION	TICKET COUNT	AUDIT COUNT	ERROR %	AUDITOR ACCEPT	ACTION REJECT

DIVISION RON MFG. CO. INVENTORY CONTROL AUDIT SHEET AUDITOR

TOTAL VARIANCE FOR THE AREA ASSIGNED

PRACTICAL TECHNIQUES FOR CONTROLLING MATERIAL COSTS 163

EXHIBIT E

Inventory Release Form.

```
                    INVENTORY RELEASE

PLANT:
DEPT:
SECTION:                                          ①   ②   ③
PLANT. REP. SIGNATURE
AUDITOR'S SIGNATURE
     THE ABOVE SIGNATURES CERTIFY THAT THE PHYSICAL
INVENTORY TAKEN IN THIS SECTION HAS BEEN AUDITED
AND FOUND TO BE IN ORDER. THE DEPARTMENT
IS CONSIDERED CLEARED AND TICKETS MAY BE PICKED UP.
              #1      LOG CONTROL DESK
              #2      AUDITOR COPY
              #3      PLANT REP. OR SUPERVISOR
```

EXHIBIT F

```
RON MFG. CO. PRE-INVENTORY TAG
PART NUMBER_____
PART NAME_____
QUANTITY_____
UNIT OF MEASURE
     PIECES    ☐
     BOXES     ☐
     POUNDS    ☐
     FEET      ☐
     GALLONS   ☐
     QUARTS    ☐
     OTHER_____
LOCATION_____
NOTES:
```

EXHIBIT G

INVENTORY TICKET			06003
PART NUMBER ①	☐ PCS ☐ LBS ☐ FT ② OTHER ___ DESCRIBE		QUANTITY ③
PART NUMBER ④	☐ PCS ☐ LBS ☐ FT ⑤ OTHER ___ DESCRIBE		QUANTITY ⑥

INVENTORY CLASSIFICATION ⑧   06003

☐ RAW ⑦
☐ IN-PROCESS
☐ FINISHED

LAST OPERATION
NUMBER ⑨   NAME ⑩
PART NAME ⑪

CALCULATIONS:

⑫

BLDG. ⑬	FLOOR ⑭	DEPT. ⑮	SECTION BAY ⑯	BIN RACK ⑰
COUNTED BY ⑱	RECORDED BY ⑲		CHECKED BY ⑳	

THIS SPACE FOR ACCOUNTING USE ONLY

	PER UNIT	EXTENSION
MATERIAL COST:		
LABOR COST:		
BURDEN COST:		
TOTAL COST:		

PRICED BY	CHECKED BY	EXTENDED BY	CHECKED BY

DO NOT DESTROY
ALL INVENTORY TICKETS MUST BE ACCOUNTED FOR

description furnished. If part number is not available, place a N/A (not available) in block.
2. Describe unit of measure—Is it pieces, pounds, feet or other. If other, describe.
3. Quantity/Number of items counted.
4. Same information as Item 1, repeated.
5. Same information as Item 2, repeated.
6. Same information as Item 3, repeated.
7. Place "X" in proper spot.
    a. Raw materials include purchase parts, supplies, and returnable containers from vendors.
    b. In-process material has had some labor expended and is not yet finished.
    c. Finished parts are those items completed and boxed ready for shipment (sub-assemblies not sold as end-items would be included in item "b" above).
8. Type of material—Major inventory sub-classifications should be put in here, such as sub-assembly, paper, steel, transmissions, etc.
9. Last operation number—If the last operation number is known, it should be indicated for costing purposes.
10. Last operation name—On all work-in-process parts, place the last operation performed (i.e., oil filter core/spot welded).
11. Part name—Place part name in this section, e.g., equals core, cam, screen, or whatever the part is usually called by shop people.
12. This space is reserved for the figuring of the calculations in aiming at the quantity in number 3 and number 6, above.
13. If applicable, indicate (see floor plan).
14. If applicable, indicate (see floor plan).
15. Inventory assignment area is indicated here.
16. If applicable, indicate.
17. If applicable, indicate.
18. Not applicable.
19. The inventory recording team number is placed in this spot.
20. Space reserved for the auditor when he is test-checking the inventory to place his signature.

VIII. *Procedure Prior to Inventory*
  A. Auditor releases the tickets to the designated plant representative based upon the preliminary estimated requirements furnished.
  B. Auditor requests inventory be taken in all vendor plants where company-paid-for material is stored. The letter from the vendor should state enough detail to insure proper material identification, i.e., quantity, size, shape, item description to afford proper pricing. Wherever practical, an audit should be made to test the count the vendor has supplied.

IX. *Procedure—Day of the Inventory*
  A. Teams meet with their respective area supervisor. Area supervisor assigns each team to the area to be counted.
  B. The teams start counting material at the northeast corner of the section following a consecutive pattern in the assignment of ticket numbers covering the items inventoried.
  C. The counter calls out the information necessary to complete the inventory ticket to the recorder (see inventory card instruction sheet).
  D. In the even a question arises on part number, part name, etc., contact the area supervisor for resolution—do not guess any answers. The area supervisor will obtain

resolution, if necessary, from the general manager or his designated representative.
E. There are to be no erasures on a ticket in the quantity area—Items No. 3 and 6; or in the units description area—Items No. 2 and 5. If a mistake appears, it should be ruled out and the corrected information written directly above it. If the ticket is messy, it must be voided and re-written. *The responsibility for accuracy on the part of the recorder cannot be over-emphasized*. This area is vital to a good count.
F. When a designated area is covered, the counter and the recorder re-check to make certain every item is tagged. After this is done, the area supervisor will be notified to contact the control desk for audit.
G. Area supervisor calls the control desk for audit of section and releases inventory team for re-assignment back to the control desk.
H. Auditor takes the exception audit of the area involved on a random basis, making certain that a composite check is made, large or small, plus weight-hand counted items. At least ten percent of the tickets in the given area should be audited (see Exhibit D). In the event discrepancies occur, they must be resolved at this time. For each count that is in error, the auditor must add (ticket) to his list, providing a higher audit percentage test check. In the event tests should indicate a 25% to 30% discrepancy factor, the auditor will bring this fact to the attention of the plant representative, who will pick up all tickets, return them to the control desk for voiding, receive new tickets from the control desk and re-inventory the areas with a different inventory crew. Cycle B through G repeats itself at this point. (It is advisable that the original team who caused this costly action be communicated with by the responsible supervisor to avoid recurrences of this nature in the future).
I. The auditor, when satisfied that sections have been properly inventoried, signs an inventory release statement in triplicate—giving the number *three* copy to the plant representative retaining the number *two* copy for his file, and submits the number *one* original to the log control desk (see Exhibit E).
J. The area supervisor upon receipt of release statements picks up the accounting sections, number two portion of the inventory ticket, arranges them numerically and accounts for all document numbers originally released to him through the control desk. All tickets must be picked up, i.e., good, voided, unused.
K. The area supervisor takes all tickets and the inventory team to the log control desk to clear the record for his section. (No department will be considered fully released until all tickets assigned have been accounted for).
L. When notified by the plant representative that an area is ready for audit, the control desk clerk will re-deploy inventory teams to the areas needing help until the total inventory has been taken and the plant has been released to go back into production 100%.

Inventory Tickets:

Two part form serially numbered for control purposes packed in lots of 50 units.

(1) Part #1—is taped to the carton, container, or part being counted for audit reference. At this time the accounting section, part 2, remains intact.
(2) Part #2—perforated portion of ticket with all pertinent data on it.

The following exhibit and numbers explain the use of the ticket.

(1) Part number—insert the part number wherever possible from the parts list description furnished. If part number is not available, place an N/A in block.

(2) Describe unit of measure—is it Pc's, LBS., Ft., or other. If other, describe.
(3) Quantity—number of items counted.
(4) Same information as #1 repeated.
(5) Same information as #2 repeated.
(6) Same information as #3 repeated.
(7) Place X in proper spot:
   (a) Raw material includes purchased parts from vendors (also supplies and returnable containers).
   (b) In process material has had some labor expended and is not yet finished.
   (c) Finished parts are those items completed and boxed ready for shipment.
(8) Type of material—i.e., paper, steel, sub-assy, major inventory sub-classification such as transmission parts.
(9) Last operation number, if known, for costing purposes.
(10) Last operation name—on all work in process parts. Place the last operation performed (i.e., oil filter core—spot welded).
(11) Part name—example equal core, cam, screen or whatever the part is usually called by.
(12) A place for authenticating figures of all calculations in aiming at quantity in #3 and #6 above is provided here.
(13) If applicable, indicate—see floor plan.
(14) If applicable, indicate—see floor plan.
(15) Inventory assignment area.
(16) If applicable, indicate.
(17) If applicable, indicate.
(18) Not applicable
(19) Recorder team number is placed here.
(20) Auditors check off.

9

EARNED HOURS—AN EASY METHOD FOR CONTROLLING LABOR COST THROUGH OPERATIONAL ANALYSIS

Many a financial man or operating manager has been perplexed by the problem of how to easily monitor the effectiveness of his labor force. Specifically, these executives are trying to solve one or more extensions of the question—How can I achieve better control of my labor cost, and thus increase labor productivity:

— in a smaller organization or business unit with limited resources.

— without depending on the computer.

— without engineered standards or an elaborate cost accounting system.

— in a unit that does not normally lend itself to labor cost control, such as a medium-size advertising firm, a customer service group, a repair center, etc.

— in a diversified multi-plant corporation where a simplified method of measuring labor effectiveness throughout all locations is needed.

An easy and economical approach is to install an earned hours reporting system.

LABOR EFFICIENCY VISIBILITY WITHOUT COMPLEX STANDARDS

Earned hours offers all levels of both financial and non-financial management visibility in the area of labor efficiency without using complex industrial engineering-type standards (time study, MTM, etc). For those companies that have varying size multi-plant and multi-product organizations, this system provides corporate management with a common insight into the operations of these organizations.

A case in point—the corporate tool that allowed a division to add 1% pre-tax, while paving the way for an acquisition that would double its size

Just the nature of the conglomerate made it difficult for corporate management to measure labor performance. The seasonality of many member companies posed the additional problem for the corporate staff in evaluating both current and future staffing against actual and projected needs.

These divisions already felt that they were submitting a great deal of paperwork to the corporate office, so whatever system that would be installed had to be of some benefit to the division's management. Unfortunately, a majority of those plants had very minimal production and labor control; most of their planning, scheduling, and staffing was based on shipping to order and not from inventory. Thus, they suffered radical production peaks and valleys, erratic staffing, late and missed deliveries.

In order to gain acceptance in the more hard-nosed divisions, the earned hours system was installed in several of the smaller units where controls were limited or non-existent. Management hoped that the success of the system in the smaller divisions would act as its own selling tool.

The forms and graphs illustrated in this chapter are exactly the same as those implemented in this plant. The installation was easy, because the approach did not require elaborate engineered standards and only slight assistance from the corporate staff. The forms[1] mentioned previously were in most cases self-explanatory, and the follow-up required little clerical effort.

One medium-sized metal fabricator installed the system in order to comply with the corporate instructions; surprisingly he found that he was able to increase pre-tax profits by almost 1%. In addition, he gained new-found confidence to accept business that was once turned away because of its difficulty to process, specialty orders, or tight profit margin. Now they were acceptable because:

— Shop loading and line balancing were tied to the financial guide line, whereas in the past, the orders flow through was hit and miss. The line loading and scheduling was erratic and thus manning was unproductive.
— Efficiency was monitored and inefficient lines and operations were quickly spotted, because of the information provided from the earned hours report.
— Front office management was able to maintain a proper ratio between direct labor, indirect support, and even office personnel. This was accomplished by simply reviewing the variances between forecast earned hours per group and the actual.

The true value of this system was realized when they were provided with the opportunity of acquiring the total inventory and equipment of their largest competitor. Their competitor, a division of a major steel company, had chosen to abandon this

---

[1] See Exhibits 9-1, -2, and -3.

marketplace. This acquisition would in fact double their size overnight and give them a virtual monopoly. The offering price was around $1,500,000, which they felt was a very attractive figure.

The earned hours system provided management with insight as to how efficiently their plant was running without an elaborate production control or industrial engineering department. With this added visibility, they felt confident in expanding their business.

Thus, this division went ahead and acquired the new plant location and equipment. Possibly, if this opportunity had been presented to management prior to the installation of the earned hours concept and their new-found confidence in handling new and close marginal business, they may have thought twice before committing $1,500,000.

UNDERSTANDING THE EARNED HOURS CONCEPT

The basis of the earned hours system is the analysis of the ratio of sales dollars generated for each hour of labor expended. This is best demonstrated by reviewing the lower left-hand section of Exhibit #9-1. The Ron Manufacturing Company's anticipated revenues are based on their financial guide line and the information that for each hour worked by all employees in November, the sales value per hour worked should be $12.95. It is computed as follows:

Manpower ratio per hour to planned sales dollars for all employees direct and indirect is illustrated:

$$\frac{\text{Planned sales dollars—Nov. } \$200,000}{\text{Planned manpower hours—Nov. } \$ 15,440} = \$12.95$$

If the computation was confined only to the *direct labor* employees, it would be $17.01 per planned hour, and is computed as follows:

Manpower ratio/per hour to planned sales dollars for direct labor employees is illustrated:

$$\frac{\text{Planned sales dollars—Nov. } \$200,000}{\text{Planned manpower hours—Nov. } 11,760} = \$17.01$$

THINK BEFORE YOU IMPLEMENT

This system is basically simple in approach and application. Its service and use should not be limited because of this factor! Management has a measurement tool which can be expanded into product offering detail, if desired. The actual case example (Laboratory Products Division) presented at the close of this chapter monitored and controlled the labor force in conjunction with close to 30 product lines. For presentation purposes, these 30 product lines have been reduced to two.

The extent of detail you wish to capture and monitor should correspond to:

—the detail in your financial guide line.

—the availability of personnel to produce the report.

—the user's ability to digest and implement the information presented.

—the emphasis provided by top management.

EARNED HOURS—AN EASY METHOD FOR CONTROLLING LABOR COST 171

EXHIBIT 9-1
Entering the Forecast or Plan

EARNED HOURS CONTRIBUTION REPORT

RON MANUFACTURING DIVISION

		NOV	DEC	JAN	FEB	MAR	APR	MAY	JU
SALES	FORECAST								
	ACTUAL								
(UNFAV.)	VARIANCE								
SALES	FORECAST								
	ACTUAL								
(UNFAV.)	VARIANCE								
SALES	FORECAST	200	200	200					
	ACTUAL	210	190	205					
(UNFAV.)	VARIANCE	10	⟨10⟩	5					
DIVISION MANPOWER HOURS									
PLANNED:									
DIRECT LABOR		11,760	11,760	14,700					
INDIRECT/SUPPORT LABOR		1920	1920	2400					
SALES MKTG.		480	480	600					
G & A		1280	1280	1600					
TOTAL		15,440	15,440	19,300					
DIVISION MANPOWER RATIO/PER HOUR TO SALES DOLLAR									
PLANNED:									
DIRECT LABOR		17.01	17.01	13.61					
INDIRECT/SUPPORT LABOR		104.17	104.17	83.33					
SALES MKTG.		416.67	416.67	333.33					
G & A		156.25	156.25	125.00					
TOTAL		12.95	12.95	10.36					

Any cost system is only as good as the management's emphasis behind its initiation and operation. *One hundred percent effort* has to be exerted by the company from the top down through the organization chain to the production worker in the shop where the time is recorded.

The important thing to remember is that any cost control system has to be built on a *common sense approach*. It must be kept simple to understand and uncomplicated to apply. The approach shown below has these two attributes.

IMPLEMENTING THE EARNED HOURS SYSTEM

Phase 1—earned hours development

The implementation of this program uses the financial guide line as the basic document for phase 1. If the financial guide line is properly prepared, every manager involved in the preparation of this document has planned the use of his manpower by cost center or department to meet his basic objectives. If the manpower is figured in head count, the head count is converted into hours by multiplication. If only direct and indirect labor dollars are considered as the basis of the plan, the conversion to hours can be made by using average rates for direct and indirect production areas and actual hourly rates in other marketing and G&A areas. If overtime is a factor, the overtime hours should also be included in this projection of total labor hours. The finalized hours are divided into the sales dollars forecast in order to arrive at the ratio rate. The arithmetic calculations used in this phase are shown in Exhibit 9-1.

DIRECT LABOR

When this approach is applied to direct labor, the computed dollar ratio will tell management the amount of sales per direct labor dollar they must achieve in order to meet their plan or target for the month (see Exhibit 9-1).

INDIRECT LABOR

All indirect labor hours (O/H, sales, and G&A) are divided into the total sales figure to arrive at the amount of sales which must be maintained in order to justify these planned levels of labor expenditures. This target figure, when compared to actual results, will allow management to keep closer surveillance over labor expenses in these areas.

TOTAL PLANT LABOR (DIRECT AND INDIRECT)

Using the same approach as listed above, total labor hours are divided into total sales to produce a total plant ratio. At the plant level, management is provided with a common denomination for measuring and monitoring profitability on a monthly, weekly, or even a daily basis.

Phase 2—recording

Actual sales information is recorded in the upper section of Exhibit 9-1. The actual labor data is compiled and summarized in Exhibit 9-2. The actual labor hours are transferred from the payroll register for the period and entered on the top third of the

EARNED HOURS—AN EASY METHOD FOR CONTROLLING LABOR COST 173

EXHIBIT 9-2
Entering the Actuals
and Computing the Ratios

EARNED HOURS CONTRIBUTION REPORT

RON MANUFACTURING DIVISION

	NOV	DEC	JAN	FEB	MAR	APR	MAY	JUN
DIVISION MANPOWER HOURS								
ACTUAL:								
DIRECT LABOR	12096	11980	15075					
INDIRECT/SUPPORT LABOR	2352	2300	2850					
SALES MKTG	480	480	600					
G & A	1584	1584	1980					
TOTAL	16512	16344	20505					
DIVISION MANPOWER RATIO/PER								
HOUR TO SALES DOLLARS								
ACTUAL:								
DIRECT LABOR	17.36	15.86	13.60					
INDIRECT/SUPPORT LABOR	89.29	82.61	71.96					
SALES MKTG	437.50	395.83	341.67					
G & A	132.58	119.95	103.54					
TOTAL	12.72	12.23	10.00					
TOTAL LABOR RATIO PLANNED	12.95	12.95	10.36					
TOTAL LABOR RATIO ACTUAL	12.72	12.23	10.00					
TOTAL $ PER HOUR GAIN (LOSS)	(.23)	(.72)	(.36)					
% GAIN (LOSS) TO PLAN	(1.8)	(5.6)	(3.5)					
$ EFFECT - VARIANCE TO PLAN	3551	21444	(6948)					
CUM $ EFFECT YTD.	3,551	24,995	31,943					

EXHIBIT 9-3
EARNED HOURS CONTRIBUTION REPORT

DIVISION _____   PAGE 1 OF 2

	NOV	DEC	JAN	FEB	MAR	APR	MAY	JUNE	JULY	AUG	SEPT	OCT	TOTAL
SALES FORECAST													
ACTUAL													
(UNFAV.) VARIANCE													
SALES FORECAST													
ACTUAL													
(UNFAV.) VARIANCE													
SALES FORECAST													
ACTUAL													
(UNFAV.) VARIANCE													
DIVISION MANPOWER HOURS													
PLANNED:													
DIRECT LABOR													
INDIRECT / SUPPORT LABOR													
SALES MKTG.													
G & A													
TOTAL													
DIVISION MANPOWER RATIO/PER HOUR TO SALES DOLLAR													
PLANNED:													
DIRECT LABOR													
INDIRECT / SUPPORT LABOR													
SALES MKTG.													
G & A													
TOTAL													

EARNED HOURS—AN EASY METHOD FOR CONTROLLING LABOR COST

worksheet. In most installations, payroll hours are picked up on a weekly basis from the payroll register and accumulated for the month. The associated arithmetic calculations of ratios are shown in the second section on the bottom portion of the form. A summary section is prepared to show total plant efficiency, and lines are also provided to show the dollar effect of monthly and cumulative variances.

Phase 3—evaluation and analysis

An example of the evaluation techniques provided from the earned hours approach is best expressed by examining the data in Exhibit 9-2. This exhibit shows that the Ron Manufacturing Co. in November is targeted for an earned dollars/sales per unit labor hour of $12.95 on planned sales of $200,000. Actual hours incurred for November were 16,512. These hours divided into the actual sales volume of $210,000, equal a ratio of $12.72 an hour or 23¢ an hour off plan or target. The dollar effect of missing the target is $3,551 (15,440 X $.23 = $3,551).

To get you off to a good start in the implementation of this phase, blank forms of pages 1 and 2 of the earned hours contribution report are included. They are Exhibits 9-3 and 9-4.

INTERPRETING RESULTS THROUGH GRAPHIC DISPLAY

The earned hours approach does not require graphic display, but its value and usefulness are enhanced as a communication tool especially to non-financial members of your management team when the results are charted. Corporate or top management upon reviewing the charts can quickly see if the various plants are achieving their targeted operating performance levels. If a target is missed, the manner in which the charts are detailed allows the analyst or manager to quickly get behind the numbers to determine the sales and/or labor area that is causing the malfunction. Similarly, the analyst can easily begin to see the early development of troublesome trends and thus begin to get ahead of the formation of unsatisfactory numbers. Exhibits 9-5 and 9-6 are examples of typical charting formats for depicting the labor contribution ratio analysis on a monthly and cumulative basis.

How to read and benefit from the charting

The financial guide line ratio sales contribution dollar line is represented on the chart as point "O" and is referred to as the plan line. The favorable variances from plan are represented graphically above the zero line. Favorable sales-dollars-generated labor ratio indicates:

—Efficient use of manpower.
—Reduction in inventory level.
—Larger share of marketplace.
—Greater profit potential.

Unfavorable conditions are portrayed graphically below the zero line. An unfavorable loss of sales-dollars-generated labor ratio indicates problems which may be in part due to:

EXHIBIT 9-4
EARNED HOURS CONTRIBUTION REPORT

DIVISION	NOV	DEC	JAN	FEB	MAR	APR	MAY	JUNE	JULY	AUG	SEPT	OCT	TOTAL
DIVISION MANPOWER HOURS													
ACTUAL:													
DIRECT LABOR													
INDIRECT / SUPPORT LABOR													
SALES MKTG													
G & A													
TOTAL													
DIVISION MANPOWER RATIO / PER HOUR TO SALES DOLLARS													
ACTUAL:													
DIRECT LABOR													
INDIRECT / SUPPORT LABOR													
SALES MKTG													
G & A													
TOTAL													
TOTAL LABOR RATIO PLANNED													
TOTAL LABOR RATIO ACTUAL													
TOTAL $ PER HOUR GAIN (LOSS)													
% GAIN (LOSS) TO PLAN													
$ EFFECT - VARIANCE TO PLAN													
CUM $ EFFECT YTD.													

PAGE 2 OF 2

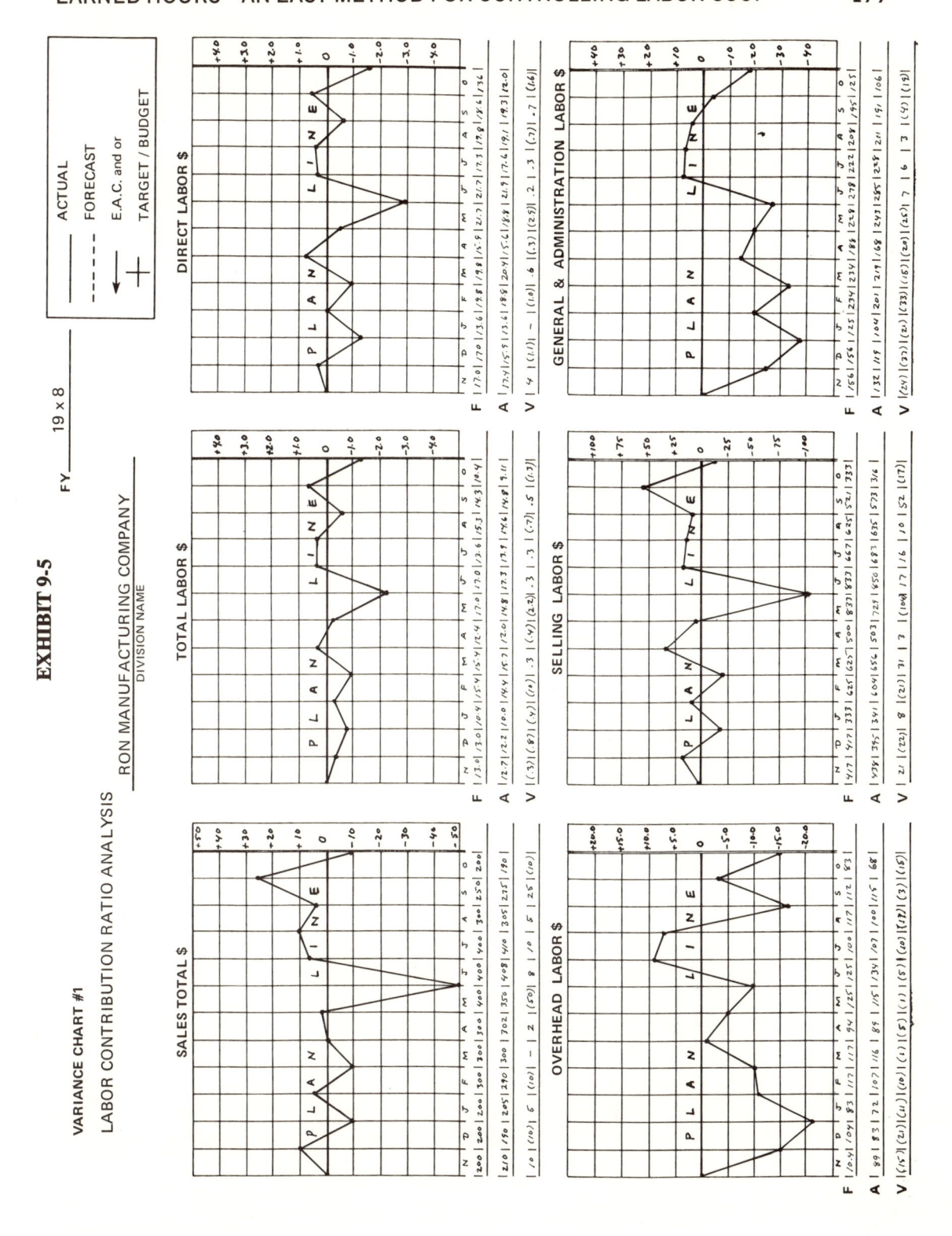

EARNED HOURS—AN EASY METHOD FOR CONTROLLING LABOR COST

EXHIBIT 9-5

FY _____ 19 × 8

VARIANCE CHART #1
LABOR CONTRIBUTION RATIO ANALYSIS

RON MANUFACTURING COMPANY
DIVISION NAME

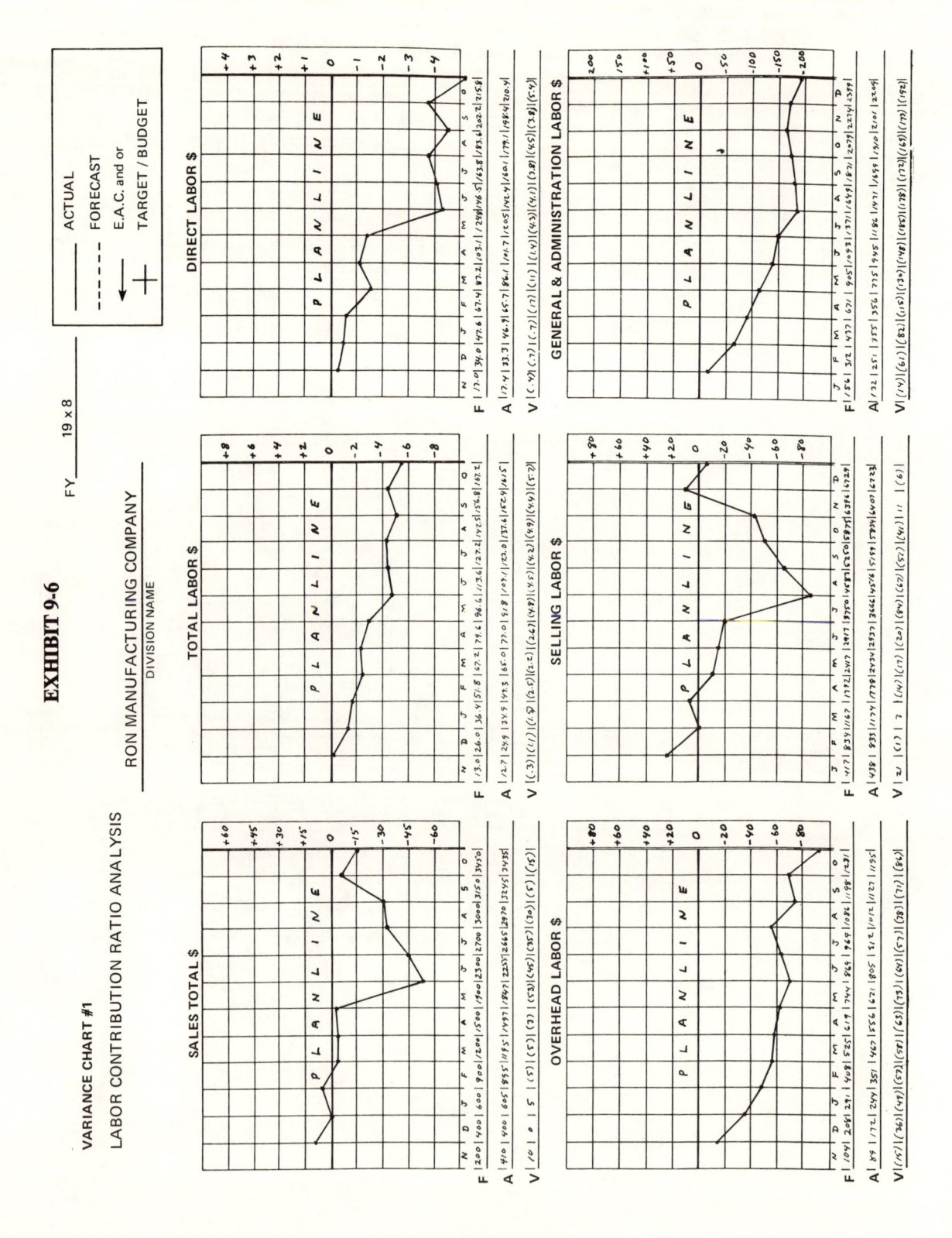

178   EARNED HOURS—AN EASY METHOD FOR CONTROLLING LABOR COST

—Inefficient use of manpower.
—Excess inventory buildup.
—Material shortage problem.
—Machinery problems.
—Other.

The charts shown in the prior exhibits were prepared on a monthly basis but if visibility was available on a weekly basis, corrective action in light of these negative results could have been taken earlier. Thus, the following corrective procedures could have been implemented:

—Eliminating all unnecessary labor hours, such as overtime.
—Reviewing current and future manpower loading.
—Checking inventory levels in order to avoid unnecessary buildup.
—Checking production processes, workflow, and methods to eliminate any redundancy of effort or bottlenecks.

HOW THE EARNED HOURS REPORTING PACKAGE CAN BE APPLIED TO YOUR ORGANIZATION

Exhibits 9-7 to 9-11 represent a live example of how the earned hours reporting package can be applied to your organization. The case example is Laboratory Products Division.

The variance charts included in this example, while using the same format, tell a different story from the previous exhibits. These charts stress percent variance from plan, which is often much easier for the non-financial managers to relate to than pure numbers.

This case has six months of actual results included on the contribution report and the first quarter on the variance charts. The second quarter has been omitted, because it was felt that the reader could gain more of an impact of the relationship between the graphs if his attention was restricted to a single quarter. The conversion of the second quarter data into a graphic presentation can serve as a training approach for introducing your management team to this technique.

In demonstrating how the technique works to your managers, ask questions, such as:

—Is Ron Manufacturing doing a good job of controlling their labor costs in all categories?
—Are they adjusting to shift in sales levels?
—Do they appear to have a good balance between labor groups, or are some overworked?

EXHIBIT 9-7
EARNED HOURS CONTRIBUTION REPORT

LABORATORY PRODUCTS — DIVISION — PAGE 1 OF 2

		NOV	DEC	JAN	FEB	MAR	APR	MAY	JUNE	JULY	AUG	SEPT	OCT	TOTAL
SALES Laboratory	FORECAST	1358	1358	1793	1363	1367	1642	1311	1381	1552	1479	1574	1980	18160
	ACTUAL	1477	1636	1734	1533	1305	1382							
(UNFAV.)	VARIANCE	119	298	<61>	170	<62>	<260>							
SALES Products	FORECAST	97	97	145	97	98	123	73	99	123	121	121	145	1340
	ACTUAL	78	134	144	123	158	146							
(UNFAV.)	VARIANCE	<19>	37	<1>	26	60	23							
SALES Total	FORECAST	1455	1455	1940	1460	1465	1765	1385	1480	1675	1600	1695	2125	19500
	ACTUAL	1555	1790	1878	1656	1463	1528							
(UNFAV.)	VARIANCE	100	335	<62>	196	<2>	<237>							

DIVISION MANPOWER HOURS

PLANNED:
DIRECT LABOR

	NOV	DEC	JAN	FEB	MAR	APR	MAY	JUNE	JULY	AUG	SEPT	OCT	TOTAL
Laboratory	81600	80947	90780	71155	66259	82824	66259	69034	86292	72298	76379	102488	946235
Assembly	4896	4733	5916	4406	4243	5304	4243	4406	5308	4233	4733	6120	59241
Maintenance	14608	14608	18040	14080	14080	17600	14080	14080	17600	14236	14236	17820	185108
Other	7357	7595	9494	7595	6949	8686	6949	6949	8686	7110	7110	8888	93768

INDIRECT/SUPPORT LABOR
SALES MKTG. } Office
G & A

	4733	4896	5916	4570	4406	5508	4406	4406	5508	4570	4570	5712	59201
TOTAL	113594	112779	130146	101806	95937	119922	95937	98875	123594	102967	107046	140948	1343553

DIVISION MANPOWER RATIO/PER HOUR TO SALES DOLLAR

PLANNED:
DIRECT LABOR

	NOV	DEC	JAN	FEB	MAR	APR	MAY	JUNE	JULY	AUG	SEPT	OCT	TOTAL
Laboratory	16.64	16.78	19.77	15.61	20.63	19.83	19.79	20.00	17.99	20.46	20.61	19.33	19.19
Assembly	19.81	20.49	24.51	22.02	23.10	23.19	17.44	22.47	22.33	25.57	25.57	23.69	22.62
Maintenance	99.60	99.60	102.54	103.69	104.65	100.28	99.37	105.11	95.17	112.23	118.97	119.25	103.34
Other	187.57	191.37	204.34	192.23	210.82	203.20	199.31	212.98	192.84	225.04	238.40	239.09	207.96

INDIRECT/SUPPORT LABOR
SALES MKTG. } Office
G & A

	307.42	297.18	327.92	319.47	332.50	320.44	314.34	335.91	304.10	350.11	370.70	372.02	329.39
TOTAL	12.81	12.90	14.91	14.34	15.27	14.72	14.44	14.96	13.55	15.54	15.83	15.08	14.51

EXHIBIT 9-8
EARNED HOURS CONTRIBUTION REPORT

LABORATORY PRODUCTS — DIVISION   PAGE 2 OF 2

	NOV	DEC	JAN	FEB	MAR	APR	MAY	JUNE	JULY	AUG	SEPT	OCT	TOTAL
DIVISION MANPOWER HOURS													
ACTUAL:													
DIRECT LABOR													
Laboratory	83,948	82,441	95,839	74,553	72,483	87,622							
Assembly	5048	4736	5946	4598	4138	5412							
Maintenance	16,173	15,615	18,873	14,150	13,793	17,182							
Other	6745	6668	8368	6805	6743	8234							
INDIRECT/SUPPORT LABOR													
SALES MKTG } Office G & A	6651	6513	7916	5986	5783	6971							
TOTAL	118,565	115,973	136,942	106,092	102,940	125,421							
DIVISION MANPOWER RATIO/PER HOUR TO SALES DOLLARS													
ACTUAL:													
DIRECT LABOR													
Laboratory	17.59	20.09	18.09	20.56	18.00	15.17							
Assembly	15.45	28.29	24.22	26.75	38.18	29.19							
Maintenance	96.15	114.63	99.51	117.03	106.07	88.93							
Other	230.54	268.45	224.43	243.35	216.97	185.57							
INDIRECT/SUPPORT LABOR													
SALES MKTG } Office G & A	233.80	214.83	237.24	276.65	252.98	219.19							
TOTAL	13.12	15.43	13.71	15.61	14.21	12.18							
TOTAL LABOR RATIO PLANNED	12.81	12.90	14.91	14.34	15.27	14.72							
TOTAL LABOR RATIO ACTUAL	13.12	15.43	13.71	15.61	14.21	12.18							
TOTAL $ PER HOUR GAIN (LOSS)	.31	2.53	(1.20)	1.27	(1.06)	(2.54)							
% GAIN (LOSS) TO PLAN	2.4	19.6	(8.0)	8.9	(6.9)	(17.3)							
$ EFFECT – VARIANCE TO PLAN	3,52,14	285,330	(156,175)	129,294	(101,693)	(304,602)							
CUM $ EFFECT YTD.	3,52,14	288,844	132,669	261,963	160,270	(144,332)							

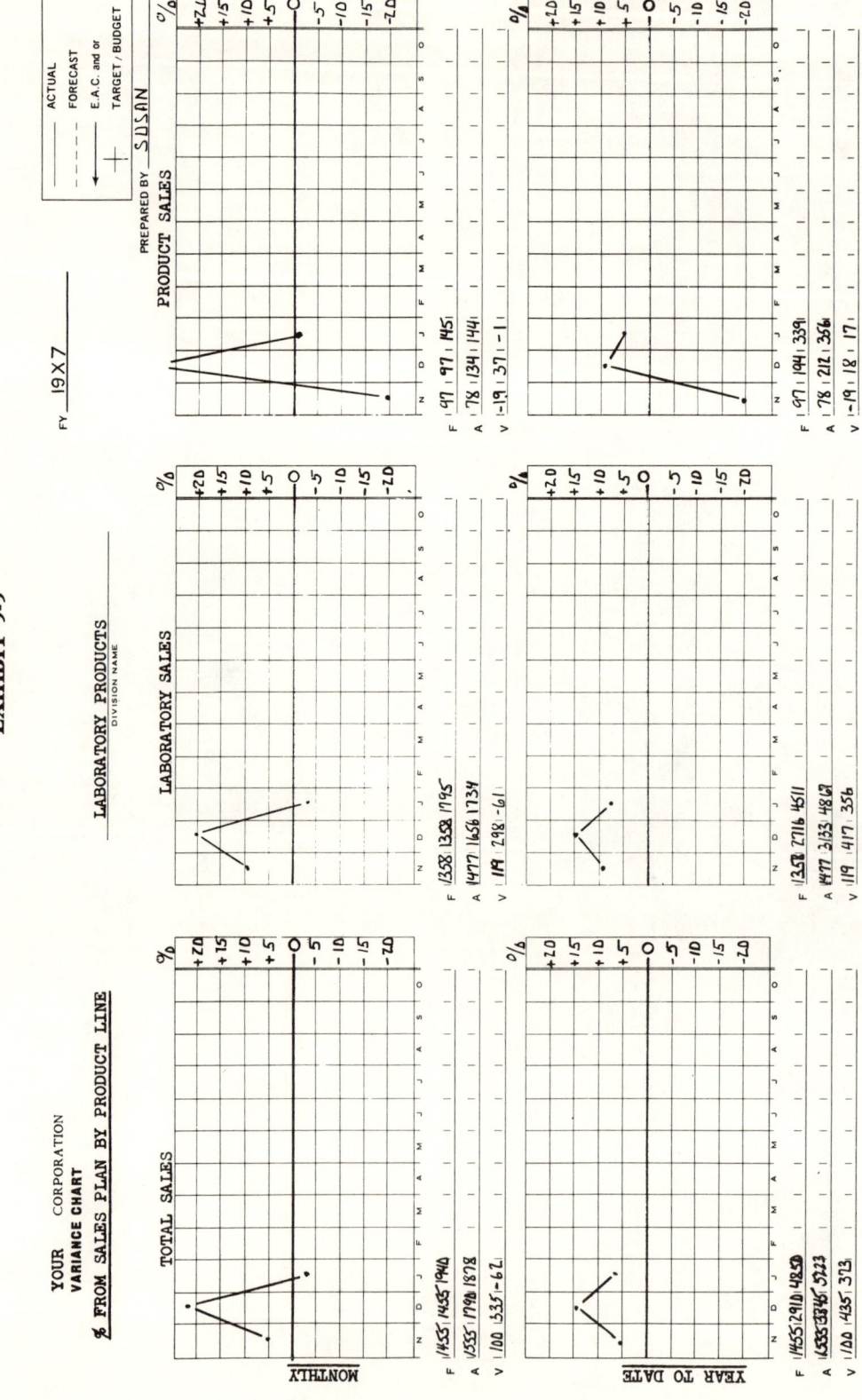

182 EARNED HOURS—AN EASY METHOD FOR CONTROLLING LABOR COST

EXHIBIT 9-9

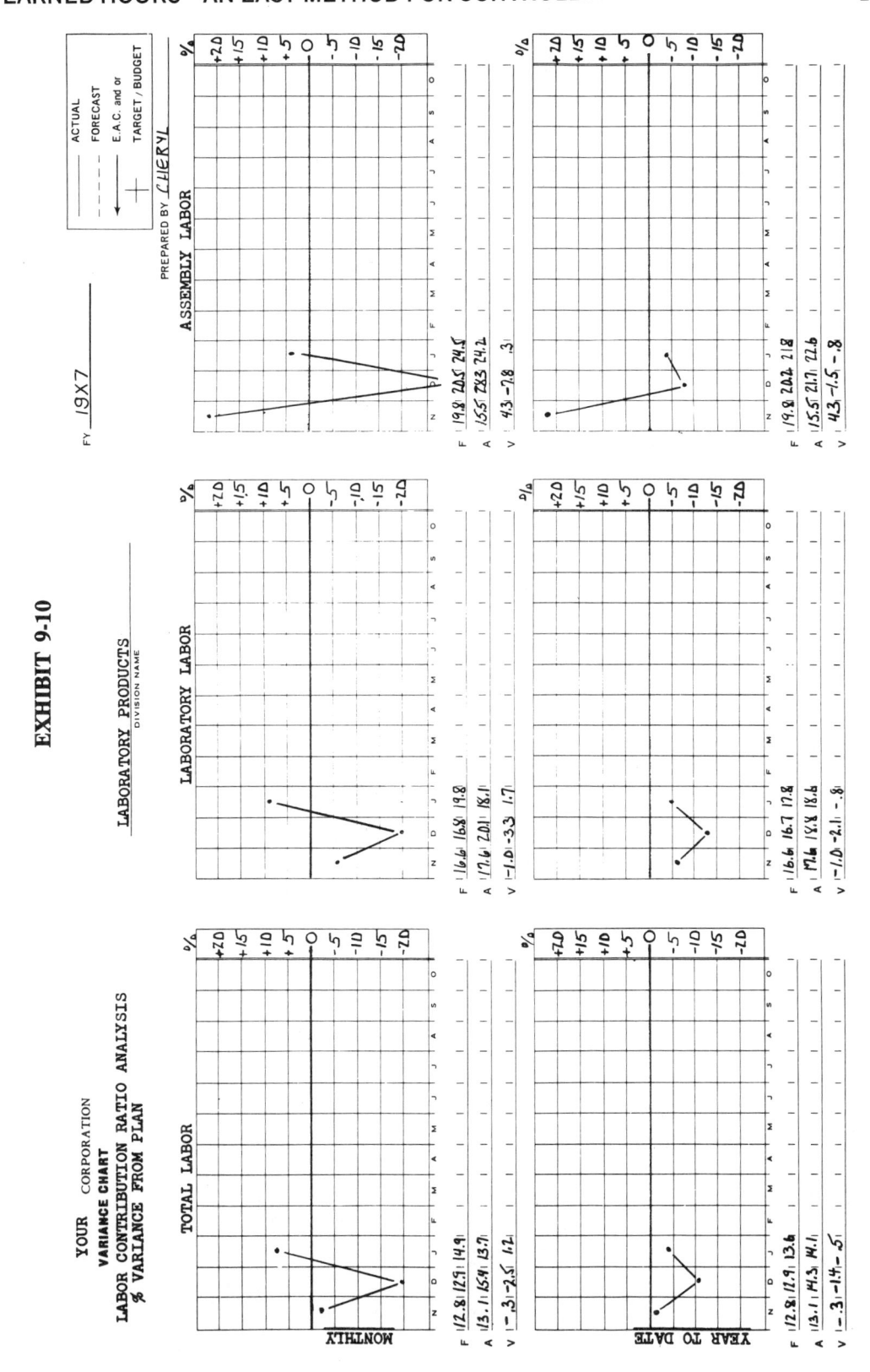

EARNED HOURS—AN EASY METHOD FOR CONTROLLING LABOR COST 183

EXHIBIT 9-10

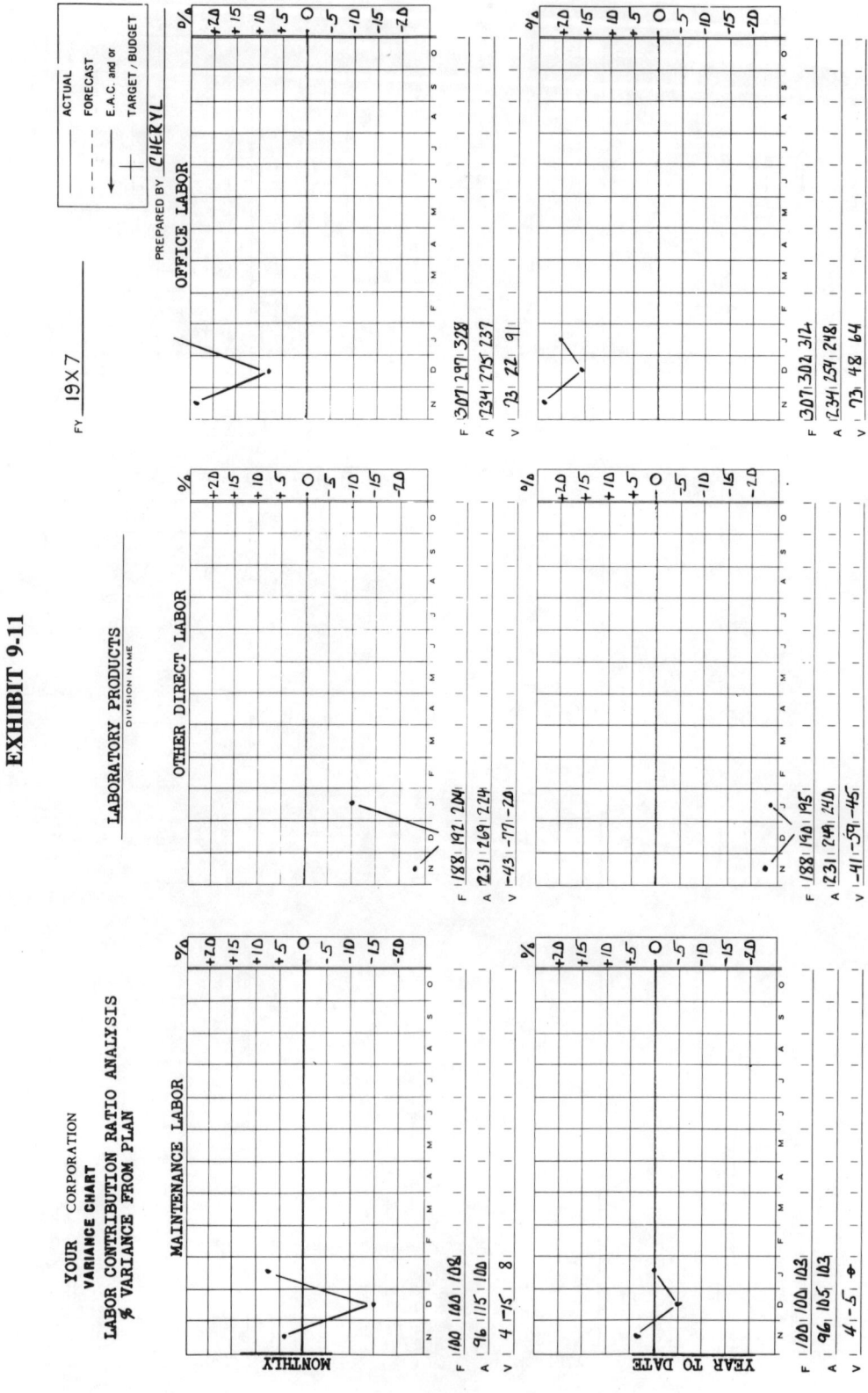

184 EARNED HOURS—AN EASY METHOD FOR CONTROLLING LABOR COST

EXHIBIT 9-11

A case in point—how a distribution company is using a modified earned hours approach to stabilize the cost per delivered case

The previous case in point and examples in this chapter have all been manufacturing or product dominated. This case in point shows that an earned-hours approach is also very applicable and beneficial to service-oriented businesses.

A large, well-run west-coast distribution company is currently using a limited and somewhat revised earned-hours application to supplement its flexible budgeting operation. In order to handle an expanding product line, this firm over the years was forced to add delivery support personnel in order to cut driver delivery cost. This was dramatized by the fact that for every delivery driver there are four back-up people in the peak part of the season. This includes order takers, dispatchers, loaders, and supervisors. While the drivers are monitored by delivery standards (a driver is expected to deliver 450 cases per eight-hour day), the large support group is loosely controlled.

In order to find out if the support group is operating at its most efficient level, each branch delivery location was monitored by using a modified earned-hours approach. The annual operating budget with its corresponding forecast case delivery schedule is the basis for the forecast phase of the system. (This replaces the financial guide used in our previous example.) The case sales delivery schedule is converted to an equivalent case basis so that all cases are equal and assigned a dollar revenue value. The equalization of the case forecast and its revenue base will eliminate product price-mix shifts, which may distort proper evaluation between locations. This optional, minor shift in approach was the only modification using the earned-hours approach.

Although it is early in the game, it is quite evident that this approach is complementing and not duplicating the existing budgeting system. Management is now getting a fresh and varied look at the operations. It can achieve proper staffing levels and be able to better anticipate changes in fixed staff that are normally excluded from the flexible budgeting reporting system.

Thus, the objective of having the cost per case remain constant will be realized, because the increased sales volume will outpace any cost increases, and the cost per delivered case will remain at current levels.

10

EXPENSE CATEGORIZATION —A PRELUDE TO IMPROVED PROFITS THROUGH STREAMLINED OPERATIONAL ANALYSIS

Operational awareness stresses the concept or need to develop the ability and skills to get behind the numbers. One of the most beneficial approaches to obtaining this objective with lasting benefits is to segregate, categorize, and analyze your firm's costs and expenses. Not until you undertake and complete this task can you truly expect to derive any lasting value from improved expense control and reduction. Because many firms do not attempt to understand their cost structure, they feel that expense reduction is the issuing of an edict that results in the following ill-conceived memo:

To: J.R. Hardworking

From: Controller's Office

Re: Expense Reduction

Considering the current economic climate and the resistance of the market to purchase our products with the same gusto as in prior periods, we will all have to tighten our belts. This has forced us to institute a 10% across-the-board cost reduction in every department. Your current budget is $343,300, so you will have to cut out approximately $35,000. (These memos always round to the high side.)

What the controller's office failed to consider is that J.R. Hardworking's section is a highly automated continuous processing operation. His departmental expenses are basically fixed, or at best semi-variable. When his department was established, it required a large capital investment, which generates a high monthly depreciation charge. J.R.'s department utilized chemical processes, thus his indirect costs for chemicals, gas, water, electricity, and maintenance personnel are basically fixed. In fact, there is very little that J.R. can do to cut his expenses.

Considering the composition of his overhead cost structure, the controller's office needs to develop an understanding of these conditions if it is to effect satisfactory results. Also, the marketing department needs to make a more intelligent effort in sales and pricing, so that J.R.'s fixed costs can be easily absorbed and spread over more future units.

DEFINING COST CENTERS ALONG FUNCTIONAL AND ORGANIZATIONAL LINES

The first step in the segregation and the analysis of expenses is to close the general ledger and look at your operation. Specifically, how does your operation perform its tasks and how is it organized? The best method for initiating this evaluation process is to examine your organization chart and determine if it is up-to-date and accurate. If your firm does not have an established organization chart, then one should be prepared. Once you begin, you will find that several supporting diagrams may be required in order to completely identify all major responsibility and reporting levels. Exhibit 10-1 is an example of a top level functional organization chart, while a second tier organization chart for administrative services would include all of the departments and functions that are predominately handled by this section. The chart would appear as follows:

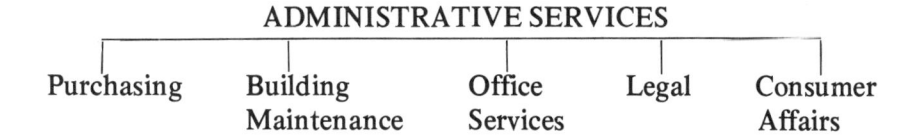

```
                    ADMINISTRATIVE SERVICES
    ┌───────────┬──────────────┬──────────┬──────┬───────────┐
 Purchasing   Building       Office     Legal    Consumer
              Maintenance    Services            Affairs
```

When this process has been completed, many firms discover that it behooves them to realign many functions and their reporting responsibilities.

Case in point—how organizational review and cost center identification resulted in the early introduction of a new product line

A prominent, independent manufacturer of exotic instrumentation, whose specialty was R&D, was acquired by a firm whose claim to fame was tight and effective cost control. The first cost control tool that the acquiring company installed was a budgeting system.

The first step in this installation was to determine the organizational and functional areas to be budgeted. Two organizational charts were developed. The first was a traditional military chain-of-command type. The second chart identified the functional tasks being undertaken by the different areas of the company. Because of the intense R&D nature of the company and the generally informal atmosphere, the two charts tended to conflict. Some functions that were engineering oriented were taking place in manufacturing, and certain test and Q.C. functions which were more manufacturing oriented were being handled by engineering personnel. Further investigation showed that the overlapping was most predominant when new products were being introduced or when a major modification was required on an existing item or line.

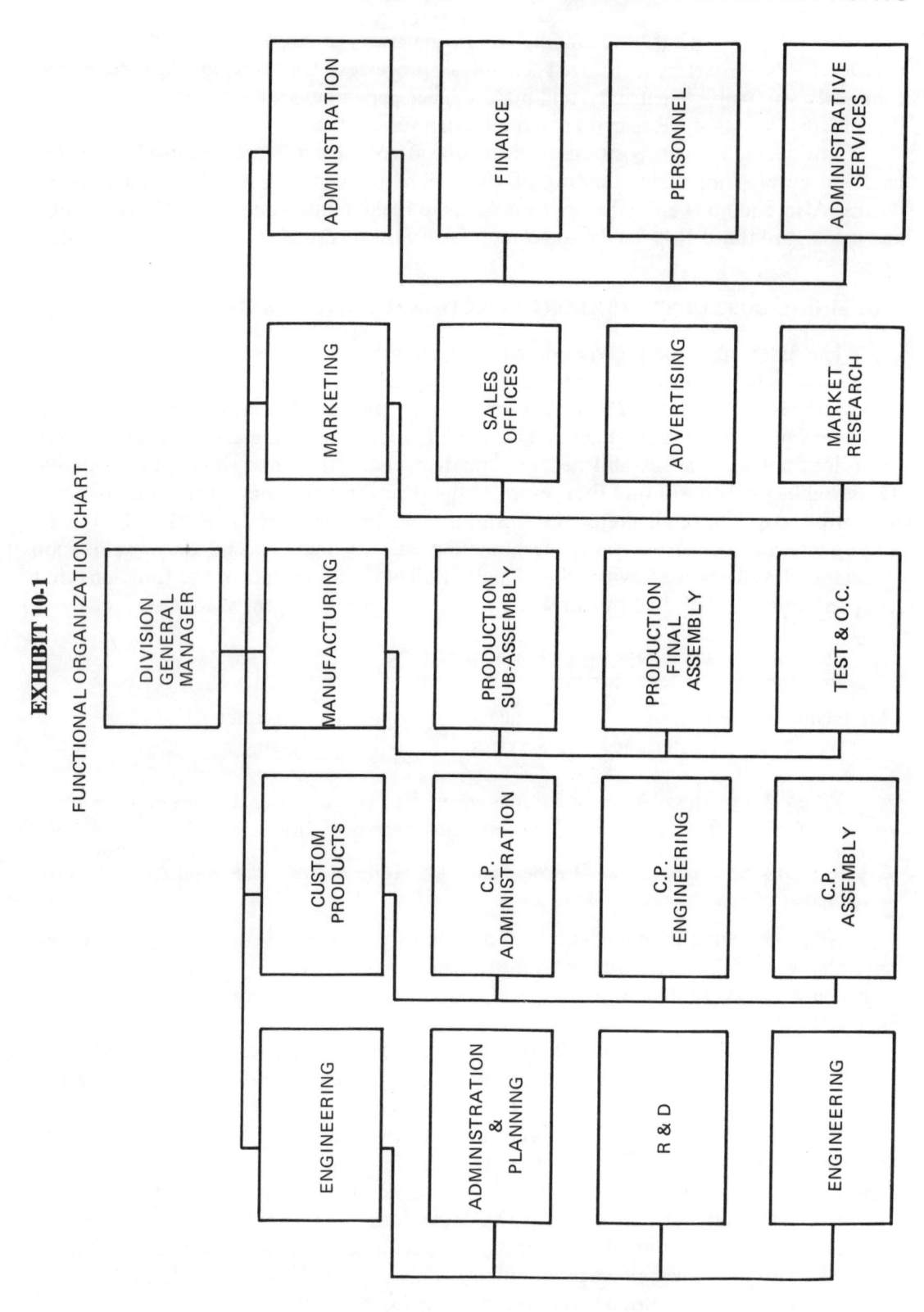

EXHIBIT 10-1
FUNCTIONAL ORGANIZATION CHART

```
                          DIVISION
                          GENERAL
                          MANAGER
         ┌───────────┬───────────┼───────────┬───────────┐
    ADMINISTRATION MARKETING MANUFACTURING CUSTOM    ENGINEERING
                                           PRODUCTS
         │           │           │           │           │
    ┌────┤      ┌────┤      ┌────┤      ┌────┤      ┌────┤
  FINANCE     SALES      PRODUCTION    C.P.      ADMINISTRATION
              OFFICES    SUB-ASSEMBLY  ADMINISTRATION  & PLANNING
    │           │           │           │           │
  PERSONNEL  ADVERTISING  PRODUCTION   C.P.         R & D
                          FINAL        ENGINEERING
                          ASSEMBLY
    │           │           │           │           │
  ADMINISTRATIVE MARKET    TEST & O.C.  C.P.       ENGINEERING
  SERVICES     RESEARCH                 ASSEMBLY
```

The solution to this overlapping problem was to reorganize production and engineering along more formal and traditional lines and to create a half-way-house between engineering and manufacturing called custom products. (The resulting organization chart is described in Exhibit 10-1.) Custom products handled all of the short run modifications and pre-production prototype assembly. In addition, tooling, jigs, fixtures, final drawings, and assembly documentation were also finalized in this area prior to being released to manufacturing. Because of custom products' specialized nature, this group was staffed by both engineers and manufacturing personnel and even included its own purchasing and production control group.

Besides deriving increased efficiency, each group was now able to concentrate on what they did best. This firm was able to introduce into production a new product line nine months earlier than anticipated. The early arrival of this new product line caught their competition off-guard, allowing the firm to secure market dominance.

COST COLLECTION HIERARCHY

When you have reviewed and solidified your organization and assigned management responsibility, you are ready to go on to the next step of assigning a cost collection numbering scheme. An easily adaptable approach is shown in Exhibit 10-2.

EXHIBIT 10-2
Cost Collection Hierarchy

```
                                           X X X - X X
Functional Area or Dept.───────────────────────────┘ │ │
(10 possible locations)                              │ │
Cost Center (99 possible locations)──────────────────┘ │
Work Station (99 possible locations)───────────────────┘
```

Functional Areas or Departments for the Exotic Instrumentation Company Would Be:
      (1 & 2 reserved for future use)
    3—Engineering
    4—Custom Products
    5—Production Subassemblies
    6—Production Final Assembly
    7—Test and Quality Control
    8—Marketing and Sales
    9—Administration

Cost Center Description for the Custom Products Department Would Be:
    410—C.P. Administration
    421—C.P. Engineering
    422—C.P. Drafting
    431—C.P. Electronic Assembly
    432—C.P. Mechanical Assembly

Work Station or Production Point Breakdown Would Be:
    431-10—Circuit Board Assembly
    431-20—Cable and Harness Assembly
    431-30—Logic Module Assembly
       ↖Work Station

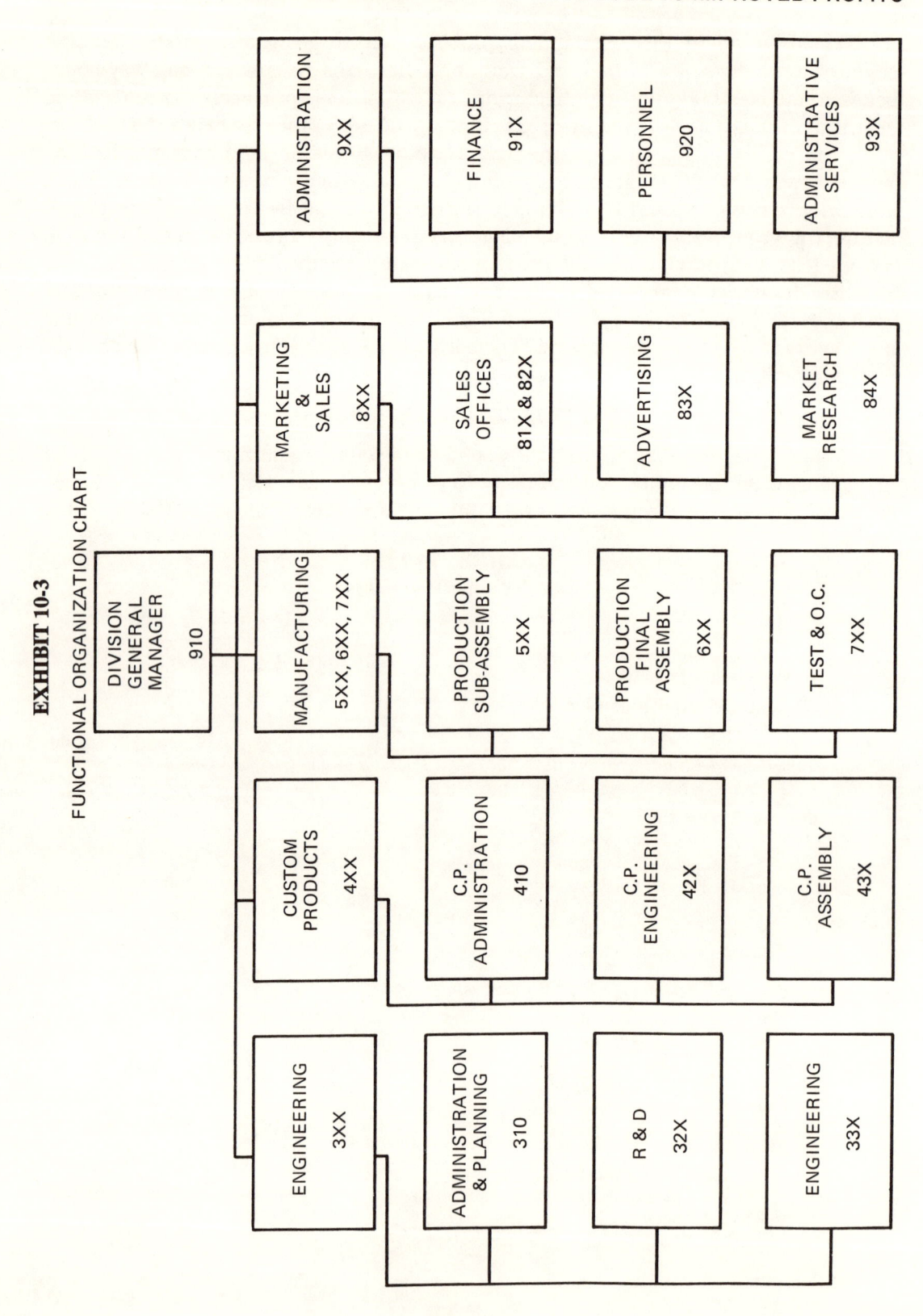

EXHIBIT 10-3

FUNCTIONAL ORGANIZATION CHART

```
                        DIVISION
                        GENERAL
                        MANAGER
                          910
                            |
    ┌───────────┬───────────┼───────────┬───────────┐
ENGINEERING  CUSTOM    MANUFACTURING  MARKETING  ADMINISTRATION
   3XX       PRODUCTS   5XX, 6XX, 7XX   & SALES      9XX
              4XX                        8XX
    |          |            |             |            |
ADMINISTRATION C.P.      PRODUCTION     SALES       FINANCE
 & PLANNING   ADMINISTRATION SUB-ASSEMBLY OFFICES     91X
    310         410          5XX        81X & 82X
    |           |             |            |            |
   R & D      C.P.         PRODUCTION  ADVERTISING   PERSONNEL
   32X      ENGINEERING   FINAL ASSEMBLY   83X          920
              42X             6XX
    |           |             |            |            |
ENGINEERING   C.P.          TEST & O.C.  MARKET    ADMINISTRATIVE
   33X       ASSEMBLY          7XX       RESEARCH    SERVICES
              43X                          84X         93X
```

EXPENSE CATEGORIZATION—A PRELUDE TO IMPROVED PROFITS

The work station number shown in Exhibit 10-2 is usually confined to the collection of direct labor and material costs while the indirect costs would be charged to the cost center. Exhibit 10-3 combines the functional organizational chart with the cost collection hierarchy in order to show how the two blend together to form a foundation for collecting, reporting, and analyzing costs and expenses along functional and management responsibility lines.

Functional reviews

After reviewing your organizational structure and determining what cost collection hierarchy is most appropriate for your organization, you are ready to examine and decide:

—what activity the cost center is engaged in.

—what natural accounts does it require.

—what statistical data does it require, such as head count by class, production statistics, etc.

Exhibit 10-4 provides a simple 12-point checklist for organizing your thoughts, asking questions, and eventually serving as a basis for creating your reporting format or print parameter, if you are computerized. An example of the natural expense classification and the reporting order for a customer service and repair department is included as Exhibit 10-5. The account grouping in this exhibit has been arranged to show cost relationship and controllability, which happens to be the next topic of discussion in this chapter.

EXHIBIT 10-4
Functional Review and Account Selection
Checkoff Sheet

1. Cost Center Name and Number _____ #_____
2. General Function:
3. Is Direct Labor (inventory) charged? Yes ☐ No ☐
4. If Yes, what categories:
5. Is Direct Materials (inventory) charged? Yes ☐ No ☐
6. If Yes, is a breakout required, and if so, what?
7. What expenses or Indirect Costs are controllable by the Cost Center manager? (List on separate sheet)
8. What fixed expenses are charged?
9. Are any costs charged to another or other cost centers (contra-credit)? Yes ☐ No ☐
10. If Yes, what?
11. What statistical data is needed by the Cost Center managers as support information (units, hours, etc.)?
12. If an existing Cost Center, what accounts should be deleted or combined, and *why?*

EXHIBIT 10-5
Account Classification and Reporting
Format for C. Lynn Distribution Co.
Customer Service & Repair

SALARIES & WAGES	SEMI-ANNUAL BUDGET
Shop & Stock Room—Salaries	$22,107
Office Salaries	16,506
Temporary—Clerical	-0-
Delivery & Installation—Labor	5,586
Field Service & Repairs—Labor	47,044
Shop Service & Repairs—Labor	56,618
Overtime Premium	165
Total salaries & wages	148,026
Payroll connected costs	37,646
Other controllable expenses	
Samples & Free Goods	292
Paint & Other Shop Supplies	13,769
Parts Used	18,419
Equipment Destruction	3,579
Janitorial Maintenance & Supplies	2,002
Office Supplies & Stationery	1,805
Uniform & Laundry	2,394
Gas, Light & Water	3,672
Telephone & Telegraph	4,446
Rent—Lease Vehicles	26,990
Repairs—Bldg., Yard & Equip.	954
Travel, Auto & Bus. Entertainment	109
Freight on Parts	2,446
Non-Recurring Expenses	1,667
Total Other Controllable Expenses	82,544
Fixed expenses	
Depreciation	15,000
Taxes	7,669
Insurance	5,000
Total Fixed Expenses	27,669
Total Dept. Expenses	$295,885
Delivery & Installation—Units	250
Field Service & Repair—Units	1,250
Shop Service & Repair—Units	1,450
Total	2,950

EXPENSE CATEGORIZATION—A PRELUDE TO IMPROVED PROFITS

UNDERSTANDING THE RELATIONSHIP BETWEEN FIXED, VARIABLE, AND CONTROLLABLE COSTS

There have been many articles and chapters written on the function of costs, whether they are variable, semi-variable or fixed, and to what extent they are controllable by a cost center manager. There are even books that show you how to track these costs by using scatter diagrams and forcing a line of best fit. As operationally-oriented financial analysts, we are more concerned with the development of a good understanding of *what costs truly can be related to changes in volume*. Furthermore, we want to be sure that this understanding can be transmitted down to the operating level, where these costs are generated and more effectively controlled. Exhibit 10-6 shows the cost/volume relationship or behavior inherent in each cost group:

— fixed—non-variable
— semi-variable
— variable

To what extent or degree a cost center manager can and should be held responsible for cost control was illustrated in our previous example of J.R. Hardworking. J.R. had very little control over the generation of costs charged to his department. Thus in reality, he had nominal fiscal responsibility, but because of the heavy investment in equipment in his department, he has a great deal of managerial responsibility for the proper operation and functioning of his section. Remember, that because of the fixed nature of his costs, when volume declines there is very little he can do to cut costs.

Classifying labor and payroll related costs

Since labor costs constitute a very large percentage of the total cost of running a business and are one area that is highly controllable by management, proper classification and analysis is essential. The classification and analysis of labor should not be confined to the broad or general classification of direct labor or indirect labor, but rather be broken down within each of these two major headings by specialty. Also, when classifying and analyzing labor costs, we want to be sure that all labor-related costs do not get lumped together. This is especially true in the case of payroll-related costs. More commonly, they are referred to as fringes, which should be segregated for visibility because of their high relationship to the payroll dollar paid. In some companies, this can be as much as 1/3 or even 1/2 of each payroll dollar paid for union personnel and 10% for salaried individuals.

In Exhibit 10-5 it would be so simple to combine all of the salaries, wages, and payroll connected costs into one line, but you would lose visibility and control of the cost/benefit relationship. Look at the following breakdown for shop service and installation:

Delivery and Installation	$ 5,586
Field Service and Repair	47,044
Shop Service and Repair	56,618
Total	$109,248

EXHIBIT 10-6
COST BEHAVIOR RELATIONSHIPS

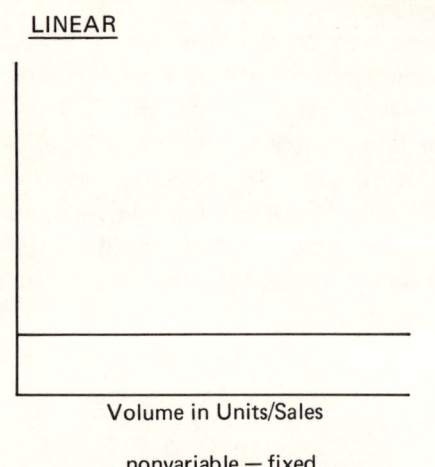

LINEAR

nonvariable — fixed
(rent, straight line depreciation)

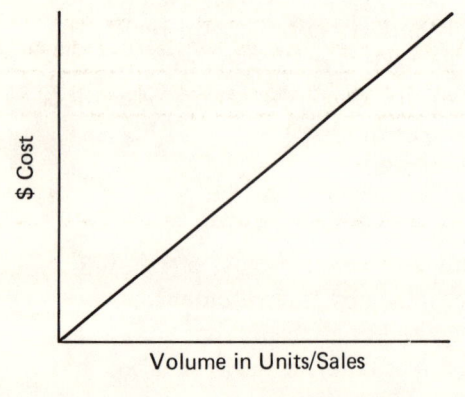

variable
(direct material, commissions)

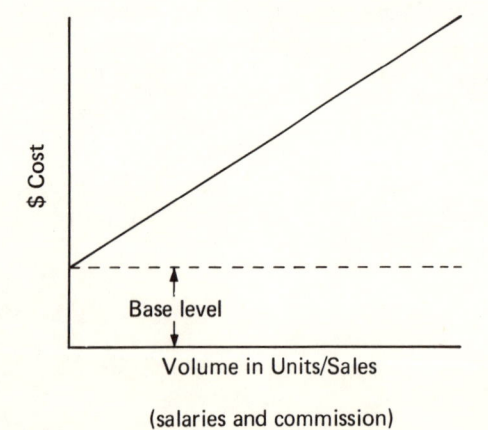

(salaries and commission)

CURVILINEAR

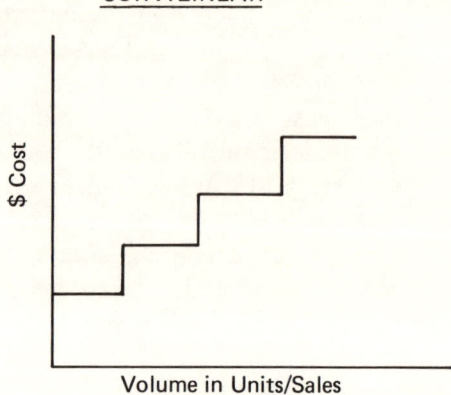

step fixed cost
(supervision)

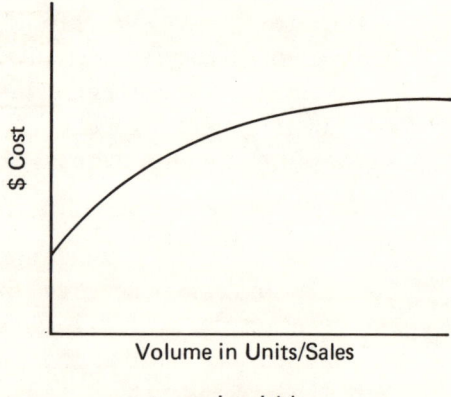

semi-variable
(utilities)

EXPENSE CATEGORIZATION—A PRELUDE TO IMPROVED PROFITS 195

If you could not measure the costs against the benefits provided, over $100,000 could easily be misspent. In addition, the following salary accounts could easily disguise inefficient overhead:

Shop and Stockroom Salaries	$22,107
Office Salaries	16,506
Temporary—Clerical	—
Total	$38,613

An expenditure of $38,613 could easily be misexplained by the statement "That is what it takes to run the operation." One more refinement: if temporary clerical is not split out, cost center managers who wish to violate head count quotas could get around these quotas by using temporary help and thus the productivity of the unit would be disguised.

PINPOINTING THE BREAKEVEN POINT

The natural fallout from the cost and expense analysis described so far is that you begin to realize what volume is required to cover your fixed nut or what volume is required to just open the doors every morning. These costs are the combination of your fixed costs and your standby costs. Standby costs are those costs which you would continue to incur if you planned to continue your business operation, even if your volume sharply declined temporarily or was eliminated, e.g., if there were a fire and the business activity was temporarily curtailed. While the standby costs will vary depending on the type of business, the classic example is a skeleton crew composed of a difficult to replace supervisor, chemist, and a token maintenance force.

While this type of analysis is adequate for providing rules of thumb that are helpful in understanding the business, a further refinement is more desirable. This refinement is the construction of a breakeven chart. As Exhibit 10-7 illustrates, no mystery or witchcraft is involved in the construction of a breakeven chart. All you have to do is plot three lines on a grid. They are:

—Fixed Costs (shown as a broken line).
—Total Costs (the area between the total cost line and fixed cost line represents your variable cost).
—Revenue.

The breakeven point is that point in either units or sales dollars where the total cost line bisects the revenue line. In our example (Exhibit 10-7), it is at $40,000 in sales. Below that volume the Sample Co. will lose money, above it there will be profit.

Exhibit 10-8 takes the classification of costs and expenses discussed in this chapter and converts them into a breakeven chart. By using a cost classification block like the one shown in Exhibit 10-8, you can better:

—understand the classification of costs used to prepare a top-notch breakeven chart.
—communicate to all levels of management the relationship of fixed, semi-variable, and variable costs upon the breakeven point.
—implement pricing decisions and tactics.

EXHIBIT 10-7

SAMPLE COMPANY

BREAKEVEN CHART

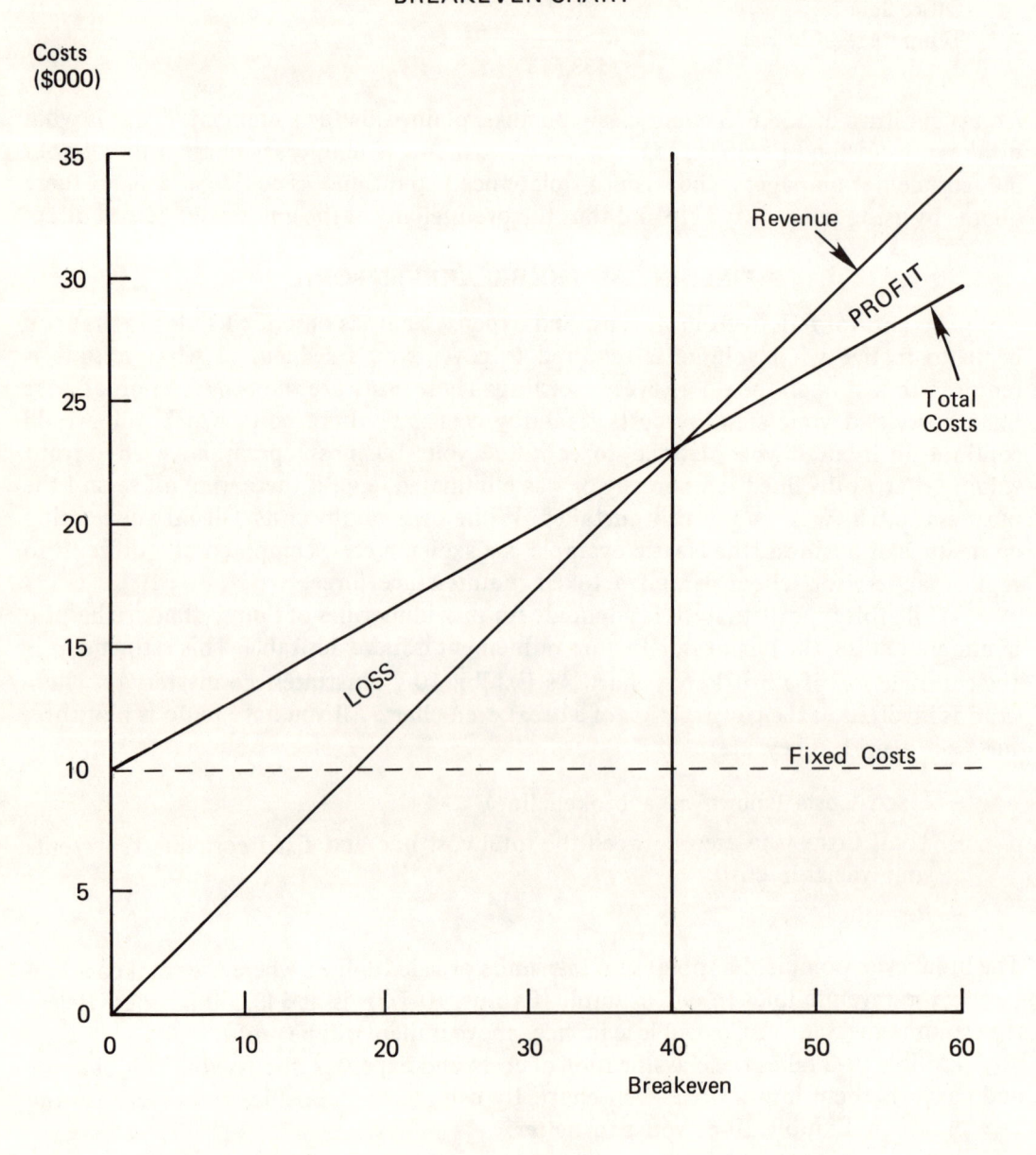

EXHIBIT 10-8

R. ROSS MANUFACTURING CO.
ANNUAL BREAK-EVEN CHART WITH COST CLASSIFICATION BLOCK

FIXED EXPENSES		VARIABLE EXPENSES				INCOME	
Fully Fixed	Semi-Variable	DIRECT MATERIALS		Variable Overhead	Variable Selling/G&A	Income Tax	Net Income

- PROFIT ZONE
- 19X7 BUDGETED OPERATING EXPENSES
- BREAKEVEN POINT APPROX. 18 MIL. UNITS
- TOTAL REVENUE
- TOTAL COSTS
- VARIABLE COSTS
- FIXED COSTS

(In Millions) 0–14
(000's of Units) 0–30

198   EXPENSE CATEGORIZATION—A PRELUDE TO IMPROVED PROFITS

—make operating decisions in order to improve profitability.

—revamp or reorganize your organization in the case of a marginal or loss operation.

A case in point—how Black & White Printing, a marginal operation, turned the corner using breakeven analysis and saved $115,000

Black & White Printing Co. is located in New York City and was for many years a successful supplier of black and white printing to the publishing industry. Most of their competition moved out of the New York area to more favorable economic climates and expanded to include color processing. True to their name, Black & White Printing did not follow suit and was losing business. A new management team took over the company and instituted an operationally-oriented financial analysis. The objective of the analysis was to determine what it would take to turn the business around, and, could it be turned around?

The analytical diagnosis was that Black & White Printing was being strangled by its fixed costs and by their frantic attempt to place marginal work on its presses in order to spread these costs. Principally, its lease payments for equipment and building were being paid out for what was basically idle capacity. If they were to eliminate five presses and sublet one-third of their facility, preferably to a bookbinder, and incorporate other savings, they would reduce their in-season quarterly breakeven by $229,000. A major part of this savings would be $143,000 for direct labor which would be eliminated by not having to crew the five presses that were being dropped. The practice in the past had

EXHIBIT 10-9
Black & White Printing Co.
The Impact of the Shrinkage Program
(000 Omitted)

	On a Breakeven Quarter			On a Minimum Sales Level Quarter		
	Current Break even	Better (worse) Savings	Shrinkage Breakeven	Minimum Level	Better (worse) Savings	Minimum Level with Shrinkage
Net Sales	634	229	405	423	0	423
Cost of Sales						
Direct Material	89	34	55	58	0	58
Direct Labor	236	143	93	157	68	89
Manufacturing Overhead	206	24	182	206	24	182
Total Cost of Sales	531	201	330	421	92	329
Gross Profit	103	28	75	2	92	94
Other Expenses						
Selling	20	8	12	20	8	12
General & Administrative	57	15	42	57	15	42
Corporate Charge	14	5	9	9	0	9
Interest Expense	12	0	12	12	0	12
Total	103	28	75	98	23	75
Net Profit	0	0	0	(96)	115	19

been to take marginal and even loss jobs in order to maintain minimum press crews; now they would not have to resort to it.

This program would save them $115,000 in their out-of-season second quarter, turning a projected loss of $96,000 for the quarter into a $19,000 profit at the new level of operations. In addition the analysis showed that if the plant could be operated for a full year at its maximum sales volume, Black & White would produce a 22.8% net profit before taxes. A badly needed four-color web press could be financed from a portion of the proceeds resulting from the sale of the five presses. Exhibit 10-9 shows the before and after impact of the shrinkage program upon Black & White's ability to break even.

USING CONTRA-CREDITS AND UNABSORBED COSTS TO MEASURE COST CENTER EFFECTIVENESS

In many companies, there are departments that exist for the expressed purpose of serving other departments within the company. Their staffing and budgets are determined by the anticipated needs of these other departments. These departments are charged for these services via a contra-credit. Hopefully, at the end of the year, the contra-credit equals and absorbs all of the costs incurred by the service department.

A case in point: how the soft drink industry uses contra-credits to measure and control service departments

In the soft drink industry, two of these support activities would be the cooler department, which installs and services vending machines and the fleet department which is responsible for keeping the delivery and transport trucks operating. In the case of the cooler department, all of the work orders orginate from the sales and distribution centers called branches. Since the branches are usually geographically scattered, the cooler department and fleet department are to some degree auxiliaries of the branch locations. In a sense, these departments exist for the purpose of servicing the branches. In turn, the branches are charged for their services at a fixed hourly rate plus parts (time and materials).

The accounting term used for charging the branches is *contra-credit*. In accounting parlance, the branch is charged or debited with the cost of repairing a vending machine and the cooler depatment receives the comparable credit for the service.

The staffing and budgeting of the cooler department is based upon the anticipated needs of the branches. When the budget is approved, the billing rate or contra-credit rate is determined. If the branches provide enough activity for the cooler department and the department keeps its cost structure in line, the billing rate should have absorbed all of the costs incurred by the department.

The measurement factor comes into play when you as the analyst begin to investigate and analyze why the cooler department did not zero out all of its costs. A few of the more obvious questions are:

—Did the branches provide enough orders?

—Did the cooler department stay within budget?

—Did the order mix change from what was anticipated?

—Are the branches satisfied with the quality of work performed?

11

HOW TO USE AND BENEFIT FROM FLEXIBLE BUDGETING— PRIME ANALYTICAL TOOL

The previous chapter showed you how to analyze, evaluate, and understand the cost and expense relationships that are present in your organization. This chapter shows you how to convert your increased knowledge of expense and cost relationships into a powerful tool called *flexible or variable budgeting*. Flexible or variable budgeting is a:

—*control tool* that allows you to evaluate expense and cost levels in relationship to varying activity levels.

—*forecasting tool* that will assist you in projecting future profit levels—now—based on current sales, backlog, or order levels.

FLEXIBLE BUDGETING AS A CONTROL TOOL

Achieving cost effectiveness when the level of activity varies

Although you have constructed your financial guide line (profit plan or master budget) to reflect varying levels of activity, it still remains a fixed or static forecast or budget. I.e., your financial guide line may indicate a shipment level of 1,200,000 units for the year, or an average of 100,000 units per month, but in reality in the off-season months, you may sell an average of 50,000 units; and in the busy season, you may sell 200,000 units. Once the static forecast has been finalized, the numbers no longer reflect the actual fluctuations in sales volume and/or production levels. Cost comparisons become difficult and in many cases meaningless. The following case in point demon-

HOW TO USE AND BENEFIT FROM FLEXIBLE BUDGETING

strates how cost control and effectiveness are eroded when you rely solely upon the static financial guide line for implementing total and complete budgeting control.

A case in point—how budgeting cost control was made ineffective by using the static financial guide line

Jules and Barry are both polishing department foremen in an automotive aftermarket manufacturing company. Jules and Barry were both budgeted to produce 1,000 units each for the month, but Jules' department was three times as busy as Barry's department.

Variance Report—Polishing Depts
(Unfavorable)

Cost Center 501	Budget	Actual	Variance
Units Produced	1,000 pcs	1,500 pcs	+500 pcs
Dollars	$1,000	$1,500	(500)
Resp. Jules			
Cost Center 502			
Units Produced	1,000 pcs	500 pcs	(500) pcs
Dollars	$1,000	$1,500	-0-
Resp. Barry			

Their boss, Herb, has called them both in to discuss their performance against budget for the previous month. As unbelievable as it seems, Jules was chewed out for being over budget by 50%, while Barry was patted on the back for hitting his budget right on the button. What Herb failed to consider in his evaluation of their performance against budget, was the production level of each department. If he had considered it, he would have applauded Jules for increasing production by fifty percent and keeping his cost (entirely variable and controllable) in line with the production increase. While in Barry's case, he should have interrogated him as to why his production level was below standard and why he hadn't monitored his costs closer.

What is a variable or flexible budget?

In order for Herb to do a more effective job of managing his two departments, he has to supplement his static budget or F.G.L. with a variable or as it is more often referred to, a flexible budget. As its name implies, a flexible budget "flexes" or adjusts the master or static budget to the current level of activity. By flexing the static budget, the cost effectiveness of an operating department is not disguised by comparing a budget based upon one level of output to the results gained from another level of activity. Thus, Herb realized that it was inappropriate to compare the current month's activity for each of his foremen to their original static budget, because the activity levels used to prepare the static budget were no longer appropriate and formed an unreasonable comparative base.

Determining what accounts to flex

In the previous chapter, we discussed the relationship between fixed, semi-variable, and variable costs and the extent each was controllable by an operating manager (remember J.R. Hardworking). This controllability factor must become the prime consideration in establishing a reporting format. The account classification and reporting format for the customer service distribution and repair department of the C. Lynn Distribution Co., which was included as an exhibit in the previous chapter, has

EXHIBIT 11-1
Comparison of Static Budget vs. Fixed Budget by Account
Classification Format for C. Lynn Distribution Co.
Customer Service & Repair

	Semi-Annual Budget	
Salaries & Wages	*Static*	*Flexed*
Shop & Stock Room—Salaries	$ 22,107	$ 22,107
Office Salaries	16,506	16,506
Temporary Clerical	-0-	-0-
Delivery & Installation —Labor (Flex)	5,586	4,190
Field Service & Repairs —Labor (Flex)	47,044	35,283
Shop Service & Repairs —Labor (Flex)	56,618	42,464
Overtime Premium (Flex)	165	124
Total Salaries & Wages	148,026	120,674
Payroll Connected Costs (Partial Flex)	37,646	30,893
Other Controllable Expenses		
Samples & Free Goods	292	292
Paint & Other Shop Supplies (Flex)	13,769	10,327
Parts Used (Flex)	18,419	13,814
Equipment Destruction	3,579	3,579
Janitorial Maintenance & Supplies	2,002	2,002
Office Supplies & Stationery	1,805	1,805
Uniform & Laundry (Flex)	2,394	1,796
Gas, Light & Water	3,672	3,672
Telephone & Telegraph	4,446	4,446
Rent—Lease Vehicles (Flex)	26,990	20,243
Repairs—Bldg., Yard & Equipment	954	954
Travel, Auto & Bus. Entertainment	109	109
Freight on Parts	2,446	2,446
Non-Recurring Expenses	1,667	1,667
Total Other Controllable Expenses	82,544	67,152
Fixed Expenses		
Depreciation	15,000	15,000
Taxes	7,669	7,669
Insurance	5,000	5,000
Total Fixed Expenses	27,669	27,669
Total Dept. Expenses	$295,885	$246,388
Delivery & Installation—Units (Flex)	250	188
Field Service & Repair —Units (Flex)	1,250	938
Shop Service & Repair —Units (Flex)	1,450	1,088
Total	2,950	2,214

HOW TO USE AND BENEFIT FROM FLEXIBLE BUDGETING 203

been modified to show those accounts which are flexed each month (Exhibit 11-1). For comparative purposes, a second budget column has been added to show the effect of flexing the semi-annual static budget. For this example, delivery, installation, and field service repairs were 25% lower than anticipated and the flexed accounts were adjusted to show the lower amount. (The 25% reflects an average for the six months, some months were up and some as low as 55%.)

In order to determine which of the accounts to flex, C. Lynn's controller had to determine which accounts were truly affected by changes in volume. As you will see, not all of the controllable accounts are flexed, because they are basically semi-variable. C. Lynn's controller also discovered that some of the flexed accounts were not as variable as he had expected, because at a certain point the costs become firm. This was determined in a very low production period, when the flexed accounts were adjusted downward by 55% to reflect a 55% lower activity level. In reality, these accounts were not totally variable, but represented a situation similar to that of standby costs. C. Lynn's controller discovered that the variability of these accounts ended at the minus 30% level of the master budget. I.e., a management decision was made to "tough it out" (be over budget at the 30% activity level until conditions returned to normal).

AVOIDING THE USE OF THE WRONG FLEXING FACTOR

Many organizations confine their flexing to changes in sales volume and/or production and fail to consider that each area of an organization may require its own tailored flexing routine. This routine need not be complicated. Exhibit 11-2 shows the many varied flexing factors used successfully for years by a large west coast production and distribution company to control its diverse but inter-related operations. The individual accounts which this large company flexes are listed as Exhibit 11-3.

EXHIBIT 11-2
Varied Flexing Factors Used to Flex a Diverse Organization
(Large Production & Distribution Co.)

Area	*Factor*
Production—Direct Labor	*Standard Labor Hours* contained as part of the computerized product data base.
Production—Direct Material	*Standard Material Dollars* contained as part of the computerized product data base. (This company produces and distributes close to 500 different products. Thus, if it relied only on total units, the budget would be incorrect because of the interaction among products, i.e., product mix.)
Production—Overhead	Specific accounts are identified and flexed based on total production units. A production unit is a case regardless of its size or whether it is made up of bottles or cans. I.e., a case is a case. Eventually the company will convert to the fluid case concept where all cases are equalized to a 182 ounce case. I.e., total current production units may be 1,250,000 in one period or 2,311,000 fluid cases.
Warehousing—Loading	Specific accounts are identified and flexed based on *cases loaded*. This relates to norm or average based on an established standard for loading different types of trucks with different load configurations.
Distribution—Delivery	Specific accounts are identified and flexed based on *cases delivered*.
Transportation—Hauling	Specific accounts are identified and flexed based on *miles driven*. The procedure is outlined in the next case in point—How a Large Distribution Firm Flexes its Transportation Budget.

EXHIBIT 11-3
Selected List of Flexed Accounts
(Large & Diverse Production & Distribution Company)

Salary & Wages
- Production Direct Labor
- Production Indirect Labor Line Support
- Production Indirect Labor—Other
- Warehouse Loaders
- Warehouse Checkers
- Transport—Long Haul Drivers
- Distribution—Local Delivery Drivers
- Distribution—Advance Salesmen
- All Areas—Overtime Premium

Non-Salary & Wages
- Payroll Connected Costs
- Uniform & Laundry
- Production, Gas, Light & Water
- Vehicle Costs (mileage basis for cars, trucks, transports, fork-lifts, etc.)
- Salesmen's Commissions
- Cash Discounts
- Advertising
- Production Loss and Damage
- Samples and Free Goods

How to flex

There are basically three approaches that you can use in flexing your budget. They are:

- Step Budget Selection
- Percentage Adjustment
- Rate Application

APPROACH I—THE STEP BUDGET

When the master budget is prepared each department does not submit a monthly budget, but an activity budget that lists its anticipated expenditures at various plus or minus activity levels, starting at the base level or zero point. Exhibit 11-4 is an example of a step budget. The budget department simply applies the appropriate step budget to the forecast activity level for each month and the annual master budget is easily prepared.

E.g.: In the preparation of the master budget you had projected October to be a plus 10% activity month and used the plus 10% budget for October's master budget. When October rolled around, it was a minus 5% activity month and not the plus 10% level as anticipated. To flex or adjust the budget to the lower than anticipated level, you simply replace the plus 10% step budget with the minus 5% budget; it is that simple. Now you are ready to compare the budget to actual results and analyze variances.

EXHIBIT 11-4
Factory Overhead—Step Budget
19XX Budget

Level of Operation	−30%	−20%	−10%	Base	+10%	+20%	+30%	Annual Total Base X 12
Total Units Produced	686,177	784,203	882,228	980,253	1,078,278	1,176,303	1,274,329	11,763,036
Direct Labor Dollars	33,331	38,092	42,853	47,615	52,377	57,138	61,899	571,380
Direct Labor Headcount	43.3	49.4	55.6	61.8	68.0	74.2	80.3	
Indirect Labor								
Management & Supvsn.	16,732	16,732	16,732	16,732	16,732	16,732	16,732	200,784
Headcount	15.0	15.0	15.0	15.0	15.0	15.0	15.0	
Indirect Labor—Line Sup.	15,711	15,926	16,307	16,538	16,902	17,200	17,432	198,456
Headcount	20.9	21.2	21.7	22.0	22.5	22.9	23.2	
Indirect Labor—Maint.	11,381	11,381	11,381	11,381	11,381	11,381	11,381	136,572
Headcount	12.0	12.0	12.0	12.0	12.0	12.0	12.0	
Overtime Premium	1,042	1,111	1,182	1,252	1,322	1,392	1,463	15,024
Total Indirect Labor	44,866	45,150	45,602	45,903	46,337	46,705	47,008	550,836
Total Headcount	47.9	48.2	48.7	49.0	49.5	49.9	50.2	
Total Payroll Connected Costs	23,727	25,491	27,323	29,104	30,933	32,738	34,505	349,248
Other Controllable Expenses								
Production Dumpage	1,890	2,160	2,430	2,700	2,970	3,240	3,510	32,400
Factory Supplies	7,000	7,400	7,900	8,350	8,800	9,250	9,700	100,200
Uniform & Laundry	1,000	1,150	1,300	1,450	1,600	1,750	1,900	17,400
Gas, Light & Water	7,000	7,500	8,000	8,500	9,350	10,200	11,050	102,000
Telephone & Telegraph	275	275	275	275	275	275	275	3,300
Vehicles	3,316	3,431	3,546	3,661	3,776	3,891	4,006	43,932
Repair & Overhaul	10,467	10,467	10,467	10,467	10,467	10,467	10,467	125,604
Travel & Auto	700	700	700	700	700	700	700	8,400
Sales of Scrap Materials	(800)	(800)	(800)	(800)	(800)	(800)	(800)	(9,600)
Total Other Controllable Exp.	30,848	32,283	33,818	35,303	37,138	38,973	40,808	423,636
Total Fixed Expenses	42,240	42,240	42,240	42,240	42,240	42,240	42,240	506,880
Total Factory Overhead—$	141,681	145,164	148,983	152,550	156,648	160,656	164,561	1,830,600

APPROACH II—PERCENTAGE ADJUSTMENT

As its name implies, those accounts that are categorized as flexed accounts are adjusted up or down in terms of percentage to correspond with the changing activity levels. When flexing labor categories there are some limitations because staffing and crewing levels do not always convert to exact percentages. Also, some activities possess a floor and a ceiling, which simply should not be flexed below or above. Remember the earlier example of the department in which the volume was off budget by 55%, but because of the standby nature of some flexed accounts, the lowest flexed percentage was 30%.

APPROACH III—RATE APPLICATION

Based upon the master budget, a rate is established for each account or group of accounts that are to be flexed. The accounts are totaled on an annual basis and divided by the activity units. This rate could be airline miles flown, hours operated, units produced, etc. The following case in point is based on an actual situation and will adequately cover this process.

A case in point—how Miles Transportation Company flexes its budget

Miles Transportation Company recently hired a new operations manager whose nickname was "Longhaul." In his new capacity, Longhaul was responsible for managing that portion of the business which was driver or road related. He was not responsible for fleet maintenance or warehousing activities. Although Longhaul was a proven administrator, he had never worked with a flexible budget prior to coming to Miles Transportation. Since he was not with the firm when his budget was prepared, he was interested in what constituted his budget, especially the vehicle account. This account collected all of the vehicle related charges—fuel, oil, repairs, fixed lease payments, licenses, and insurance.

As Longhaul began to review his budget with the assistant controller, it became quite evident that the vehicle account was being flexed incorrectly, because cases hauled and not miles driven was the flexing factor. Using cases hauled ignored varying case configurations per load, empty back-hauls, or specialty runs that could not be classified as a case. At the conclusion of the indoctrination session, Longhaul asked the assistant controller to provide him with a synopsis of their meeting. This synopsis is shown below:

New Flexing Procedure

Per our conversation, the flexing of the vehicle account will be based upon actual miles driven and not cases. In order that you can audit this calculation each month, you simply subtract $6,180 from the budgeted amount, divide this by 24¢ per mile. The answer will be the miles driven by your drivers during the month. Exhibit 11-5 shows how the budget was flexed using miles driven and then compares them to the static budget and actuals for the same period.

Calculations Used in Preparing the 19X7 Static Budget

For your records, I am including the calculations used to compute the 19X7 budget

HOW TO USE AND BENEFIT FROM FLEXIBLE BUDGETING

data. The 19X7 budget was based on the following miles to be driven and expenses to be incurred:

Miles	90,155
Variable Expenses (Fuel and Oil)	$4,704
Other Controllable Expenses (Repair Parts/Labor, Sublet)	16,905
Fixed Expenses	6,180

The following calculations substantiate the revised year-to-date flexed vehicle charges:

Base Budget Dollars/Month[1]	$27,789
Less Fixed Expenses	(6,180)
Variable/Other Expenses	$21,609
Divided by 90,155/Miles	
Equals Budget Cost/Mile	.2397¢

With the added insight coupled with his trucking experience, Longhaul was better able to administer his section.

EXHIBIT 11-5
Flexing Application—Miles Transportation Co.

Year-to-date Adjustments Using Miles Driven as the Flex Factor

Base Cost/Mile .2397 X Actual Miles + Fixed Expenses = Flexed Dollars

Month	Actual Miles	X Rate =	Flexed Var/ Other Exp.	+ Fixed = Exp.	Total Charges
Jan.	64,892	.2397	$15,555	$ 6,180	$21,735
Feb.	59,014	.2397	14,146	6,180	20,326
Mar.	45,810	.2397	10,981	6,180	17,161
TOTAL	169,716	.2397	$40,682	$18,540	$59,222

Year-to-date Comparison to Static Budget & Actuals

A comparison of revised flexed dollars to base budget dollars (27,200/Month) and actual dollars follows:

Month	Flexed Budget $	Static Budget $	Actual $	Variance Budget vs. Flexed	Variance Actual vs. Flexed
Jan.	$21,735	$27,200	$28,979	(5,465)	(7,244)
Feb.	20,326	27,200	20,255	(6,874)	71
Mar.	17,161	27,200	14,492	(10,039)	2,669
TOTAL	$59,222	$81,600	$63,726	$ (22,378)	$ (4,504)

---

[1] *Note:* Budget dollars/month were reduced from 27,789 to 27,200 by top management directive. However, no support received to indicate where the reductions occurred. Considering fixed expenses remain constant, dollar reduction in variable/other expenses would reduce miles proportionately, thereby retaining an identical cost/mile rate of .2397¢.

FLEXIBLE BUDGETING AS A FORECASTING TOOL

Preparing weekly profit projections

The application of flexible budgeting techniques need not be restricted to that of a control tool. The same approach that flexes or adjusts individual accounts to reflect volume fluctuations can be put to work as a forecasting tool. The use of flexing as a forecasting tool is best performed at the income statement level. The same results can be achieved with a lot less effort than working at the detail account level within each and every cost center. The procedure is simple, all you have to do is to determine what portion or percentage of each individual income statement line can be related to changes in volume and what portion is static. E.g.: If warehousing and transportation costs appear on your income statement as a line item, possibly 65% of the dollars shown reflects volume and 35% is relatively fixed.

PROJECTION USING FLEXIBLE BUDGETING TECHNIQUES

Case in point—how R. Ross Mfg. Co. prepares its weekly profit projection using flexible budgeting techniques

The R. Ross Manufacturing Company has a P&L category labeled Distribution Expense. This company knows that for each unit it distributes, its variable cost will be 30 cents per unit. In their static budget for the month of August, their distribution cost was forecast at $750,000 and they anticipated handling 1,200,000 units. Unfortunately, July, a comparable month, was down by 200,000 units and August seems to be following right along. Every week the finance manager quickly prepares a current month's and quarterly forecast for his senior management. In order to forecast his August distribution cost, he simply reduces the $750,000 by the anticipated lost cases multiplied by the variable distribution cost rate of 30 cents per unit.

Distribution Cost Per Master Budget	$750,000
Less Anticipated Loss (200,000 @ 30c)	- 60,000
Anticipated August Distribution Cost	$690,000

This process can be repeated in all areas that can be identified as being affected by the decreased volume. Exhibit 11-6 shows the format and approach used to convert R. Ross Manufacturing's static budget into the August forecast. Exhibit 11-7 shows another format adapted by one company for monitoring various divisions using a minimum, most likely, and maximum level. Based on these inputs, senior management can make the timely and vital decisions.

The pocket profit projector

How many times has someone walked into your office and said, "How does the bottom line look this month?" or "With our current backlog, how much profit do you think we will generate next quarter?" Depending on how much accuracy and support data is required, your answer can be derived by using one of two alternate methods.

The first method is to convert your static budget projection into a more updated forecast by using the method described in the previous section of this chapter. This would be the approach if you wished to insure that all the known variables were included in your forecast. I.e., develop a forecast that is as accurate and complete as possible.

The second method will not provide you with a great deal of detail, but will be fairly accurate and will give you an answer in a matter of seconds. This approach is to develop a pocket projector.

Of course, the initial development will require investing four or five hours to develop this table, but once completed and tested, you and other key managers of your organization can easily project for themselves what the current period's anticipated results will bring

EXHIBIT 11-6
R. Ross Manufacturing Co.
Weekly Projection #32 Month of August
(000s)

	Prior Year August	Static Budget	Current Week Project'n	Prior Week Project'n	Variance From Prior Year	Variance From Static Budget
Units						
Budget	---	1,200	1,200			----
Actual or Project'n	1,150	----	1,000		(150)	
Change—Units			(200)			
%			(16.7%)			
Revenue	$ 5,465	$ 6,000	$ 5,000		$ (465)	$(1,000)
Cost of Sales						
Labor	655	720	600		55	120
Material	1,640	1,800	1,500		140	300
Variable O.H.	983	1,080	900		83	180
Fixed O.H.	78	85	85		(7)	----
Mfg. Variances	32	(85)	(35)		67	(50)
TOTAL	3,388	3,600	3,050		338	550
Gross Profit $	2,077	2,400	1,950	SAME AS PRIOR WEEKS	(127)	(450)
%	38%	40%	39%			
Expenses						
Development	124	145	135		(11)	10
Distribution	683	750	690		(7)	60
Advertising	173	180	150		23	30
Selling	218	240	240		(22)	----
Administration	109	120	120		(11)	----
Interest & Other	3	5	5		(2)	----
TOTAL	1,310	1,440	1,340		(30)	100
Profit Before Taxes	767	960	610		(157)	(350)
Taxes @ 50%	384	480	305		$ 79	$ 175
Net After Tax $	$ 383	$ 480	$ 305		(78)	(175)
	7.0	8.0	6.1			

Note: For this example Prior Weeks was the same and thus not entered. Advertising is accrued at 15c per unit.

EXHIBIT 11-7

PUBLIC CORPORATION
VISUAL & GRAPHIC COMMUNICATIONS GROUP

PROFITABILITY ANALYSIS

EXPECTED SALES LEVEL	BREAKEVEN $ Heads %	MINIMUM $ Heads %	MAXIMUM $ Heads %	MOST LIKELY $ Heads %	PRODUCT MIX DOLLAR ANALYSIS Hds. Hds. Hds. Hds. Hds.
SALES					
Direct Labor					
Direct Material					
Variable O.H.—Labor					
Variable O.H.—Non-Labor					
Fixed O.H.					
Total Overhead					
Total Cost					
Gross Margin					
Selling Expense					
Salesmen's Salaries/Comm.					
Other Salaries					
Non Labor					
Total Selling Expense					
General & Administrative Exp.					
Management Salaries					
Other Salaries					
Data Processing Costs					
Other Non-Labor Costs					
Total G & A Expense					
Corporate Charge					
Total Selling & G & A					
Operating Profit					
Non-Operating Expense					
Non-Operating Income					
Net Before Tax					
Fixed Cost Analysis					
Depreciation/Amortization					
Lease Payments					
Rent					
Utilities					
Taxes					
Other					
Total Fixed Costs					

NOTES:

HOW TO USE AND BENEFIT FROM FLEXIBLE BUDGETING

EXHIBIT 11-8
Pocket Profit Projector—Alternative Base Lines—Units

New Orders Booked (Weekly)		Current Backlog Level		Units Shipped	
Units (000)	Extended Dollars N.A.T.	Units (000)	Extended Dollars N.A.T.	Units (000)	Extended Dollars N.A.T.
.3	(12,145)	3	(12,145)	1	(12,145)
3.0	(8,950)	30	(8,950)	10	(8,950)
10.0	-0-	100	-0-	35	-0-
21.5	14,250	215	14,250	75	14,250
28.5	23,000	285	23,000	100	23,000
43.0	41,250	430	41,250	150	41,250
71.5	76,250	715	76,250	250	76,250

Notes: *How The Numbers Used In This Exhibit Were Derived*

— In order to break even, they need to ship 3,500 units per month.
— The production cycle is 2 1/2 months or 10 weeks.
— In order to break even, they need a backlog of 87,500 units, without any cushion for production delays. A cushion of approximately 14% has been added as a safety factor which brings the breakeven backlog level to 100,000 units. To determine any other point, multiply shipments X 2.5 production cycle + 14% safety factor and round.
— Continuing our example of a 10 week production cycle, in order to maintain a continuous production flow your "through-put" must be one week's production.

if orders continue at a certain rate, or if backlog remains at a specified level, or if shipment goals are reached. In its simplest form, the pocket profit projector is two vertical scales. By picking a point on the left-hand scale and drawing a horizontal line to a corresponding point on the right-hand scale, you can read the forecasted profit. Exhibit 11-8 demonstrates how your profit projector need not be confined to shipments or revenue levels, but may be used to forecast your profit levels based on orders booked or current backlog. Regardless of what projection techniques you are employing, you must always be aware of the extent mix shifts in either orders, backlog, or sales affect your gross profit. For more on mix shifts, see Chapter 6.

Once you have decided on what basis you wish to develop your profit projector (i.e., the left-hand scale), you will need to determine the following per unit figures:

—Revenue
—Gross Profit (assume a standard mix)
—Fixed Cost
—Net Before Taxes
—Net After Taxes

The reason these figures are computed on a per unit basis is to allow for the easy spreading of the fixed costs and any semi-variable costs. E.g.: the first 100 units each cost $1.00 and the second 100 units cost 50 cents each, etc. After you have computed the per unit profit at various levels, these figures multiplied by the corresponding volume level equal an estimated net profit level in total dollars *before* special adjustments. Exhibit 11-9 shows the development of a pocket profit projector. Exhibit 11-10 shows the results of consolidating a nine-column worksheet into the two-column pocket profit projector. Another format or alternative is to include a column showing fixed costs as part of the profit projector. Exhibit 11-11 will demonstrate to your management team how many units are required to cover your fixed costs.

You may also wish to develop several similar profit projectors, the only difference being that the gross profit margin will vary. In our example 40% was used, but two other projectors could be easily developed to show the effect of changing volume and gross profit at 35% and 45%.

A case in point—how various company executives use their pocket profit projector

The pocket profit projector could offer a wide range of possible uses to operating executives. The following applications are offered as a means of stimulating ideas of how you and your company can apply and benefit from the introduction of the pocket profit projector.

The chief executive officer of a multi-divisional company finds his pocket profit projector invaluable when conducting on spot plant visits or when talking to division general managers on the phone. This allows him to convert current activity levels into dollars and cents. These numbers can then be compared to the results of prior months or years or to the current period's profit plan or financial guide line. With live numbers easily at hand, a more meaningful dialogue can transpire.

HOW TO USE AND BENEFIT FROM FLEXIBLE BUDGETING

EXHIBIT 11-9
Pocket Profit Projector—Worksheet

Units Shipped (000's)	Average Revenue	Gross Profit	Variable Cost	Fixed Cost	Net before Taxes	Net After Tax @ 50%	Extended Dollars Net After Taxes	%
1				25.00	(24.29)	(12.145)	(12,145)	
5				5.00	(4.29)	(2.145)	(10,725)	
10				2.50	(1.79)	(.895)	(8,950)	
15				1.67	(.96)	(.480)	(7,200)	
20				1.25	(.54)	(.270)	(5,400)	
25				1.00	(.29)	(.145)	(3,625)	(4.1)
30				.83	(.12)	(.060)	(1,800)	
35				.71	--	--	--	
40				.63	.08	.040	1,600	
45				.56	.15	.075	3,375	
50	3.50	1.40	.69	.50	.21	.105	5,250	3.0
55				.45	.26	.130	7,150	
60				.42	.29	.145	8,700	
65				.39	.32	.160	10,400	
70				.36	.35	.175	12,250	
75				.33	.38	.190	14,250	5.4
80				.31	.40	.200	16,000	
85				.29	.42	.210	17,850	
90				.28	.43	.215	19,350	
95				.26	.45	.225	21,375	
100				.25	.46	.230	23,000	6.6
125				.20	.51	.255	31,875	
150				.16	.55	.275	41,250	
175				.14	.57	.285	49,875	
200				.12	.59	.295	59,000	
250				.10	.61	.305	76,250	8.7

Note: Total Fixed Costs per month—$25,000

EXHIBIT 11-10
Pocket Profit Projector

Units Shipped (000's)	Extended Dollars N.A.T.
1	(12,145)
5	(10,725)
10	(8,950)
15	(7,200)
20	(5,400)
25	(3,625)
30	(1,800)
35	------
40	1,600
45	3,375
50	5,250
55	7,150
60	8,700
65	10,400
70	12,250
75	14,250
80	16,000
85	17,850
90	19,350
95	21,375
100	23,000
125	31,875
150	41,250
175	49,875
200	59,000
250	76,250

EXHIBIT 11-11
Pocket Profit Projector

Units Shipped (000')	Fixed Cost Absorption	Extended Dollars N.A.T.
1	25.00	(12,145)
5	5.00	(10,725)
10	2.50	(8,950)
15	1.67	(7,200)
20	1.25	(5,400)
25	1.00	(3,625)
30	.83	(1,800)
35	.71	-----
40	.63	1,600
45	.56	3,375
50	.50	5,250
55	.45	7,150
60	.42	8,700
65	.39	10,400
70	.36	12,250
75	.33	14,250
80	.31	16,000
85	.29	17,850
90	.28	19,350
95	.26	21,375
100	.25	23,000
125	.20	31,875
150	.16	41,250
175	.14	49,875
200	.12	59,000
250	.10/1,000 units	76,250

HOW TO USE AND BENEFIT FROM FLEXIBLE BUDGETING

The chief financial officer of a construction products company employs a set of pocket profit projectors using current backlog levels, each of which reflects a somewhat different mix and thus varying gross profit returns to complete his long range planning charts. Because of the long delivery lead time, he wants a glimpse at his profit levels and cash generation levels a year or a year and a half from now without going through a lot of detail. Only when the profit projector indicates future problems will he consider undertaking the lengthy process of forecasting future results based on current backlog levels.

The group controller of a highly diverse multi-plant company uses his pocket profit projector as a means of evaluating the weekly flash numbers that each division is required to call into his office each week stating their key financial data and projecting monthly profit levels. He also uses it as a training and incentive tool for the division's general managers and sales managers so they may continually reappraise themselves as to what volume levels are required in order to meet their profit objectives. As an example, in the first or second week of the month, he will remind them that of this date, with shipments at a certain level, they haven't begun to cover their fixed and variable costs.

12

MACHINE-HOUR RATES— PROVEN PROFIT GENERATOR

Chapter 6 initiated a series of chapters which addressed specialized areas and techniques. The techniques covered in the prior half dozen chapters provided you with a kit of tools which when implemented would allow for the easy introduction of machine-hour rates (MHR) in your company. Thus, the machine-hour rate is a bonus analytical and control tool. MHR is a natural by-product of those steps already implemented in achieving an operational approach to financial analysis.

FIRST STEP—UNDERSTANDING AND APPLYING OVERHEAD

Understanding the overhead pool

Overhead costs are those indirect production costs which are not prime costs, such as labor and materials. Some organizations expand this concept to include *all* indirect costs. (See Exhibit 10-5, C. Lynn Distribution Co.) In reviewing this exhibit, C. Lynn's expense pool for its customer service department is $295,885 for six months. C. Lynn arrived at this amount by using a three-step process. Chapter 10 showed you how to segregate, categorize, and analyze your firm's cost and expenses in the following three-step process:

The first step was to study and analyze your firm's organization and define a cost center structure for collecting, budgeting, and analyzing your costs and expenses along organizational and functional lines.

The second step was to understand the relationship between fixed, variable, and controllable costs. Special attention was also directed to the classification of labor costs, because this is one area that is truly controllable by operating managers.

MACHINE-HOUR RATES—PROVEN PROFIT GENERATOR

The third and final step was to show the conversion of these cost groupings into the formation of a breakeven chart. This transition was accomplished by adding a simple but highly effective cost control block to the chart that allows the breakeven to be a control tool usable by various segments of management.

C. Lynn, because of its excellent service record, had found there was a growing demand for its service. C. Lynn decided to expand this function and planned to eventually spin-it-off as a separate venture. These requirements, with a desire to become more cost effective, forced C. Lynn to examine their overhead pool further. In examining their pool of dollars, they decided on three labor classifications:

Delivery & Installation —Labor	$ 5,586
Field Service & Repairs—Labor	47,044
Shop Service & Repair —Labor	56,618
Total Direct Labor	$109,248

Total direct labor would now be a direct cost. This would now reduce the pool by $109,248 and create a new pool for six months of $186,637.

Four ways of applying the overhead pool

Once the overhead pool has been developed, it is necessary to find an easy and appropriate base for distributing a portion of this pool throughout the year (in our example six months) and to each production order.

Although there are many methods for applying or spreading the overhead pool, four methods are generally accepted:

—As a percentage of direct labor dollars.
—Units produced.
—Direct labor hours.
—Machine-hours.

What these four methods have in common is that they all produce an overhead rate. This rate is computed simply by dividing the overhead pool by the selected divisor. Using C. Lynn's overhead pool, it could be spread as follows:

Percentage of direct labor

$$\frac{\text{Pool}}{\text{Direct Labor}} = \frac{\$186,637}{\$109,248} = 171\%$$

Units—Products

$$\frac{\text{Pool}}{\text{Units}} = \frac{\$186,637}{2,950} = \text{OH rate per unit of } \$63.27$$

Direct Labor Hours

$$\frac{\text{Pool}}{\text{Hours}[1]} = \frac{\$186,637}{19,863} = \text{OH rate per hour of } \$9.40$$

$$[1]\frac{109,248}{\$5.50/\text{hr}} = 19,863 \text{ hours}$$

These three methods are appropriate for C. Lynn's expanded service function because their repair function does not require a heavy or extensive machine capability.

UTILIZING THE MACHINE-HOUR RATE

MHR is the most desirable overhead application method when machines dominate the production or conversion process. The MHR is best applied when a production facility is departmentalized or arranged by machine center. A machine center can be developed based on several criteria:

—*Type*—   (In a printing plant, equipment type would be press dept., composition dept., binding)

—*Capabilities*— (Sheet fed press vs. a web press or 2-color press vs. 4-color press or letter press vs. offset)

—Value—   (High or low investment)

—Usage—   (High or low hours)

—Crewing—   (Automated vs. semi-automated or none)

Once the MHR center has been established using any one of the above criteria, the indirect costs and direct labor costs associated with the center should be identified. These dollars will form the MHR dollar pool, which will become the basis for the computation of the MHR hourly rate.

Computing the MHR or C. Lynn's conversion to a machine-hour rate

C. Lynn Distribution Co. feels it can best capitalize on its expansion plans by specializing and converting to semi-automated equipment, planning eventually to curtail all outside activities. Since they will not have to lay off any employees, their cost structure for six months will be $295,885 (remember the direct labor is included) plus additional fixed costs for the new equipment of $25,000 (for the six-month period). This will bring the total pool to $320,885.

They anticipate operating the equipment on a five day basis consisting of two ten-hour shifts with the remaining four hours for maintenance. In addition, every six months they plan to shut down the process for a one-week overhaul. A six-month period will contain 2430 available MHR's. The available hours were computed as follows:

```
  365 days per year
 -104 less weekends
 -  8 less holidays
 - 10 less plant shutdowns for overhaul
  243 days
X  20 hours per day (2-10 hour shifts)
4,860 available hours
```

In C. Lynn's case, they are only concerned with a six-month period or half of the available hours (2,430 hours). Remember, when considering any period greater or shorter than a year to count the number of available workdays in order to reflect the correct number of weekends and holidays.

Example: If you were computing the number of workdays in the fourth quarter and your plant was closed the day after Thanksgiving and half days prior to Christmas and New Year's, you would have half of your eight holidays occurring in the fourth calendar quarter.

So to compute the Machine-Hour Rate, simply divide the increased pool of $320,885 by the 2430 available hours.

$$\frac{\text{Pool}}{\text{Hours}} \quad \frac{\$320,885}{2,430} = \$132.05 \text{ per machine hour}$$

As C. Lynn expands and adds more and different equipment, it will adopt the machine-cost-center concept.

Why does C. Lynn's management use and value the MHR

C. Lynn, as many other management teams, uses the MHR because it:

— Provides financial management with complete cost information for measuring product line profitability.

— Provides cost estimating with accurate data for pricing, thus insuring that a product is not over- or under-priced.

— Provides manufacturing with information as to the value of each machine-cost-center, thus curtailing idle time.

— Provides marketing with product mix relationships. This identifies the amount of cost absorption so that slow moving products do not tie up production's most expensive equipment.

— Provides an accurate product cost picture for both product and manufacturing engineering, so they can spot the need to make changes in product design, tooling, and/or processing methods.

— Provides sales with accurate data so they can quote the best available price to their customers.

— Provides senior management with the assurance they have the best insight into gross margin, the relationship between their product cost and selling price, which in reality is set by the law of supply and demand.

13

PLUGGING THOSE OFT-TIME OVERLOOKED PROFIT LEAKS WITH PROFIT ENRICHMENT PROGRAMS

This chapter tells you how to identify and plug those hidden cost leaks which day in and day out erode your profits. This action program is called P.E.P. P.E.P. is more than a series of checklists, it is the vehicle for:

1. Making cost control and profit improvement a continuing way of life.
2. Instituting profit improvement actions which do not fade when the emphasis on cost reduction lessens.
3. Plugging cost drains at the user level.

I.e., it is easier and more effective to stop expenditures when the purchase order requisition is written rather than when the invoice is paid.

What P.E.P. is not!

P.E.P. is not a typical cost reduction program, because most cost reduction programs are single-shot activities and the results are not continually measured. Most cost reduction programs do not attempt to get behind the scenes and to get to the true source of increased costs. Unfortunately, in many cases managers and supervisors are not aware of these hidden areas which are shrinking their profits, and they offer the wrong type of direction to their subordinates when costs have to be cut.

A case in point—the cost reduction memo as an ineffective cost cutter

When many firms embark on a cost reduction program, they feel a need to offer specific cost cutting recommendations. They fall into the "you must cut costs by X%" trap by writing a cost-cutting memo similar to the one received by J.R. Hardworking in Chapter 10. Thus they issue memos like the following:

To: All Department Heads

Re: Today's Cost Reductions & Tomorrow's Profits

This year's sales could come up short as a result of supply problems. Costs could skyrocket during the shortage period, without *daily* attention.

Think before you spend! Hold purchases that can be held. Get production for your dollars. Analyze overtime requirements.

TIGHTEN UP ON ALL FRONTS!!!

Be aware—escalating prices and costs on all fronts could cause a negative, psychological reaction in your troops—a "What's the use attitude." Guard against this in your areas.

In spite of the spiraling costs of supplies and services, volume limiting shortages, *we are going to make a profit.* Your contribution helps determine how much.

Cost Reduction Memo #2

To: Supervision

Re: Cost Cutting

Both internal and external business conditions dictate an awareness and improved implementation of such basic management credos as the following:

* Productivity is essential, thus non-performance and poor attitudes will not be tolerated.
* Working hours will be rigid!
* You will reduce the use of supplies.
* You will restrict telephone usage to company matters.
* Be vigilant regarding use of the copying machine.

Both of these memo writers had the best of intentions, but they were ineffective in cutting costs because they attempted to be dictatorial rather than helpful. Management relied on a memo to motivate their employees, but the recommendations were not specific because they did not stimulate in-depth ideas which could have a lasting, corrective impact.

What is P.E.P.?

P.E.P. is short for profit enrichment program. P.E.P. is a systematic approach to developing information, diagnosing, and identifying conditions which erode profits. This profit erosion syndrome need not be confined to business, but is also apparent in hospitals, governmental agencies, and other institutions.

P.E.P. is the result of a highly diversified company's attempt to find a common denominator or approach in cost improvement for similar, but unrelated businesses.

P.E.P. was their first attempt at a systematic approach. The program at first was designed to provide an answer to the division manager's or controller's question—"But, how can we improve our division's profits, when you don't understand our business, and anyway our business is unique."

Thus P.E.P.'s conception and birth was out of necessity to provide an answer to the "our business is unique" syndrome. To meet this need, an umbrella program was developed that would identify cost drains in varied businesses such as film processing, metal working, printing, etc. The task was easy, simply identify those types of expenditures and functions which are common to all organizations. Over the past several years the concept has resulted in a series of checkoff lists or questionnaires. Their objective is to surface those hidden actions, approaches, techniques, methods, and procedures which are counter-productive and profit eroders. The questions are designed not just to point an accusing finger, but to initiate lasting corrective action. Exhibit 13-1 identifies 12 areas where those often overlooked profit leaks may occur and also serves as a table of contents for the lists which follow the exhibit (Exhibits 13-2 through 13-13). An additional checkoff list relating to profit erosion at the supervisory level is included as Exhibit 14-1 in the next chapter.

EXHIBIT 13-1
Table of Contents
P.E.P.'s 118 Questions for Profit Leak Detection

Exhibit	Topic
13-2	*Clerical Services*
	—files, paper processing, stenographic services
13-3	*Computerized Data Processing*
	—systems, programs, hardware, users
13-4	*Employee Turnover*
	—selection, indoctrination, training, promises, termination
13-5	*Forms*
	—control, coordination, completeness
13-6	*Housekeeping*
	—responsibility, program, obstructions
13-7	*Loss Prevention*
	—program, fire, security, safety
13-8	*Preventative Maintenance*
	—scheduling, productivity measurement, cost control
13-9	*Material Handling and Space Utilization*
	—handling techniques, space usage
13-10	*Standard Operating Procedures*
	—value checkoff list
13-11	*Supplies and Small Tools*
	—cribs and supply rooms, special tooling, pilferage
13-12	*Quality Assurance*
	—more than inspection, techniques, scrap control, training
13-13	*Utilities Conservation*
	—electrical, heat, air, water, sewage, communication

EXHIBIT 13-2
P.E.P. Profit Leak Detection Questionnaire
Clerical

1. When was the last time you conducted a *ruthless purge* of your files, or are you continuing to buy needless files and misuse valuable floor space?
2. Are you using either *micrographics* or *microfiche* to preserve key records?
3. Have you considered a *centralized record retention center* to eliminate personal files?
4. Does your internal correspondence have a *retention block,* and do you require the originator to specify how long this piece of correspondence or report should be kept active or filed?
5. Do you have *centralized typing* and *stenographic services* available, or must every manager have his own secretary?
6. How often do you survey your *reproduction equipment,* needs, location, utilization, security, etc?
7. When was the last time you listed, reviewed, and analyzed the *paperwork and reports* flow?
8. Are you sure you are not *staffing to meet peak clerical* work load periods?
9. Have you evaluated the *efficiency of clerical work stations* to insure the most efficient use and design of desks, tables, file cabinets, office machines, etc?
10. Do you seriously listen to employee complaints about excessive paperwork requirements?
11. Does every job have a *job description* and position manual complete with examples and techniques?
12. Do you apply an organized approach to paperwork by:
    a. Splitting up paperwork processing into three work periods per day?
    b. Pre-sorting and routing before it reaches your desk?
    c. Acting immediately to save handling it again?
    d. Keeping paperwork moving by handling small batches?
    e. Splitting large jobs into smaller jobs?
    f. Using tickler files for follow-up on uncompleted jobs?
    g. Retaining only necessary paperwork?
13. Do you adopt the "single file concept" where possible?
    —The single file concept requires only one four-drawer file. On New Year's Eve, move the contents of the first two drawers down one drawer. Remember to destroy or send to storage anything you can. The following diagram shows what should be contained in each drawer.

    Single File Concept
    1. *Current Year's Files*
    2. *Last Year's Files*
    3. *Necessary Records Older than Last Year*
    4. *Catalogues, Books, Reference Materials*

EXHIBIT 13-3
P.E.P. Profit Leak Detection Questionnaire
Computerized Data Processing (MIS)

1. Have you considered that some applications are best left in a manual mode?
2. Have you truly defined your *informational needs and data base* requirements?
3. Do you have a *master implementation plan* for incorporating your data processing needs that represents a complete management information system?
4. Do you screen and approve all requests for *subsystem development* to insure that they comply with the master plan or is subsystem design implemented to fight a fire?
5. Are *system design and programing efforts* planned, budgeted, and monitored, and most important, are they held to original objectives with modifications and changes being approved by all?
6. Is adequate program documentation provided so that changes can be easily instituted?
7. Are *user manuals* prepared and explained to ensure proper data input once a system is on line?
8. Do you have *adequate hardware backup* and are *up-to-date duplicate programs* kept in a remote fireproof area away from day-to-day operations?
9. Are users presented with a detailed list of their *computer usage and programing changes* on a monthly basis by job?

EXHIBIT 13-4
P.E.P. Profit Leak Detection Questionnaire
Employee Turnover

1. Are your supervisors aware of how expensive employee turnover can be?
2. Do your supervisors know the difference between "bossing" and *intelligent direction and leadership?*
3. Are new employees properly interviewed and selected based on the proper qualifications for the job to be done?
4. When a new employee arrives is he *properly indoctrinated,* introduced, and basically treated in a friendly manner? Is he acquainted with the unpleasant or dangerous parts of his job or is he left on his own?
5. Are *promises* made that cannot be fulfilled, especially those relating to wages, promotions, etc?
6. Do employees clearly understand management's aims and policies toward work and what constitutes a full day's work, or are they treated like mushrooms—kept in the dark and fed a lot of B.S.?
7. Do your supervisors rate employees on grounds other than competence, such as fraternal, religious, etc.?
8. Is a job description available for each employee, and is he allowed to remain in a position for which he is not mentally nor physically prepared?
9. Are men discharged without sufficient cause and is the pink slip used as a penalty?
10. Do you question men who leave of their own volition in order to seek out the true cause of their leaving and their attitude toward the company and supervision?

EXHIBIT 13-5
P.E.P. Profit Leak Detection Questionnaire
Forms

1. Who is responsible for systematizing, coordinating, and controlling your forms activity, or is it left to individual departments, which often over- or mis-order, mis-design, or fail to consider the impact upon other departments?
2. When was the last time you conducted a forms survey to determine the need to continue using existing forms and if there is a need for a new form?
3. Can a form have a multi-use or can it be combined with another form?
4. Before printing the form is the form checked to insure:
   a. The form has a title that expresses its purpose?
   b. A form code number has been assigned to aid identification in job description manuals and re-ordering?
   c. All data required has been included and organized in a simple and systematic manner?
   d. Consecutive numbering has been applied to those forms requiring it?
   e. Forms which are to be mailed are designed so they can be placed in window envelopes?
   f. Specifications and design criteria are adhered to, such as typewritten tab stops, color, weight of paper, ink, etc.?
   g. If your form travels outside of your office, have you checked with the user and public relations before printing in regard to image, logo, etc.?

EXHIBIT 13-6
P.E.P. Profit Leak Detection Questionnaire
Housekeeping

1. Does your firm understand that supervision is the key to achieving a beneficial and cost effective housekeeping program? Does it clearly assign responsibility?
2. Does the head of housekeeping make regular inspections and does he get cooperation from department foremen?
3. Is your housekeeping program planned or a haphazard one which reduces efficiency and hikes costs?
4. If you do have a program, does it include minimum standards, balanced work schedules, training courses, and inspection criteria?
5. Are work stations kept neat in order to provide an efficient workplace that fosters quality, or do you find oily rags, idle equipment, and clutter scattered on the floor?
6. Are salvagable materials isolated so that they can be sold or reclaimed, or are they left around or swept away with the trash?
7. Are yards and aisles cluttered and obstructed so materials do not easily flow through the production process?
8. Is your production floor littered with excess tables, benches, racks, cabinets, and old and unused equipment that collects clutter and impedes the production process?

EXHIBIT 13-7
P.E.P. Profit Leak Detection Questionnaire
Loss Prevention

1. Do you have a loss prevention plan that includes security, safety, fire prevention, and is it one individual's major or full-time responsibility?
2. Do you have a fire protection and safety committee with an organized training program which is more than just posters and handouts?
3. Do you conduct regular loss prevention surveys?
4. Are you making full use of insurance company accident prevention services?
5. Do you have up-to-date automatic fire and security detection and protection equipment; if so, when was it last tested and inspected?
6. Have you considered replacing or supplementing watchmen with closed-circuit television and other detection devices?
7. Do you have too many time clocks and are they located strategically to discourage punching co-workers' cards? Is employee pilferage allowed to run rampant, because employees check out at scattered time clocks and leave through mass exits?

EXHIBIT 13-8
P.E.P. Profit Leak Detection Questionnaire
Preventative Maintenance

1. Is there a scheduled preventative maintenance program, and is it conducted with a production schedule to minimize conflict and lost time?
2. Do you control your maintenance activities via work orders, with time and materials applied to that task?
3. Do you apply labor standards to your maintenance activity (especially repetitive jobs) and monitor them according to some form of work measurement to achieve the highest possible productivity level?
4. Are maintenance supervisors provided with cost feedback in the form of cost accounting reports?
5. Are maintenance supplies and critical spare parts inventoried so that lost time does not occur awaiting parts?
6. Do you have an on-going training program which instructs the employee as to the proper use of equipment to minimize damage and wear?
7. Is there an equipment malfunction card maintained for each piece of equipment—service and repair?
8. Does your firm use "cause codes" spotlighting repetitive repairs, and do you regularly review the results of procedure to identify trends?

EXHIBIT 13-9
P.E.P. Profit Leak Detection Questionnaire
Material Handling and Space Utilization

1. Do you pay enough attention to the routing of materials through the plant and to the placement of machines and other permanent equipment?

PLUGGING THOSE OFT-TIME OVERLOOKED PROFIT LEAKS

2. Are workers allowed to leave portable tools, ladders, wheelbarrows, etc., in the way of other workers at both work stations and in passageways?
3. Is needed space kept unusable awaiting roof or floor repair?
4. Do you fail to take advantage of vendors' warehousing capabilities for carrying your inventory, especially materials that can be delivered in one hour?
5. Do you handle drums instead of pumping from storage tanks or continue to handle 50- and 100-pound bags when your usage is over 1,000,000 pounds?
6. Are you assigning material handlers (loaders) by area and not by job, and are crew sizes based on custom rather than by labor standards?
7. Do you fail to ship in bulk containers between plants, and once inside the plant, are you handling single pieces rather then combining to make unit loads?
8. Are your conveyors flexible, and are they designed to do secondary operations such as automatic weighing, counting, sorting, etc.?
9. Do you allow improper and inefficient lighting that curtails the use of badly needed space?
10. Are work stations properly laid out with lockers and supplies and are tool cribs easily accessible?
11. Are unnecessary materials, scraps, and surplus parts kept at work stations?
12. Are unused machinery and equipment which could be sold allowed to take up valuable work and storage space or interfere with the efficient flow of materials?
13. Do you make maximum use of material handling equipment such as cranes, lifts, conveyors, etc.?

EXHIBIT 13-10
P.E.P. Profit Leak Detection Questionnaire
Standard Operating Procedures—Their Values

By not having standard operating procedures you are wasting profits by:

1. Not providing employees with a guide to an approved method of operation and therefore keeping them uninformed and ineffective.
2. Not furnishing a means by which inter-departmental activities are co-ordinated and thus unnecessary operations and costs not eliminated.
3. Not allowing current practices to be scrutinized, analyzed, simplified, and standardized.
4. Not eliminating the need for relying on snap judgments, trusting to memory, and oral instructions.
5. Hindering the establishment of cost controls because the best way of getting something done has not been defined.
6. Not monitoring the work as to proper sequence and coordination so that waste is avoided and assets are properly used and maximized.
7. Impeding supervision, thus not allowing for the proper evaluation of employee effectiveness and productivity.
8. Hampering the transfer and interchange of personnel between departments thus not providing the best people match for the need.

9. Slowing down the decision-making process and allowing for repetition of the same wrong or incomplete decision.

EXHIBIT 13-11
P.E.P. Profit Leak Detection Questionnaire
Supplies and Small Tools

1. Are your tools and supplies standardized throughout all departments so as to cut down on the number of items carried in inventory plus the paperwork associated with maintaining these items?
2. Do you maintain a tool and supply room that issues items by requisition and inventories the contents regularly?
3. Have you trained your tool and supply room personnel to be alert to abnormal consumption levels?
4. Do your craftsmen supply their own standard tools so they will exercise more care, and is there a cash allowance provided for this purpose?
5. Does your engineering department approve all purchase requisitions for special tools and supplies?
6. Do you ever consider renting before purchasing special tools?
7. What steps do you institute against pilferage of tools (especially those that could be used at home) once the tools are issued from the crib?

EXHIBIT 13-12
P.E.P. Profit Leak Detection Questionnaire
Quality Assurance

1. Does your Q.C. department understand that their job is more than inspecting but improving product quality?
2. Is Q.C. involved in vendor selection and setting and reviewing raw material specifications?
3. Does your Q.C. department have the authority to stop production when quality falls off, and is Q.C. protected from being overruled by the department foreman?
4. Does Q.C. receive and evaluate customer complaints, rather than the department foreman, and are these complaints evaluated on a percent defective basis?
5. Do you use statistical techniques (sampling) rather than the less effective 100% inspection, and are specification control charts maintained to prevent processes from getting out of hand?
6. Do you take the following steps to control scrap? (see Chapter 7):
    a. Compare scrap generation ratio and percentages to industry average.
    b. Segregate avoidable scrap from scrap.
    c. Have cost accounting issue scrap, spoilage, yield, and re-work reports.
    d. Attempt to re-work or re-cycle rejected materials.
    e. Receive competitive bids from scrap dealers and have physical control over what leaves the plant as scrap.
7. Do you involve your Q.C. department in value analysis to reduce cost and improve reliability?

8. Does Q.C. establish adequate training programs and competition between shifts and crews in order to maintain worker interest in product quality and reliability?

EXHIBIT 13-13
P.E.P. Profit Leak Detection Questionnaire
Conservation

1. Is everyone in your organization sensitive to *electrical conservation* and achieving the most efficient use of electrical equipment and lighting? Has a program been formalized complete with objectives?
2. Have you evaluated your heating needs? Have you checked *heat* recovery potential and checked insulation for heat leaks along with the relation between space, heat, and needs?
3. How often do you check your *compressed air system* for leakage and inefficient operation so that tool efficiency will not be cut or electrical power wasted?
4. At how many points in your production process could you re-use *water*, and have you recently checked all obvious water wasting techniques and practices?
5. How closely are you monitoring *sewage* costs to insure that they are based on contribution to the sewage system and not water consumed? Can you re-use treated water?
6. When was the last time you conducted a *communications* survey to match costs with needs?

QUESTIONING IS NOT THE END BUT THE BEGINNING

P.E.P. is a program and the P.E.P. profit leak detection questionnaires are just one part of the program. The total program is outlined in Exhibit 13-14.

EXHIBIT 13-14
10-Point Checkoff List for Achieving
a Successful Profit Enrichment Program

1. Plan your program.
2. Gain support at all levels for your plan and program.
3. Ask your questions with tact and understanding.
4. Analyze your answers.
5. Develop solutions in conjunction with the people who are responsible.
6. Set a timetable for implementing solutions along with measurement milestone points.
7. Determine the cost effect, if any, of the corrective action on other areas of the organization.
8. Follow up by asking the same questions over again at a later date. This will help to curtail backsliding into old habits and routines.
9. Add new questions to your P.E.P. checkoff list that are especially tailored to your organization.
10. Don't try to run the program from behind your desk; get out into the field or plant and see first hand what is happening!

14

PEOPLE INVOLVEMENT— KEY TO LASTING COST REDUCTIONS

Most articles and texts on cost reduction and many unenlightened businessmen feel that all incentive and leadership for cost reduction and profit improvement flows from the top downward, but rarely ever seeps upward from the ranks. Organizations subscribing to this philosophy are excluding one of their most valuable resources for profit leak detection and the implementation of solutions—the person who works on the job daily. If provided with proper data, he is in the best position for making a lasting impact. There are many methods for harnessing this power and incorporating it into your business. This chapter will tell you how to tap this valuable resource by:

1. Reminding you that your first level of supervision is your first line of defense against profit erosion.
2. Establishing a suggestion system, so that profit leak detection and profit improvement are not confined exclusively to the higher levels of management.
3. Organizing three special teams with a prescribed approach and discipline rather than the "it's time we got together and cut costs" teams which are so prevalent.
4. Installing incentive, bonus, and profit sharing plans as a means of making the personnel of your firm profit partners rather than just employees.

FIRST LEVEL SUPERVISION—YOUR FIRST LINE OF DEFENSE

Put your indicators and management information to work

The previous chapters have provided you with many beneficial approaches on how to obtain, interpret, and analyze data. But are you disseminating this data outward and

KEY TO LASTING COST REDUCTIONS

downward to those who can truly control costs? Many organizations choose to hold operating data and financial information within the confines of top management and fail to channel the data downward into the lower management and supervisoral ranks. Furthermore, they fail to provide the instructions of how to use this data effectively.

As operational financial analysts, it is our job to assist those members of our management team who daily man our forward cost control positions with simple indicators and programs, and not lengthy reports. All a department head may need to monitor his day-to-day operations effectively is a few simple ratios, percentages, key data, etc. This data coupled with the tools provided in the previous chapters can provide him with a fighting edge. To insure that this data is properly used and not wasted, be sure to work and coach these individuals. I.e., don't just prepare the reports, be sure they are being implemented and of some use. Don't treat first level supervisors as the forgotten people of business.

The forgotten people

Much is said and written today about the first level supervision being the forgotten people of business, especially the production foreman. He always seems to be caught in between workers, unions, upper management, rules, schedules, etc., and thus his time is divided so severely that his effectiveness is watered down. First level supervision, especially the production foreman, is your first line of defense for insuring that costs, quality, and productivity schedules are all controlled and maximized. Failure to do so will cause permanent damage. Exhibit 14-1 forms a checkoff list for stopping 23 negative factors that will erode profits in the areas of communication, productivity, misuse of machines, and quality.

EXHIBIT 14-1
Foreman and First Level Supervision Cost Erosion Prevention
23-Point Checkoff List

Foreman and first level supervision can erode profits by inadvertently:

Communications

1. Not cooperating 100% with management in its goals, objectives, educational programs, suggestion systems, safety programs, etc.
2. Not understanding or interpreting orders and instructions correctly received.
3. Not making orders and instructions clear to subordinates.

Productivity

4. Not communicating to employees what constitutes a full day's work.
5. Not policing workers in regard to intentionally doing less work than they can or ordering overtime work that could have been avoided.
6. Not pre-planning a worker's schedules as to starting time, and after he starts, insuring there are no delays between jobs or waiting for materials.
7. Not organizing his own time and work, being unnecessarily absent or tardy or getting into the habit of visiting, talking, killing time, and delaying the rendering of decisions.

Misuse of Machines

8. Not seeing that the men are supplied with the proper tools and equipment and abusing small machines on large or heavy work.
9. Not making regular inspections of equipment and keeping it in good operating condition.
10. Not planning nor understanding machine capacity, so there is full and proper machine utilization, i.e., large and powerful machines are not wasted on small jobs.
11. Not allowing needed repairs or allowing men to make "shoestring repairs" or repairing equipment that should be scrapped.

Quality

12. Not tracing down or following-up defective work to the man who performed the work so it can be corrected.
13. Not monitoring employee health and eyesight as a possible cause of poor quality work.
14. Not checking production documents, instructions, blueprints, or machine calibrations and settings. Giving improper instructions plus not following each job through to completion.
15. Not stopping defective material from going through as standard or scrapping materials that could have been salvaged.
16. Not knowing what type and quantity of parts and supplies should be ordered, ordering more materials than necessary, and not returning excess to stock and failing to see that materials are properly piled or stored.

Employee Relations

17. Not treating people as individuals and taking for granted their abilities and shortcomings, especially as it relates to their ability to produce.
18. Not showing an interest in a worker's progress and personal affairs and forgetting to commend him for a job well done.
19. Not properly screening an employee before assigning him to do a job for which he is not mentally or physically qualified or permitting him to remain on the job when he is ill.
20. Not considering problems relating to wages, promotions, working conditions, and safety.
21. Not setting a good example as regards safety practices, allowing men to work without protective devices (goggles, helmets, etc.), and not conscientiously conducting safety inspections.
22. Not cooperating with other foremen, departments, and functions.
23. Not halting gossip and tale-bearing, cliques, agitation by disgruntled employees, and generally failing to promote friendliness and cooperation at all levels.

SUGGESTION SYSTEMS GET EVERYONE INVOLVED

In 1975, the National Association of Suggestion Systems, Chicago, released its latest figures stating that for every dollar invested in a plant suggestion system, the return on investment averages 570%, and this return is increasing every year. The Association also states that where these systems are installed, management can count on an average of 40 suggestions per 100 workers.

A suggestion system can be installed for under fifty dollars. All you need is a couple of boxes, three-part speedy memos, and the appointment of a suggestion system administrator. Many companies fail to receive all of the benefits that a suggestion system can generate, because of a lack of publicity, true employee involvement, and the appointment of a competent and interested administrator.

KEY TO LASTING COST REDUCTIONS

A case in point—how 7 different companies handled their suggestion systems

Company A—The job of evaluating the ideas submitted and the potential cost saving was assigned to the chief industrial engineer. He squashed all of the truly good ideas, while letting the mediocre ones pass. He felt that the good ideas were a reflection of his department's inability to do a good job of cost cutting.

Solution—His attitude changed when he realized the company wanted to tap this source and that it was not a reflection on him.

Company B—This company has a few scattered shoe boxes placed in obscure locations with no procedure or awards. Although unproductive, they still have a program.

Solution—With the appointment of a responsible administrator, the system was brought to life.

Company C—The supervisors in this company do not encourage their subordinates to generate ideas because they feel it is a poor reflection on them as supervisors.

Solution—After the company implemented improved supervisory training classes, foremen were made aware of the benefits. The company then began to receive many worthwhile ideas. Cash awards were given along with recognition to the employees.

Company D—A large steel company has developed a double-page magazine advertising campaign based around the award winning employee and his suggestion.

Company E—A very prominent weapons system company has the local press cover their quarterly awards presentation dinner. Because of the large employment afforded the community by this company, they are eager to demonstrate how it rewards its employees for ideas. This is a way to attract other qualified personnel.

Company F—A large motion picture film processor is very quick to tell you how one of their foremen submitted an idea which allowed them to generate well over one million dollars in additional revenue. It also earned them a most coveted Academy Award Oscar.

Company G—This firm has instituted "Call Now." The employee dials an extension where his idea is recorded, i.e., the idea is only a phone call away.

The value of special teams

In many instances one of the best and most productive means of cost reduction and profit improvement is the combining of different disciplines and approaches into special teams or task forces. Unfortunately, in many companies these teams evolve only when there is a problem or fire to fight. In a metal manufacturing company these teams would include a member from engineering, fabrication, assembly, inspection, and finance. These teams are organized and meet on a regular basis to update, communicate, and exchange ideas with other members of the team in regard to on-going projects, or they can be formed and only meet under special conditions such as the assembly team. The assembly team is only called into service when a new product or subassembly is close to entering into the production cycle. The remainder of this section discusses three types of special teams:

—Value Analysis Teams
—Work Simplification Teams
—Production Assembly Teams

The reason you should consider these particular teams is that they are goal oriented and offer an easily implementable approach and discipline. Other forms of cost-cutting teams are usually undisciplined in approach and method and thus are ineffective.

Value analysis teams

Value analysis teams usually consist of three members of the organization with different disciplines, such as manufacturing, engineering, and cost accounting. Whereas cost-cutting and reduction programs strive to eliminate the item or replace it with a lower cost item, value analysis is *function* oriented, i.e., the item itself is not examined and analyzed, but the function it serves. While traditionally V.A. is primarily applied to product cost reduction, the technique can be applied elsewhere in the organization wherever an expenditure is made.

Value analysis sets into motion a simple systematic technique called the value analysis program or job plan. The steps are as follows:

STEP 1: SELECTION OF ITEM TO BE ANALYZED

A choice is made based on the following considerations—production quantities, design status, production status and present value of item, especially if it has high value and multiple uses.

STEP 2: GATHERING OF INFORMATION

This is accomplished by asking a series of fundamental questions:

a. What is its function, and is it required?

b. What are the customer's requirements?

c. What are the current costs?

d. What should it cost?—Define a target.

STEP 3: CREATION OF ALTERNATIVES

Explore alternative approaches to fulfilling the function. Remember, the emphasis is always on the function. The goal of the study is *not* to produce the same item at a lower cost, which is the fundamental approach of traditional cost-cutting methods.

STEP 4: COST EVALUATION

Each alternative is analyzed and evaluated to determine which is the lowest cost method. The method or alternative is only selected if it will accomplish the function and will result in a net overall saving without downgrading design.

STEP 5: FEASIBILITY EVALUATION

The new method or approach should be technically evaluated to assure complete and satisfactory implementation into the production process.

KEY TO LASTING COST REDUCTIONS

STEP 6: IMPLEMENTATION AND FOLLOW-UP

In order to properly introduce a proposal, the implementation package should include method instructions, production and procurement instructions, drawing, etc. At this point, it is imperative not to impede the receptiveness of future ideas or kill the program completely, i.e., don't blow the game in the last inning.

A case in point—how V.A. saved Meredith Electronics $10,500

Meredith Electronics found themselves with voids or gaps in one of their major product lines. If the voids were going to continue, their competition would eventually make inroads into their product line and gain market dominance. Meredith's marketing strategy was to be dominant and command at least 75% of this market, so they decided to fill the gaps. They designed and introduced into production an expanded line capable of filling all gaps and maintaining market share. Unfortunately, the products were not price competitive. To remedy this problem, a value analysis program was undertaken to examine the functional parts of their product offerings.

Teams were organized to examine the high cost and high usage parts. Their findings allowed for substantial cost savings, which were passed on to their customers in the form of price reductions. Typical of these savings was a tape cleaner cartridge. The original cost was $5.50 each and the usage was forecast at 2,250 units. To correct a misdesign, a $530.00 investment was made in engineering and drafting. The part was now obtainable for 60 cents, a net saving of $10,495.

Remember value analysis should not be confined to the plant, it is also applicable in the office, institutions, or any area where a function is performed. Next time you create or approve a purchase order request, ask the question—What function is being provided by this expenditure and can it be achieved in another manner?

Work simplification teams

Work simplification teams share the same common benefits as value analysis teams; they both require the user to follow a specific discipline. Work simplification has been described as the organized approach to common sense. The purpose of work simplification is to:

—eliminate all unnecessary work, activity, or effort.

—arrange the remaining work in the best possible order.

—develop standardized work methods.

—assign accurate time standards for the work.

These points all have one common goal, and that is the elimination of wasted effort. A wasted effort is any that does not:

—plan a decision.

—calculate.

—provide or receive critical information.

There are four types of non-productive effort which do not add value to the product or process.

1. *Transportation*—Movement between two points, e.g., work stations, locations. Process Chart Symbol—Arrow.
2. *Inspection*—Examination for quality, count, or information. Remember, quality should be built into the product to eliminate inspection steps. Process Chart Symbol—Square.
3. *Delay*—For whatever reason the work-flow is interrupted. Process Chart Symbol—Square with rounded side.
4. *Storage*—An idle situation, when something is kept protected against unauthorized removal. Storage and delay are sometimes combined as is the case of Exhibit 14-2.

The method for eliminating wasted effort is similar to the V.A. method:

STEP 1: SELECTIVITY

Choosing a project to be evaluated.

STEP 2: GATHERING INFORMATION

Prepare the universal tool of work simplification—the process flow chart (see Exhibit 14-2). The form is simple and complete in detail. All steps in the process are listed and defined as to whether they are an operation, transportation, inspection, delay, or storage.

STEP 3: CREATION OF ALTERNATIVES

Apply brainstorming challenge to every detail and develop as many new and innovative steps as possible.

STEP 4: FORMULATE AN IMPROVED METHOD

Gather, organize, and evaluate your alternatives into an improved method.

STEP 5: IMPLEMENTATION AND FOLLOW-UP

The important aspect of this phase is in the proper training of those who are going to perform the work. Many installations fail after a successful *pilot run* because the workers were not adequately trained, and the success of the pilot run was the result of constant handholding and not informed workers. Always follow-up to insure that the workforce has not gravitated back to the old methods.

A few hints on establishing effective work simplification teams

If the organization is large enough, a steering committee should be established to coordinate the various individual W.S. teams. In the beginning, there should be only one or two project teams organized on a vertical basis in order to delegate detail work to newer members of the team. As the new members become seasoned, they in turn can become leaders of their own teams. In this manner, work simplification becomes a company way of life. Projects that are currently under evaluation should be posted on a bulletin board in order to solicit ideas from other members of the organization.

KEY TO LASTING COST REDUCTIONS

EXHIBIT 14-2
SYSTEM FLOW CHART

SYSTEM: DEPOSITING PERSONAL PAYCHECK
DATE: OCT. 5, 19X7
ANALYST: RUTH
INTERVIEWED: BARBARA
POSITION: OPERATIONAL FINANCIAL ANALYST

SEQ. NO.	OPERATION ○	TRANSFER ⇨	STORAGE △	CHECK □	TIME IN MINUTES	DISTANCE IN FEET	WORK DESCRIPTION
1	●						Check rec'd by secretary @ 9:30AM
2			▲		Approx. 30		Held until payee returns from coffee break to prevent loss or theft
3		■				22'	Delivered to payee (Barbara)
4	●				1		Check opened and stub detached
5				■	2		Checked for accuracy
6	●				1		Deposit slip is filled out
7	●				1		Check is properly endorsed
8	●				1		Check and deposit slip are placed in prepaid envelope
9			▲		Approx. 30		Envelope is held until secretary's visit
10		■				28'	Check is delivered to mail station by secretary
11			▲				Check held for mail pick-up
12		■				188'	Check taken to mail room on mail cart
13			▲		360		Held until post office trip
14							
15							
16							
17							Recommended solution - Barbara should
18							sign up for the automatic payroll deposit
19							service offered by her company's bank.
20							Thus, freeing her and the secretary's
21							time for more productive activities.
22							
23							
24							
25							
26							
27							

Remember, when establishing the teams, the foreman and if possible the person responsible for doing the task should be included. Besides tapping a storehouse of knowledge, it fosters good inter-personal relations and aids in gaining acceptance of the new method when installation time rolls around.

Production assembly teams

When a new product or subassembly initially enters the production cycle, does your company have an organized team whose purpose it is to minimize start-up problems? These teams are usually composed of a representative from engineering, manufacturing engineering, production, and purchasing. The first task of a newly established team is to develop a checkoff list for new production items. A simple list is not provided because of the peculiarities of individual plant processes, but some common areas to consider could be:

—Timetable and lead times.
—Documentation package, including working drawings, process sheets, etc.
—Tooling requirements.
—Work-flow and area, including storage.
—Purchasing—availability and lead times, identification of critical parts.
—Special problems, requirements, test and customer specifications.

Remember, it is preferable not to leave things to chance, but to identify all possible weaknesses as early in the production process as possible. This will eliminate future costly delays, shortages, and interruptions in the production, delivery, and eventually the revenue cycle.[1]

Incentive plans—making your employees your partners

The common thread running through this and the previous chapter is creating an environment that fosters and stimulates day-in and day-out cost effectiveness and control. The specific theme of this chapter is to gain employee involvement in accomplishing perpetual cost effectiveness. Because of the extensive nature of this subject, a financial handbook of this type can only scratch the surface. The intent is to make the operational financial analyst aware of the following tools that are available for enriching profits. Hopefully, the analyst in reading the brief commentary relating to:

—Production and Distribution Incentive Plans
—Profit Sharing Plans
—R.O.I. Management Incentive Plans

will be prompted into further investigation and eventual implementation of these programs.

---

[1] In Chapter 10, a half-way house was described between engineering and manufacturing called Custom Products. In reality, a permanent production assembly team had been established.

KEY TO LASTING COST REDUCTIONS

Production and distribution incentive plans

In the production areas, it is a known fact that when a company switches from a straight hourly payment plan to a well designed and maintained incentive plan productivity increases. Distribution firms should also consider the possibility of incentive systems for their operations. One major weil-run parcel delivery service has used an incentive system very effectively for years. The major problem of these systems has been determining what constitutes a fair day's work. Much of this problem is eliminated with the use of predetermined work standards such as methods—time—measurement (M.T.M.).

EXHIBIT 14-3
Profit Sharing Consideration Checkoff List

1. Does management truly feel that its employees are part of a productive team capable of adding more to the company's profits?
2. Has the scope of the plan been developed along with a list of objectives and qualifications, including vesting periods?
3. Are current salaries equal to the prevailing rate, so that employees will not misinterpret the intent of the plan?
4. Has a preliminary list of qualifiers been prepared along with a profit impact study?
5. How much of your profits are you going to share, and is it sufficient to qualify as an award, yet small enough to allow for ample reinvestment (the plow-back concept) into the business for future growth?
6. Is the profit sharing formula viable and thus capable of stimulating results?
7. Has consideration been given to rewarding those with longevity with the firm, such as bonus points for each year of service?
8. Do the employees truly have confidence in management's ability, honesty, and intentions?
9. Have you checked legal, tax, and union considerations as they relate to your plan?

Profit sharing plans

Whereas production and distribution incentive plans are oriented toward the individual, profit sharing is a means of forming a joint venture or partnership between the company and the employee. The employee now has a direct concern or stake in the profitability of their company; he is aware of the fact that the success of the profit sharing plan depends on making a profit. Profit sharing plans have a way of penetrating even the crustiest of employees. For example, a young cost accounting supervisor was cleaning out the desk of a recently terminated employee who was an abysmal housekeeper. Instead of taking a few moments to sort through the debris, he decided to dump the contents of the desk (paper clips, notebooks, pencils) into the nearest wastebasket. Upon seeing him begin this procedure, an old-line staff accountant promptly reminded him that he was throwing away profit sharing dollars.

In order to achieve a responsiveness and responsibility in your employees similar to that demonstrated by the old-line staff accountant and to get you started in a program, a few considerations are listed in Exhibit 14-3.

R.O.I. management incentive plans

A group orientated management incentive plan will have the same effect in generating an overall profit contribution as was described in the previous section (remember the poor cost accounting supervisor). Many management incentive plans or bonus plans are not designed to motivate the management group as a whole, but individually. These plans award the bonus dollars based on the general success of the business during the year or on the attainment or completion of incentive tasks or objectives. Whereas the incentive task or objectives form of bonus does foster individual effort, it does not motivate the total management group. I.e., each individual agrees to accomplish certain tasks during the year, but each individual isn't really concerned about his fellow management team member's goal unless they have a common goal.

Basing the management incentive plan (bonus) on a return on investment (R.O.I.) concept, the individual funnels his efforts into a common goal where each participant can make a positive contribution to the firm's profits and his incentive compensation. As the following steps will show you, the R.O.I. approach is simple, flexible, and is adjustable to the individual needs of your company.

The first step is to determine what return you expect to receive from the capital employed in your business. This will include setting a minimum level, and if it is a high risk business such as exotic R&D, you will probably expect a higher return than a food processing firm. If you are a division of a larger firm, you may also have to add corporate requirements such as corporate overhead, profit sharing, etc. In order to keep the following exhibits neat and simple, the minimum that is expected will be 10% and a target of 30%, both in pre-tax dollars. Thus the bonus payment range is established, and you can select any point in between as your base point.

The second step is to define the investment base or capital employed. The trick is to remember that you are not relating the system to other accountants or financial analysts, but to fellow members of your management team who may have a limited accounting background. So base your capital employed figures on items they can relate to, such as inventory, building, etc. The following example strives to accomplish this fact:

Machinery & Equipment	$ 2,240
Owned Buildings	1,500
Inventories	4,450
Accounts Receivable	2,100
Reserve for Bad Debts	(10)
Notes Receivable	40
Annualized Lease Payments (25 x 8.33 = 199.0)	200
	$10,520 [2]

---

[2]Note: $ 000 omitted.

KEY TO LASTING COST REDUCTIONS

The third step is to convert the percentages determined in Step One (min.-10%—target-30%) into the lower and upper dollar limits to form the bonus spread. To calculate the spread, simply multiply the expected return by the capital base.

Lower $10,520 x 10% = $1,052[2]
Upper $10,520 x 30% = $3,156[2]

Remember, the base can be any point your management chooses.

The fourth step is to calculate the bonus dollars that would be paid if and when the return has been made. For our example, the base will be the 10% minimum level.

R.O.I. of 10% and below

A 1% bonus is earned for every 10% increment of the *base* R.O.I. dollars generated. I.e., every $105,200 of return is worth 1% extra pay. If the base target is $1,052,000, then a 1% bonus is earned for every $105,200 of pre-tax R.O.I. generated. Thus, in order to get a 4% bonus the business would have to earn 420,800 pre-tax dollars. You may wish to limit your bonus to zero unless a certain R.O.I. level is obtained, because if 10% was your minimum goal, then a 4% R.O.I. would be considered mediocre.

R.O.I. of 11% to 12.5%

In order to discourage short-term gains, which could produce one-shot peak years in which your management creams the bonus plan while leaving the firm with a legacy of problems caused by:

—curtailing maintenance
—spending less on tooling and tool repairs
—stopping the advertising program
—slowing down R&D expenditures
—abandoning capital expenditures
—trimming the field sales and service force
—cutting back inventories so that customers complain
—raising prices—gouging customers
—stopping all training programs
—reducing expenditures on improved methods and processes

To discourage these practices, the base is upped from 100% to 140%. Once the R.O.I. dollar level has been achieved, the business must then earn $147,280 additional R.O.I. dollars in order to earn the additional 1% bonus pay, e.g., $105,200 x 1.4 = $147,280.

R.O.I. of 13% and above

To earn another 1% extra pay in this bracket, your business must generate an additional $294,560 R.O.I. or double the previous bracket.

The fifth step is the review of bonus brackets.

R.O.I. Brackets	Achievement for Every 1% of R.O.I. Earned	Index
1% to 10%	$105,200	100% base
11% to 12.5%	147,280	140% base
13% to infinite	294,560	280% base

Exhibit 14-4 summarizes the dollar brackets used in this example.

EXHIBIT 14-4
Table of Extra Pay Percentages at Various Levels of Performance

R.O.I. Performance Level	Earned Bonus Percent	Index
$ 105,200	1	
210,400	2	
315,600	3	
420,800	4	
526,000	5	100%
631,200	6	(Base)
736,400	7	
841,600	8	
946,800	9	
1,052,000	10	
1,199,280	11	
1,346,560	12	140
1,420,200	12.5	
1,567,480	13	
1,862,040	14	280
2,156,600	15	
2,451,160	etc.	

The sixth step reminds you to modify and tailor this procedure to your needs. The purpose of this type of bonus plan is to develop a team approach to profit enrichment.

The seventh step is to run a pro-forma income statement and cash flow to determine the impact of your bonus plan.

The eighth step is to implement the payment or settlement of the bonus plan. Payments should be made quarterly in order to keep everyone involved and motivated. Payments should coincide with a meeting that reviews the results that activated the payment of the bonus. Payment should represent no more than 75% of the monies earned in order to allow for a possible downturn in results.

When the final results for the entire fiscal year are determined, pay the remaining 25%.

15

GENERATING PROFITS THROUGH ACCELERATED CASH FLOW

This chapter continues the evaluation of functional areas by addressing an area in which the operationally-oriented financial analyst can make one of his most significant contributions—the generating of profits through accelerated cash flow.

HOW DOES ACCELERATING CASH FLOW BUILD PROFITS?

The acceleration of cash flow will increase profits because business will be able to:

—restrict the use of outside funds, whether it be bank borrowing, venture capital funds, leasing, debt, or equity. Subsequently, the cost of funds will be reduced.

—retire existing debt obligations thus reducing interest costs.

—free-up cash for expansion in the form of working capital or new plant and equipment.

—make available cash for implementing innovative ideas and techniques for increasing productivity.

—generate sufficient cash to institute needed equipment replacements and repairs. This will reduce maintenance costs and waste caused by worn or obsolete equipment.

—make business acquisitions to gain a greater share of the available market and/or provide for product diversification. The existing fixed administration costs can then be spread over a wider base.

—be able to take advantage of large purchase quantity discounts.

—be able to take cash discounts for prompt payment.

PINPOINTING CASH FLOW BLOCKAGE

Pinpointing cash flow blockage is a four-step process:

Step 1—Defining Cash Requirements (forecasting)
Step 2—Monitoring
Step 3—Analyzing
Step 4—Taking Corrective Action

Step 1—defining cash requirements (forecasting)

Before you can determine when the cash flow blockage will occur and what is causing the stoppage, you must define the extent of the problem. I.e., define the task to be accomplished:

—How much cash is or will be available in order to meet payroll, taxes, debt payments, accounts payable, etc?

—What will be the sources of the funds, and more important, will the timing coincide with the need?

—If this timing is not compatible, why?

Determining your cash needs is best accomplished by cash forecasting. There are two generally accepted cash forecasting techniques:

Short Term—daily, weekly, quarterly, using the *cash receipt and disbursement method*—Exhibit 15-1.

Long Term—semi-annual or annual projections using the *adjusted net income approach* or as it is sometimes referred to *the source and application of funds method*—Exhibit 15-2.

Because the second method addresses cash flow forecasting in aggregates and not components, its use is most effective in the long run. Unfortunately, as the analyst moves further away from his current position, it becomes more difficult for him to clearly define the components. Thus, the ideal situation is to prepare an adjusted net income cash forecast in order to define long term needs and problems in addition to the cash receipts and disbursements forecast as a short-term tool. These forecasts can be adjusted and shaped to combine both current and future requirements.

Step 2—monitoring

The key in pinpointing cash flow blockage is in the monitoring of the short-term forecasts. In order to determine if you will be able to meet your long-term commitments, you need to concurrently maintain at least three interlocking short-term cash flow forecasts based on the cash receipts and disbursements format:

1. A quarterly forecast similar to Exhibit 15-1.
2. Current quarter-monthly—again Exhibit 15-1 is suitable.
3. The current month-weekly.

GENERATING PROFITS THROUGH ACCELERATED CASH FLOW

EXHIBIT 15-1
FOUR WEEK CASH PLAN

SUBSIDIARY / DIVISION _____   SUBMISSION DATE _____

	DESCRIPTION	WEEK ENDING	WEEK ENDING	WEEK ENDING	WEEK ENDING
1	CASH RECEIPTS				
2	CASH SALES				
3	ACCOUNTS RECEIVABLE COLLECTIONS				
4	SALE OF FIXED ASSETS*				
5	OTHER*				
6	TOTAL CASH RECEIPTS				
7	CASH DISBURSEMENTS				
8	CASH PURCHASES				
9	ACCOUNTS PAYABLE PAYMENTS				
10	PAYROLL				
11	PURCHASE OF FIXED ASSETS*				
12	TAXES				
13	OTHER*				
14	TOTAL CASH DISBURSEMENTS				
15	NET CASH GAIN OR (LOSS)				
16	BEGINNING CASH BALANCE				
17	CUMULATIVE CASH POSITION				

*EXPLAIN SIGNIFICANT ITEMS

EXHIBIT 15-2
Long-Range Financial Plan
Funds Flow Statement

(DOLLAR AMOUNTS IN THOUSANDS)

	EST. CURRENT	19X1	19X2	PLANNED 19X3	19X4	19X5
FUNDS PROVIDED BY:						
Net Income	$	$	$	$	$	$
Depreciation						
Disposals of Property						
Deferred Taxes						
Other						
Total Funds Provided	$	$	$	$	$	$
FUNDS APPLIED TO:						
Capital Expenditures	$	$	$	$	$	$
Returns to (from) Corporate						
Debt Service						
Change in Working Capital						
Other						
Total Funds Applied	$	$	$	$	$	$
INCREASE (DECREASE) IN WORKING CAPITAL						
Cash and Securities	$	$	$	$	$	$
Receivables and Inventories						
Current Liabilities						
Other						
Total Changes	$	$	$	$	$	$

If you can confine your disbursements to one or two days a week, you will find it easier to plan and monitor your expenditures and maintain the monitoring of your cash forecast worksheets. As in any systematic decision-making tool or problem solving approach, don't become the victim of an elaborate system—remember to keep it simple!

Step 3—analyzing

Here is where you can cash in on your efforts because weekly and even daily you will be able to see and evaluate the extent to which your forecasts were correct and the reasons why when they are not. I.e., you will be able to pinpoint the blockage.

Step 4—taking corrective action

Don't stop with the pinpointing, take corrective actions. Make current decisions

GENERATING PROFITS THROUGH ACCELERATED CASH FLOW

now! It will improve your cash flow and also improve profits. The following case in point illustrates this critical step.

A case in point—how a large printer improved profits by analyzing and making cash flow timing decisions

A low margin, high-volume printer was continually having cash flow problems. Payments were stretched and made on a basis of how much money was in the bank account and who yelled the loudest. I.e., he wasn't taking his prompt payment discounts on his accounts payable. When his bank asked him to show support or justification of his need for a new working capital loan, he reluctantly adopted the four-step approach outlined above using the cash receipts and disbursements method. This analysis indicated that he was *not* timing his payable payments to cash collections, and he was not aggressive enough in collecting overdue accounts receivable. His reason for not aggressively pursuing his debtors was he did not want to endanger the accounts to the point where they would cease or limit their doing business with his firm. He could not afford to lose the volume as the volume was needed to cover the fixed costs generated by over-equipmentization of the plant.

When the cost of money was computed on these completed but not paid jobs, many were found to be marginal while others were at a loss. To correct his cash flow timing problems, a customer rebuilding program was developed and a major vendor payment program strategy was instituted based on collections. Salesmen were enlisted to help collect money and the average day's sales in receivables were cut significantly. Once the key vendor payment program (paper and ink companies) was under way, this printer was able to take advantage of prompt payment discounts, which at his purchasing levels added between $3,500 to $5,000 per month to his before tax profit. Previously, these were lost profit and cash dollars.

Another side benefit which affected profits occurred when a paper shortage developed and our printer found himself on the favored customer lists. He was able to obtain paper while his competition could not. Thus customers, who had specific paper requirements, were usually assured by this printer that he could handle their needs—he had the production capacity and now he had the paper.

Can you imagine what an adverse position he would have been in if he could not have obtained paper when the shortage occurred:

—His previously slow paying customers could have drifted to the competition. His job of collecting the overdue accounts would have become even more difficult.

—Being caught with an over-equipmentized plant and reduced volume, he probably could not have fully absorbed his fixed costs.

—He would have had to drop his high hourly press machine-hour rate in order to maintain volume, which was a result of over-equipmentizing. (Machine-hour rates are discussed in Chapter 12.)

What else do you think could have happened to him, and could it happen to your firm, or one of your divisions?

19 WAYS TO ACCELERATE CASH FLOW

The previous case in point demonstrated a few techniques and ideas which, if not currently being used in your organization, can be easily implemented. The following checkoff list, Exhibit 15-3, is designed to serve as an idea stimulator. The implementation process in most cases is easy and can be obtained with a little further investigation in the form of reading, conversations with your banker, or possibly an outside processing service or time-sharing—all of which can help you form a workable solution.

EXHIBIT 15-3
19-Point Checkoff List for Accelerating Cash Flow

How organized is your cash management program? Does it include:
1. Assigning functional responsibility for cash management to a single person?
2. Centralizing, where possible, cash flow functions, whether it be the number of banks, accounts with banks, or collection points?
3. Insuring the prompt collection and depositing of cash?

    Idea!—Have you considered introducing a procedure whereby your customers remit directly to a bank lock-box, where cash can be deposited around the clock?

4. Establishing proper banking relationships, number of member banks in the line, level of compensating balances, etc?
5. Evaluating and monitoring bank account balances so idle or excess cash can be invested?

    Idea!—Have you investigated the practicality of establishing "zero level bank accounts"?

6. Selecting the proper investment mode for excess cash?

    Idea!—When investing excess cash in marketable securities, do you fully evaluate:
    - What portion of your excess cash is to be invested in securities?
    - What should be the proper timing and sequencing of these purchases?
    - What should be the composition and mix of the investment portfolio including maturity dates of the securities?

7. Analyzing the "float," so you can take advantage of the lags in the commercial banking system check clearing process, thereby adding a day or more float before you must deposit the funds to cover the checks written?

    Idea!—One large company, who had both east and west coast operations but very few mid-west locations, found they could generate as much as four days' float, thereby holding $2 million which could be earning interest.

Are you making full use of your cash budget by:
8. Basing it upon realistic and reliable data?
9. Operating within its limits?
10. Observing future weaknesses well in advance, and belt-tightening when needed? Do you notify your bank well ahead of time of future needs in order to cover lean periods?

GENERATING PROFITS THROUGH ACCELERATED CASH FLOW

Belt-tightening Idea!—One national retailer, in efforts to reduce its short-term debt, floated a 9% debenture. They then began zeroing in on reducing inventory. Their reasoning was that every dollar tied up in excess inventory would result in ten plus cents of needlessly incurred interest expense.

11. Reserving adequate cash for future expenses or new equipment needs?

Do you have a cash conservation program which includes:

12. Granting credit along established and proper guidelines, while remembering a sale is not complete until the cash is collected?

    Example—Assume your average accounts receivables were $5,000,000 and you shortened your average collection days, so as to cut your accounts receivable balance by 25%. This would reduce your receivables' level by $1,250,000. If you had to borrow that sum for a year at 8%, it would cost you $100,000 in interest.

13. Timing payments so as to avoid conflicts?

    Idea!—The printing company discussed in the previous case in point staggered their payments by arranging for the payment of paper invoices on the 1st of the month, ink on the 15th, and supplies on the 21st, etc. Also, consider the value of this approach in dealing with your suppliers, who in turn can better plan their cash flow.

14. Placing proper controls and authorizations on negotiable assets and check signing?
15. Offering discounts when necessary, especially to cover those tight times during the month?
16. Analyzing aged accounts receivable and monitoring collections, especially delinquent accounts?

    Idea!—Check and see if there is a relationship between your most difficult customers and those who are the slowest paying. Maybe they are too costly to keep as customers.

17. Gaining bank assistance in collections by adopting the lock-box concept and having the bank apply your accounts receivable payments, thereby freeing your accounts receivable clerks to become researchers and not just posters.
18. Being assured that other areas of the business are supporting your cash conservation measures, such as checking to see that purchasing is buying raw or basic materials at the best price? Remember, cash conservation occurs at the time the purchase requisition is written.
19. If you are a privately held business by not comingling your personal and business funds. Monitor your withdrawals from the business and maintain a salary level which will not place a cash burden on the business.

IDLE ASSETS ARE NOT ALWAYS IDLE

Idle assets come in many forms and are not always easily distinguishable as an idle asset. Classically, the idle asset is conceived of as the old plant with the boarded windows. Normally they are not so apparent. An idle asset can be:

1. Excess cash which is not invested.
2. High receivable levels with lengthy agings.
3. Temporary investments which should be cashed in and the proceeds re-invested or otherwise re-directed.
4. Permanent investments in product lines or businesses which have been moderately successful, but may be draining cash and other business resources.
5. Inventories—too much or too old (see chapter on material cost control).
6. Equipment which is seldom used.
7. Plant and warehouses which are cluttered. They are generally inefficient or useless.

All of the above items provide drag on your organization and thus impede the profitability and growth of business. This drag occurs because in addition to the cost of money or carrying cost associated with accounts receivable and inventories, there are other costs associated with these idle assets:

—Debt payments in the form of lease or debt arrangement.
—Depreciation costs while a non-cash item continues to erode profits.
—Property and/or floor taxes.
—Security costs in the form of insurance, guards, A.D.T. services, etc.
—Maintenance costs.
—Alternative use costs—the lost profit resulting from not placing the asset into a more productive mode.

A case in point—how Sangray Advanced Technology Company discovered a hidden source of expansion capital

INTRODUCTION

Sangray Advanced Technology Co. (SATCO) was able to develop and maintain a very successful and unique operation, even though they did not possess a proprietary product line. SATCO was able to command a distinctive competitive edge and premium pricing because they were the undisputed technical leader in their field. While enjoying their success, they did not have at least one or two core products which could be expanded upon to achieve future growth goals.

One day SATCO's chief engineer and marketing director jointly reported a technical breakthrough which enabled them to develop their own proprietary line.

PROBLEM

SATCO's new product line was received with excitement, acceptance, and orders. This new-found opportunity produced several challenging and unexpected problems. Prime among these problems was the need for production and warehousing space and expansion capital. Over the years as pioneers in their field, they had acquired machinery, equipment, parts and supplies which they no longer required to complete current contracts. The technology which SATCO sold was so advanced that their customers were willing, within reason, to pay the costs required to deliver SATCO's technology. This aspect allowed SATCO to recover the out-of-pocket cost associated with acquiring the needed machinery to meet the contract. I.e., for all intents and purposes, the machinery was free and clear.

SATCO was located in an out of favor, low rent industrial area, which allowed them in the past to easily rent or lease cheap buildings, establish the line required for the new contract, and use the facility for storage once the contract was finished. This practice was tolerated because management believed they might require the equipment and facility for future contract requirements. This course of action was also tolerated since SATCO's management was technically oriented and the contracts were profitable and there was always enough cash in the bank.

Now they needed additional contiguous production and warehouse floor space and expansion capital.

SOLUTION

The solution to their cash problem was reached as a result of solving their contiguous space problems. SATCO, in surveying their neighborhood, discovered that they were now the area's largest renter and there was no additional space available. Behind SATCO's original and main plant was a large warehouse which over the years had collected the surplus excess parts and equipment from the other locations.

The warehouse was large enough to meet their requirements, and since they had no place else to move, they decided that the most expedient way was to dispose of the equipment. To their surprise the used equipment was in demand, because of the lack of availability and the inflated cost of equivalent new equipment. The success of their first disposal action spurred them into examining and analyzing the equipment stored or under-utilized at the other locations.

In examining the excess equipment at the other locations, they discovered certain pieces of equipment could be modified and placed into service, thereby making planned purchases of equipment required to produce the new products unnecessary. As the equipment was removed and the buildings became vacant, they were able to terminate their lease and rental arrangements. This action fired up more cash flow as period costs, such as phone, utility, and protection services were reduced.

SUMMARY

SATCO was able to find the necessary space required to establish an efficient and cost-effective production, warehousing, and shipping arrangement. In addition, they cut their potential interest expense and the future debt repayment demands on their cash flow because their borrowing requirements were cut back substantially. They reduced period costs and needed to spend less on new capital equipment and support tooling. Thus they were able to convert idle assets into active assets.

Case in point—how idle assets added to the final collapse of Terminal Printing Company

Terminal Printing Co. had been a moderately profitable operation prior to its being acquired. It was acquired for the purpose of rounding out the total printing capability of a fast growing printing company. Even at the time of the merger, management stated they were not sure of its exact position in the company's printing capabilities, but they felt the additional $4.5 million in revenues would add to their growth.

Some of Terminal's customers were marginal accounts because sales were geared to maintaining a volume level capable of covering high fixed costs. In addition, the difference between making a profit and breaking even hinged on two key customers, both of whom were unfortunately controlled by the same salesman.

About two years after the merger, a new competitor entered the market who had a much lower cost structure and thus a lower machine-hour rate. This new company was able to undercut Terminal in what had become a very fierce competitive market. To make matters worse, the salesman who held the key accounts left Terminal to join the new competitor. The two key accounts followed after a respectable time.

Terminal limped along for awhile and then began to look at their cost composition from a more operational viewpoint and observed the following:

1. Outside rental costs were greater than the lease on the main plant, which was in theory more than adequate for a plant with their current volume.
2. Interest costs were high because of the need to finance paper purchases.
3. Because warehouses were loaded and they did not want to incur the expense of any additional rental space, premiums were being paid to paper companies for short lead times.
4. Insurance and transportation costs were high due to the need for outside storage.

Although other facts emerged, these formed the basis for further investigation which disclosed the following:

1. Obsolete equipment was taking up too much room. Two out of three presses were found to be unoperational, and a hot metal typesetting process was totally incompatible with current technology. The hot metal process and one press were sold, and the other press repaired for a surprisingly small amount. These removals along with other space saving moves and operational changes allowed for the availability of more storage space and improved product flow.
2. A survey of the outside rental revealed:
   —A dockside warehouse contained a paper inventory, some of which had recently been ordered at premium prices.
   —A smaller warehouse area was being shared with a metal fabricator who frequently cut magnesium, thus creating a formidable fire hazard.
   —A vacant suite of offices and an abandoned parking lot, both of which no one had bothered to sublet or negotiate a termination of the lease.
   —Another storage area where spare parts and an ancient press were stored. The owner of this space had been trying to get these items cleared out to no avail and was ready to sue.

3. In a survey of the equipment list and maintenance cost, a direct mail list surfaced which was being carried on the books at $65,000. In reality, it was of little value because the equipment required to process the list was quickly becoming obsolete. They discovered vehicles in poor repair or sitting idle which should have been sold or repaired. While they were waiting to be repaired or held for infrequent use, they had to be licensed and insured. In one case, lease payments were being made. In addition, there were entire storerooms filled with cannibalized parts from old presses, which were not inventoried, categorized, and otherwise useless.

When Terminal's management was questioned as to why these occurrences had been allowed to take place, they usually answered with the following statement, "We were too busy with the day-to-day operation, and really all of these items were idle and weren't really costing anything."

In the end, it did cost them something, because the president of the parent company decided it would take too much time to rebuild the customer base and the idle asset problem could best be resolved by liquidation. Thus Terminal's idle assets weren't idle, they were corrosive. They were burdening the business with extra costs which could not be passed on to the customer in a very tight and competitive market.

A final note on accelerating cash flow

Every two years as an operational financial analyst you need to evaluate and provide answers to the following critical business question—Knowing what your firm currently knows about product line X or business Y, would you re-enter and invest in these products and/or this business? This concept was brought to the forefront during the recession of the 1970's, when numerous companies closed entire units or eliminated product lines which were acquired during the go-go years of the 60's in the name of growth. These firms failed to realize in the 60's that not all growth is good. Thus, what had been a marginal operation in the past, was now unprofitable or unacceptable and was consuming vitally needed cash, which could be employed elsewhere in a more advantageous manner.

16

OPERATIONAL FINANCIAL ANALYSIS AND THE ECONOMIC JUSTIFICATION OF BIG-TICKET ITEMS

The previous chapter concluded with a discussion of how idle assets and their attendant costs can debilitate the profitability of a business. These idle assets were at one time acquired with the purpose of being active contributors and not passive profit eroders. This chapter addresses the analysis and evaluation of significant cash outlays or those big-ticket decisions which, once made, will have a long term effect upon the operational and financial performance of the business. This chapter is a preventative maintenance chapter. By doing your homework today, you will prevent tomorrow's crisis.

IDENTIFYING BIG-TICKET ITEMS

Capital budget items

Big-ticket items are usually associated with capital expenditures, and subsequently capital budgeting plays a vital role. As a rule of thumb—most companies consider a capital budget big-ticket item as any item with a useful life of more than two years and an acquisition cost of over $200. It may also be an item which does not meet these criteria, but which management wishes to control, and thus chooses to include these items in their capital budgeting process.

These capital items usually fall into the following categories and should be grouped accordingly for control and evaluation purposes:

OPERATIONAL FINANCIAL ANALYSIS

- Land and Building
- Tools and Dies
- Laboratory and Test Equipment
- Autos and Trucks
- Furniture and Fixtures
- Leasehold Improvements
- Others depending on the nature of your business, such as returnable containers and drums
- Major repairs and overhaul projects, although not capitalized, should be presented along with the capital budget for control and evaluation purposes

The individual items should also be cross-referenced in order to improve evaluation and justification of each capital request. The categories are:

- Business Expansion—new product introductions or current product expansion
- Replacement—wear, loss, etc.
- Support Equipment—material handling, test, etc.
- Productivity Increases—volume or efficiency
- Cost Savings—dollar identifiable
- Safety—protection of people
- Civic Code Requirements—O.SH.A., F.D.A., etc.
- Security—protection of plant, equipment, and goods

Remember, it is vital to back up accompanying requests for capital items and major expense projects with a written form to facilitate:

- Determining if the request is justified
- Ranking the items to be approved if the total dollar value of all of the requests exceeds the total amount of dollars available
- Providing a starting point for post-auditing of the expenditures

An example of a completed capital appropriation request has been included as Exhibit 16-1.

Beyond the capital budget

There are other big-ticket items which require analysis and evaluation which do not necessarily fall into the category of items covered by the capital budget. They represent those business decisions and commitments which have a long-lasting effect upon the business because they:

- require a sizeable investment in time, money, and effort.
- will affect the financial condition for a considerable number of years.

EXHIBIT 16-1
Capital Appropriation Request
Financial Plan—Page 5

SUBMISSION DATE _____ 9-1-X7 _____

DATE TO BE COMMITTED _____ 12-15-X7 _____

DOLLAR AMOUNT
(NET OF TRADE-IN ALLOWANCE) $910,000

SUBS/DIV NUMBER: 5 5 5 Ronald Mfg. Co.
SUBSIDIARY/DIVISION NAME

DIV.#	ITEM#	YEAR

CAPITAL ITEM NUMBER   555   011   X7

TITLE AND DESCRIPTION Wenthur Perforating Press—300 Ton Model WPP-3
High speed, 60' wide perforating press, capable of handling sheet and coil, and intricate spacing variations. Unit includes mini-computer for numeric and trace control.

CLASSIFICATION
- ☐ LAND & BUILDINGS
- ☐ FURNITURE & FIXTURES
- ☐ TOOLS & DIES
- ☐ LEASEHOLD IMPROVEMENTS
- ☐ LABORATORY & TEST EQUIPMENT
- ☒ MACHINERY & EQUIPMENT
- ☐ AUTOS & TRUCKS
- ☐ OTHER

JUSTIFICATION
- ☐ SAFETY
- ☐ CIVIC-CODE RELATIONS
- ☐ COST SAVINGS
- ☒ BUSINESS EXPANSION
- ☐ SUPPORT EQUIPMENT
- ☐ REPLACEMENT EQUIPMENT

This press will enable us to add $1,000,000 to sales on a multi-shift basis and reduce raw material handling time and scrap. This unit requires less labor and reduces die wear which reduces scrap level. This unit will add sales by providing early entrance into the new 60' market. (Present market limited to 48'.) Additional sales to also be developed by our ability to offer various pattern combinations using basic die configurations.

APPROVALS:

R. R. Feiner 9/1/X7
DIVISION CONTROLLER   DATE

a. Shore 9/1/X7
DIVISION MANAGER   DATE

GROUP EXECUTIVE   DATE

FINANCIAL PLANNING   DATE

CAPITAL ASSETS COMMITTEE   DATE

EXECUTIVE V.P.   DATE

OPERATIONAL FINANCIAL ANALYSIS

- —will change to some degree the manner in which you conduct and manage the business.
- —may require sizeable future cash injections to continue viability and growth, e.g., a new product or business venture.
- —could severely damage the business organization at its market or industry position, along with its financial stability, if you should choose to abandon the endeavor.

In reviewing the previous criteria for what constitutes a non-capital big-ticket item, you will be able to identify those commitments which fit your particular business environment.

Four typical areas which fit this criterion are:

- —*Business Acquisitions*—either in the form of complete or partial product lines or entire business entities.
- —*New Product Development*—a business should begin to analyze its future return at the inception stage.
- —*Product Line Expansion and New Product or Service Introductions*—before committing further resources to the project or accepting a new product provided by an outside source.
- —*Business Systems Installations*—whether the application is a manual or computer system, it should be evaluated from a "hard dollar savings," even though the "soft dollar savings" may dictate its immediate adoption. Once a business system has been implemented and personnel have been re-assigned and trained to operate the new system, it is very difficult to withdraw.

For the remainder of this chapter, examples of big-ticket items will be confined to:

Capital Budget Items—normal (primarily replacements)
Capital Budget Items—extraordinary (a new plant)
Business Acquisitions
New Product Introductions

The above examples should not limit your choice of items which your firm classifies as big-ticket items, because each industry and company will have its own particular items which fall into this category.

A SIMPLE FRAMEWORK AND METHOD FOR EVALUATING BIG-TICKET ITEMS

In order to provide a sound economic justification for acquiring a big-ticket item, a sound framework and method of evaluation is required.

The framework

The following checkoff list should serve as a basic framework which you can easily tailor to your organization.

EXHIBIT 16-2
Checkoff List for Developing a
Framework for Evaluating Big-Ticket Items

1. Has your company a written set of business objectives? Are they backed up by approved functional responsibility and assigned operational goals? Do these objectives serve as a guide for making, analyzing, and evaluating big-ticket item decisions?

2. Does your company have a written annual business and five-year long-range plan which acts as a timetable for implementing big-ticket decisions?

3. Are your monitoring devices effective in evaluating your business plans and planning systems? This insures the proper evaluation of big-ticket items according to plan.

4. Have preliminary benchmarks been developed which allow each division of a large company to predict the size of its big-ticket pool? This will allow for preliminary screening and ranking of all projects and will provide ample notice to the treasurer's office of a division's need for extra funds in order to finance a special project which it cannot afford to finance out of its normal cash flow.[1]

5. Is the formalized capital budgeting procedure followed, and does it include established R.O.I. criteria for evaluation and post-audit follow-up. Subsequently, the processing of the more routine capital requests would be simplified and provide ample time for the critical evaluation and analysis of the extraordinary big-ticket items.

6. Does a formal, specialized big-ticket item checkoff evaluation procedure exist for evaluating those particularly large or special items such as an acquisition or a new product introduction? The same consumer products company referred to in point no. 4 has an acquisition evaluation review book. This book is divided into sections such as marketing, production, distribution, financial, etc., and within sections pertinent operational questions are listed. Typical questions are:

    Marketing—Are the products properly packaged and priced to meet competition?
    Production—How much and what type of production equipment is available, and what manning levels are required to operate this equipment line?
    Distribution—Can products be efficiently hauled from existing production centers?

7. Is there a written procedure for presenting big-ticket candidates to senior management? Is there a common understanding of the procedure by all those concerned?

8. Do you have a standardized approach or method for determining the financial and economic feasibility of items which fall outside of the capital budgeting framework (acquisitions, new products, etc.), such as the approach described in the next section?

The method

Part of a standard approach is the preparation of a big-ticket evaluation guide which states clearly what the evaluation techniques and criteria are. Exhibit 16-3 provides a starting point in the preparation of your guide.

In reviewing this matrix, two evaluation techniques are presented:

---

[1] One west coast company (divisionalized) uses 70% of a division's cash flow (N.A.T. + Depreciation = Cashflow) as a guide-line for determining the size of its capital budgeting pool.

OPERATIONAL FINANCIAL ANALYSIS

—The Time Payback Method
—The Discounted Cash Flow Method

Remember to limit the evaluation techniques to two methods, so the non-financial members of your management will not be confused or spellbound by fancy financial footwork. For ease of understanding, payback should be expressed as a period of time.

EXHIBIT 16-3
Big-Ticket Evaluation Guide

BIG-TICKET ITEM CLASSIFICATION[2]	PAYBACK METHOD[2]	CRITERIA[3]
CAPITAL BUDGET ITEMS		
Ordinary Capital		
Civic Code & Safety	None Required	
Normal Replacements	None Required	
Other—Below $24,999	Time Payback	
Other—Above $25,000	Discounted Cash Flow	
Extraordinary Capital	Discounted Cash Flow	
NON-CAPITAL BUDGET ITEMS		
Business Systems—Low Cost	Time Payback	
Business Systems—High Cost	Discounted Cash Flow	
Product Line Acquisition	Discounted Cash Flow	
Business Acquisition	Discounted Cash Flow	
Product Development (R & D Stage)	Discounted Cash Flow	
New Product Introductions (Pre-Production Stage)	Discounted Cash Flow	
Alternative Situations (Lease or Buy/Purchase or Build)	Discounted Cash Flow	

The Time Payback Method is used for quick evaluation and will normally be adequate for evaluating low to medium capital budget (rule of thumb—$25,000 and below) requests which do not fall into the mandatory purchase requirements. The formula is simple and is designed to tell you how many years it will take the cash benefits or savings from the new item to repay the investment.

$$\frac{\text{Original Investment}}{\text{Annual Cash Benefits}} = \text{Time Payback}$$

1. Original Investment less salvage value: $95,000 less salvage value of $9,500 (1/10 original cost) equals $85,500.

2. After taxes profits plus depreciation: Estimated savings per year are $13,850 as a result of improved labor efficiency, plus depreciation of $8,550 per year equals $22,400 per year.

3. $\dfrac{\$85{,}500 \text{ Invested}}{\$22{,}400 \text{ Benefit}} =$ a payback in 3.82 years.

---

[2] Dollar amounts should be included where possible and have been omitted due to varying company requirements. Also, this list should be adjusted to meet your company needs and requirements.

[3] ROI% and payback amounts have been omitted due to varying company requirements and needs.

The discounted cash flow method, sometimes referred to as the investors method, is used for those heavy long-term cash commitments (rule of thumb—$25,000 plus). This method is extremely valuable because it brings the *time value of money* into your evaluation. This is essential when you are making a large dollar commitment which will affect your business for a long period. Remember, a dollar is worth more today than it will be tomorrow, i.e., present value. If you were to take a $5,000 note, payable one year from now at 10%, the bank would pay you the discounted amount of $4,545 or the present value of $5,000 at 10% for one year. By using the 10% factor on a present value table, the value of $1.00 will be worth .909 one year from now. The same dollar will be worth .826 and .751 two and three years hence respectively.

The discounted cash flow method entails two features:

Present worth feature discounts future costs and revenues in order to compare the present value of future rewards or benefits with the current value of the investment needed to reap the future rewards. I.e., if the present value of the reward is not greater than the investment, don't make the investment.

Example: Your company wishes to invest $10,000 and expects a 10% discounted return computed on a five year base. If the return was $3,000 per year, it would be discounted as follows:

YEAR	AMOUNT	10% P.V.	DISCOUNTED AMOUNT
1	$ 3,000	.909	$ 2,727
2	3,000	.826	2,478
3	3,000	.751	2,253
4	3,000	.683	2,049
5	3,000	.621	1,863
	$15,000		$11,370

You can expect a return of $11,370 on your investment, which means you should go ahead with the investment.

Rate of return feature does not consider the interest rate element, and thus the objective is to determine the percentage return which will equate the discounted cash flows to the amount to be invested. When done manually, this method requires trial and error in order to determine the percentage.

Example: Assuming the same $10,000 investment and a return of $3,000 for each of the five years, what would be the discounted rate of the return? Because 10% is your minimum return, you should first discount the cash flow stream at 10%. Discounting the stream at 10% equals $11,370, an amount greater than $10,000. Because it is a trial and error factor, lets pick 15% and 16% as your next selections.

YEAR	AMOUNT	15% P.V.	DISCOUNTED AMOUNT	16% P.V.	DISCOUNTED AMOUNT
1	$ 3,000	.8696	$ 2,609	.8621	$2,586
2	3,000	.7561	2,268	.7432	2,230
3	3,000	.6575	1,973	.6407	1,922
4	3,000	.5718	1,715	.5523	1,657
5	3,000	.4972	1,492	.4761	1,428
	$15,000		$10,057		$9,823

OPERATIONAL FINANCIAL ANALYSIS

As the example shows, 15% was a lucky guess because at that rate, the cash flow stream equaled $10,057, thus exceeding the $10,000 investment. At 16%, it did not equal the $10,000 investment.

If you have access to computer support, the guess-work and all of the mathematics can be eliminated. Once you have determined your benefit dollar stream, there are many time sharing financial analysis packages which accomplish discounting as a simple sideline and they are worthy of your investigation.

Establishing criteria for D.C.F.—R.O.I.

After reviewing the two previous examples, you will realize the need for having previously established criteria. In the previous example, 10% was used as the criteria. In surveying different companies, you will find different rates in use for various reasons. As operational financial analysts, be sure you choose a practical and not theoretical rate: a rate should reflect your industry and your company.

As a general rule of thumb, the percentage rate of return should reflect your cost of borrowing and the risk factor you associate with the project requiring the investment. The higher the risk, the higher the R.O.I. percentage. As an example, assume a 10% interest rate, then you may wish to develop a R.O.I. percent as follows:

TYPE OF PROJECT	FACTOR[4]	R.O.I.%
Absolute minimum (Very special activities)	1.0	10% - 12%
Normal	1.5	15% - 17%
Some Degree of Risk	2.0	20% - 25%
High Risk	3.0	30% - 35%

A case in point—how the Big Company applies an easy five-step D.C.F. approach to acquisition reviews

The Big Company along with several other firms had for many years been interested in acquiring the Tiny Co. because of its technology in an emerging area. Tiny Co. finally approached each of its suitors and said they were interested in selling, but their opening bid was $750,000.

The Big Co. sent in its acquisition review team to gain both operational and financial information, both of which were willingly supplied by the Tiny Co. This evaluation was aided by the use of an acquisition analysis checkoff list containing close to 300 key operational and financial questions. This list was prepared in advance to provide the comprehensive approach to evaluating acquisition candidates. Typical questions are:

—Could they expand or contract the product line?

—Can pricing be adjusted?

---

[4] Factor is based upon the cost of borrowing. Eg. 10% rate X 3 = 30 R.O.I.

—What cost-cutting techniques can be implemented and when?

—Can departments and functions be combined or eliminated?

—What distribution techniques should be changed?

—How much additional capital will be required?

—What are the tax advantages?

When the team finished their evaluation, a meeting was held to determine what improvements could or could not be made in the operation of the busines, the following steps were undertaken:

Step 1.— Prepared the list of criteria for review and assumptions. Exhibit 16-4 lists the criteria and assumptions which were prepared, thus completing step one.

Step 2.— Converted these assumptions into a projected income statement, which showed that over ten years, the firm would produce $810,000 of after tax income.

Step 3.— Projected the cash flow. They calculated a cash flow of $900,000 over a ten-year period. This is exclusive of the tenth year residual value used in computing the value of the business.

Step 4.— Discounted the cash flow by 15% and 19% as stipulated in the evaluation criteria and found the business should be valued at $654,100 and $531,700.

Step 5.— Showed management that if they met the opening bid criteria of $750,000 and operated it as projected, they could expect a D.C.F.—R.O.I. percent of approximately 12 1/2%.

Armed with this information, management decided to submit their bid at $757,000. They decided to accept the lower rate of return in order to enter this allied technology, even though the return did not measure up to their previously stated criteria. The $7,000 was a kicker added to act as a tie breaker in case of a tie.

Big Co. was not successful in its bidding, because the Tiny Co. was acquired by the Not So Big Co. Not So Big Co. was the winner as the Tiny Co. was afraid of losing its identity in an organization the size of the Big Co. Although the exact number was not known, it was rumored Not So Big Co. was to have paid around $850,000, a lot more than the Big Company's estimate of the company's value. In trying to determine why Not So Big Co. and another firm were willing to pay around $850,000 for Tiny, it was concluded that both of these firms failed to realize the future cash need required to replace Tiny Company's production line #2.

OPERATIONAL FINANCIAL ANALYSIS

EXHIBIT 16-4
Big-Ticket DCF Evaluation
Acquisition Review
Step 1
Criteria for Review and Assumptions

Criteria for Review

1. The acquiring company normally expects a return on its investment of 15% after taxes, but wishes, in this particular acquisition, to also consider what price it should pay in order to gain a 19% after taxes return on its investment. The reason for conducting the additional analysis is management anticipates having to spend more of its time than is normally required to bring an acquisition on board. This additional effort is required due to its smaller size, lack of market penetration, etc. These factors in no way prohibit it from being a worthwhile acquisition.

   Thus, management has requested a financial analysis which will establish a purchase price yielding to them an ROI of 15% and 19% on an after taxes discounted cash flow basis.

2. The selling company has stipulated that its opening bid is $750,000.

   Thus, management has also requested a financial analysis which will establish what return on its investment will be yielded on an after taxes discounted cash flow basis if it were to pay $750,000, i.e., will the 15% and 19% ROI level be achieved?

Assumptions to be Used in Preparing the Analysis

1. The latest financial statement showing an N.A.T. profit of $100,000 is satisfactory for forming a base line.

2. The marketing department has analyzed the market (not shown) and predicts sales will be increased greatly. This will be accomplished by introducing pricing and packaging improvements, plus a generally more aggressive approach to the market. This will result in added profits in years one through six as follows: $10,000, $12,000, $14,000, $16,000, $18,000, and $20,000 respectively.

EXHIBIT 16-5
Big-Ticket DCF Evaluation
(Acquisition Review)
Step 2
Projected Income Statement

Assumptions	1	2	3	4	5	6	7	8	9	10	Total
Profit Before Taxes from latest stmt.	100	100	100	100	100	100	100	100	100	100	1,000
Added profits from pricing and market improvements	10	12	14	16	18	20	30	30	30	30	210
Cost Reduction after 2nd year	--	50	50	50	50	50	50	50	50	50	450
Added Depreciation from new equipmt.							(10)	(10)	(10)	(10)	(40)
	110	162	164	166	168	170	170	170	170	170	1,620
Tax Rate of 50%	55	81	82	83	84	85	85	85	85	85	810
After Tax Profit	55	81	82	83	84	85	85	85	85	85	810

EXHIBIT 16-6
Big-Ticket DCF Evaluation
(Acquisiton Review)
Step 3
Projected Cash Flow Statement

Periods	1	2	3	4	5	6	7	8	9	10	Total
After Tax Per Step 2	55	81	82	83	84	85	85	85	85	85	810
Normal Depreciation	15	15	15	15	15	15	15	15	15	15	150
Depreciation— New Equipment	--	--	--	--	--	--	10	10	10	10	40
Cash out— New Equipment	--	--	--	--	--	--	(100)	--	--	--	(100)
Projected Cash Flow	70	96	97	98	99	100	10	110	110	110	900
Residual Value[5]										850	850
Final Cash Flow	70	96	97	98	99	100	10	110	110	960	1,750

[5] Represents the value which the company would be sold for in the tenth year. Computed at ten times tenth year's earnings of $85,000.

3. The production department has reviewed the equipment and states in year seven, production line two will have to be replaced at a cost of $100,000. This new equipment will add plant capacity, which marketing predicts can be easily marketed, and thus the added profits in years seven through ten will be $30,000 for each year.

4. Through improved systems and converting to parent company approaches, additional after-tax profits of $50,000 in each year, beginning in the second year, will be generated.

5. Tax rate will be 50%, and the investment tax provision will be ignored on the new equipment because it is always subject to repeal.

6. The residual value will be based on ten times the tenth year's earnings.

EXHIBIT 16-7
Big-Ticket DCF Evaluation
(Acquisition Review)
Step 4
Determining the Discounted Cash Flow Value

DISCOUNTING

Periods	Cash Flow Per Step 3	At 15% Factor	$	At 19% Factor	$
1	70	.8696	60.9	.8403	58.8
2	96	.7561	72.6	.7052	67.7
3	97	.6575	63.8	.5934	57.6
4	98	.5718	56.0	.4987	48.9
5	99	.4972	49.2	.4190	41.5
6	100	.4323	43.2	.3521	35.2
7	10	.3759	3.8	.2959	3.0
8	110	.3269	36.0	.2487	27.4
9	110	.2843	31.3	.2090	23.0
10	960	.2472	237.3	.1756	168.6
Discounted Value			$654.1		$531.7

OPERATIONAL FINANCIAL ANALYSIS

EXHIBIT 16-8
Big-Ticket DCF Evaluation
(Acquisition Review)
Step 5
Determining the Discounted Cash Flow Percent R.O.I.

First, we already know from the previous step, the discounted R.O.I. will be less than 15%. So by trial and error we begin to focus on a present value factor which will discount the $1,750 cash flow to $750,000. As the following discounting will show, if the firm pays the $750,000 and the predicted cash flow develops, they can expect a return approximating 12 1/2%.

		DISCOUNTING			
	Cash Flow	At 12%		At 13%	
Periods	Per Step 3	Factor	$	Factor	$
1	70	.8929	62.5	.8850	62.0
2	96	.7972	76.5	.7831	75.2
3	97	.7118	69.0	.6931	67.2
4	98	.6355	62.3	.6133	60.1
5	99	.5674	56.2	.5428	53.7
6	100	.5066	50.7	.4803	48.0
7	10	.4523	4.5	.4251	4.3
8	110	.4039	44.4	.3762	41.4
9	110	.3606	39.7	.3329	36.6
10	960	.3220	309.1	.2946	282.8
Discounted Value			$774.9		$731.3

D.C.F. approach summary

The five-step approach listed in the case in point can be applied in evaluating any big-ticket item using the D.C.F. technique. The key is not in having a lot of data, but in having the right information in an easy and presentable format. Remember to always organize your conclusions, support paperwork, and findings in an easily understood and interpretable form so those who are commissioned with making the final decisions can do so without getting bogged down in the numbers.

A REMINDER TO POST-AUDIT AND CONTROL

This is not a "how to" step in the succession of operational financial analysis steps, but a "must do" step. Too many financial analysts and their management fail to post-audit and control the big-ticket item once it is a permanent fixture because they approach it as a *fait accompli*. Thus they fail to learn from their mistakes and successes. They are too busy fighting today's fires to ask—Did:

— the acquired company provide the expected R.O.I.?

— the new computerized accounts receivable and cash application system reduce head count and speed-up cash flow?

— the $30,000 investment in new equipment produce labor savings of $20,000, reductions of $3,000 in maintenance costs and $3,000 in operating supplies in the first year, and are these people off the payroll?

Post-auditing is simple—do it!

The Savings Analysis Calculator, Exhibit 16-9, should be completed twice, once when the request is submitted prior to acquiring the item and a second time one year after the item is in place and operative. In completing both analyses, you will be able to confirm if the payoff did in fact really occur. Remember, the intent is not to play "Now, I've got you!" but to build an arsenal of knowledge for making future business decisions.

Controlling is not difficult—do it!

Many companies do not properly keep close tabs on their big-ticket items. In small companies or smaller divisions of bigger companies, records are not always complete and are often scattered. In larger firms where records are maintained and even computerized, control in many cases is still weak. The weakness occurs because there is no adequate life history recorded. The big-ticket item is so labeled because it is a valuable productive resource. Productive resources, whether they are business acquisitions or fixed assets, have one thing in common with the new product introduction—they all have a life cycle. During their life cycle they move, are maintained, eventually wear out, become obsolete, or surplus. What could be more wasteful than in a large organization requesting, analyzing, and committing funds for a particular type of machine tool in one division of a company while another division has made the decision to deem surplus similar equipment because of a decision to cease operations on a particular product or function. For this reason, there needs to be a surplus equipment availability list.

EXHIBIT 16-9
Big-Ticket Savings Analysis Calculator

Savings Analysis (Annual Basis)

Category of Expenses	Present	Proposed	Annual Savings/(Loss)
1. Direct Labor	$	$	$
2. Indirect Labor			
3. Overtime Premium			
4. Payroll Connected Costs			
5. Scrap and Re-work			
6. Maintenance of Facility			
7. Tool Cost			
8. Operating Supplies			
9. Outside Services			
10. Incremental Fixed Costs			
11. Incremental Inventory Costs			
12. Improved Product			
13. Increased Output			
14. Other (specify)			
15. Total Annual Amount	$	$	$
16. Net Annual Savings			$

(front)   EXHIBIT 16-10

FIXED ASSETS ADDITION – EQUIPMENT RECORD CARD

[Form with key punch data fields along left and right margins, containing fields: 1 Entity No., 5 Acct., 8 Loc., 11 Cost Center, 14 Dept., 17 Category, 21 Asset Number, 36 Description of Asset, 38 Corp Salvage Value, 46 Ins BS YR, 48 Insurance Value(s), 55 Acq Date, 59 Date Instld, 63 Tax Est. Life, 67 Tax DM, 70 TPC, 71 N/U, 72 IT, 36 Tax Cost Basis, 45 Tax Acc. Reserve, 54 Tax Salvage Value, 62 Assessed Value, 69 ME, 36 Tax Loc. No., 46 Corp Est. Life, 50 Corp. D.M., 53 TPC, 54 Corp. Cost Basis, 63 Corp. Acc. Reserve. Card codes FA01, FA02, FA03, FA04. Prepared By, Date, Entity Name fields.]

EQUIPMENT/ASSET STATUS:

ACTIVE ☐   RESERVE ☐   DATE OF CHANGE _____   SURPLUS ☐   DATE OF CHANGE _____   DISPOSITION DATE _____

GENERAL INFORMATION:

MAKER _____

BOUGHT FROM _____

ADDRESS _____

INVOICE NO. _____ INVOICE DATE _____

MAKERS IDENTIFICATION NO. _____ MODEL NO. _____

SIZE _____ H/P CONSUMPTION _____

OTHER REMARKS: _____

(SEE OVER)

REPAIR & MAINTENANCE RECORD:

DATE	REF.	AMOUNT	DATE	REF.	AMOUNT	DATE	REF.	AMOUNT

SEE OVER

COST INFORMATION: **AUDIT DATES:**

PURCHASE _____   1ST YR _____   9TH YR _____

FREIGHT _____   2ND YR _____   10TH YR _____

MATERIAL _____   3RD YR _____   11TH YR _____

LABOR _____   4TH YR _____   12TH YR _____

BURDEN _____   5TH YR _____   13TH YR _____

INSTALLATION _____   6TH YR _____   14TH YR _____

TOTAL _____   7TH YR _____   15TH YR _____

         8TH YR _____   16TH YR _____

TRANSFER INFORMATION   **FROM:**

DATE	DIV.	PLANT	BLDG.	COST CENTER	DEPT.	DEPRECIATION	NET COST

TO:

FINAL DISPOSITION OF ASSET TO: _____   SALVAGE VALUE _____

(back)

REPAIR & MAINTENANCE RECORD CONTINUED

DATE	REF.	AMOUNT	DATE	REF.	AMOUNT	DATE	REF.	AMOUNT	DATE	REF.	AMOUNT	DATE	REF.	AMOUNT	DATE	REF.	AMOUNT

REMARKS

_____

_____

_____

_____

_____

_____

_____

267

Whether you are large or small, all of the above tasks begin when you acquire the asset and accomplished when you complete a Fixed Asset Addition—Equipment Record Card—(Exhibit 16-10). The card provides several values:

—Records the complete life cycle of the asset.
—Allows for the updating of accounting records because the Key Punch Data is a two-part form. The top portion can be sent to the computer to initiate a new record on your fixed asset accounting control system. This function can also be completed manually.
—Maintains the detailed acquisition history which often gets separated from the equipment, vendor, invoice number, etc.
—Records the audit dates of each annual audit of the equipment's location and who the auditor was.
—Provides for a complete maintenance and overhaul record, which should be reviewed for cost effectiveness on a periodic basis.
—Continues this maintenance record on the reverse side (not shown) to allow for notations and comments which are pertinent to the history of the unit.

A case in point—what can happen to a company which does not follow a capital evaluation framework

The Diversified Company began as a high-flying mini-conglomerate. After completing an acquisition binge which saw them acquire over seventy small-to-medium-size companies, Diversified's management decided it was necessary to consolidate its efforts into four primary business areas. These areas were not based upon any business growth prescription or according to a set of written business objectives, but were chosen by sorting out what they owned and forcing a fit into four so-called synergistic unrelated groupings. Each of these groups were equal in sales dollar volume (the only common denominator).

The group directors were charged with the charter of tying together loosely-knit companies into viable business units which could eventually be spun-off as separate independent companies. Diversified's management realized that to implement their charters, a large injection of capital equipment was required. The division presidents, many of whom had sold their businesses to Diversified on the promise of expansion capital, rallied to the cause. Soon Diversified added over one million square feet of plant under construction and several million dollars of equipment on order to fill these plants.

As long as Diversified could find ways to finance these new ventures, they kept adding plant and equipment. The "Piper" was to be paid out of internally generated operating cash flow. The plan was as soon as each subsidiary went on-stream, it would begin to retire its debt, pay its leases, etc. What they failed to anticipate were the numerous start-up problems which would plague them, such as:

—The failure of a new type of conveyor system to function properly. Eventually it was torn out by the new owners of the plant after Diversified was forced to sell this fledgling venture.

- The failure of the ground to freeze over unpaved, muddy roads, so heavy processing equipment could not be moved onto the plant site in a new industrial park. Once the equipment was installed, it took eight months to de-bug.
- The failure to have enough profitable orders ready at two existing plants when the new plant finally went on-stream. These plants barely broke even for almost two years.

What happened to our go-go company? Each of the requests for capital equipment was presented in accordance with the established processing procedure, and each had the appropriate return on investment attached. Unfortunately, Diversified's capital budget was not prepared, analyzed, and allocated in accordance with an established written capital evaluation framework as the one shown in Exhibit 16-2.

The capital budgeting review committee passed on all items they felt had a satisfactory R.O.I. as long as they could currently finance the project. Diversified's president's decision-making ability was influenced by his desire to pacify disgruntled subsidiary presidents who were also large stockholders. He would try to calm the subsidiary presidents by saying, "By the way, why don't you purchase that new equipment you have been wanting, if you agree to..."

Thus, Diversified authorized capital expenditures had neither a framework for evaluation, a capital spending plan, nor a long range plan—not even a method for determining how much could be spent and where it was to be best spent.

As you will recall from Chapter 2, Diversified fell upon hard times when money became tight. This forced the ouster of the president, and his successor began a rebuilding program. This rebuilding program could not truly begin until many of the businesses and plants were sold to avoid throwing the company into bankruptcy.

17

SYSTEMATIC PROFITS
VIA OPERATIONAL FINANCIAL ANALYSIS—
AN ORGANIZATIONAL CASE STUDY

The adoption of a systematic operationally-oriented approach to financial analysis with accompanying improvements in decision-making, communications, cost control, profits, and cash flow has its application in both financially weak and strong businesses. This organizational case study is based on how one successful company, who takes pride in their financial strength and acumen, has organized to implement a systematic operationally-oriented approach to financial analysis.

This company for ease of presentation is referred to as the Abron Company. They offer a regionally well-known, high unit volume consumer goods product. They are expansion oriented with revenues exceeding $100,000,000. This company was chosen as a case study because it is a medium-sized company, and thus its organizational approach can serve as a prototype for both larger and smaller companies.

In examining Abron's organizational approach to financial analysis, business planning, and control, six basic fundamental concepts must prevail:

1. Establish *goals* and *objectives*.
2. *Plan* how these goals and objectives can best be achieved.
3. *Organize* in a manner which would facilitate the implementation of the plan (under Step 2).
4. *Staff* the organization with the proper mix of people and support. (Support refers to the trade-off which can occur between permanent staffing, outside

SYSTEMATIC PROFITS

consultants, and/or computer support. Computer support could be in the form of either computer capabilities or external via computer timesharing.)

5. *Direct* the effective implementation of the plan through the organization which has been established and staffed.
6. *Control* or coordinate the results achieved and adjust to changing circumstances.

ESTABLISHING GOALS AND OBJECTIVES

When firefighting is the order of the day

As financial analysts, financial administrators, or non-financial executives, you have undoubtedly witnessed the firefighting which takes place in response to an unforeseen crisis. Review your own experiences to see how your company and other companies have reacted to an excessive finished goods inventory level by doing one or more of the following:

1. Production lines were slowed or stopped
2. Special sales campaigns were developed with a company customer promotion
3. Rebates
4. Task forces of all types were developed

Thus, the unsystematic firefighting, which could have been prevented by some preplanning and preventative action, continued until the crisis was over or was eclipsed by another more demanding crisis.

We sometimes fail to realize or accept the fact that our own financial analysis and cost control functions are operating in a firefighting mode. This firefighting occurs because little or no early warning systems exist which would alert the financial analyst and his management of pending problems.

The granting of an operational charter

At Abron, even routine financial analysis and control assignments were originally treated in a firefighting mode. The turning point was reached when a bright new controller was hired and directed by Abron's senior management to:

1. Improve current financial and accounting techniques and approaches while laying out the groundwork for future expansion of the business and his functions.
2. Develop a financial staff which would be sales-and people-oriented and which would understand all facets of the business, rather than a group of green-eye-shaded bookkeepers.
3. Eliminate the firefighting, especially the war dance associated with preparing the annual budget.
4. Improve timeliness, accuracy, and decision-making ability of all financial reports and assignments.
5. Realize that the business was in an accelerated growth mode, and not to lose sight of the key factor which had gained Abron success to date. This was their

ability to manage the business at the detail level and thus continually monitor the pulse beat of the business.

6. Strengthen and encourage a more responsive reiterative process in light of the increased growth due to acquisition of related businesses and new product introductions. This process was viewed as follows:
   a. A problem or negative trend is detected and additional analytical work is performed.
   b. The affected manager is notified of the problem and supplied with observations and conclusions derived from the analytical process.
   c. A corrective action is defined and implemented.
   d. The corrective action is monitored to insure that its implementation was effective.

Functional responsibilities and operating objectives

As time passed, the financial analysis and budget department (F.A.B.D.) introduced under management's direction a modified management by objectives approach which was based on the definition and implementation of a written set of functional responsibilities and operating objectives for each major segment of the business. These are based upon the general charter described earlier plus the evaluation of what is the group's charter. The functional responsibilities are as follows:

Business planning and control

1. Strategic Planning: Coordinate the preparation of the five-year long range plan.
2. Tactical Planning: Administer preparation and presentation of all phases and aspects of the annual capital budget, operating budget, and business plan.
3. Shorter Range Planning: Perform those intermediate business forecasts and reviews which are required to monitor performance and profitability on an interim basis. Currently, these are the bi-weekly income statement trend (flash reports) and the quarterly performance reviews.

Financial and economic analysis

4. Perform a financial and economic review of all proposed acquisitions.
5. Evaluate capital equipment and plan expansion decisions and investment decisions prior to purchase.
6. Analyze the profitability of proposed new product introductions, new business segments, and long term contracts.
7. Review all pricing decisions to be sure they will generate satisfactory margins.
8. Monitor key ingredient cost fluctuations and make recommendations where appropriate in order to preserve satisfactory margins.
9. Conduct those special management economic and financial studies usually associated with business expansion, contractions, or significant change in operating method.

SYSTEMATIC PROFITS

Operational financial analysis

10. Maintain all facets of the budgeting system including the monthly flexing and reporting system.
11. Issue a monthly operating variance letter (prime operational analysis and control tool) in sufficient time to be a useful management tool.
12. Conduct an operational awareness program (cost control at the detail level) stressing the monitoring to trend and conditions, area assignments, regular field contacts, etc.

Operational analysis

13. Prepare those analytical studies which are more business and operationally related than financial, independently or in conjunction with various line managers.
14. Observe all aspects of the operation, being constantly vigilant for significant opportunities to improve methods and approaches and thus profits.
15. Interpret financial and other reports (primarily outlying branch operations reports) for cost reduction and improvement opportunities.

Systemization and education

16. Investigate and add those analytical tools and aids which will increase the group's ability to measure, analyze, and control operating and financial results.
17. Harness the computer wherever possible and profitable in order to allow for more pure analytical time and effort.
18. Document and simplify all financial analysis procedures, tools, and analytical routines.
19. Conduct a continuing user education program using a "how to" approach in the form of lecture programs, procedure manuals, etc.

In addition to its functional responsibilities, the group elects and/or is assigned the completion of certain operating objectives. While these objectives may appear to overlap, they are considered to be those tasks not currently being accomplished which will aid the profitability, efficiency, or generally improve the company's overall performance. While Abron's F.A.B.D. is charged with the functional responsibility to harness the computer wherever possible and profitable in order to allow for more pure analytical time and effort, it is also held responsible for implementing the following operating objective (this is a new and innovative approach for this firm):

Evaluate Time-Sharing techniques, make a limited introduction

Approach and Timing: The introduction of time sharing into F.A.B.D. will be an orderly approach in order to ensure an interlocking building block approach. At the present time, this building block has not been fully defined, but initially appears to be assuming the following configuration:

1. Define approach.
2. Evaluation of time-sharing financial analysis programming languages.
3. Further investigation of time-sharing budgeting systems at other locations.
4. Definition of tasks.
5. Establish implementation schedule.
6. Begin adding applications to Abron's financial analysis library.

Responsibility and Timing: Responsibility will fall upon the director of financial analysis and budgets, director of management information systems, and senior financial analyst. Timing to begin after the budget has been wrapped and in between the following year's budgeting activity while striving to get as much as possible accomplished by July 1, 19X8.

PLANNING

The F.A.B.D. uses several tools to insure the successful completion of its functional responsibilities and operating objectives and is organized and controlled as if it were an in-house consulting staff. Projects and objectives which are to be accomplished are controlled in the same manner as a production control department plans and controls a small job shop, R&D project, and/or engineering prototype activity. Such project planning and control techniques as:

— Maintaining project backlog list. This monitors and directs the analytical talents so they are effectively utilized. It also increases the analyst's productivity, because he can shift his efforts to another project when he is held up awaiting data or information.

— Developing an annual master budgeting, planning, and reporting calendar. This monthly program acts as a master planning, scheduling and staffing guide.

— Establishing PERT networks for the more involved projects to insure all details and interdependences are considered and included.

A mini-case in point

One of Abron's prime objectives was to improve and simplify the preparation of the annual budget and accompanying business plan. Due to a very short and inflexible preparation schedule, every year the budgeting and business planning process was a major firefight which was costly both in time and energy. During the budgeting period, the F.A.B.D. ceased to perform all other forms of financial analysis and cost control. Furthermore, not only was it debilitating to the planning system, but the work was so chaotic that each year saw a new team tackling the budget beast because no one was willing to come back for a second try.

It was not until a systematic approach was undertaken and applied for taming the beast that the firefighting element disappeared. The budget became just another large analytical project. This approach was accomplished by:

1. Applying a systems analysis approach similar to that used by data processing personnel when developing a computerized system.

2. Documenting the current system.
3. Preparing a master PERT network.
4. Developing a major accomplishment calendar consisting of 77 major milestone events.
5. Gaining user department involvement in the budget preparation. (This added momentum to the operational effectiveness of the individual departmental budget.)

In addition to demonstrating to line managers that the budgeteers were more than just numbers crunchers, they were able to build a basic system with a useful life of more than just one budgeting cycle, which had been the case in prior periods. They also cut out-of-pocket costs by $12,000 by reducing computer usage, outside temporary clerical help, and overtime. Most important, they shifted their efforts from routine numbers crunching to more analytical efforts—they worked smarter, not harder.

ORGANIZING AND STAFFING

The previous sections basically described how Abron's operationally-oriented financial analysis staff determined what had to be done and how to address the task of completing the budget. No matter how carefully you plan the "how to get it done" portion, it cannot be completed without properly skilled people. Before determining the type of staffing required, they first had to develop a functional organization chart grouped by what had to be done and the experience level required to accomplish these tasks. In reviewing the functional organization chart (Exhibit 17-1), you will see the functions divided into three categories:

— Planning and Control
— Financial and Economic Projects
— Operational Projects

The supporting outside consultants are used primarily to provide expertise in the completion of specific operational projects. If a distribution problem were to develop, a material handling specialist or industrial engineer would be called if needed. Abron also uses the services of a former employee who had left the group to form his own practice to handle overload situations. Rather than adding future staff members, the director is striving to develop timesharing as a support tool. In fact, two of the analysts were hired because of their time-sharing exposure.

While there are position descriptions (see Exhibit 17-2) covering each of the individuals on the payroll, the staffing is primarily determined by the task and skills grid. Examples of the task and skills grid for the budget analyst, financial analyst, and senior financial analyst are shown as Exhibit 17-3. In reviewing this grid, three terms are used in referring to the level of experience or competence required to accomplish and successfully complete the functional responsibilities and operating objectives:

Theoretical or awareness

The analyst has not necessarily applied or worked with this area in the past, but has been more than just exposed to the subject or area in question. The individual has

EXHIBIT 17-1

```
                    ┌─────────────────────┐
                    │     DIRECTOR,       │
                    │  FINANCIAL ANALYSIS │
                    │     & BUDGETS       │
                    └─────────────────────┘
                              │
            ┌─────────────────┼─────────────────┐
  ┌──────────────────┐                 ┌──────────────────┐
  │  ADMINISTRATIVE  │ - - - - - - - - │    SUPPORTING    │
  │     SECRETARY    │                 │ OUTSIDE CONSULTING│
  └──────────────────┘                 └──────────────────┘
```

OPERATIONS ANALYST —OPERATIONAL PROJECTS	FINANCIAL ANALYST —FINANCIAL & ECONOMIC PROJECTS	SENIOR FINANCIAL ANALYST —PLANNING & CONTROL
—Operational Studies —Business Plan —Operational Awareness	—Acquisitions —Pricing New Prod. Intros —Quarterly Reviews —Long Range Plan —ROI —Computerization—"What If" —Post-Audits	—Capital Budget —Operating Budget —Operational Awareness —Computerization-Budget
BUDGETING SPECIALIST ◁ SUPPORT DATA	**BUDGETING ANALYST**	**TEMPORARY BUDGET SUPPORT**
—Distribution (Branch) Reporting and Analysis	—Budget Maintenance —Flexing —Monthly Variance Letter —Head Count Control —Bi-Weekly Trend	

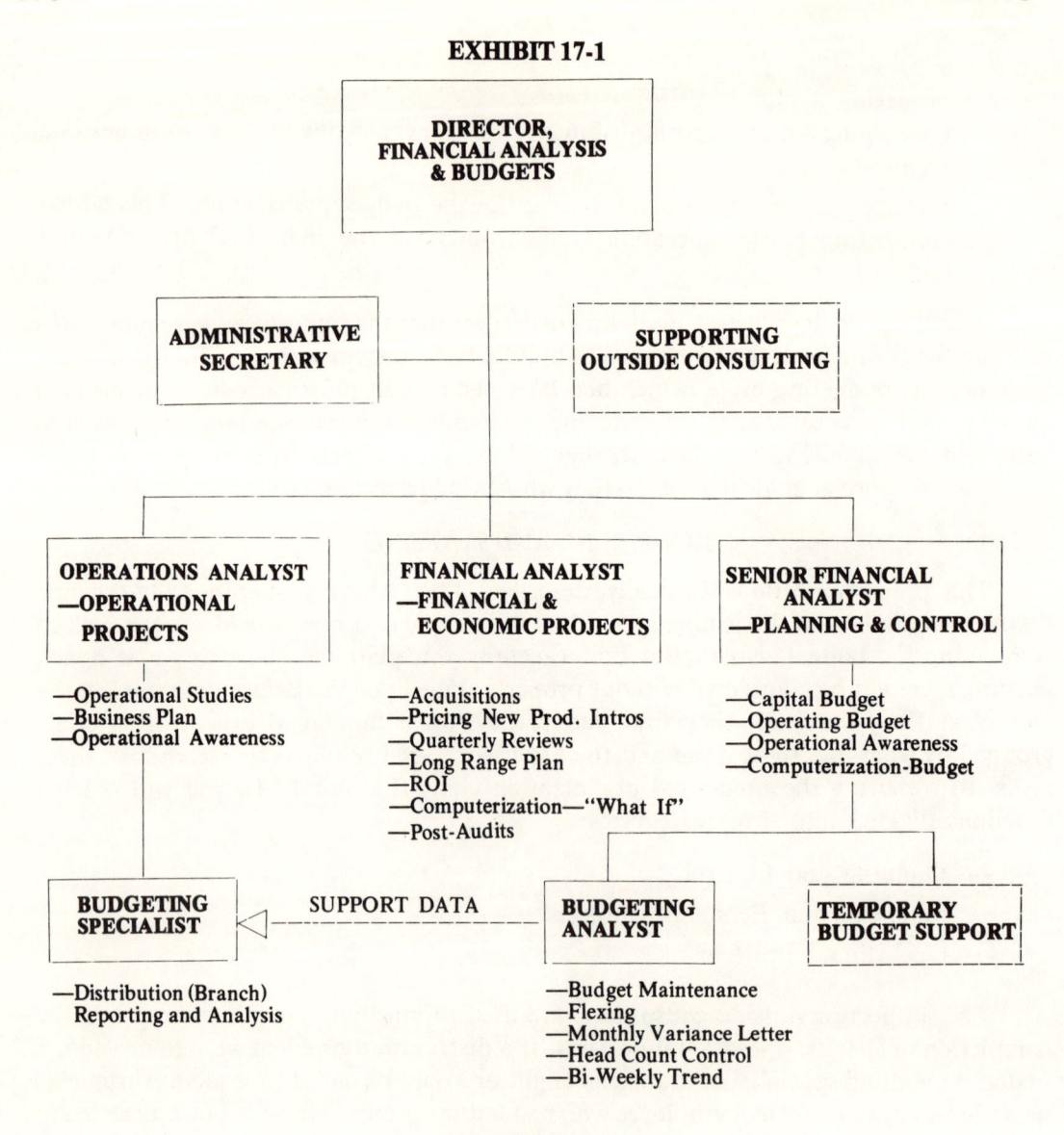

EXHIBIT 17-2
Position Description

Budget Analyst

General: Performs duties and makes studies that may be varied and somewhat difficult in nature, but which usually involve limited responsibility. Some evaluation and ingenuity required.

(Experience Level: 3—5 years)

Position: This position is generally responsible for the preparation, consolidation, and distribution of corporate profit and loss and capital expenditure budgets, the analysis and interpretation of results, and the preparation of financial and operating statistical reports to provide a basis for management planning, operating controls, and the performance appraisal.

Specific Functions:
1. Recommends budgetary policies and practices.
2. Develops methods and procedures for the preparation of budgets.

3. Prepares economic and sales forecasts and provides for their periodic adjustment.
4. Participates in formulating projected income budget and forecasts of cash requirements.
5. Prepares or reviews capital expenditure budgets.
6. Assembles product line's profit and loss statements and consolidates and summarizes profit and loss budgets as well as inventory and capital expenditure budgets.
7. Prepares and analyzes operating and financial reports and maintains graphic charts for management use.
8. Assists individual department heads in the preparation of their operating budgets.
9. Reviews actual performance against budgeted performance and prepares reports explaining budget deviation.
10. May also prepare projections of material and labor costs, and various control and statistical reports as required.

EXHIBIT 17-3

TASKS AND SKILLS PREPARATION OF:	BUDGET ANALYST - THEORETICAL OR AWARENESS	BUDGET ANALYST - WORKING KNOWLEDGE	BUDGET ANALYST - EXPERT	FINANCIAL ANALYST - THEORETICAL OR AWARENESS	FINANCIAL ANALYST - WORKING KNOWLEDGE	FINANCIAL ANALYST - EXPERT	SENIOR FINANCIAL ANALYST - THEORETICAL OR AWARENESS	SENIOR FINANCIAL ANALYST - WORKING KNOWLEDGE	SENIOR FINANCIAL ANALYST - EXPERT
1. OPERATING BUDGETS: Including		X			X				X
Cost center budgets, Income Statement, Balance Sheet, Cash Flow, Supplementary Data		X			X				X
2. CAPITAL BUDGET	X				X				X
3. BUSINESS PLAN	X				X				X
4. LONG RANGE PLAN	X				X				X
Modeling, Simulation	X			X			X		
5. QUARTERLY MANAGEMENT REVIEWS		X				X			X
6. MONTHLY BUDGETING: Including Flexing, Variance Analysis, Head Count Reporting, Variance		X			X			X	
7. PRICING	X				X				X
8. RETURN ON INVESTMENT Payback, ROGA, DCF, etc.		X			X				X
9. ACQUISITION ANALYSIS	X				X				X
10. NEW PRODUCT INTRODUCTION	X				X				X
11. BREAKEVEN ANALYSIS	X				X				X

EXHIBIT 17-3 (Cont.)

12. GROSS PROFIT ANALYSIS	X	X	X
13. POST-AUDIT OF CAPITAL	X	X	X
14. ASSET MANAGEMENT REVIEWS			
Receivables, Inventory, etc.	X	X	X
15. INDUSTRY RELATED	X	X	X
16. PROFIT IMPROVEMENT THROUGH OPERATIONAL AWARENESS	X	X	X

	BUDGET ANALYST			FINANCIAL ANALYST			SENIOR FINANCIAL ANALYST		
TASKS AND SKILLS PREPARATION OF:	THEORETICAL OR AWARENESS	WORKING KNOWLEDGE	EXPERT	THEORETICAL OR AWARENESS	WORKING KNOWLEDGE	EXPERT	THEORETICAL OR AWARENESS	WORKING KNOWLEDGE	EXPERT
1. ANALYTICAL ABILITY		X			XX				XX
2. BREAKEVEN ANALYSIS	X				X				X
3. COMMUNICATION SKILLS (Especially Written)		XX				XX			XX
4. CONCEPTUAL BUSINESS KNOWLEDGE		X			XX				X
5. COMPLETED STAFF WORK		X			XX				XX
6. CONTRIBUTION ANALYSIS	X				X			X	
7. COST ACCOUNTING— Overhead Absorption		X			XX			XX	
8. CAPITAL BUDGETING		X			X				X
9. CASH BUDGETING	X				X				X
10. DIRECT COSTING	X				X			X	
11. FINANCIAL STATEMENT									
a. Preparation		X			X				X
b. Analysis	XX				X				X
c. Projection	X				X				X
d. Consolidation	X				X				X
e. Income Statements		X			X				X

NOTE: XX indicates dual importance.

SYSTEMATIC PROFITS

EXHIBIT 17-3 (Cont.)

TASKS AND SKILLS PREPARATION OF:	BUDGET ANALYST - Theoretical or Awareness	BUDGET ANALYST - Working Knowledge	BUDGET ANALYST - Expert	FINANCIAL ANALYST - Theoretical or Awareness	FINANCIAL ANALYST - Working Knowledge	FINANCIAL ANALYST - Expert	SENIOR FINANCIAL ANALYST - Theoretical or Awareness	SENIOR FINANCIAL ANALYST - Working Knowledge	SENIOR FINANCIAL ANALYST - Expert
f. Balance Sheets		X			X				X
g. Source & Uses of Funds	X				X				X
12. FLEXIBLE BUDGETING		X			X			X	
13. INVENTORY ANALYSIS & CONTROL	X				X			X	
14. OPERATIONAL AUDIT ANALYSIS	X			X				X	
15. PAY BACK		X			X				X
16. PRESENT VALUE	X				X				X
17. RATIO ANALYSIS		X			X			X	
18. RETURN ON INVESTMENT		X			X			X	
19. RESPONSIBILITY ACCOUNTING	X				X			X	
20. SYSTEMS									
a. Computerized	X				X				X
b. Manual	X				X				X
21. VARIANCE ANALYSIS		X			XX				X
22. "WHAT IF" BUDGETS				X				X	
23. ZERO BASE BUDGETS	X			X				X	

NOTE: XX indicates dual importance

either taken a course or seminar or read a book or article on the subject. I.e., the analyst should be able to understand and comprehend how this subject could be applied to the resolution of the financial analysis assignment or business decision.

Working knowledge

The analyst has a working knowledge of the particular area in question. He can successfully work out and solve problems in this area, but could require direction and/or assistance in order to insure that the maximum result is achieved.

Expert

The analyst has fully mastered this skill or task in a manner that allows him to complete the tasks with little or no direction. In addition, his understanding and mastery of the subject would allow him to direct or teach others.

DIRECTING AND CONTROLLING
(OPERATIONAL FINANCIAL ANALYSIS IN ACTION)

Applying direction and control

Abron's financial analysis team as described earlier is charged with the role of supporting in a staff capacity both functional line managers and senior management. This circumstance primarily occurs when management, because of a very full work load resulting from a number of legitimate causes, cannot independently resolve certain operational and financial problems and opportunities. Acting as a staff of internal consultants, watchdogs, etc., they are implementing the concept which concluded Chapter 1—profits don't happen, they are engineered.

Engineering by definition or connotation suggests an organized, well thought out approach, an approach which arranges a set of facts or conditions into a rational, interlocking connection with one dependent upon the other or creating a network. This network is carried through to completion in a thorough and concise manner. Also problems which will affect the profitability of Abron and the manner in which the financial analysis department completes its tasks are spotted easily, and the solutions are approached with logic. By adopting a systematic approach and getting involved in the day-to-day activity as participators and not spectators or reporters they can apply analytical and control tools which probe the cause and effect of actions and decisions. The financial analysts at Abron are establishing a sense of direction and control for their function while improving the cost control capability and profitability of their company.

Results of this application

The proof of the pudding is that the department was able to:

1. Minimize the firefighting by identifying weakness, documenting existing approaches, and pre-planning large activities.
2. Improve the quality and thus the credibility of the department's efforts.
3. Demonstrate to line management that the financial analysis staff was sincerely interested in assisting them to do a better job and not just there to spy.

4. Open up communications in all directions so the key operational causes and conditions are presented jointly and accurately.
5. Prove to senior management that they can successfully monitor an expanding organization in sufficient detail to spot problems and trends early, before they get out of hand, and generally keeping their fingers on the pulse of the organization.
6. Continue to develop and add new skills and techniques to their analytical and control tool-chest.

A mini-case in point

After a two-year period of applying and evolving their concept of systematic operational financial analysis, Abron began to feel the economic pinch of a recession mixed with inflation and stepped-up competition. Abron's management wanted to be sure that their analysis group had literally thrown their arms around the cost structure of the organization and were squeezing out all of the excess costs. They decided to overlay an intensified cost control program which they labeled operational awareness. Their approach, used in conjunction with their existing budgeting system, was successful. This success resulted from a combination of groundwork previously developed and their ability to get at the cost at the detail level. Managers, who up to this time believed cost control was meeting or beating their budgets, began to examine ways of curtailing costs which had previously been considered unreducible. The cost structure was re-examined to insure those variable and semi-variable costs were truly under control. Head count control and analysis became the order of the day. Operating standards and existing approaches were reviewed and tightened, and then reviewed again, i.e., their long-haul transportation department introduced a new driver relay or exchange system which alleviated the costly practice of the same driver staying with his vehicle until his destination was reached. This cut out driver overtime, shortened the time the truck was in use, made more trucks available, and reduced the need to acquire more vehicles (a fixed cost), while adding only slightly to the driver head count (a variable cost). Equipment maintenance and replacement programs were also re-examined and changed.

Abron weathered the storm without reducing the quality of their products or the service offered to their customers. They finished the year reporting one of their most profitable years in their long and successful history. The principle they practiced was one which seems to prevail in a majority of profitable companies: it is okay to understand the big picture, but keep your eye on the key details of your particular operations.

INDEX

A

ABC class, 151
A.B.C. inventory control, 134-135
Accelerated cash flow:
    adjusted net income approach, 244
    aged accounts receivable, 249
    analyzing, 246
    analyzing "float," 248
    belt-tightening, 248-249
    build profits, 243
    cash conservation program, 249
    cash discounts for prompt payments, 243
    cash management program, 248
    cash receipt and disbursement method, 244
    centralizing cash flow functions, 248
    check signing, 249
    collections, 249
    defining cash requirements (forecasting), 244
    delinquent accounts, 249
    discounts when necessary, 249
    evaluate every two years, 253
    free-up cash for expansion, 243
    full use of cash budget, 248
    future expenses, 249
    future weaknesses, 248
    granting credit, 249
    idle assets, 249-253
        cases, 250-253
        costs, 250
        drag on organization, 250
        equipment seldom used, 250
        excess cash not invested, 250
        high receivable levels, lengthy agings, 250
        inventories, 250
        liquidation, 253
        many forms, 249
        permanent investments, 250
        plants and warehouses cluttered, 250
        temporary investments, 250
    idle or excess cash, 248
    implementing innovative ideas, 243
    increasing productivity, 243
    large purchase quantity discounts, 243
    lean periods, 248
    level of compensating balances, 248
    limits, 248
    lock-box concept, 248, 249
    marketable securities, 248
    monitoring, 244-246
    needed equipment replacements and repairs, 243
    negotiable assets, 249
    new equipment needs, 249
    not commingling personal and business funds, 249
    number of member banks in line, 248
    pinpointing cash flow blockage, 244-248
    product diversification, 243
    prompt collection and depositing of cash, 248
    proper banking relationships, 248
    proper investment mode for excess cash, 248
    reducing interest costs, 243
    restrict use of outside funds, 243

Accelerated cash flow: *(cont.)*
    retire existing debt obligations, 243
    salary level, 249
    source and application of funds method, 244
    taking corrective action, 246-247
    timing payments, 249
    "zero level bank accounts," 248
Accountant, management, 30
Account classification and reporting format, 192
Accounting, 30, 130
Accounts payable, 244
Achievements, measure, 118
Acquisitions, business, 257
Action plan, 50
Activity, 30, 48
Adjusted net income approach, 244
Administrative expense, 42, 47-48
Administrative services, 187
A.D.T. services, 250
Advertising, 81
"After inventory," 156
Aisles, 225
Alternatives, creation, 234, 236
Alternative use costs, 250
Analyst, financial, 30-31
Analyzing, 246
Assembly of customer orders, 156
Asset management, 30
Assumptions, clearly defined, 79
Auditor, inventory, 158
Autos, 255

B

Backlog list, 274
Balance, 30
Balances report, 148
Bank borrowing, 243
Banking relationships, 248
"Before inventory," 156
Big picture analysis, 34
Big-ticket items:
    capital budget items, 254, 255, 257
        beyond capital budget, 255, 257
        business acquisitions, 257
        business systems installations, 257
        categories, 255
        new product development, 257
        new product or service introductions, 257
        product line expansion, 257
    evaluating, 257-265
        D.C.F.-R.O.I., 261-265
        framework, 257-258
        method, 258-261
        present worth feature, 260
        rate of return feature, 260
        time payback method, 259
        time value of money, 260
    identifying, 254-257
    post-audit and control, 265-266
    savings analysis calculator, 266
    significant cash outlays, 254

INDEX

Blanket purchase orders, 145-146
Borrowing:
    restrict, 243
    short and long term capital, 81
"Bossing," 224
Bottlenecks, 37, 179
Breakdowns, 37
Breakeven point, 195-199
Budgets, 30, 81
Building, 255
Business acquisitions, 257
Business planning, 30, 48
Business systems installations, 257

C

Capabilities, 218
Capital budget items, 254, 255, 257
Capital needs, 48
Cash drains, 38
Cash flow, accelerated, 243-253 (*see also* Accelerated cash flow)
Cash receipt and disbursement method, 244
Cause codes, 226
Centralized purchasing:
    better inventory control, 146
    blanket purchase orders, 145-146
    clerical effort is cut, 146
    cost cutter, 146
    early insight into needs and problems, 146
    enjoying benefits of specialization, 146
    improved price negotiations, 146
    pays its way, 145-147
    responsibility is pinpointed, 146
    what it is, 145
Charter, 271-272
Charting:
    earned hours, 175, 179
    profit impact, 85-120 (*see also* Profit impact charting)
Check signing, 249
Civic code requirements, 255
Clerical services, 223
Closed-circuit television, 226
Communication, 30-31, 79, 229
Compensating balances, 248
Components, 134
Compressed air system, 229
Computerized data processing, 224
Conceptual analysis, 34
Conservation, 229
Consigned material, 157
Consumption of resources, 35
Containers, 157
Contra-credits, 199
Control, 30
Controllable costs, 193-195
Controller, 30
Controllership, 49
Controlling, 265, 266, 280-281
Corporate level, data, 52
Corrective actions, 38
Correlation technique, 82-83
Cost:
    absorption, 219
    fixed, variable, controllable, 193-195
    gross profit changes, 122

Cost Centers:
    defining, 187-189
    effectiveness, 199
Cost collection hierarchy, 189-192 (*see also* Expense categorization)
Cost estimating, 219
Cost evaluation, 234
Cost of sales, 40, 42, 45-46
Cost relationship and controllability, 191
Cost savings, 255
Cost system, 44
Counts, 157
Credit, granting, 249
Crewing, 218
Customer consigned material, 157
Customers, polling, 82
Cutoff, 156

D

Daily log, 148
Data base requirement, 224
Data gathering:
    action matrix, 37-38, 48-54
        action plan, 50
        bottlenecks, breakdowns, 37
        cash drains, 38
        corrective actions, 38
        developing markets, 49, 51
        employee relations, 49, 51
        financial management, 49, 51
        fixed and variable cost relationships, 38
        general management, 49, 51
        inefficiencies, 37
        key objectives, 49
        organizational relationships, 37
        pricing and gross profit, 49, 51
        product data, 37
        product research and development, 49, 51
        production management, 49, 51
        profit eroders, 38
        reporting structure, 37
        selling, 49, 51
        specific end result, 49-50
        strengths and weaknesses, 37
        system deficiencies, 37
        timing and due dates, 50
    corporate level, 52
    diagnostic approach, 38-39
    division level, 54
    group level, 52-54
    questionnaire/matrix technique, 38
    questionnaires, 39-48
        cost of sales, 42, 45-46
        divisional cost systems survey, 42, 43-45
        president's operating report, 46-48
        profit enrichment program, 39-42
    value analysis teams, 234
    work simplification teams, 236
D.C.F., 261-265
Debt, 243, 250
Debt obligations, 243, 244
Decision-making, 79
Deficiencies, systems, 37
Delay, 236
Delivery expense, 47
Delphi technique, 82

Depreciation costs, 250
Detection devices, 226
Diagnostic approach, 38-39
Dies, 255
Directing, 280-281
Direction, 224
Direct labor, 45, 172, 217
Discounts:
    offering, 249
    quantity, 132, 144, 243
Distribution:
    inefficiencies, 37
    marketing plan, 81
Diversification, 243
Divisional cost systems survey, 42, 43-45
Division level, 54
Division Manager, 46, 158
Documentation package, 238
Double handling, 131
Due dates, 50
Duplicate programs, 224
Dynamics, financial, 34-35

E

Earned hours:
    common sense approach, 172
    efficiency without complex standards, 168-170
    graphic display, 175, 179
    implementing, 172-175
        development, 172
        direct labor, 172
        evaluation and analysis, 175
        indirect labor, 172
        recording, 172, 175
        total plant labor, 172, 175
    product offering detail, 170, 172
    reporting package, 179-185
    think before implementing, 170-172
    understanding, 170
Econometric technique, 83
Economic analysis, 272
Education, 273
Electrical conservation, 229
Employee relations, 49, 51
Employee turnover, 224
Engineering, 56, 129
Equipment:
    malfunction card, 226
    new, 249
    replacement and repairs, 243
    seldom used, 250
Equity, 243
Estimating and pricing, 44-45
Excess items, 151
Executives, polling, 82
Expansion, 243, 255
Expense categorization:
    contra-credits, 199
    cost center effectiveness, 199
    cost collection hierarchy, 189-192
        account classification and reporting, 192
        cost center activity, 191
        cost center description, 189
        functional areas, 189

Expense categorization: *(cont.)*
    cost collection hierarchy, *(cont.)*
        functional reviews, 191
        natural accounts, 191
        numbering scheme, 189
        statistical data, 191
        work station or production point breakdown, 189
    defining cost centers, 187-189
    fixed, variable and controllable costs, 193-195
        classifying labor and payroll related costs, 193, 195
        cost/volume relationship, 193
    organization chart, 187
    pinpointing breakeven point, 195-199
    unabsorbed costs, 199
Extrapolation technique, 82

F

Facilities, 56-57
Factory, 41, 47
Fast moving items, 151
F.D.A., 255
Feasibility evaluation, 234
Files, 223
Financial administrator, 130
Financial analysis, 30, 272
Financial analyst, 30-31
Financial data, market plan, 80
Financial dynamics, 34-35
Financial Guide Line, 58-60, 63-64, 73-77, 108, 134, 170 (*see also* Planning mechanism)
Financial management, 49, 51, 54
Finished goods, 134
Fire prevention, 226
Fixed and variable cost relationships, 38
Fixed, variable and controllable costs, 193-195
Fixtures, 255
Flexible budgeting:
    control tool, 200-203
        static budget vs. fixed budget, 202
        what flexible budget is, 201-203
        when level of activity varies, 200
    flexing application, 207
    forecasting tool, 208
    percentage adjustment, 206
    projection, 208-215
        alternative base lines—units, 211
        pocket profit projector, 208-215
    rate application, 206-207
    selected list of flexed accounts, 204
    step budget, 204-205
    varied flexing factors, 203
    weekly profit projections, 208
    wrong flexing factor, 203
"Float," 248
Floor, litter, 225
Floor plan, 155
Floor taxes, 250
Flow of production, 81
Forecasting, 81-84, 208, 244
Foreman, 231
Forms, 225
Forward looking, 31

INDEX

Functional reviews, 191
Furniture, 255

G

General Manager, 46
Goals, 80, 271-274
Government consigned material, 157
Graphic presentations, 87, 175, 179
Gross margin, 219
Gross profit, 35, 49, 51, 54, 212
Gross profit analysis:
    calculating effect of mix shift, 123
    cost, 122
    ignoring mix, 124-125
    knowing your business, 129-130
    pricing, 121
    segregating mix, 125-128
    touching the hardware, 128
    what gross profit margin is, 121-122
    why analyze, 122-123
Group level, data, 52-54
Guards, 250

H

Handling, double, 131
Hardware, 128
Hardware backup, 224
Heat, 229
Housekeeping, 156, 225

I

Idle assets, 249-253 (*see also* Accelerated cash flow)
Implementation plan, 80
Incentive plans, 238-242
Indirect labor, 172
Indoctrination, new employee, 224
Industrial relations, 56
Inefficiencies, 37
Informational needs, 224
Inspection, 236
Insurance, 250
"Intelligence," 49
Interdisciplinary, 31
Interest costs, 243
Inventory:
    auditor, 158
    checking levels, 179
    components, 134
    control, 134-135, 146
    day, 154, 165-167
    excess buildup, 179
    finished goods, 134
    levels, 81, 131-134
    physical, 151-167 (*see also* Physical inventory)
    procedure prior, 165
    raw materials, 134
    reduction, 175
    sub-assemblies, 134
    team, 158
    tickets, 158, 165
    too much or too old, 250
    turnover, 135-137

Inventory:*(cont.)*
    updating, 134
    work-in-process, 134
"Investment" area, 48

J

Job description, 223

L

Labor, direct and indirect, 172
Labor area, 41, 45, 47
Laboratory equipment, 255
Labor cost:
    classifying, 193, 195
    earned hours, 168-185 (*see also* Earned hours)
Labor relations, 48
Land, 255
Leadership, 224
Lead times, 238
Learning curve, 132
Lease, 250
Leasehold improvements, 255
Leasing, 243
Liquidation, 253
Lock-box concept, 248, 249
Long term capital, 81
Loss prevention, 226
Lost items, 151

M

Machine-hour rate:
    amount of cost absorption, 219
    capabilities, 218
    conversion, 218-219
    cost estimating, 219
    crewing, 218
    curtailing idle time, 219
    direct labor costs, 218
    financial management, 219
    gross margin, 219
    indirect costs, 218
    overhead pool, 216-218
        applying, 217
        direct labor hours, 217
        percentage of direct labor, 217
        understanding, 216-217
        units produced, 217
    processing methods, 219
    product cost picture, 219
    product design, 219
    product mix relationships, 219
    provides sales with accurate data, 219
    senior management, 219
    slow moving products, 219
    tooling, 219
    type, 218
    usage, 218
    use and value, 219
    value, 218
    value of each machine-cost-center, 219
    when best applied, 218
Machinery problems, 179

Maintenance preventative, 226
Maintenance costs, 250
Management:
    general, 49, 51, 54
    senior, 219
Management accountant, 30
Management performance tool, 79
Manager:
    plant or division, 158
    smaller units, 86
Manpower:
    efficient use, 175
    inefficient use, 179
    reviewing, 179
Manuals, user, 224
Manufacturing, 43-44, 56
Marketing, 41-42, 56, 81, 129
Marketing plan:
    advertising sales promotion, 81
    alternative courses of action, 79
    assumptions clearly defined, 79
    basic business, 80
    checkoff list, 80-81
    communication, 79
    complete, 79-80
    current market situation, 79-80
    decision-making, 79
    distribution, 81
    external factors, 79
    financial data, 80
    goals and objectives, 80
    good planning precepts, 79
    implementation plan, 80
    internal limitations, 79
    long-term objectives and needs, 79
    management performance tool, 79
    marketing, 81
    markets, 80
    measuring, 79
    opportunities, 80
    organized approach, 79
    preface, 79
    prior year review, 79
    products, 81
    responsibility for achievement, 79
    sales forecasting, 81-84
        borrowing short and long term capital, 81
        correlation techniques, 82-83
        Delphi technique, 82
        econometric technique, 83
        extrapolation techniques, 82
        flow of production, 81
        levels of inventories, 81
        polling customers, 82
        polling key executives, 82
        polling sales force, 82
        setting budgets, 81
        setting sales quotas, 81
        spending of purchasing dollars, 81
        timely and reasonably accurate, 81
    selling, 81
    strategy, 80
    tasks and programs, 79
    top-management support, 79
    warning device, 79
    what to expect, 79-81
    written, 79
Marketplace, larger share, 175
Markets:
    developing, 49, 51
    marketing plan, 80
Market situation current, 79-80
Master shipment schedule, 134
Material, 41, 45, 47, 129, 179
Material costs:
    A.B.C. inventory control, 134-135
    analyzing, 131-140
    benefits of learning curve, 132
    centralized purchasing, 145-147 (*see also* Centralized purchasing)
    components, 134
    controlling, 141-167
    detailed production schedule, 134
    double handling, 131
    economical quantity orders, 132
    financial guide line, 134
    finished goods, 134
    inventory levels, 131-134
    master shipment schedule, 134
    Pareto's Law, 134
    parts numbering, 141-145 (*see also* Parts numbering)
    physical inventory, 151-167 (*see also* Physical inventory)
    plan work, work plan, 131-132
    production lines slowed, 132
    production runs, 131, 132
    projecting material usage, 131-134
    purchase commitment, 148-151 (*see also* Purchase commitment)
    quantity discounts missed, 132
    raw materials, 134
    scrap reporting and analysis, 137-140
        benefits, 137-138
        material rejection tag system, 140
        scrap ticket, 138
    sub-assemblies, 134
    tooling methods, 132
    understanding inventory turnover, 135-137
    updating inventory, 134
    work-in-process, 134
Material handling, 226-227
Material movement, 157
Material rejection tag system, 140
Meetings, review, 107-119
Microfiche, 223
Micrographics, 223
Mind joggers, 89, 91
Mix:
    ignoring, 124-125
    segregating, 125
    shift, 123-124
Modification phase, 33
Monitoring, 244-246
MTM, 168

N

Negotiable assets, 249
Net, 212

O

Objective phase, 33
Objectives:
    business and planning, 60-63
    establishing, 271-274

INDEX 287

Objectives: *(cont.)*
    key, 49
    marketing plan, 80
Observation phase, 32
Obsolescence, 151
Office, inefficiencies, 37
Operating procedures, 227-228
Operational, 31
Operational analysis, 186-199, 273 (*see also* Expense categorization)
Operational financial analysis, 273
Opportunities, 80
Organization, 56
Organization chart, 187
Organizing, 275-280
Out of stock conditions, 144
Overhaul projects, 255
Overhead, 41, 46, 47, 216-218 (*see also* Machine-hour rates)
Overplanning vs. underplanning, 59-60
Overtime, 179

P

Pallets, 157
Paperwork and reports flow, 223
Pareto's Law, 134-135
Parts list descriptions, 155
Parts numbering:
    example, 142-144
    first control step, 141-145
    general description, 142
    know what you are controlling, 141
    out of stock conditions, 144
    quantity discounts, 144
    specific description, 142
Payroll, 244
Payroll hours, 175
Payroll related costs, 193, 195
People involvement:
    first level supervision, 230-232
        forgotten people, 231-232
        indicators and management information, 230-231
    incentive plans, 238-242
        production and distribution, 239
        profit sharing, 239
        R.O.I., 240-242
    production assembly teams, 238
    special teams, 233-238
    suggestion systems, 232-233
    value analysis teams, 234
        cost evaluation, 234
        creation of alternatives, 234
        feasibility evaluation, 234
        gathering of information, 234
        implementation and follow-up, 235
        selection of item to be analyzed, 234
    work simplification teams, 235-238
        creation of alternatives, 236
        delay, 236
        establishing, 236, 238
        formulate an improved method, 236
        gathering information, 236
        implementation and follow-up, 236
        inspection, 236
        purpose, 235
        selectivity, 236
        storage, 236

People involvement: *(cont.)*
    work simplification teams, *(cont.)*
        transportation, 236
        wasted effort, 235-236
Percentage adjustment, 206
Performance, 30
Performance indexes data, 57
PERT networks, 274, 275
Physical inventory:
    aids, 155
    assembled customer finished goods orders shipments on inventory date, 156-157
    auditor, 158
    classification, 151
    consigned material on site, 157
    counts, 157
    cutoff, 156
    day of inventory, 165-166
    floor plan, 155
    forms requirement, 155
    functions affected, 154
    housekeeping, 156
    lost or excess items, 151
    material movement, 157
    obsolescence, 151
    operations affected, 154
    parts list descriptions, 155
    personnel, 155
    planning inventory day, 154
    plant or division manager, 158
    pre-inventory instructions, 155
    procedure instructions, 154-167
    procedure prior, 165
    receiving, 156
    returnable containers, 157
    scope, 154
    scrap, 157
    shipping, 156
    slow and fast moving items, 151
    slow-moving inventory areas, 157
    statistical information, 156
    team, 158
    tickets, 155, 158, 165, 166-167
    times, 155
Pilferage, 226
Pink slip, 224
Planning, 274-275
Planning mechanism:
    business and planning objectives, 60-63
        American industrial giants, 61
        areas of business first to benefit, 61
        basic everyday problems, 61
        cases in point, 61-63
        detail presented, 60
        management's top priorities, 61
        new ideas generated, 61
        objectives, benefits, purposes, 60
        reporting methods, 61
        resources available, 60
        results and actions, 61
        time periods covered, 60
        updating and maintaining, 61
        workable blueprint, 61
    Financial Guide Line, 58-60, 63-64, 73-76, 76-77
        evaluating, 76
        fundamentals, 63-64, 73-76
        greater profits, 58-60
        importance, 58-59

Planning mechanism: *(cont.)*
    Financial Guide Line, *(cont.)*
        in action, 76-77
        need and/or purpose, 59
        overplanning vs. underplanning, 59-60
        presenting to senior management, 76-77
        "reporting unit," 60
        updating and tracking, 77
        what profit center can achieve, 60
Plant, cluttered, 250
Plant manager, 158
Pocket profit projector, 208-215
Polling, 82
Post-auditing, 265, 266
Preface, marketing plan, 79
Pre-inventory instructions, 155
Pre-production activity, 129
Prerequisites of total systematic approach, 30-31
Present worth feature, 260
President's Operating Report, 46-48
Preventative, 31
Price negotiations, 146-147
Pricing, 35, 44-45, 49, 51, 54, 121
Prior year review, 79
Processing methods, 219
Product cost picture, 219
Product data, 37
Product design, 219
Product mix relationships, 219
Production:
    assembly teams, 238
    control, 129
    floor, 130
    flow, 81
    incentive plans, 239
    inefficiencies, 37
    management, 49, 51, 54
    procedures, 130, 179
    runs, 131
Production point breakdown, 189
Productivity increases, 255
Product research and development, 49, 51
Products, 81
Profit enrichment programs:
    achieving success, 229
    at first, 222
    developing information, 221
    diagnosing, 221
    identifies conditions eroding profits, 221
    not typical, 220
    "our business is unique" syndrome, 222
    profit leak detection, 221-229 (*see also* Profit leak detection)
    systematic approach, 221, 222
    what it is, 221
Profit eroders, 38
Profit impact charting:
    activating charts, 89, 91
    considering, 87-88
    dramatic supplement, 87
    list key data, 89
    mind joggers, 89, 91
    planning and control techniques, 86-87
    possible problems, 89
    putting charts to work, 93
    questionnaire, 39-42

Profit impact charting: *(cont.)*
    recommended list of charts, 88-89
    review meetings, 107-119
        chart selection, 108, 117
        checkoff list, 118-119
        financial guideline, 108
        measure your achievements, 118
        structure, 117
        Unison Computer, 107
    sharpening, use, 91
    smaller business unit, 86-87
        for and against, 86-87
        reticent managers, 86
        size not a limitation, 86
    suggest opportunities, 89
    trends, 89
    vehicle, 87
    visibility to deviation from plan, 89-105
Profit leak detection:
    clerical, 223
    computerized data processing, 224
    conservation, 229
    employee turnover, 224
    forms, 225
    housekeeping, 225
    loss prevention, 226
    material handling, 226-227
    preventative maintenance, 226
    quality assurance, 228-229
    space utilization, 226-227
    standard operating procedures, 227-228
    supplies and small tools, 228
Profit sharing plans, 239
Projecting material usage, 131-134
Projection, 208-215
Promises, 224
Promotions, 224
Property taxes, 250
Purchase commitment:
    balances report, 148
    current period balance, 148
    current period invoices paid, 148
    current period purchase order commitment, 148
    daily log, 148
    opening commitment balances, 148
    step-by-step installations, 151
    summary information, 148
    today's view of tomorrow, 148-151
Purchasing, 56, 238
Purchasing dollars, spending, 81

Q

Quality assurance, 130, 228-229
Quantity discounts, 132, 144, 243
Quantity orders, 132
Questioning, 31
Questionnaire/matrix technique, 38
Questionnaires, 39-48

R

Rate application, 206-207
Rate of return feature, 260
Ratio, 170, 175
Raw materials, 134
Receivables, 48, 249, 250

INDEX

Receiving, 156
Record retention center, 223
Redundancy, 179
Reiterative, 31
Relationships, organizational, 37
Repairs, 243, 255
Replacement, 243, 255
Reporting methods, 61
Reporting package, earned hours, 179-185
Reporting structures, 37
Reproduction equipment, 223
Research and development, 49
Resources available, 60
Responsibilities:
    functional, 272
      physical inventory taking, 158
    purchasing, 146
Result, end, 49-50
Retention block, 223
Revenue, 212
Review, marketing plan, 79
Review meetings, 107-119
R.O.I., 261, 265, 269
R.O.I. management incentive plans, 240-242

S

Safety, 226, 255
Salary level, 249
Sales, 40, 47, 54, 129
Salesforce, polling, 82
Sales forecasting, 81-84
Sales promotion, 81
Sales quotas, 81
Salvagable materials, 225
Savings analysis calculator, 266
Scrap, 157, 228
Scrap reporting and analysis, 137-140
Scrap ticket, 138
Securities, 248
Security, 226, 255
Security costs, 250
Selling, 41-42, 47, 49, 51, 81
Senior management, 219
Sewage, 229
Shipping, 156
Shipping expense, 47
Short term capital, 81
Skids, 157
Slow moving items, 151, 157, 219
Smaller business unit, 86-87
Source and application of funds method, 244
Space utilization, 226-227
Specialization, 146
Special teams, 233-238
Staffing, 275-280
Standards, 168-170
Static budget vs. fixed budget, 202
Statistical information, 156, 191, 228
Statistics, 57
Stenographic services, 223
Step budget, 204-205
"Stop Loss" area, 48
Storage, 236, 238
Strategy, 80
Strengths, 37
Sub-assemblies, 134

Subsystem development, 224
Suggestion systems, 232-233
Supervision, first level, 230-232
Supplementary, 31
Supplies, 228
Support equipment, 255
Systematic, 31
Systematic approach:
    active, 30
    balanced, 30
    communicative, 30-31
    control, 30
    "evaluation link," 33
    evolutionary process, 31-34
    "feedback loop," 33
    financial analyst, 30-31
    forward looking, 31
    "goals link," 33
    "how to" tools, 35
    interdisciplinary, 31
    "matched," 35
    modification phase, 33
    objective phase, 33-34
    observation phase, 32
    operational, 31
    people oriented, 31
    preventative, 31
    profits are engineered, 35
    questioning, 31
    reiterative, 31
    supplementary, 31
    systematic, 31
    understanding financial dynamics, 34-35
    understanding phase, 32-33
    understanding total business, 34
Systematization, 273
System design, 224
Systems and procedures, 130

T

Tags, rejection, 140
Target, 49-50
Taxes, 244, 250
Team, inventory, 158
Test equipment, 255
Ticket requirements, 155
Tickets, inventory, 158, 165, 166
Tickler files, 223
Time clocks, 226
Time Payback Method, 259
Time periods covered, 60
Time-sharing techniques, 273-274
Time study, 168
Timetable, 238
Time value of money, 260
Timing, 50
Tooling:
    methods, 132
    MHR, 219
    requirements, 238
Tools:
    capital budget items, 255
    small, 228
Total business, understanding, 34
Tracking, F.G.L., 77
Transportation, 236

Treasurer, 30
Treasury, 49
Trucks, 255
Turnover, inventory, 135-137
Type, 218
Typing, 223

U

Unabsorbed costs, 199
Underplanning, overplanning vs., 59-60
Understanding phase, 32-33
Units produced, 217
Updating:
    continually, 134
    F.G.L., 77
    inventory, 134
Usage, 218
User manuals, 224

V

Value, 218
Value analysis teams, 234-235
Variable budgeting, 200-215 (*see also* Flexible budgeting)

Variable costs, 193-195
Variances, 46
Venture capital funds, 243
Volume, 122

W

Wages, 224
Warehouses, cluttered, 250
Water, 229
Weaknesses, 37
Weekly profit projections, 208
Workflow, 179, 238
Work-in-process, 134
Work simplification teams, 235-238
Work station, 189, 191

Y

Yards, 225

Z

"Zero level bank accounts," 248